THE UNIVERSITY OF NORTH CAROLINA PRESS ● CHAPEL HILL

SOVIET
COMMUNISM
AND
WESTERN
OPINION
1919-1921

E. Malcolm Carroll

Edited by Frederic B. M. Hollyday

Preface

The appearance of Bolshevik Russia in 1917 was a new historical phenomenon and one that the Western powers were ill-equipped to counter. Their poorly co-ordinated and conflicting attempts at armed intervention had revealed their impotence by the time the Russo-Polish War broke out in 1920. America took the strongest stand against the Communists but was unwilling to implement its words by deeds. Germany stood expectantly on the sideline, hoping that the Russo-Polish conflict would embroil all her recent enemies and bring an accession of power. The French feared most of all a revision of the Versailles Treaty. Subordination of their Polish policy was the price they paid to secure Lloyd George's continued adherence to their German policy. The prime minister moved cautiously in the direction of establishing trade relations with Soviet Russia and according diplomatic recognition. His naïve belief that he could tame the Communists in this fashion was faced by an equally unrealistic reaction from the Liberals, while Labor saw a working-class utopia in the making and put intense pressure on Lloyd George to hold him to his conciliatory policy. Only Tory opinion, spurred on by Winston Churchill, perceived the real danger from communism but flinched from using armed force against it.

The divisions in the policy and opinion of the West toward Soviet Russia that have persisted to the present day first appeared in these early years.

The author of *Soviet Communism and Western Opinion, 1919-1921,* Dr. Eber Malcolm Carroll, James B. Duke Professor Emeritus of History, died at Bussum, Holland, December 28, 1959. Among his papers was found the typed and revised manuscript of this book. Before his death he had confided to his colleague, Professor John R. Alden, that the manuscript was complete.

Readers of his pioneer works on foreign policy and public opinion will perhaps find his last work surprising. *French Public Opinion and Foreign Affairs, 1870-1914* and *Germany and the Great Powers, 1866-1914* are massive monographs, characterized by an imposing wealth of material, a minimum of conclusions, and a departure from strictly "diplomatic" history, based upon the belief that foreign and domestic affairs were closely linked in the minds of statesmen. True, *Soviet Communism and Western Opinion, 1919-1921* is marked by the same meticulous attention to detail as the writings on the pre-1914 epoch. But, doubtless as a result of his experiences in military service and in editing the German Foreign Office documents and in constant thought, he came to believe that history must be emphatically interpretative, a feature not conspicuous in his early publications. Moreover, he decided that the historian's style must be more vigorous and evocative than that he had been accustomed to employ in his previous works, though his lectures were remarkable for forceful diction and adept choice of illustrative examples. Thus, increased interpretation and a more robust style distinguish the present volume. Quotations from newspapers and journals are used with greater skill and selectivity. Indeed, these chapters rest upon the underlying assumption that history is of definite utility in formulating policy. Had Professor Carroll completed his contemplated volume on the interaction of public opinion and foreign affairs between the world wars, of which only some research notes survive, these qualities would have become even more pronounced.

The present volume must stand as Professor Carroll's historical testament, though had he lived he would have wished to incorporate the findings of the latest research and documentation, particularly that contained in the recently published volumes of *Documents on British Foreign Policy, First Series.* Believing that the fruit of forty years' research, writing, and teaching deserves unaltered presentation and that Professor Carroll would have wished his forthright, individual, and independent conclusions to be published without excision or embellishment, I have refrained from all "improvements," with three exceptions. The original first chapter, entitled "Years of Indecision, 1917-1919," has been overtaken in many details by recent scholarly works, especially those of George F. Kennan and Richard H. Ullmann. As a result, the first chapter has been drastically abridged; Professor Carroll's conclusions, largely in his own words, are added to the chapter "Western Opinion, Bolshevism, and Soviet Russia, 1919-1920," as the seven opening paragraphs. The second alteration is the omission of a final chapter "Past and Present," originally entitled "Looking Forward: Conclusions and Reflections," which reviews the interaction of Western opinion and Soviet Russia from 1921 to 1959. Despite its interest as a summary of Professor Carroll's views and reflections, it has been omitted, because it is obviously not an integral part of this study, it is not up-to-date, and no evidence is presented to support any of its conclusions. Finally, the original title, "The Western Powers and Soviet Russia, 1917-1921," has been altered to *Soviet Communism and Western Opinion, 1919-1921*. The present title, I believe, presents without ambuiguity the intent of the author to describe the reaction of the West to Bolshevik policy; the original title, perhaps, would have led the reader to expect a detailed analysis of the policy of Soviet Russia from the original sources. With these three exceptions, my editorial task has been limited to preparing the Preface and Editorial Note, standardizing reference forms, correcting typographical errors, reparagraphing, and compiling the index.

My work has been facilitated by aid from many sources. This volume would not have been possible without the generosity of Mrs. Mary Carroll-Pos (now Mrs. Pos-Dowdswell), who presented her late husband's notes and papers to the institution he served for thirty-six years. The Duke University Council on Research has been very liberal with grants for clerical assistance and publication. Professor William R. Rock of Bowling Green University provided useful information. Professor William A. Jenks of Washington and Lee University gave me both support and counsel. Mr. Ashbel Brice, Director of the Duke University Press, furnished much helpful and friendly advice. Without the aid and encouragement of my colleagues at Duke University, Professors John R. Alden, Joel Colton, William B. Hamilton, John Tate Lanning, and Richard L. Watson, Jr., this book would never have appeared. A special debt of gratitude is owed to Professor William E. Scott, who has been unstinting of his time and knowledge of diplomatic history. Dr. Mattie Russell, Curator of Manuscripts, and Miss Gertrude Merritt, Chief of Technical Processes, of the Duke University Library, have been most helpful. Finally, I am indebted to the staff of The University of North Carolina Press for the benefit of their experience.

FREDERIC B. M. HOLLYDAY

Editorial Note

E. Malcolm Carroll's career is briefly summarized by William T. Laprade in Lillian P. Wallace and William C. Askew, editors, *Power, Public Opinion, and Diplomacy: Essays in Honor of Eber Malcolm Carroll by His Former Students* (Durham, N.C., 1959), pp. ix-xiv, and in Robert H. Woody's obituary notice in the *American Historical Review*, LXV (April, 1960), 780-81.

A list of Carroll's writings is given in Frederic B. M. Hollyday, compiler, "The Printed Writings of Eber Malcolm Carroll: A Preliminary Bibliography," in Wallace and Askew, *Power, Public Opinion, and Diplomacy*, pp. 370-81. To this should be added an obituary of Charles S. Sydnor, *American Historical Review*, LIX (July, 1954), 1079-80, and a review of International Press Institute, Zürich, *The Press in Authoritarian Countries* (New York: Frederick A. Praeger, Inc., 1959) *Journal of Modern History*, XXXIII (December, 1960), 437-38. Dr. Carroll once spoke of an early review or two in North Carolina newspapers, which I have been unable to locate. These newspapers contain his letters to the editors and reports of his public address. A not entirely complimentary reference (which greatly amused Dr. Carroll) to his work with the German diplomatic documents

Editorial Note

appears in Ernst von Weizsächer, *Memoirs* (Chicago, 1951), p. 307. Unprinted addresses, delivered after 1948 and preserved in the Manuscript Room, Duke University, include: "Germany and the World Crisis," "What Is to Be Done about Germany?" "Germany Reviews Her History," "The Nature of the U.S.–U.S.S.R. Crisis," and "History and America's Cultural Relations with Europe, 1945-1951." These addresses, his review articles, and remarks to his students in classes, seminars, and conversations of recent years testify to his increasing concern with the applicability of history to present-day events.

An example of Dr. Carroll's meticulousness is of general interest to historians. During his free evenings in Berlin while heading the team microfilming the captured German diplomatic documents he carefully compared the original files with the "Kautsky Documents" (*Die Deutschen Dokumente zum Kriegsausbruch,* edited by Karl Kautsky, Graf Max Montgelas, and Walther Schücking, 4 vols. [Charlottenburg, 1919; new, enlarged edition, 1929]). He concluded that the Kautsky selection was pre-eminently fair, impartial, sound, and reliable.

F. B. M. H.

Contents

Contents

SOVIET
COMMUNISM
AND
WESTERN
OPINION
1919-1921

I

Western Opinion, Bolshevism, and Soviet Russia, 1919-1920

Few, indeed, were those anywhere, during the first critical year after the Bolshevik seizure of power in Russia, November 7, 1917, who foresaw the survival of the Soviet regime. To the Central Powers, however, it seemed to offer the hope that victory might be wrested from their opponents. But in the end neither they nor the Allies derived any decisive military advantages from their policies toward the Bolsheviks. As a result of greed for territory, the Germans were unable to withdraw as many troops as their operations on the western front required or to satisfy their need for food and raw materials. While the Allies reaped negative advantages from Germany's errors of judgment, it cannot be said that their cause was materially advanced by their treatment of Soviet Russia. The idea of a revived eastern front was never more than a fantasy, born of wishful thinking. The Czech Legion, still in Siberia at the war's end, was powerfully drawn by the desire to get out of Russia and go home. Japan's interests were restricted to the Maritime Provinces, and she had no intention of advancing farther west. The White Russians, whose zeal for fighting was directed against the Bolsheviks rather than the Germans, were not a significant military factor before the end of the war. It remained to be seen whether the Allies could find a solution or act more vigorously when their hands were freed by the Armistice.

But Allied efforts after November, 1918, were crowned with no greater success. Woodrow Wilson, David Lloyd George, and Georges Clemenceau wrestled with the Russian question for many hours at Versailles. They considered three basic tactics: negotiations among the Russian factions, peace with the Bolsheviks, and all-out intervention. Their invitation to the White Russians and Bolsheviks to meet at Prinkipo Island in the Sea of Marmora was flatly refused by the White Russians. The mission of the American agent, William C. Bullitt, who brought back from Lenin an offer of moderate peace terms, was ignored by Wilson. Finally, Winston Churchill's proposal for an efficient centralized Allied campaign of anti-Bolshevik intervention in Russia was turned down by Wilson and Lloyd George. Whatever else might be done, there would be no concerted action on the grand scale against the Bolsheviks.

In desperation to make some decision for action, the Big Three extended considerable aid, which granted implied, though not official, *de facto* recognition, to the White Russian government established at Omsk by Admiral Kolchak. But here too they were frustrated. In the absence of unlimited intervention and of a supreme Allied command in Russia, the eventual doom of the White Russians was sealed by the shortcomings of their leadership, the lack of co-ordination between their widely separated armies, and, above all, by their inability to capture the confidence and loyalties of the peasants, factors which were beyond the power of the Allies to correct.

Lloyd George's meditations in the "wilderness" of Fontainebleau in March, 1919, focused his attention upon the shortcomings of the Versailles Conference and, among others, upon the failure to agree upon a policy toward Russia. He was more impressed than ever before by the dangers of bolshevism. "Bolshevik imperialism," he wrote in his famous memorandum of March 25, "does not merely menace the States on Russia's borders. It threatens the end of Asia and is near to America as it is to France [*sic*]. It is idle to think that the Peace Conference can separate, however sound a peace it may have arranged with Germany, if it leaves Russia as it is today."[1] This, however, was precisely what happened. A solution of the Russian problem was no nearer when the Allied chieftains signed the Treaty of Versailles and left for home. At bottom, they were agreed for the moment that none should have any truck with the Bolsheviks and upon little else; and even this tacit and negative agreement was not to survive for more than a few months.

On the Bolshevik side, these first turbulent years of the revolution materially influenced, if they did not irretrievably determine, the future development of its international relations. Despite the dogmatic certainty of Lenin and his associates in regard to the historical inevitability of world revolution, their zealous efforts to accelerate its pace were restrained only by the meager resources at their command. For the time being, subversive propaganda was their only weapon. They, nevertheless, demonstrated an unexpected capacity to trim their sails to unfavorable winds for the sake of survival in Russia. If bourgeois institutions failed to collapse under the strains of the war and the immediate postwar problems, this disappointment meant to them only a delay of uncertain duration in the revolutionary timetable.

The significance of the German Revolution and its results was, in fact, far more serious: the failure of the German working classes to borrow Bolshevik methods—violence, terror, and proletarian dictatorship—meant that the prospect of successful Bolshevik revolutions within the Allied countries was virtually hopeless. But, from another point of view, German reactions to the Bolshevik regime in Russia were not without encouragement from the future. Already it was clear that part of the former ruling circles in Berlin would not permit ideological hostility to bolshevism within Germany to interfere with deals advantageous to Germany's interests. Even the Majority Social Democrats, irreconcilable enemies of bolshevism as they were, were receptive at least to economic co-operation with Soviet Russia as necessary for Germany's recovery.

Unlike Germany, the Allies, in part perhaps because Russia had fought on their side but mainly because of their wish to restore peace and stability to the world, felt some responsibility for a solution of Russia's internal problems, although this sense of responsibility was visibly declining after repeated failures by the summer of 1919. From the beginning their approach was far more swayed by ideological hostility than was German policy. It was the decisive obstacle to co-operation with the Soviet Regime and to material assistance in February and March, 1919. It was an important, though largely unacknowledged, factor in the origin of Allied intervention in Russia and the resulting Civil War. It was also responsible in large measure for the failure of President Wilson and Lloyd George during the Peace Conference to substitute some form of negotiations for armed intervention. In general, however, the Allies failed to translate their anti-bolshevism into effective action. In the case of the United States, the trend was away from armed intervention and toward the high ground of moral denunciation. Nowhere was public sentiment and opinion in the Allied countries an adequate basis for decisive action of any kind. It was toward a more passive and defensive role, the containment of bolshevism, that Allied policy and Western opinion seemed to be moving.

The influence of the Bolshevik ideology of world revolution upon the relations of the Western countries with Soviet Russia has been a powerful factor in determining their official policy and in the development of Western opinion. Nevertheless, this ideology was by no means an entirely satisfactory explanation of either official policy or of public opinion; if the Bolsheviks had not controlled Russia with her vast territory, resources, and population, bolshevism would have remained the faith of just another underground conspiracy. The Bolsheviks were not at first themselves entirely aware that this was so. If they believed with fanatical conviction that their seizure of power would set off a chain reaction ending in the world revolution, the reason was not their control of debilitated Russia but the demonstration of the infallibility of their revolutionary technique: absolute discipline of a minority under a professional revolutionary elite in the name of the proletariat. One of their first moves was, in fact, to dissociate themselves from historic Russia, more especially from its traditional national interests in the Straits and in the control of its minority peoples. Lenin was ready to transfer the center of the revolution to Berlin should, as he expected, Germany go Communist.[2] When the chain reaction of revolutions did not begin on schedule, the Bolsheviks awoke to the use that could be made of Russia and her resources in the cause of world revolution. From the beginning in November, 1917, the significance of the union between bolshevism and Russia was more or less clear to the governments concerned but less so to public opinion, because of Russia's obvious weakness and constant assurances that the collapse of Bolshevik rule was just around the corner. By and large, therefore, it was their ideology rather than their status as the rulers of Russia that accounts for the dominant reactions of Western opinion to the Bolsheviks, at least until the winter of 1919-20, when their eventual victory in the Civil War was unmistakably indicated.

In many ways, circumstances were not conducive to sober and enlightened opinion about bolshevism and Soviet Russia. There was a dearth of reliable information on the part of the governments as well as the general public after the withdrawal of all Allied missions during the autumn of 1918. The Allied blockade of Soviet-controlled territory severed most of the means of communication, including the telegraph, telephone, and mail.[3] No official circles showed any interest in furnishing the public with unbiased, factual information after the Allies' blockade made the normal operation of the news services largely impossible. The contrary seemed nearer the truth.[4] Raymond Recouly, the nationalist French publicist, complained that the public was kept "in practically complete ignorance" so that Russian affairs were as mysterious as if "they were happening upon the moon," and he doubted that the governments were much better informed.[5] There was a tacit conspiracy of silence against news and views that went counter to prevailing opinion. A Socialist member of the French Chamber blamed the government when an "enlightened" series of articles was ignored by the rest of the press.[6] An anglicized Russian and a mortal enemy of the Bolsheviks protested vigorously against this boycott of information about Russia. "We now see," he wrote in an English review, "what a colossal mistake has been committed by European statesmen in building around Bolshevism a sort of Chinese Wall of silence. . . . The only way to fight Bolshevism is by letting light in on the situation. Light, more light, and always more light."[7]

The wall was not entirely impassable, and the boycott was not absolute. Moscow had already become the mecca of the extreme left. In March of 1919 small bands of sympathizers made their way there, in spite of all difficulties, for the formation of the Third International Association of Workers, and the same thing occurred in July, 1920, on the occasion of the Association's Second Congress. Such information and opinions as these visitors communicated publicly after their return home doubtless reached few and convinced still fewer outside the membership of their particular coteries. Occasionally, however, the Bolsheviks welcomed and assisted visits by less dedicated persons, such as that of the sizable delegation from the British Labor party, to which Bertrand Russell attached himself, from May 11 to June 16, 1919. The unfavorable impressions upon some members as well as the more favorable report from the delegation as a whole attracted wide attention and doubtless influenced opinion in other countries as well as Britain.[8] Arthur Ransome, the British journalist who had witnessed the various phases of the revolution in 1917, returned to Russia during February and March, 1919, and in the same year published an abbreviated version of his not unfriendly journal.[9]

In the absence of day-by-day reporting at first-hand of the Russian situation by reliable observers with sufficient background to understand the Russian scene, occasional pieces such as these and the rumors reported from the Baltic listening posts were insufficient to restrain the understandable but unfortunate trend of opinion toward opposite extremes. Such tales as that of the nationalization of women found ready credence, just as the delusion that the Soviet government was a workers' government assured an uncritical audience for the rose-colored reports of George Lansbury, the British Labor leader and pacifist, in 1920. A far more serious consequence of the lack of reliable *reportage* was the almost universal failure of the most responsible newspapers to estimate correctly the Soviet government's prospects for survival. Walter Lippmann and Charles Merz gave the classic demonstration in a critical examination of the coverage of Russia in the

New York Times during this period. The *Times* had repeatedly announced the impending fall of the Soviet government, only to be invariably contradicted by events.[10]

More news from Russia would perhaps have changed in no important respects the general reaction to bolshevism whose essentials were sufficiently known or sensed by the leaders of Western opinion.[11] That it furnished a model worthy of adoption by Western countries was the conclusion of only a small minority on the extreme left, out of which was organized the various Communist parties affiliated with the Third International.[12] Except for these sectarians and some intellectuals whose judgment was warped by their fascination with the Bolshevik's apparently successful use of force,[13] opinion unanimously rejected bolshevism as a guide for Western action. There was also virtual unanimity in condemning the Bolshevik methods: the dictatorship of the proletariat and the Red Terror. No one, whatever his politics might be, could speak or write about Soviet Russia without a scathing moral denunciation.

On the practical question of relations with Soviet Russia, the difference was, however, profound. Lloyd George, with an eye to such Bolshevik sympathies as existed in the Labor party, yielded to none in the violence of his castigation, yet his policy of British Prime Minister aimed at the establishment of trade relations and a *modus vivendi*. After describing the Soviet regime as "without excuse or defence," "a grinding and oppressive tyranny," and as "one of the most bloody and brutal despotisms," Lord Robert Cecil roundly condemned armed intervention and advised the White Russians to settle down in the territory they controlled and to set an example in good administration.[14]

Generally typical of conservative opinion everywhere, Germany alone excepted, was the interjection of a Tory back-bencher in the House of Commons: "You cannot approach this leprous thing without actual defilement."[15] The elections of December, 1919, for the House of Commons and of November for the French Chamber of Deputies resulted in large majorities that consistently echoed this moral abhorrence of any dealings with Soviet Russia. This moral tone had not formerly been characteristic of the conservative point of view in foreign affairs. In the past it had usually regarded the effective exercise of power as the test that should determine the recognition of foreign governments and relations with them.

Since the conservative attitude toward Soviet Russia would seem to have been the more realistic in view of later developments, it is significant that the explanation for this change on the part of the British Tories is not to be found entirely in their reactions to Russian bolshevism. Economic and social problems at home, intensified by the war and productive of social unrest, seemed to make the Bolshevik regime in Russia a dangerous example for the British working classes. After the brief postwar prosperity, the excessive wartime expansion of industry soon flooded the markets with consumer goods, and some pre-1914 markets had ceased to exist (as in Russia) while others had greatly diminished in purchasing power. Industrial production declined, unemployment increased, and labor unions struggled to maintain wartime living and wage standards. Many felt that the "brave new world" for which, they had been told, the war had been fought should be installed at home as well as in international relations.

Fear of revolution or of serious social disorder accounts in considerable measure for the conservatives' uncompromising hostility in Great Britain and the United States. Duff Cooper recalled that it was widespread in Britain, although its existence was later largely forgotten since the revolution never occurred and many of its aims were obtained by constitutional means.[16] To Field Marshal Sir Henry Wilson, the Chief of the Imperial General Staff, the revolution seemed at the time to be just around the corner; Lloyd George's and the Cabinet's refusal to accept Wilson's estimate of the danger and to take the necessary police and military precautions was conclusive proof, in his view, of their incapacity.[17] The private letters of Paul Cambon, France's ambassador to London since 1898, were peppered with prophecies of doom: conditions in England were *"des plus graves," "terribles"*—the situation was *"révolutionnaire."*[18] The Tory *Morning Post* (January 14, 1920) feared the worst when the railroad workers refused the terms which the government had recommended: "And . . . what we mean is not merely a strike, but a Revolution." More than a year later, the same journal agreed (March 2, 1921) with the Duke of Northumberland's denunciation of the international revolutionary movement as a conspiracy whose purpose was the destruction of the British Empire. Bolsheviks had inspired the Irish Rebellion in order to force the dispersal of Britain's troops so that she would be "too weak to deal with the Communist rising which was being prepared here." The Conservative candidate who was contesting the by-election in East Woolwich against Ramsay Macdonald was fighting, it insisted, "against Bolshevism" (!).

Such indications of hysteria reminded St. Loe Strachey of Disraeli's remark that there was "no more unpleasant sight in the world than that of a patrician in a panic." The entire English speaking world, including the United States, was infected. "Our world is oppressed by the fear of Revolution. . . . The spectacle is like that of a herd of powerful and stately cattle thrown into terror and confusion by the barking of an impudent little cur." Nevertheless, Strachey regarded the danger as serious, warning that revolutions were always the work of minorities. When Labor, on the model of the Soviets, organized the Councils of Action against possible intervention in the Russo-Polish War of 1920, the British government offered "a capital example of the failure to govern, a failure which may be fraught with direst consequences."[19]

With considerably less cause than in Britain, the United States experienced the same scare in an even more exaggerated degree. President Wilson appealed to his attorney-general, A. Mitchell Palmer: "Do not let the country see red,"[20] but because of illness or his own increasing anti-bolshevism, he failed to translate his words into action. Palmer, in fact, did see "Reds," in the words of a sober historian, "behind every bush and every demand for an increase of wages." In many instances, the victims of judicial prosecution were moderate Socialists who believed in the democratic process. Those who were elected to the New York State Legislature were not permitted to take their seats. Victor Berger, the Milwaukee Socialist, was sentenced to a term of twenty years' imprisonment in January, 1920, and was prevented by the action of the Congress of the United States from taking the seat in the House of Representatives to which he was twice re-elected. Some hundred aliens were deported to Russia, against some of whom the most serious grounds of suspicion were apparently their Slavic or Russian names.[21] Neither the organization of a tiny Communist party in Chicago, September, 1919, nor the noisy activities of other extremists constituted a sufficiently serious threat to social order to account for these repressive measures. Indeed, the intensity of the "Red Scare" increased, contrary to all logic, in direct proportion to the distance from the source of the infection, Soviet Russia.

In France and Germany the worst symptoms were largely over by the end of 1919. Fear of revolution as well as the German problem helped the election of the predominantly conservative and nationalist "horizon bleu" French Chamber of Deputies in November. During the electoral campaign, walls were plastered with posters picturing a bewhiskered ogre, dagger between clenched jaws, and bomb in hand. The result was a decisive set-back for the Socialist party. On May Day, 1920, the government mobilized the army against the general strike sponsored by the General Confederation of Labor and reduced syndicalism temporarily to comparative impotence.[22] Thereafter, thanks in part to effective security measures, not even the Bolsheviks thought of revolution in France as a serious possibility, although a nervous deputy scented a Soviet-German plot to create a revolutionary situation when Germany failed to make the stipulated monthly deliveries of coal in full.[23] Each parliamentary vote of confidence on the government's anti-Bolshevik policy resulted in resounding majorities and the few critics spoke mainly for the record keeping in view an eventual shift in the political balance.

Germany continued to disappoint Lenin's persistent hopes that the world revolution would begin there. Much use was made of the danger of revolution in German propaganda addressed to the victorious Allies in the hope of military and economic concessions, but it is doubtful that many German conservatives were seriously alarmed. If a government controlled by Social Democrats, whose firmness is dealing with social disorders was normally held in low esteem, had crushed the Spartacists and their sympathizers, surely there was little cause to fear after the political balance began to shift toward the center and the right. There was some support even at this early date for an association with the Allies against Soviet Russia that doubtless reflected some fear of revolution as well as hopes for a beginning in the revision of the Treaty of Versailles.[24] While some good democrats like the philosopher and Reichstag member, Ernst Troeltsch, voiced the moral abhorrence of bolshevism that was generally characteristic of Western opinion, German conservatives, and other groups as well, were inclined to accept the Soviet regime as, at least for the time being, the *de facto* Russian government and to consider the possibility of using Russia to advance the recovery of Germany. It was, however, still too prostrate in 1919-20 for positive action of this kind, although the question of the exchange of prisoners served as the occasion for the first semi-official contracts.[25] The brusque rejection of the Allies' invitation to join in the blockade of Soviet Russia registered Germany's repudiation of intervention in no uncertain fashion.[26]

Practically everywhere, even in France and Germany where fear of revolution at home was not a really serious factor, conservative opinion was alert to the danger of Bolshevik propaganda—as were the governments. Nothing good could be expected from it. More significant, however, was the latent fear of the expansion of bolshevism by the force of arms, although conservative opinion usually counted upon its collapse in Russia almost from day to day. Each success of the White Russians was hailed as a harbinger of its impending fall, while their defeats inspired fearsome prophecies of the invasion of Central and Western Europe by Slavic and oriental hordes. On the part of those whose thinking was still conditioned by the traditional motives and procedures of power politics—and this state of mind persisted in France especially—there was also alarm. Having exhausted what remained of the resources of Russia and lacking the capacity to create anything but armies, Lenin and Trotsky might resort to foreign conquests to keep themselves in power. Such traditionalists detected also a revival of Russia's historic imperialism in the guise of the ideology of world revolution, and they recalled the messianic mission that the Pan-Slavism of the nineteenth century had conferred upon Russia.

More important, because the French government never forgot it, was the logic of the postwar situation that pointed to a Russo-German rapprochement and an eventual alliance. The Germans, it was feared, would always be ready to co-operate with the Bolsheviks or the White Russians, whichever succeeded in consolidating themselves in power, in order to overthrow the peace settlement.[27] These fears, and worse, were occasionally expressed in Britain. A Tory back-bencher, perhaps influenced by the ideas of Halford Mackinder, conjured up a geopolitical nightmare. Germany might draw China as well as Russia into her orbit. "What chance would the nations at the outskirts have to curb the ambitions of a Russo-German-Chinese block established astride the Urals, with the advantage of interior lines, a colossal reserve of man-power, and far greater unity of control than anything which could be put up against them by the League of Nations?"[28] A French commentator drew somewhat similar conclusions from the anti-colonialism of Bolshevik propaganda in Asia. In it he saw, prophetically it must be said, the seeds of Europe's loss of world preponderance and of a declining way of life.[29] The prophets of doom probably impressed few since the predictions implied a success for the Bolsheviks which then seemed highly improbable, and those who cried "wolf" too frequently doubtless did so with diminishing effect.

Even in these early years, there was, of course, considerable justification for seeing in bolshevism a world conspiracy. The movement began as a conspiracy, it had triumphed in Russia as such, and it counted upon conspiratorial methods for the success of the world revolution. The Third International was a move in that direction, and the Russian Bolsheviks imposed the methods by which they had seized power upon the member parties at its Second Congress. As yet, however, it was for the most part the Socialists, especially in France and Germany, and British Laborites, whose ranks were being raided for the organization of affiliates for the Third International, who had firsthand experience of the *modus operandi* of Bolshevik agents.

The general public had no special reason to be alarmed about a purely Bolshevik conspiracy. In fact, the tendency was to associate it with other real or fancied enemies against whom emotions and prejudices had already been inflamed. It was only too easy to associate bolshevism with Germany and also with the Jews. The widely credited charge that the Bolshevik leaders were paid German agents during the war undoubtedly conditioned many to believe that Germans controlled the Bolshevik conspiracy. This version was further elaborated in the American press. The conspiracy, it was said, was controlled by the Prussian militarists and included the Egyptian and Indian nationalists and Mustapha Kemal of Turkey as well as the Bolsheviks.[30] While it is true that Bolshevik propaganda was already exploiting anti-colonial sentiment against the British Empire and that the Turkish nationalist leader, Mustapha Kemal, was willing to accept aid from Russia in the service of Turkey's regeneration, there is no evidence that any German or Prussian militarists were involved and that anything more than minute fractions of the Egyptian and Indian nationalists had become even nominal Bolsheviks.

Another hatred, anti-Semitism, was more universal and of much more ancient origin, and its revival in a virulent form was one of the more ominous features of the postwar situation. In many countries the *Protocols of the Elders of Zion,* the forgery of the Tsarist secret police at the turn of the century that purported to expose the existence and methods of a worldwide conspiracy to establish the world domination of the Jews, received wide circulation for the first time.[31] The fateful significance of these developments in Germany—their part in the rise of Hitler and National Socialism—is well known. Less familiar is the association between anti-Semitism and anti-bolshevism and the form it took in Britain. In view of the presence of a number of Jews among the Bolshevik leaders and, at the same time, of the upsurge of anti-Semitism, it was perhaps inevitable that anti-Semitic circles should proclaim bolshevism as a tool of the world Jewish conspiracy. This myth was, however, by no means confined to the lunatic fringe, for there are traces of it in the otherwise respectable Tory press. When Lloyd George spoke out against armed intervention in Russia, November 17, 1919, a review said, editorially, that he was "even more in the hands of the International Jew than any of his predecessors."[32] The same editor attributed the criticism of Poland's invasion of the Ukraine in April, 1920, to the influence of "the Jew-ridden portion of our Government . . . and of all of the world's Jews." The dominant role of Jews among the Bolsheviks "is enough to predispose in their favor Jewish opinion the world over."[33]

Anti-Semitism found sponsors in unexpected and high places. Carried away by a passionate desire for action against the Bolsheviks, Winston Churchill played up to it briefly in a speech at a coalition demonstration in Sunderland, January 3, 1920. "They [the Bolsheviks] believe," he said, "in the international Soviet of the Russian and Polish Jews."[34] On the same day the ultra-Tory *Morning Post* (January 3) expounded and endorsed the essence of the *Protocols,* without naming it, in a leading editorial. "Lenin . . . is not, in fact, Lenin at all, but a secret organization—directed by revolutionary Jews to the destruction of the world. That organization has its plan of campaign. . . . It has its members and its agents in all countries and in unsuspected places . . . it sees in the temporary exhaustion of Christendom the best chance of a victory for anti-Christ." That the *Times,* under Lord Northcliffe's ownership at this time, came close to committing itself to the same views was perhaps the best witness to the prevailing hysteria. While nothing was said of the matter in its leading articles, a communication "from a correspondent" on the *Protocols* was featured on May 8, 1920. There was a virtuous appearance of reserved opinion; the "correspondent" called for an investigation of its allegations of an international Jewish conspiracy because of the wide circulation of the *Protocols.* Since, however, he proceeded to draw his own conclusions, the "correspondent's" good faith and that of the *Times* in printing his communication were at least questionable. The Soviet government was acting in accordance with the principles of the *Protocols.* "We see this, and it seems uncanny. . . . Have we been struggling these tragic years to blow up and extirpate the secret organization of German world domination only to find beneath it another more dangerous because more secret? Have we, by straining every fibre of our national body, escaped a 'Pax Germanica' only to fall into a 'Pax Judaeica'?"[35] Needless to say, there was no investigation of the *Protocols.* At least one contributor to a reputable review attributed the Labor party's efforts to prevent intervention in the Polish-Russian War to penetration by Russian Jews. "Who were these men? The cousins, aunts and uncles of Trotsky, innumerable members of the same tribe."[36]

Uncompromising as the anti-bolshevism of conservative opinion was almost everywhere, it was by no means of one mind as to what should be done. Only in Germany was there at least potential support in these circles for any dealings with the Bolshevik regime, and they would doubtless have preferred the White Russians if Germany's interest could be served equally well. While the disappearance of the Bolsheviks would have been received with great relief and satisfaction, the partisans of their destruction by force of arms, if those arms had to be those borne by their own soldiers, were not representative even of rightist opinion. The French conservatives, the most ardent interventionists of all, would certainly have approved a French contingent to an international army, but they were too conscious of the drainage of French man power during the war, of the German problem, and of the doubtful effectiveness of French troops for operations in Russia to approve the assumption of the major burden. And so it was with the others. During the Red Scare of 1919-20, at least conservative opinion in America held that the Bolsheviks should be destroyed by any and all means but at the same time it insisted that the responsibility should be shouldered by the European allies. It was largely the same with the British Tories. They were all for supporting the White Russians, and here and there the thought that Germany might be enlisted was given consideration. Like many of their opposite numbers elsewhere, they generally clung to the illusion that the Bolshevik regime was doomed for internal Russian reasons: its own failure, the supposedly irreconcilable hatred of the peasant masses, and the ultimate triumph of the White Russians.[37]

At the opposite extreme of Western opinion, a small minority of left-wingers of the Socialist movement and a scattering of unattached intellectuals responded favorably to the Bolsheviks' announced purpose of achieving the millenium by violence and dictatorship. They organized local Communist parties and sent delegations to the congresses of the Third International. Not all of these pilgrims, however, were won over to the Bolshevik cause. If Marcel Cachin returned from Moscow to Paris in the summer of 1920 to lead the Communist schism in the Socialist party, Crispien and Dittmann of the delegation from the German Independent Social Democrats courageously repudiated violent methods on behalf of the German Revolution during the Second Congress.[38] Neither in numbers nor in quality of leadership were the Western converts to bolshevism as significant as the ado that was made about them would suggest. George Bernard Shaw might proclaim his sympathetic approval and say that the Bolsheviks had "on the whole, pounced upon the right things, and shot the right people (from the Marxian point of view)," but his views on politics never enjoyed the influence of his literary pen.[39]

On the whole, the Communist left was probably most influential in causing the Socialist and Labor parties to emphasize their differences with the Bolsheviks. The German "revisionist" Social Democrats moved so far to the right that one of them, writing in their principal review, repudiated the thought of an exclusively Social Democratic government even if it enjoyed a clear majority of the popular votes. Since the peasants were irreconcilably hostile and no one could govern against their will, an exclusively Socialist government would be impossible.[40] The Socialists went almost as far as the conservatives in the vigor of their moral denunciations of the Bolsheviks. They drew the line, however, at anything that smacked of intervention in Russian affairs and they generally favored economic cooperation (in the case of the German Social Democrats), the resumption of commercial relations (the British Labor party in particular) and to some extent official recognition (especially British Laborites and French Socialists).

What counted most, especially in terms of influence upon official policy, was not the relative weight of conservative opinion in comparison with the extreme left but rather the comparative importance of conservative and liberal opinion. This alignment was perhaps less significant on the Continent than in Britain and the United States for, in regard to bolshevism and Russia, liberals, like conservatives, were inclined in France and Germany to react in the terms imposed by the perennial Franco-German problem. From the nineteenth century, the liberals of the English speaking countries, especially, had inherited a profound confidence in the essential goodness of man and in the progress of the world toward political democracy. More recently, the liberal outlook had also acquired a conviction of the need for social justice, a point of view that perhaps weakened to some extent its traditional attachment to the liberty and rights of the individual. It was, therefore, not altogether the result of fortuitous circumstances that the historic Liberal party in Britain was already declining and that the Labor party was moving into its position as the chief opponent of the Conservatives. Thanks to the "revisionist" movement within the continental Socialist parties, something like this evolution was also taking place there; as Marxian orthodoxy weakened, liberal values and ideas tended to take its place. Liberal opinion was bound to reject Soviet bolshevism's reliance upon violence and dictatorship, especially as a model to be copied by Western countries.

Conservatives regarded the critical conclusions of members of the Labor delegation as among the most effective weapons of anti-Bolshevik propaganda. One noted, especially, Mrs. Philip Snowden's "lapidary definition of Lenin as 'Prince of slaves and slave of dogmas'" and Bertrand Russell's "epic sentence" about "the doubts raised in him by the contact with those who had no doubts."[41] Of Russell's impressions, Gilbert Chesterton wrote: ". . . he did admire them [the Bolsheviks] until he saw them: what he saw, and what he makes us see under a dead daylight of lucidity [is] more dreadful than the flarerockets of any number of raving reactionaries...."[42] Russell's penetrating comment that the Bolsheviks meant what they said about dictatorship but that they did not mean what Westerners thought they meant when they spoke of the proletariat was not only true but effective against those who persisted in seeing in the Soviet government a workers' government.[43]

Given their intellectual inheritance and outlook, liberals, in other respects, saw different aspects of the Bolshevik experience and reached different conclusions from those of the conservatives. They were thoroughly skeptical, for one thing, as to the reliability of almost all accepted reports about Russia, and were inclined, perhaps naturally but certainly unwisely, to accept the opposite as nearer the truth. According to Arthur Ransome, the knowledge that the Bolsheviks were not Germany's paid agents was one of the reasons why he and Raymond Robins came to their defense.[44] In view of the pronounced austerity of Lenin's own manner of life and that of his associates, as well as the puritanical tendencies of bolshevism, the constant references to them as immoral criminals could not but be regarded as intentional perversions of the truth. Walter Lippmann's and Charles Merz's devastating demonstration of the unreliability of even the *New York Times*'s Russian news has already been noted. The same point had been made months earlier on the editorial page of the *Manchester Guardian*. "We were first asked to believe," it stated, January 15, 1920, "that a mere touch of the Allied finger was needed to topple the Russian Soviet Government into destruction. That was found to be untrue. Then we were told that the Soviet Government was, anyhow, on its last legs, as 95 per cent of Russians...would welcome Denikin and Koltchak [*sic*] with open arms. That was found to be untrue. At another time we were told that Bolshevism was run by a little gang of Jews. That was found to be untrue. . . . It will not do." There was a feeling that the public had been purposefully misled. "The governments chose to picture Bolshevism as a fabulous monster; to exaggerate its vices, or to invent them . . . to present its work as a carnival of human malice and corruption."[45] Across the Atlantic, a weekly of similarly radical but not Bolshevik tendencies noted the obvious consequence. "They have tried to paint that government so terribly black, and have been caught in so many lies, that from believing nothing good of Russia there is a reaction towards believing nothing bad. . . . The Russia of the western world has been largely a fiction, a horrible fiction to the conservatives, a glorious fiction to the revolutionists."[46]

In crediting the Bolsheviks with sincere aspirations for a better world, no matter how utopian they might be or how perverted and wrong their methods, liberal opinion sensed an element of strength that was to account in large part for bolshevism's world-wide appeal which the conservatives never understood. "For Bolshevism as an idea, as a dream," wrote a British observer, "is perhaps the temptation of this generation...."[47] Unlike right-wing conservatives, liberals did not fear revolution at home, for they were confident that the reforms they advocated would avert such tendencies in that direction as might exist. They were not, therefore, hypnotized by the influence Soviet Russia might exert in their own working class circles.

As an example to be emulated, there was little to commend bolshevism as it manifested itself in Russia. It was "a dreary ideal" even if it were practicable, according to an influential liberal American weekly.[48] Aside from its unacceptable reliance upon force, the claim that the Socialist ideal could be attained so quickly encouraged impossible hopes whose inevitable disappointments would do irreparable damage to true socialism. This, in Russell's view, was one of the major reasons for rejecting bolshevism.[49] He deplored the failure of many Western Socialists to tell the truth as he—

Russell—saw it, for that truth would require its complete rejection, but it was not without merit for the time being as a purely Russian phenomenon. "For their international program there is, in my mind," he reported on his return from Russia, "nothing to be said. But as a national government, they are performing a necessary though unamiable task in disciplining a lazy population and in preparing to develop Russia's natural resources through state capitalism."[50]   It was doing more, in his opinion, "to prevent chaos than any possible alternative government could do."[51]   Although Russell's silence suggests his disagreement, liberal opinion, especially in Britain and the United States, was confident, obviously on the basis of British and American political experience, that the responsibilities of power would, in time, tame the Bolsheviks and moderate their most objectionable practices. A hostile critic noted fairly enough that many British liberals thought that Lenin would act as they themselves would act in similar circumstances. "They think that the responsibilities of Lenin must sober and modify him as they would sober and modify an English Socialist." Lenin, on the contrary, was a fanatic who was incapable of change.[52]   The Red Terror would normally have itself sufficed to damn the Bolsheviks in the eyes of Western liberals, but they discovered extenuating circumstances. Even a pacifist like George Lansbury discounted it as a temporary phenomenon and perhaps as a necessary weapon against the hostility with which the Bolshevik leaders were surrounded.[53]   The Liberals' sense of fair play was outraged by the silence of the militant anti-Bolsheviks about the atrocities of the counter-revolutionaries and White Russians. "The limited Red Terror was at least less sanguinary than the Finnish White Terror, and it is over."[54]

In contrast to the trend of liberal opinion, British Labor believed, mistakenly for the most part, that the Soviet regime was a workers' government. Therein was to be found the explanation of the Tories' uncompromising hostility and of the policy of armed intervention. If the Bolsheviks had failed to improve the lot of masses in Russia and had been guilty of excesses, the reason was that the opposition of the Allies, their support of the White Russians and the blockade, had not given them a "fair chance."[55]   As this strongly emotional reaction became increasingly an article of faith, Labor as a whole took the position that the blockade should be lifted, trade relations resumed, and an end be made to the support of the White Russians. Increasingly restless because of depressed economic conditions at home, hope for improvement came to center far more than the facts warranted upon peace and trade with Russia, and the trade unions furnished powerful pressure for a reversal of official policy.

While the Liberals did not share Labor's worst illusions about the nature of the Bolshevik regime, they were in substantial agreement as to what should be done. There was, in their opinion, no reason to fear that friendly relations with Russia, even if the doors were opened to Soviet emissaries and Bolshevik propaganda, would convert the British working classes to bolshevism if for no other reason than its foreign origins. "It is probable that any Russians who get through Sir Basil Thomson's sieve turn English revolutionaries into moderate men about as fast as Sir Basil Thomson is turning moderate men into revolutionaries. We are in all our classes a conservative people, prejudiced against any idea that comes from abroad."[56] If Bolshevik sympathies had penetrated the ranks of labor, it was the result of the military effort to overthrow the Soviet regime and to set up a reactionary government in its place.[57] Bertrand Russell spoke for most British and American liberals when he wrote: "The policy of crushing Bolshevism by force was always foolish . . . peace and trade" would alone solve the problem.[58]

Everywhere in the Western world, except on the extreme left, bolshevism and Soviet Russia aroused a moral abhorrence that differed only in degree between countries and parties. Nowhere, however, did this almost universal anti-bolshevism and hostility to the Soviet government constitute a sufficiently solid basis for armed intervention of sufficient scope to assure its destruction. The spokesmen for conservative opinion, otherwise uncompromising enemies of the Bolshevik regime, who frankly called for such action on the part of their own governments, were few indeed. The climate of opinion in the immediate aftermath of the war could scarcely have been less favorable. A French commentator correctly characterized the situation everywhere when he wrote that the times were not appropriate for decisions and sacrifices of heroic proportions.[59]

While the die-hards on the extreme right sometimes breathed fire and brimstone and the Bolsheviks gave as good as they received, there were indications of impending changes. These polemics, according to a recent historian of the League of Nations on the situation at the beginning of 1920, had a "hollow sound" as if they expressed not a policy but a sentiment.[60] The hopes placed in the White Russians, even with the support of Allied arms and supplies, were declining after repeated disappointments. In the French Chamber of Deputies, voices were occasionally raised from surprising quarters for a revision of the interventionist policy. A member of the Radical party asserted that the atrocities of which the White Russians were guilty rivalled in horror those of the Bolsheviks; he was certain that "the Soviets, who are Russians, will have the same attitude toward us that we have toward them."[61] If the parliamentary economic expert Anatole de Monzie endorsed an indictment of the qualifications of the Quai d'Orsay's experts on Russia properly to assess the situation there, the basis for the official policy was not quite as solid as it seemed.[62] Usually, however, those who spoke up for a change did so because of concern for France's position with reference to Germany and a desire for the recovery of Russia as an ally. The conservative and nationalist Louis Barthou spoke of the unreality of French policy and, rather contemptuously, of the *cordon sanitaire* and of the *fil de fer barbelé* as a policy of metaphors.[63] In his maiden speech, Éduoard Daladier, a Radical Socialist and a future president of the council, urged that France should revise her attitude toward Russia before it was too late to prevent Germany from approaching Russia and using her man-power against France. The ovation he won was, however, a tribute to his war record and not an endorsement of the policy for which he pleaded in vain.[64] None of these speakers reduced in any significant degree the mas-sive votes that monotonously approved the interventionist policy of which the existing Millerand government was an ardent advocate, but that there were spokesmen at all against the prevailing sentiment was a matter of some significance. Public support for a new departure was by all odds strongest in Britain where it had a powerful champion in the person of Prime Minis-ter Lloyd George. Besides his own personal following, he could count, if he so decided, upon the support of Labor as well as the Liberals.

II

Lloyd George's Russian Policy,
July, 1919, to March, 1920

On August 25, 1919, the Allies declared a blockade of the Soviet-controlled Russian coasts, which at that time were restricted to the Baltic area. This action was intended to prevent any "increase in the strength of the Bolsheviks," and the participation of the neutrals in its enforcement was invited.[1] Depriving the Soviets of the possibility of securing essential commodities such as medicines from abroad, it was a powerful addition to the policy of containment which Clemenceau described as the *cordon sanitaire* and *fil de fer barbelé.*[2] The blockade, however, was by no means universally approved. The American government refused to adhere to it, citing the legal difficulty of blockading a country against which it was not officially at war.[3] Germany rejected a special invitation to co-operate, and the neutrals showed little enthusiasm. The effectiveness of the blockade, although France was its ardent champion, ultimately depended upon the British fleet, and the war just ended testified to its efficiency as an offensive weapon. Although the declaration could not have been made without the approval of the British Prime Minister, it was soon evident that his heart was not in it. His consent was perhaps the result of French pressure, the views of the Foreign Office and of the British service departments, and the momentary successes of the White Russians.

The prospects of joint allied action in regard to Russia were nevertheless dimmer than ever, especially if that action took the form of vigorous intervention. Indeed, the common front established at the time of the promised material assistance to Admiral Kolchak in May, 1919, promptly disintegrated after the signing of the Treaty of Versailles. On August 21, the British Foreign Office vainly initiated, with the Cabinet's approval, a new effort for Allied unity. Writing to Arthur Balfour, the Foreign Secretary, then in Paris, Lord Curzon stressed the inconsistencies that had developed in dealing with the Russian problem, doubted the existence of an Allied policy, and proposed a conference of the Allied and Associated Powers on Russia.[4] Weeks passed without action until Curzon finally lost patience. A memorandum listing the decisions the British government had reached independently moved him to write: ". . . if any one is sanguine enough to believe that this moribund Conference [the Paris Peace Conference] is capable in its death throes of producing a Russian policy, I am not that man. I consider it more profitable to formulate and pursue our own Russian policy within the limits (financial, political, and geographical) open to us and to inform Paris when we have done so."[5] Curzon's pessimism was fully shared by Sir Eyre Crowe, a permanent Foreign Office official then attached to the British Peace Delegation in Paris, but he had his own views as to where the responsibility lay. The treatment of Russian problems, he wrote, "has been a hand-to-mouth affair sometimes arranged between France and England, sometimes with America, at other times based on decisions of the British and French governments." It seemed to him that this evasion of the conference "was deliberate and intentional" on the part of the British government.[6]

Crowe's impression was substantially correct, but he might have added that the prime minister's own frequently independent action in foreign affairs, without regard to the Foreign Office, also played a part.[7] What Lloyd George's personal attitude was on the Bolshevik experiment escapes exact definition and it may well be that he had no clear-cut or lasting opinions. Some official observers of his policy, Lord Hardinge and Sir Henry Wilson, especially, felt as the former wrote later that the prime minister had a "sneaking sympathy" for the Bolsheviks,[8] and he once told a close friend that the Communist experiment had to be tried.[9] Certain it is that the fervent moral denunciations with which his speeches were seasoned did not reliably indicate his purposes. These objectives, which repeatedly yielded, however, to expediency, were first of all the liquidation of direct intervention as incapable of restoring peace and order to Russia and Europe, and then the restoration of normal relations, at least in the form of trade but perhaps also by formal diplomatic recognition.[10] Since any attempt to carry out this policy would, and did, challenge the essential Tory element of the coalition that supported his government, it required considerable political courage on his part, although he could rely upon the support of Liberal opinion. In any event, this master politician could be counted upon to choose the approaches toward his goals that would be least offensive, and his retention of Winston Churchill in the Cabinet, despite his well-known hostility to the prime minister's Russian policy, was an anchor to the windward.

The first moves toward the liquidation of Britain's part in intervention were, in fact, approved or accepted almost unanimously. By the end of July, 1919, it was decided that the largest contingent of British troops in Russia should be withdrawn from Archangel and Murmansk before the onset of winter, a decision that was later extended to the small units with Denikin in South Russia and in Vladivostok with scarcely a protest. As the head of the War Office, the evacuation was Churchill's responsibility which he fulfilled promptly (except for the military mission with Denikin whose withdrawal was delayed in the obvious hope of a change for the better in his military fortunes), despite his passionate certainty that Britain's long-term interests required the overthrow of the Bolsheviks. In September, 1919, he warned the Cabinet that Russia would soon be "thoroughly militarized, with nothing but its militarism to live on, bitterly hostile to the Entente, ready to work with Germany, and already largely organized by Germany."[11] Even he had to accept as a fact that opinion would not support the continued employment of British troops for combat purposes, and an obstinate confidence in the ability of the White Russians with material support to do the job doubtless eased the necessary readjustment. "We have," he wrote in a message read at a meeting of Liberals in Dundee in October, 1919, "steadfastly adhered to our principle that Russia must be saved by Russian manpower, and all our own fighting troops have now been safely and skilfully withdrawn from that country."[12] His Tory admirers (on matters relating to Russia) were silent when Balfour, the Foreign Secretary, asserted in the House of Commons, November 17, 1919: "Nobody, so far as I know, defends the use of a single British soldier in these internal conflicts in Russia."[13]

Far more bitter to Churchill must have been the gradual cessation of shipments of war supplies to the White Russian forces. When Lloyd George repeatedly acknowledged a debt of honor arising from the encouragement and assistance given the White Russians, he was perhaps thinking of Churchill as well as the many others who felt this obligation, but he believed that the large supplies already sent had paid the debt in full.[14] The decision, in fact, had already been taken to send nothing more to Kolchak (the United States was to be asked to assume the burden), although Denikin was to be further provisioned.[15] There was no noticeable objection when Balfour announced in the House of Commons, November 17, 1919, that a date had been set for the termination of all supplies for Denikin: ". . . nobody . . . defends the further expenditure of British money after the present contributions are concluded on the 31st March [1920]."[16] While Labor and Liberal opinion greeted the approaching end of the military phase of British intervention with satisfaction, the Tory bitter-enders resigned themselves silently to the inevitable.

Concerning what further steps to take, Lloyd George was pulled in opposite directions by his own impulses toward the restoration of normal relations and by pressure on the part of those, including the French, who were determined to maintain at least the close containment of Soviet Russia. Clemenceau exaggerated the extent of his success in committing British policy during the Anglo-French conversations in London, December 11-12, 1919, in addressing the Chamber of Deputies ten days later. Only in a formal sense could Lloyd George be said to have committed himself, as Clemenceau claimed, to the "barbed-wire encirclement" of Soviet Russia.[17] While the agreements reached provided that Bolshevik Russia was "to be left, as it were, within a ring fence," that "a strong Poland was in the interests of the Entente Powers," and that the border states of non-Russian population would be assisted "as may be found desirable," it was also stipulated that no further commitments beyond those already made should be undertaken, that "the form and extent" of the aid promised for the defense of Poland were left for further determination, and aid for other border states would be such "as may be found desirable in the circumstances of each case as it arises."[18] During the discussion, Lloyd George had, in fact, expressed serious doubts about Clemenceau's version of the *cordon sanitaire:* "a federation of anti-Bolshevik States," whose effectiveness was dependent upon Allied money, guns, and equipment, "was, he thought, not very helpful."[19]

The two governments reacted quite differently to the first signs that the new Baltic states wished to make peace with the Soviets. As early as September 25, 1919, the Baltic States were told that, because of the inability to continue its material support, the British government was not entitled "to exercise any pressure upon the free initiative of the Baltic States and that their governments must be at liberty to decide upon such action as may be most conducive to the preservation of their own national existence."[20] The French, however, assumed a menacing attitude when Estonia, refusing to subordinate her decisions to those of the Baltic States as a group, moved for a separate peace. The Allies, they said, would be compelled "to take all necessary measures to meet this danger" to the blockade of Soviet Russia.[21] Without British support, the French were powerless in the Baltic, and the British, despite the vague London agreements, continued to leave the decision to the Baltic governments. On February 2, 1920, Estonia was the first to sign a treaty of peace with the Soviets.[22]

Meanwhile, Lloyd George was cautiously moving toward direct contacts and a possible settlement with the Soviet government. In contrast to the silent acceptance of military withdrawal from Russia, each step in this direction aroused violent protests from Conservative opinion which was unalterably opposed to the acceptance of the Soviet regime as a partner in negotiations. The prime minister put out a feeler in his Guildhall speech, November 8, 1919: "I hope the time is not distant when the Powers will be able to renew that attempt [the Prinkipo invitation] with better prospect of success."[23] The *Times* (November 10) was enraged, as was to be expected, partly because of the vendetta its owner, Lord Northcliffe, had declared against Lloyd George; the speech, the *Times* reported "disturbed and chilled the company" and its leader stirred up anti-Semitic feeling by attributing the Prinkipo affair to "prominent Jewish financiers in New York, whose interest in Trotsky and his associates is of long standing." More significant for the reaction of sober conservatives was the immediate response of R. W. Seton-Watson's well-informed weekly; it was "frankly appalled,"[24] although its attitude was soon to be reversed. Addressing the Commons, and more especially its Labor members, the prime minister asserted that bolshevism inevitably led to "black reaction"; it was the enemy of everything they held to be good. In his opinion, however, bolshevism could not be beaten with force of arms but "by sympathetic justice in all countries, by planting justice in all countries, by planting confidence in all classes, rich and poor. . . ."[25] The *Times* (November 17) captioned its leader, "A Pitiable Exhibition," and a Tory back-bencher replied: "You can no more expect Bolshevism to live within its own boundaries than you can expect a man-eating tiger to live in a stall and feed on carrots."[26]

For some months, the British and Soviet governments had, in fact, been exchanging communications on the question of the exchange of military and civilian prisoners. These negotiations, even from the technical point of view, encountered serious difficulties. In the absence of diplomatic representatives, the messages between Curzon[27] and Chicherin were exchanged directly via the wireless, often being sent to the Eiffel Tower station in Paris for transmission. Delays and imperfect reception were not infrequent. Of greater moment was the intrusion of a brutal tone into the traditionally restrained language of diplomacy because of the passions aroused by the ideological conflict, for it foreshadowed one of the deplorable characteristics of later international relations. As a result of a Soviet threat to discriminate between the treatment of British volunteers "who came of their own free will and for the sake of money to kill Russian workers and peasants" and drafted men to the disadvantage of the former,[28] Curzon threatened that Chicherin, Lenin, Trotsky, and all others concerned would be held "personally responsible" and that retaliatory treatment would be meted out to Russian prisoners.[29] Chicherin's reply was likewise couched in "insolent" terms. After charging that Soviet soldiers had been clubbed with rifle butts or killed on being taken prisoner in northern Russia, he spoke of Curzon's "insolent threats" and declared "that no blackmail" could influence the policy of the Soviet government. It would continue to treat working-class prisoners more liberally than officers unless they were volunteers. "Any repetition of such threats addressed personally to members of the Russian Government will cause the Soviet Government to consider whether they can entertain further negotiations with the present British Government even on questions like that of the exchange of prisoners."[30] Although this arrogant message was treated with scornful silence,[31] Chicherin continued the main negotiations as if nothing had happened.

By November, 1919, arrangements were finally concluded, after the other Allies had agreed, for direct negotiations with Litvinov in Copenhagen for an exchange of prisoners. Captain James O'Grady, Labor member of Parliament and a trade union official, was chosen as the head of the British mission, doubtless on the erroneous theory that a man of his background could negotiate more effectively with Bolsheviks than a professional diplomat.[32] He was instructed not to permit the negotiations to extend beyond the exchange of prisoners and the repatriation of civilians who wished to return to their native countries. In France the selection of O'Grady was regarded with suspicion from the first, and it promptly protested against his alleged willingness to communicate whatever proposals Litvinov decided to make even if they concerned general political problems such as peace. Curzon at once called O'Grady to order, warning that "your mission is being subjected to the most intense scrutiny by the press and public of all the countries interested." O'Grady was to observe his instructions scrupulously, yet in conceding that he might discuss matters concerning the blockade on receiving appropriate instructions, Curzon was himself extending the limitations of the mission.[33]

Litvinov in fact seized upon every favorable circumstance, especially Britain's anxiety for the repatriation of her nationals, to broaden the scope of the conversations and to secure diplomatic recognition or, at least, the resumption of normal trade relations. To the great indignation of those concerned, he communicated the peace proposals of the Seventh All-Russian Congress of Soviets of December 5, 1919, to the Entente legations in Copenhagen four days later. The British and French ministers agreed "that we cannot better mark our sense of the breach of good faith than by refusing to accept this letter," and their American and Italian colleagues likewise returned it unopened.[34] Nevertheless, O'Grady saw to it that the Soviet peace offer and Litvinov's covering letter were brought to Curzon's attention[35] and personally handed a second Litvinov letter to Curzon, at the Foreign Office, December 26. It contained a direct appeal for peace, as the indispensable condition for Russia's recovery. If the formal guarantees of the Soviet government were insufficient to allay the "bogy" of Communist propaganda, "could not means of preventing this propaganda be devised without barring the way to mutual representation?"[36]

Whatever Lloyd George's response might have been had he been able to act in accordance with his instincts, Curzon, now the Foreign Secretary, was not willing to abandon hope of the overthrow of the Bolsheviks, as was clearly indicated in his instructions to Halford Mackinder for his special mission to General Denikin. Mackinder was to explain the reasons why British aid would cease on March 31 (1920), but he was also to keep in mind (and these instructions received the Cabinet's approval, December 2, 1919) "that there is . . . no reason to conclude that the wheel of fortune has finally turned in favor of the Bolshevik armies."[37] Curzon quickly brushed aside Litvinov's letter as raising questions that O'Grady was not authorized to consider; it "cannot be answered by him."[38] Despite irritation with Litvinov's maneuvers, Curzon still did not break off the negotiations, and the agreement for the exchange of military and civilian prisoners, with freedom for the latter to decide for or against repatriation, was signed at Copenhagen, February 2, 1920. It was followed by similar agreements between Soviet Russia and a large number of governments, including those of Belgium, Italy, and France, as well as of neutral states.[39] While these first sensible and humanitarian arrangements had no immediate or large significance for amelioration of the East-West conflict, they did show that contacts and agreements for specific and limited purposes were possible. Moreover, they offered no provocation to anti-Bolshevik sentiment, although the possibly inevitable delays in carrying them out did nourish suspicion of the good faith of the Soviet government.

Coincident with these favorable developments, a situation appeared in Soviet Russia that might in other circumstances have given a further impetus in the same direction. The Red Army seemed to have gained the upper hand against the White Russian forces on all fronts, the apparently decisive turn in the fluctuations of the Civil War taking place during the autumn of 1919. On two of them, organized resistance on any considerable scale had practically ceased early in 1920. In the Baltic area, General Yudenich's forces, after entering the suburbs of Petrograd in mid-October, were thrust back by Red Army units already operating there under Trotsky's galvanizing leadership, and the White Russian forces retreated across the Estonian frontier where they were disarmed and interned. More significantly, Admiral Kolchak, upon whom the Allies had mainly relied for the overthrow of the Bolshevik regime and whose leadership the White Russian generals had recognized, was driven out of his capital, Omsk, on November 14. The authority of his government in Siberia rapidly disintegrated, with the Allies being among the first to abandon him. The American government had not, as the British hoped, taken over the burden of provisioning him. In January, General Graves's small expeditionary force was largely withdrawn from Vladivostok and eastern Siberia, and the Czech Legion had retreated into an attitude of neutrality. But Kolchak's doom was sealed by his failure—or that of the men around him, the responsibility being disputed—to recover the loyalty of the population. On January 4, 1920, he put himself under the protection of the Allies and into the hands of the Czechs, who, fearing renewed hostilities, surrendered him to the Bolsheviks and to his execution, February 7. In the backwater of northern Russia, General Miller maintained precarious control of the Archangel region after the withdrawal of the last British troops, September 27, 1919, until he himself fled, February 19.

Only in South Russia, where General Denikin seemed almost to have had Moscow within his grasp in the summer of 1919, was there at least some hope at the beginning of the following year. He had, however, lost both Orel and Voronezh before the end of October and, thereafter, outflanked repeatedly by Budënny's cavalry and unable to rely upon the loyalty of his rear areas, was forced into continuous retreat. The successive losses of Kursk, Kharkov, and Kiev in November and December gave the control of the entire Don area and much of the Ukraine to the Bolsheviks by January, 1920, although Denikin still held the Crimea at the end of March.

At the beginning of 1920, the question of gravest concern to the outside world was the use that the Bolsheviks would make of what seemed to be their definitive victory. Lack of reliable information about the economic situation in Russia was a major obstacle to sensible conclusions. The productive and distributive systems were in a condition verging upon complete paralysis. Only the iron military dictatorship of "war communism" had made the war effort possible. With the virtual disappearance of consumer goods and of currency of any value, food for the declining urban population was secured from the peasants only by the use of force. Industrial production, except perhaps for the Red Army, which, however, equipped itself in part from the captured stores of the White Russians, disappeared almost entirely; and the dispersal of the small body of trained workmen into the army or to the villages and the deterioration of machines were most serious obstacles to its revival. Where surpluses beyond the starvation rations existed, they could be distributed only with the greatest difficulty, especially while military necessities monopolized the broken-down railways. If victory in the Civil War was in sight, the Bolshevik leaders were aware of the perhaps still most difficult economic problem, particularly since the lessening danger of counter-revolution would presumably stimulate dissatisfaction of peasants and urban folk alike with the hardships of their lot.

Lenin, in fact, announced that the next campaign would be on the economic front for the revival of production, and Trotsky urged the formation of labor armies for this purpose.[40] The Third Army in the Urals was declared to be a labor army on January 15, 1920.[41] This was a period of lively controversy in party councils over Trotsky's support of central economic planning and of Lenin's proposal for Russia's electrification.[42] In any event, these new developments were certain to affect Soviet Russia's international situation, and the Bolshevik leaders repeatedly affirmed their desire for peace in Chicherin's direct appeals to the Allied governments, in resolutions adopted by various Soviet governmental assemblies,[43] and in interviews in the foreign press.[44] Karl Radek developed the thesis that co-existence was the policy of the Soviet government in the *Manchester Guardian* (January 8, 1920). The struggle against capitalism, he said, would be won in each country "from within the growing struggle between the peoples and governments. Revolutions never originate in foreign affairs, but are made at home." It is reasonable to conclude, in view of hard economic fact, that Lenin and his associates meant what they said up to a certain point. The need for at least a "breathing spell" was almost as imperative as it had been at the time of the Treaty of Brest-Litovsk. His long term aims, however, remained the same. He was still confident in the certainty of world revolution beginning in Germany, and it remained to be seen whether or not he would be able to resist the temptation to use Russia's Red Army to advance its time table. Trotsky's scheme for the militarization of labor could, in fact, be interpreted as a convenient means to keep that army in being for just such circumstances.

In the West, news of the Bolshevik victories was a principal reason for the scare discussed in the preceding chapter. While liberal and labor opinion generally accepted the Bolsheviks' peaceful assertions because it seemed reasonable they should desire peace under the circumstances, the leaders of right-wing opinion sounded the alarm. Few, apparently, understood the real danger: that the Bolsheviks would intervene to aid a revolutionary movement already in being in Central Europe. On the contrary, the menace was more often seen as the result of the fact that the Bolsheviks were Russians after all and had inherited Russia's historic aggressiveness. The similarities between bolshevism and Pan-Slavism were pointed out.[45] In the *Action Française* (January 15, 1920), Jacques Bainville saw nothing new in the prospect of Bolshevik aggression: "It is eternal Russia that is on the move, that seeks space and air in the same ways in which she has always sought them."[46] The country's economic paralysis was not seen as a reason for expecting a period of peace but as an imperative compulsion forcing the Bolsheviks to seek the loot of foreign conquests in order to survive.

The conclusion usually drawn was that the Allies should take steps to meet the danger at their meeting in Paris in mid-January, 1920, when the Treaty of Versailles was to be ratified. In the discussion as to what measures should be taken, significant differences developed between conservative opinion in Britain and France. J. L. Garvin offered a program of action in his weekly journal, the *Observer* (January 4) which was in general sympathetic with Lloyd George's policies, that attracted wide attention. Force should be resorted to only after every possible approach to peace had been explored and exhausted. The Allies must then understand that Germany would be essential for either the containment or the overthrow of the Bolshevik regime. "The Bolsheviks can only be hemmed in by Germany on one side, Japan on the other side, and Britain's Eastern Power. . . . If Germany entered into a common policy towards the Bolsheviks—solid peace if possible, effective war if not—the success of that policy would be assured." In order to attract Germany, it would be necessary according to Garvin to reduce her reparations burden, to provide her with raw materials, to revise the territorial settlement in Upper Silesia and to allow Austria to choose between the *Anschluss* and membership in a Danubian Confederation.

Between Churchill's direction of the continued withdrawal of British troops from Russia and his anti-Bolshevik public pronouncements at this time there was a curious contradiction explainable by the approaching showdown with Lloyd George on the latter's Russian policy. Churchill's memorable speech at Sunderland, January 3, was obviously intended to enlist opinion behind him for this test. Disputing the Liberal and Labor idea that the Bolsheviks had not been given a "fair chance," he declared, "they can never have such a chance, and for this grave and vital reason, that the theories they have held are fundamentally opposed to the needs and dictates of the human heart, and of human nature itself." He predicted that "something very menacing to civilization and very dangerous to the peace of Europe and Asia" would result "from the immense and horrible catastrophe of Russia." He reproached the Allies for their inaction and warned of the danger to British interests in the Middle East. "The ghost of the Russian bear comes paddling across the immense field of snow. Now it stops outside the Conference in Paris, in silent reproach at their uncompleted task. Now it ranges widely over the enormous countries which lead us to the frontiers of India, disturbing Afghanistan, distracting Persia, and creating far to the southward great agitation and unrest among the millions of our Indian population, who have hitherto dwelt in peace and tranquillity under British rule." Although he spoke of the "wise and courageous" German government and recommended a policy of moderation toward it, he did not at this time declare openly for enlisting Germany against the Bolsheviks.

What pleased Tory opinion, which was only less anti-German than anti-Bolshevik, was Churchill's efforts to arouse opposition to any dealings with the Soviet regime.[47] Had the truth been known, declared the *Daily Telegraph* (January 6), the Allied peoples "would never have rested until the infamous despotism of Lenin had been overthrown." It was a "vain illusion" to think that Russia could be left to work out her own salvation. "The world will find with horror that it is chained to the corpse of a great nation. . . ." Bolshevism could not settle down. "It is like the rush of the Mongol hordes. It devours and passes on. There is no possibility of peace with Bolshevism." The *Times* (January 5) held that bolshevism "has failed unless it has conquered everywhere: it lives on propaganda and dies the moment it ceases to attack; it is all or nothing with it. . . . With such a movement there is no question of peace, but only the kind of war that must be waged against it."

The dominant trend in French opinion and official circles was as firmly opposed as ever to any truck with the Bolsheviks, but French suspicions were aroused by the role being assigned to Germany and by Churchill's choice of the Middle East as the area where the danger was greatest. To Garvin's list of concessions that the enlistment of Germany would require, the *Temps* (January 10) replied indignantly that he had not offered to return the former German colonies or the German merchant ships, and in Churchill's speech (January 8) it discerned an effort to involve France in defense of British imperial interests where the two countries were themselves at odds. "It is," the *Temps* (January 8) declared, "on the Eastern frontier of Poland that civilization will be preserved." For the time being, the cry of "wolf" resounded more loudly in Britain than in France, despite the contrary impression of left-wing labor opinion.[48]

Instead of seeing in the Soviets' military successes against the White Russians cause for alarm and a return to aggressive intervention, Lloyd George evidently concluded that the time had arrived to move toward the re-establishment of normal relations. There is little doubt, although documentary proof is lacking, that he was personally prepared for full diplomatic recognition, but, in his view, this final step was not essential and, moreover, it was for the time being not a matter of practical politics. Not only were the Allies and the United States firmly against it, but it would probably have meant the fall of the coalition government and a dangerous division of public opinion. He, therefore, chose a gradualist approach.

On January 7, 1920, a few days after Churchill's anti-Bolshevik blast at Sunderland, Curzon circulated a memorandum on "Economic Aspects of British Policy concerning Russia" to the Cabinet. Its author, E. F. Wise, an official of the Ministry of Food and a British representative on the Supreme Economic Council, began by stating that "political and military considerations had so far mainly determined Allied policy" toward Russia while he was concerned with the economic aspect of the problem. Though crudely developed, "the vast resources" of Russia had been "a factor of enormous importance in the economic stability and organization" of the pre-1914 world. Her exports in 1912 had included 8,898,000 tons of grain and flour (about one-fourth of the world's total exports), 5,500,000 tons of timber, and 311,000 tons of flax (Russia harvested four-fifths of the world production). As Wise pointed out, the bulk of these and other exports went to European countries, Germany taking 30 per cent, the United Kingdom 21 per cent, etc., with the result that there was in 1920 50 per cent unemployment in Belfast and Dundee whose linen mills had formerly relied upon Russia for three quarters of their raw materials. Britain had also relied upon it for one-third of its imported butter. In terms of current values, British exports to Russia had totalled about £75,000,000.

The prospects for exports were bright. "The demand of the Russian market for goods as soon as trade is possible will undoubtedly be on a colossal scale, and will only be limited by the power of Russia to organise exports for payment." Concerning a revival of Russian exports on a large-scale and their beneficent effect, Wise was unrealistically optimistic. The grain harvest was said to be "of almost record size," and the amount available for export from the area controlled by General Denikin was estimated at from one to four million tons. Reliable reports indicated the existence of considerable quantities of flax and timber. As a result of the Civil War and the Allied blockade, Europe had been forced to buy American grain at high prices or "starve," but these prices would fall on news of "substantial exports" from Russia. "Broadly, the opening of Russia to trade would go further than any other factor to reduce the cost of living. . . ."

After indicating the importance of Russian food in Central Europe, Wise then drew certain conclusions: (1) that the prospective peace between Soviet Russia and Estonia (and the other Baltic states) would make the blockade impossible, and, in any event, the existing policy was a source of increasing difficulties with the neutrals, Germany, and above all with "the industrial classes in this country"; (2) that the same economic benefits could be secured without the formal diplomatic recognition of the Soviet government; and (3) that the blockade should be abandoned without diplomatic recognition and with safeguards against "Bolshevik propaganda outside Russia" and "the import of war materials into Russia." He warned against expecting its immediate and "complete economic recovery," while forecasting an appreciable revival of trade at least on a barter basis for which a useful mechanism was already at hand in the "Agricultural Co-operative Organizations" in Bolshevik Russia. The longer the decision was delayed, "the more formidable will be German and American competition."[49]

Curzon's circulation of this memorandum did not, however, mean his approval or that of the Foreign Office. Indeed, he had recently passed an unfavorable judgment upon an essentially similar proposal by a member of his own staff; it would probably result in as "much grief and . . . lack of success" as the author had attributed to the policy of limited intervention.[50] Lloyd George, nevertheless, welcomed Wise's counsel, and on January 14, during the Allied Conference in Paris, he submitted a memorandum based upon Wise's and secured the appointment of a committee to report on the possibility of resuming trade with Russia through the Russian Co-operative Societies. For its chairman, ignoring the Foreign Office, he secured the appointment of Wise.[51]

Lloyd George's proposal was a sharp break with Allied policy and, as was to be expected, a determined effort was made to defeat it, although, curiously enough, not by the French. It was intensely distasteful to them, but their attention was largely concentrated upon Clemenceau's defeat in the National Assembly for the presidency of France by a relative nonentity, Paul Deschanel (January 17). Moreover, if Lloyd George's British critics had their way, it might mean concessions to Germany and support of rival British interests in the Middle East. His greatest difficulties came from within his own government, especially from Winston Churchill.

Curzon first initiated a diversionary move. Personally interested in the Caucasus from a visit many years before and determined for India's sake—he had served as Viceroy—to keep it out of Bolshevik hands, he secured the *de facto* recognition of the Menshevik Republics of Georgia and Azerbaijan, a step which, he said, would be "equivalent to according them support."[52] In this area, Lloyd George was less determined to scuttle the policy of active intervention, for he was seriously impressed by the danger that the Turks and the Bolsheviks might join hands. On the same day, January 10, warning the heads of the Allied governments that their co-operation might "throw the States of the Caucasus into a desperate situation," he secured the reference of the question of arming them to the Allied military authorities.[53] They thought favorably of a military line in the Caucasus to be defended by perhaps two European divisions which would be replaced later by native troops with Allied arms.[54] Some Allied troops, British as well as Italians, were sent along with arms but as usual not in sufficient number or quantity. Batum fell in April and Azerbaijan became an autonomous Soviet republic.[55]

While the Allied discussions continued in Paris, efforts were made in the conservative press and by the War Office to create a crisis atmosphere at home. The purpose was obviously to influence the statesmen in Paris. The *Manchester Guardian* (January 15) warned its readers that the press was being "drenched, from some unknown source, with what is simply war propagandist 'information' about Russia." It was about ready to cry "a pest on both your houses." Englishmen were "like a jury who had not heard both sides . . . but only a confused bawling of abuse by the litigants and their friends." The sensible course was "to stand off and mind our own business." Warsaw was the source of many alarming reports from press correspondents. Writing under the date of January 13, the *Times's* (January 15) "Our Correspondent" asserted that "it may be regarded as certain that if they are not forestalled, the Bolsheviks will attack the Baltic States, or Poland, or both," and the *Times* editorialized that only a "firm decision on a considered policy and immediate preparations to execute it" could avert the menace. "There is not room in the world for Bolshevism and civilization." The *Morning Post's* (January 15) "Special Correspondent" likewise wrote from Warsaw (January 13) that the Polish General Staff and public opinion expected the Red Army to attack without waiting for the more favorable conditions of spring in order to forestall an Allied-sponsored Polish offensive.

For the moment, Churchill's War Office wished to center attention upon the Middle East where British imperial interests were directly involved. It issued an alarmist statement (supposedly through a "subordinate spokesman") that appeared in the morning newspapers of January 16—the date was important. In the *Times*, it was captioned "The Threat to India," and in the *Daily Telegraph,* "Grave Spread of the Bolshevik Menace," "Threat to the Middle East," and "Subdued Combustion." The entire Middle East, it asserted, was "in a state of subdued combustion which may break out into flame at any time in the next three months." A more cursory survey of the western Russian borderlands led to only somewhat less disturbing conclusions. The duty of the authorities was to prepare for "this new and probably very dangerous situation" and this would "probably mean military commitments on a large scale." The result was a serious war scare. From London, the Associated Press reported to its subscribers in America: "Before peace with Germany is a week old the British public has been brought up sharply against the possibility of another war."[56]

The timing of the War Office's tocsin was important for two reasons: the Allied heads of governments were to consider the report of the Wise Committee on the resumption of trade with Soviet Russia on January 16, and the chieftains of the British armed services—some of whom broke important speaking engagements—crossed the Channel during the night of January 15-16 and arrived in Paris the next morning in response to a summons from Paris. They included Field Marshal Sir Henry Wilson, Chief of the Imperial General Staff; Walter Long, First Lord of the Admiralty; and Earl Beatty, First Sea Lord of the Admiralty.[57] Coupled with the scare in London and the article inspired by the War Office, the summoning of the service chiefs led inevitably to the conclusion that war-like measures impended. A well-informed American press correspondent assured his newspaper that the meeting had been called, according to the general impression outside the Big Three, "to make war plans against the Bolsheviks."[58] The Paris press expressed the same view. Under the heading, "Le péril rouge," the *Temps* (January 17) identified the purpose as the discussion of "a vast plan of operations against Bolshevism," but it significantly added that France, always alive to the Bolshevik peril had no need of alarmist agitation and that she would not act hastily.[59] In London, the Tory *Morning Post* (January 16) warned that England could keep out of another war only if she aided her friends in Poland and Russia. The left-wing Labor journal, *Daily Herald* (January 16) expected to hear cries "that the white women of India are in danger," and it predicted (January 17) that the new war, like the old, would be one "of defense against aggressive Imperialism; it is to be a war of civilisation against barbarism; a war for democracy; a war for Christianity." Liberals were also skeptical of Britain's case. J. A. Spender's *Westminster Gazette* (January 16) suspected that the Bolsheviks' aggressive activity in Asia was the logical reaction to Western intervention in European Russia.

What was said when the British authorities met in Paris still remains a mystery. Sir Henry Wilson's diaries are still about the only source, and they are not illuminating on this point. For him the domestic danger of revolution was more important than the Bolshevik menace, and he succeeded in having it placed first upon the agenda to no great purpose, it would appear. The forecasts of far-reaching plans for the destruction of the Bolsheviks were not confirmed by events. According to Wilson, Earl Beatty's proposal that British crews should take over Denikin's warships in the Caspian Sea was the nearest approach to a vigorous plan of action, and Wilson seems to have blocked even that modest plan by showing the difficulty of holding the bases necessary for the operation of these ships.[60] For the moment, Churchill's intrigue against Lloyd George, if such it was, collapsed completely.

Within a few hours after the arrival of British service chieftains in Paris, Lloyd George secured the adoption by the heads of governments of the report of the Wise Committee recommending the resumption of trade with the Russian people through the Co-operative Societies. He agreed that this decision meant the end of the blockade which he thought had been implied by the earlier withdrawal of the British warships from the eastern Baltic. The Supreme Council thereupon issued a carefully drafted communiqué announcing its approval of negotiations for the resumption of commercial relations between the Allied and neutral countries and the Russian people through the co-operatives and declaring, with something less than complete candor, that no change was implied in Allied policy toward the Soviet government.[61] At any rate, it was clear that Lloyd George did not intend to rely upon Curzon or the Foreign Office for the development of his new Russian policy. According to Curzon's reply (January 22) to a request from Hardinge, Permanent Under-Secretary of State for Foreign Affairs, for information about the communiqué, the prime minister's decision on trade with Russia "was taken by them [the members of the Supreme Council] in the absence of any Foreign Office representative" and Lloyd George had told him "in private conversation that this was not the affair of Foreign Office, but of Food Ministry, who should control procedure."[62]

In contrast to its hitherto consistently intransigent attitude on Russian questions, France had been surprisingly co-operative. Its representative, Kammerer, on the Wise Committee had approved the report favoring the resumption of trade relations, and Clemenceau readily seconded Lloyd George's move to accept, just as he had the earlier motion to refer the matter to the Wise Committee, practically without argument. By that section of the French press which usually reflected the official attitude and was extremely anti-Bolshevik, the Supreme Council's communiqué was received, if not cordially, at least in a business-like spirit. The *Temps* (January 18) insisted that the contacts must be restricted to economic matters, but it also urged that the new policy be given a fair trial. To those who claimed that Russia had nothing to export or, if she did, that there was no way to transport it to a port, it replied *"essayons."* It hoped that the Quai d'Orsay and the French business world would be sufficiently adaptable and enterprising to assure a fair share of the trade of France.[63]

In view of the influential, even decisive influence of American policy in regard to Russia in the past, it was natural that the Supreme Council should desire the approval of the American government for its new departure. Hugh Wallace, American Ambassador in Paris, still attended its meetings, but since the Senate's failure to ratify the Treaty of Versailles in November, 1919, he had not been empowered to commit his government. From Lloyd George's point of view, knowing he could not expect France's wholehearted co-operation, especially in the further development of his Russian policy and because he had to expect Conservative opposition at home, American support was particularly desirable. It was he who proposed, January 19, that Clemenceau, who was still the president of the Peace Conference, should cable Washington an explanation of the decision to reopen trade with Russia. This message, which was sent in the name of the Peace Conference, began by citing the defeats of Kolchak and Denikin as meaning that "the attempt, supported up to the present time by the Allies, to overthrow the Bolshevik régime by anti-Bolshevik forces has definitely failed." On the basis of representations on the part of officials of Russian Co-operative Societies present in Paris that these societies with a membership of twenty-five million "are the only organizations which have survived the Bolshevik efforts at destruction," the Allies had decided to permit the free exchange of products needed by the peasants in return for grain and raw materials. There was reason to believe last year's crop had made a record and that enormous quantities of food-stuffs and other raw products were available for export to meet "the acute food shortage which is the principal encouragement to Bolshevism in the West." In saying that "the reorganization of commerce is the best means of destroying the extremist forms of Bolshevism in Russia itself," the message expressed one of Lloyd George's favorite ideas. There would be no negotiations with the Soviet government, no "recognition of the Bolsheviks," and no "authorisation of Bolshevik representatives to enter the Allied countries." The management of this trade would be in the hands of the co-operatives. While the Allies had agreed for the future upon a policy of non-intervention, they had recognized the independence of "the neighboring states," including Georgia, Azerbaijan, and Armenia, and if they should become the victims of Soviet aggression "the Allies would accord these States the fullest support in their power."[64]

Lloyd George had already dispatched virtually the same cable to Washington, and it was this version which Secretary of State Lansing sent to the White House. In asking for the president's views, Lansing offered his own: that the general statement about the growth of the Bolshevik movement he had proposed, December 4, 1919 (as a special message to Congress), might be revived.[65] Given the state of the president's health and the creeping paralysis of his administration, a firm decision of any kind was scarcely to be expected. Lansing's advice was not followed—the "general statement" he had in mind would have implied a denunciation of Lloyd George's policy—but no official reply was made to Clemenceau.

In the prevailing climate of American opinion, anything other than a refusal was highly unlikely. The decision arrived at in Paris did not, it is true, entirely lack support. The liberal New York *World* (January 19) claimed that Herbert Hoover shared Lloyd George's confidence that trade would destroy the Bolsheviks in the long run. The renewal of trade was wholeheartedly, but unrealistically, welcomed by the *Nation* (New York, January 24), as "the opening wedge" from which "complete peace will come," because it would make it possible for Russia "to disarm, to restore the peace for which its people long, and to come to a decision, unaffected by foreign intervention, as to the kind of government the majority of its people desire." But these views, inspired, unfortunately, in most part by wishful thinking or based upon the mistaken assumption that Western political experience was a reliable guide to the Russian scene, were significant only for a small group of intellectuals.

In the atmosphere of the Red Scare which was then rampant, judicial consideration of a move in the direction of normal relations with Soviet Russia was not to be expected. The responsibility was rightly attributed to Lloyd George. The decision, according to the *Washington Post* (January 18), would never have been made had it not been for the collapse of the executive branch of the American government. "If the foreign policy of the United States had not become a myth, this sinister surrender would never have been made." British Labor would eventually turn against Lloyd George, "and will go very far on the road to bolshevism...." The *New York Times* (January 18) dubbed the decision "Peace by Surrender," and "Peace, New Style" (January 19), and thought it was an example of the "brilliant improvisations" by which Lloyd George vaulted from pinnacle to pinnacle, "displaying the agility of the Rocky Mountain goat." There was "a certain novelty in a peace which may permit partial demobilization of armies, but will necessitate material increases in the Secret Services of every nation."

There was little solid support, however, for effective American participation in an active effort to overthrow the Bolshevik regime, for the *Washington Post's* war cry (January 19) had virtually no echo. "There can be no compromise with bolshevism. The cause of liberty requires that Americans shall fight bolshevism with just as much energy as they fought against Prussianism." The Washington correspondent of the Tory *Morning Post* (January 17) was under no illusions as to the meaning of the Red Scare for the practical problem that confronted Europeans. The Americans, he wrote, see "the deportation of the Reds, the passage of more stringent laws, and the asinine performance of the New York Legislature in refusing to permit Socialist members to take their seats" as the solution of the problem as far as America was concerned. It was, in his opinion, "highly improbable that America will give any material assistance to the military measures against Bolshevist Russia. . . ." The decision to withdraw the American forces from eastern Siberia tended, in fact, to confirm this conclusion.

In the main, the British Conservatives reacted in much the same way as the Americans. There was the same moral indignation and also the same silence when it came to the matter of using military force. Words were inadequate to express their opinion of the prime minister. The proposal to trade "with that power of evil," declared the *Morning Post* (January 17), would "fill all decent people . . . with horror and disgust. This country is being betrayed against its will into a desertion of its friends in Russia and a gradual peace with its enemies," and these enemies were "more hideous, savage and cunning" than the Germans. For the *Daily Telegraph* (January 20), only the destruction of Leninism would end the threat. "Bolshevik hostility to this country, as a bulwark of the civilisation which Bolshevism exists to destroy will never be, can never be, brought to an end; for that hostility is a principle of its very being, and all words and pledges and agreements are meaningless which pretend otherwise." It was clear, however, that Labor and Liberal opinion was solidly behind Lloyd George, and there were increasing indications that the Labor people were in a mood to use the economic weapons at their disposal to prevent open war or a return to military intervention. The exodus of the service chieftains to Paris on the night of July 15-16 moved Arthur Henderson to issue a public statement that the Labor party would not "regard itself as bound by military and political commitments entered into in secret as part of a general policy against which it has never failed to protest."[66] J. R. Clynes and eighteen other Labor leaders joined in saying, "The course of least risk all round is complete peace."[67] The *Daily Herald* (January 19) hailed the lifting of the blockade as "the first step towards the peace which Labour has demanded for 18 months." More significantly for the probable direction of Lloyd George's policy, the Liberal press assumed as a matter of course that trade would be followed by political negotiations, and perhaps political agreements. Such was the *Manchester Guardian's* (January 19) assessment of the situation. The government had decided "at last, it seems, to make peace.... Naturally, that is not the way in which the thing is put.... But there is the fact, dress it up as nicely as you will.... Obviously they cannot at the same time open up trade relations with Russia and go on hitting her." In the *Observer* (January 18), J. L. Garvin was even more explicit: "their policy would be unintelligible unless they [the government] were prepared seriously to explore the possibilities of solid peace with Soviet Russia, before embarking themselves upon wider war or giving their sanction to it." If Garvin was willing to consider at least the possibility of war, J. A. Spender's *Westminster Gazette* was not. It agreed (January 19) that the crimes of Bolsheviks were great, that they "have horrified a world hardened to brutality," but it accepted the Soviet government as the only stable authority in the greater part of Russia. The only alternatives were peace or war, and war offered no solution unless it resulted in conquests such as no invader of Russia had ever won. Even if all Russia were occupied, "we have nothing to set up in Russia which would be accepted as a government by the people. The facts have only to be stated to convince that the attempt to crush Bolshevism in Russia itself is madness."

Churchill was still not prepared to yield in his struggle with Lloyd George over the shaping of Allied policy. Disclaiming personal responsibility for the War Office's alarmist statement, he told the prime minister privately that its contents were, nevertheless, true.[68] Their differences culminated, January 19, during the Supreme Council's discussion of military aid for the Caucasus states. The trend of Churchill's questioning of Marshal Foch revealed his hope to align him against the prime minister. Did Foch consider the Caucasus a separate problem or a part of the larger question of the general defense against bolshevism? Did he regard Poland as in danger? Was he aware of concentrations of Bolshevik forces against her? Did he think a Bolshevik attack probable, and if he did, when?

Foch's responses, perhaps reflecting the disquietude he must have shared with his government and with French opinion at Churchill's attitude toward Germany, must have disappointed him. Foch, of course, regarded the Caucasus as a phase of the general problem of stopping the advance of bolshevism, but he was deplorably vague about Bolshevik strength and intentions. In his opinion, there was no doubt about the Bolsheviks' ascendancy over the White Russians, a superiority which he seemed to attribute to the presence of "a great number of German officers." Since they were able to penetrate "various countries under various guises," it was high time to establish at least a barrier wherever possible. In regard to Poland, he did not know that Bolshevik concentrations were in progress, but it was "quite possible at some undefined future date.... I do not know that they are going to attack, but such an attack might well take place."

It was then Lloyd George's turn. When he asked the marshal whether he had offensive or defensive purposes in mind in his advice that an understanding between the border states should be arranged and that Poland should be armed, he perhaps was countering Churchill; if so, Foch's reply that he was thinking of defense served the prime minister more than Churchill. Lloyd George then asked: "Do you know whether the Bolsheviks are preparing to attack those countries?" Foch's reply that "one cannot know till after the event" was obviously not what Churchill wanted. Pressed to name a single country "against which the Bolsheviks contemplate a military attack," Foch was again evasive: "When that attack takes place, I shall be in a position to reply. I could not do so beforehand." The decisions reached were in accord with Lloyd George's views: an agreement in principle to furnish arms and ammunition to the Transcaucasian states, but not to send the three divisions recommended by the Inter-Allied Military Council.[69]

Rising criticism of Churchill in the British press undoubtedly strengthened Lloyd George's hand. It began with an attack upon the War Office's scare statement. The Liberal *Westminster Gazette* (January 17) saw it as "a last attempt to stampede the public and to alter if it were possible the decision known to be impending in Paris." The *Manchester Guardian* (January 21) devoted a leading editorial to "Mr. Churchill's Vagaries" in which Lloyd George was credited with blocking his coup. "Instead of plunging into a new war with Russia it was decided to buy some butter from her and to sell her some cotton goods. And very good sense, too." Foreigners were astonished by the fiery cross Churchill had sent out "on the eve of his chief's dispatch of the first small sprig of olive," and they ask if "it is the normal thing for a subordinate Minister to break out into yellow semi-official journalism against the policy of the Premier." When the nonconformist religious *British Weekly* (January 22) took up the same refrain, it meant that the conscience of a powerful sector of the British people was aroused. "War No More," headlined an article that covered the entire first page. Up to a certain moment, Churchill had been the winner, "until the masses of our people insisted that this endless waste should cease." The prime minister, who understood British opinion better, had finally asserted himself, but none too soon. "Anyone who thinks that the alarmist dispatch which has caused the trouble was the work of a mere underling . . . is more simple than Simon." In the war that Churchill desired, Britain would be alone: "we wish to see Mr. Churchill out of the Cabinet, or at least out of the War Office." His driving force might be useful in house-building, "but he must not drive us over the precipice—as he will if he can."

Despite this pressure—which Labor joined—Churchill remained in the Cabinet, doubtless as a sop to anti-Bolshevik and Conservative opinion for the sake of the coalition government but possibly also because he stood for an alternate policy if that of the prime minister became unworkable. Both men stood their ground. "We have failed," Lloyd George told the Commons, February 10, "to restore Russia to sanity by force. I believe we can save her by trade. . . . The simple sums in addition and subtraction which it inculcates soon dispose of wild theories."[70] In addition to undermining or moderating the Bolsheviks, he believed that Wise's calculations of the economic benefits to Britain and Europe were sound. For a moment, he believed, as he privately told a confident, that Churchill, who had been prepared "to sacrifice men and money" at Paris, had moderated his views probably as a result of the *British Weekly's* "able and bitter" article which he had called to his attention. Churchill had thought of going to the people in a full and official statement of his position, but he had vetoed this project. " 'You can withdraw, if you like,' " the Prime Minister had warned him, " 'but I will not be a party to any justification.' "[71]

Winston Churchill was not to be silenced, however, although he did adjust his views somewhat to the unmistakable trend of opinion against war and for some sort of an arrangement with Soviet Russia. At Dundee he vented his feelings publicly, February 14, just four days after the prime minister reaffirmed his government's Russian policy in the House of Commons. Trade, Churchill conceded, might perhaps mellow the Bolsheviks, but he doubted it. The despotism of Lenin and Trotsky was not "fit company for a democratic country." None could tell what would come out of the "Russian cauldron, but it will almost certainly be something full of evil, full of menace for Britain, France, and the United States." He warned the great powers that they would "learn to rue the fact that they could not take more decided and more united action to crush the Bolshevist peril at its head and centre before it had grown too strong" and that Britain should do all she could to help the existing German government, if it made a genuine effort to carry out its obligation, in view of the grave danger of a Russo-German coalition.[72]

Churchill unburdened himself more frankly, especially in regard to his acceptance of at least a temporary arrangement while reaffirming his basic estimate of the situation, in a memorandum to the prime minister in March.

He began by defining their differences: "Since the Armistice my policy would have been 'Peace with the German people, war on the Bolshevik tyranny.' Willingly or unavoidably, you have followed very near the reverse." The results, he thought, had been "terrible"; "we may well be within measurable distance of universal collapse and anarchy. . . ." What was left of Russia "is in the power of these deadly snakes." He felt that Germany could still be saved by warning France that she could have a defensive alliance with Britain against Germany only if she "loyally accepts a British policy of help and friendship towards Germany." Yet, he himself mentioned a condition which would have irreparably antagonized France when he recommended "the early revision of the Peace Treaty by a conference to which New Germany shall be invited as an equal partner in the rebuilding of Europe." He was, however, prepared as a part of this policy "to make peace with Soviet Russia on the best terms available to appease the general situation, while safeguarding us from being poisoned by them." While he, of course, did not believe "any real harmony is possible between Bolshevism and present civilisation," he admitted "in view of the existing facts a cessation of arms and a promotion of material prosperity are indispensable, and we must trust for better or for worse to peaceful influences to bring about the disappearance of this awful tyranny and peril."[73]

When the implications of the Supreme Council's raising of the blockade (January 16) as a preliminary to political relations and eventual recognition became clearer—they were spelled out in British journals that were understood to reflect Lloyd George's views—the American and French governments did what they could to restrain the British Prime Minister. The former's hands were tied by increasing isolationist sentiment at home, but its attitude still counted for a good deal. When Lansing asked, February 2, about the meaning of press reports of possible recognition, there was no doubt of Washington's displeasure,[74] but Lloyd George's reply could have given it little satisfaction. He wanted the restoration of peace in Russia, believed that the Bolsheviks were "changing color," that peace would put an end to their aggressive designs, and that trade would bring about a stable regime. Even in regard to the question of recognition, he said nothing more than that there was no intention of granting it "for the present."[75] In France, the surprising co-operative attitude of Clemenceau and the press, at the time of the Paris meeting of the Supreme Council in January, rapidly deteriorated after the Millerand government took over from Clemenceau in January, 1920. While leftist opinion approved the resumption of trade with Soviet Russia, the nationalist Émile Buré called upon Millerand to repudiate Clemenceau's commitment of France to the decision of January 16.[76] So sharp a break was impractical, as Gustave Hervé, the one-time revolutionary firebrand turned nationalist, pointed out,[77] since the failure of the United States to ratify the treaty guaranteeing France against a German attack increased her need of Britain. The need of caution and moderation was stressed by one of the commentators whose voice carried weight with sober opinion. Millerand's policy, he was convinced, would be one of reason as was required by the times. "We have left the epic period when nations reacted heroically to events; . . . the moment . . . is one for cool resolves, political calculations, for undramatic but realistic activity."[78]

That Millerand did not intend, however, to follow Lloyd George unquestioningly in the application of the January 16 decision was evident from his statement to the Chamber of Deputies, February 6, a speech that diverged markedly from the prime minister's views. He was not even willing to accept the defeat of the White Russians as definitive. While he agreed to the termination of material aid and the reopening of trade, he gave greater weight to his assurances that Poland and Rumania "could count upon the most complete support of the allied powers" if either were attacked and that there would be no relations with the Soviet government. Such relations were impossible while that government continued to flout the most elementary rules of international behavior and to seek the establishment everywhere of a class dictatorship. To Millerand it seemed an especially presumptuous challenge to the France of the Revolution and of the Declaration of the Rights of Man![79]

At the same time, France's stiffer attitude was making itself felt in the Supreme Economic Council which had been entrusted with the arrangements for the reopening of trade. Its representatives insisted upon the greatest prudence in carrying out the decision of January 16 and there could be no question whatever of any French official relations with the Soviets, while the British, supported by the Italians, held that the risks in failing to ameliorate the economic situation exceeded those involved in allowing a Soviet agent or two to leave Russia.[80]

There was more talk than ever, even in responsible British circles, of official relations with the Soviet government. They were being prepared, according to a telegram dispatched by American Ambassador John W. Davis, February 24, "by officially inspired articles in the press for resumption of direct relations. . . ." Even officials who opposed official recognition were saying that "such action must come eventually and it is of little moment whether this occurs within the next few weeks or months. . . ."[81]

Moreover, Lloyd George's hand was strengthened by the Italians who continued their traditional support of British policy. Although faced at home by a more truly revolutionary situation, one aspect of which had been the workers' occupation of factories in the first sitdown strikes and another was to be the prompt formation of a Communist affiliate of the Third International, the Nitti government and Italian opinion were in essential accord with or even in advance of Lloyd George's policy. The Italian Chamber of Deputies had expressed itself in favor of the *de facto* recognition of the Soviet government in December, 1919.[82] The Paris correspondent of *Giornale d'Italia* (Rome, February 24) noted reports from London that Millerand would be confronted there by an accord between Great Britain, Italy, and Japan favorable to Soviet Russia's recognition.

The official communiqué of the Supreme Council's London meeting, February 24, and the British government's statement show that Lloyd George's views prevailed in the main. The decision of January 15 on trade was reaffirmed (without specific mention, apparently, of the role of the Co-operative Societies), and it was proposed that the Council of the League of Nations should send the commission of inquiry to Soviet Russia which the International Labor Office had initiated. On the other hand, Millerand secured a firmer declaration against official recognition. According to Bonar Law's statement in the House of Commons, the Allies had agreed not to enter into diplomatic relations until they were convinced "that Bolshevik horrors have come to an end, and that the government of Moscow is ready to conform its methods and diplomatic conduct to those of civilized governments."[83]

There was, at first, reason to believe that this restrictive condition would not block permanently Lloyd George's solution of the Russian problem. Although the left-wing Labor journal, *Daily Herald* (February 25), denounced what it regarded as the "insolence" of the Allies' language—in its opinion, it simply meant the refusal of these "gentlemen" to treat with a Socialist government—it boasted immediately that its "policy has triumphed; definite peace cannot now be long delayed." The Italians were undoubtedly prepared, even eager, to move in that direction.[84] Since the hostility of American policy to official contacts with the Soviet government, not to mention its recognition, was known to the French, Millerand probably hoped for American support in trying to prevent this development, but contrary interests were at work in both countries. A part of the American business world was eager for a share of the prospective Russian trade. As a result of the pressure of certain industries, the State Department instructed the embassies in Paris and London to press for early dates, March 20 and then April 10,[85] for the removal of all restrictions on that trade, although it was by no means willing to provide the necessary positive conditions regarding Russian payments, etc., that its encouragement would require. The moderate republican *République française* reported that

French business wanted peace,[86] but in this instance economic interests do not appear to have exerted much influence upon official policy.

On March 13, the situation was complicated by the attempt of the German reactionaries and nationalists to overthrow the Weimar Republic in the Kapp Putsch. Among the many who were dominated by the fear of Germany's recovery of her lost military might, some regarded the Putsch as a reason for a change in attitude toward Soviet Russia. This was especially true of Louis Barthou who interpellated the Millerand government on its foreign policy, March 25. He predicted that the Supreme Council's decision on February 24 was only the first step; willingly or not, the president of the council would take another and another "in the interests of France." Millerand's reply was a dogged refusal to change his Russian policy and also an affirmation of American support. He read a communication from the American Embassy dated March 11 stating the firm objection of the United States to official relations with the Soviet government, and he also mentioned an earlier agreement with Great Britain that there should be a common front in regard to Russia.[87]

When Millerand sent French troops into Frankfurt, April 6, as a reprisal for the violation of the demilitarized zone without consulting the Allies or the United States,[88] he gravely compromised the chances of having his way in the Russian question. President Wilson's suspicions of his motives, even in regard to Russia, had already been aroused. When the president's attention was called to evidence of an equivocal attitude on the part of the British and French military in Berlin toward the Kapp Putsch, he felt that both governments "are on the watchful lookout for any material advantage of any kind that they can get out of the situation in Germany or the situation in Russia, and I hope that the Department [of State] will take the necessary means to keep on their track and know *exactly* what they are doing."[89] The seizure of Frankfurt, April 6, turned him away from France and resulted in his approval of the British and Italian protests,[90] despite France's efforts to exploit the American government's anti-bolshevism.

On April 5, the eve of the march into Frankfurt, the Quai d'Orsay emphasized to the American Embassy France's agreement with the American point of view on relations with Russia. Three days later, April 9, Millerand replied to the American note of April 2 (it urged an early date for the opening of the Russian trade) insisting upon guarantees that Russian payments would not involve illegally acquired securities or the alienation of the public domain in the form of concessions, and demanding that claims arising from the Russian debts should remain intact.[91] As a sign of his displeasure, the president instructed the State Department personally that the United States should not be officially represented at the San Remo Conference which was to open on April 19. There should only be an observer "who sits and reports."[92] Millerand's involvement in Germany and the poor prospects of America's effective support argued successfully against a break with Lloyd George over his Russian policy. As a result, the final step toward negotiations with the Russians (ostensibly on trade) was taken with the French premier's approval.

When the Russian delegation arrived in Copenhagen where it awaited Britain's permission to proceed to London, its composition, especially the presence of L. Krassin (an industrial executive under the Tsarist regime and President of the Council of Foreign Trade under the Soviets since 1918) and Maxim Litvinov (later Chicherin's successor as Commissar for Foreign Affairs), created an embarrassing problem for the British Prime Minister. He had always insisted that the contacts would be with the Co-operative Societies and, indeed, it had been agreed that the Supreme Economic Council would speak for the Allies. In soliciting America's approval of the January 16 decision, he had taken the position that no representatives of the Soviets would be allowed to enter an Allied country. He did not allow these matters to interfere with his plans. Although he knew that Krassin as well as Litvinov were agents of the Soviet government and that the co-operatives had been taken over by it,[93] Lloyd George continued to maintain the fiction that only the co-operatives were involved. Replying to Labor members of the Commons, he denied that the Soviet government had requested permission to send a delegation to London and asserted that such a request had been received from the Central Board of the Co-operative Societies. The delegation included, he said, Krassin and Litvinov, and with the exception of the latter who had earlier been expelled from Britain for violating the conditions of his stay, the government, after consulting the Allies, would admit it.[94]

Even Lloyd George, having apparently decided to bypass the Supreme Economic Council and to negotiate directly with the Russian delegation once it arrived in London,[95] seems to have seen the advisability of regularizing the situation by consulting the Supreme Council. When it assembled at San Remo, April 19, with the German problem and the allocation of the mandates as its principal business, he again resorted to legerdemain to achieve his purposes. He introduced the Supreme Economic Council's request for specific authority to "make such arrangements with the Russian delegation as are necessary to enable trade with Russia to be resumed as rapidly as possible," and the other Allies, including France, approved it apparently with little or no debate. They also accepted without material change the British draft of a reply to Krassin's telegram of February 21 requesting permission to bring a Russian delegation to London. It declared that the Allies had "decided to authorise representatives of the Allied Governments" (thus was the door opened to direct negotiations between the Soviets and each of the Allies, including Britain) to negotiate with "M. Krassin and the Russian Delegation [with the exception of Litvinov] now at Copenhagen with a view to the immediate restarting of trade relations with Russia and other countries through the intermediary of the co-operative organisations and otherwise."[96]

Thus Lloyd George had apparently successfully laid the foundations for negotiations with Soviet Russia that would at first be limited to trade, but no one at that time could have safely predicted their ultimate scope. Moreover, he had finally carried reluctant France along with him. A few hours before the final decision was reached at San Remo, Poland launched the invasion of Ukraine, which was to pose a serious threat to the negotiations that were the heart of Lloyd George's Russian policy.

III

The Western Powers
and the Russo-Polish Problem,
1918-1920

Germany's defeat precipitated another of the armed conflicts that have plagued Russo-Polish relations over the centuries. The provision in the Armistice by which the Allies might ask the German invaders to remain on Russian soil[1] was not applied on the Polish front, and their withdrawal left a temporary military and political vacuum that both sides were impelled to fill. Both were weak, the Bolsheviks because the main theaters of the Civil War, which were elsewhere, . required all of the military strength they could muster, the Poles on account of the chaos incidental to the organization of a new state. The ragged, ill-armed Bolshevik bands were the first to seize the initiative, driven by the revolutionary compulsion to push as far westward as possible, especially in view of Germany's importance in their scheme of world revolution. They were much too weak to overrun all of Poland and thus to reach the German frontier, but they did occupy Vilna.[2] Meanwhile, the Poles were hastily organizing an army from troops that had fought on both sides during the Great War in the German, Austrian, and Russian armies, and, in the case of General Haller's divisions which returned to Poland across Germany after the Armistice, with the Allies on the western front. Trained under a variety of military systems, they were at first armed with weapons of diverse national manufacture. Thanks in large part to the aid of France and the counsel of General Henry's large military mission, twenty-two divisions and supporting units were organized within a period of two years under Pilsudski's command.[3]

Like the Bolsheviks, Polish leaders rarely hesitated to acknowledge the far-reaching extent of their aims. In the one case, it was world revolution; in the other, the recovery of Poland's historic boundaries before the first partition of 1772,[4] regardless of the non-Polish character of many millions living in the territory to be recovered. Some years later, Pilsudski, the Chief of State and Supreme Commander, represented Poland's defensive needs as the supreme consideration. "I determined from 1918 in complete independence the goal of our war against the Soviets. I decided especially to make the greatest effort to thrust the Bolshevik danger to our young society as far away as possible. In 1919, I accomplished that task. . . ."[5] The failure of the Allies to delimit Poland's eastern frontiers in the Treaty of Versailles and their declared intention to do so later[6] suggested the advantages of prompt action in order to confront them with a *fait accompli.*

Although the reorganization of the army was far from complete and border troubles had been precipitated with the Germans and Czechs, the Poles moved against the weaker Soviet forces early in 1919, taking Vilna in April and launching something like an offensive in July when the fortunes of war were running strongly in favor of Denikin and Kolchak. The Polish advance took them far eastward to a line from Stucz northward through Ubroc and the Berezina to the Dvina River.[7] They were still considerably short of the 1772 frontier, but the line lay far eastward beyond Poland's true ethnographical limits and would, if permanent, put some millions of White Russians under Polish rule. It approximated the boundary that was laid down after Poland's victory in 1920 by the Treaty of Riga, March, 1921,[8] which separated the two countries until Poland was once more partitioned in September, 1939. As noted above, Pilsudski wrote later that it satisfied Poland's defense requirements against Soviet Russia.

It is far from certain, however, that Pilsudski and the Polish government were, in fact, content with their gains in the east. Impoverished and devastated as Poland was from the years of fighting on her soil and dangerous as was the state of public health, the Polish people, or at least their leaders, had no intention of settling down to the humdrum tasks of recovery. The state of flux in the power relationships of Eastern Europe offered irresistible temptations to their romantic aspirations for the role of a great power. On all sides there were opportunities to expand at the expense of smaller or temporarily weaker neighbors, and so far-flung had been medieval Poland and so potentially perilous was her position between the German and Russian giants that history and strategy furnished facile excuses for forgetting that the principle of self-determination applied to others as well as to Poles. Besides the industries of Upper Silesia and the plebiscite that was to be held there in 1921, Teschen's coal on the Czech frontier, Vilna and even East Prussia, the boundaries of 1772 lured them eastward and there was also the far richer prize of the Ukraine. The feeling that Poland was the main bulwark of Western civilization against bolshevism[9] in which they were encouraged by Western opinion stimulated still more grandiose designs. Marshal Pilsudski's ultimate objective was a federation of all of the border states from Finland to Rumania, possibly including the Ukraine, under Poland's leadership. The protracted negotiations with Finland and the Baltic States in 1919-20 foundered, however, upon Poland's determination to have Vilna regardless of the consequences in Lithuania's irreconcilable hostility and in militating against Pilsudski's larger aims.[10] For the accomplishment of these purposes, which in the estimation of all true Poles should have had the blessing of the Allies, there was need of more assistance than even the French were furnishing them. This theme dominated Poland's relations with the Allies from September, 1919, to the spring of the following year.

In the agonizing dilemma of the Allies' Russian policy (their desire for the disappearance of the Bolshevik regime and their unwillingness or inability to act accordingly), the Poles saw their chance and tried, somewhat contemptuously, to exploit it. Paderewski, the great musician who was then the president of the council and foreign minister, journeyed to Paris in September, 1919, with a fantastic scheme that must have had Pilsudski's approval. Speaking privately to Lloyd George and then in the full meeting of the Supreme Council, he explained that Poland was prepared to put half a million men in the field for an offensive against Moscow with the purpose of overthrowing the Bolshevik regime and thus to do what the Allies would like to but could not do for themselves, provided only that they would foot the bill. Time was pressing, since Poland could not go on fighting indefinitely. In order to hasten a favorable decision, he pointed out that Poland could choose an alternate course. "If the decision of the Allies should be for peace, he was most anxious to know this as soon as possible for very advantageous terms of peace had been offered by the Bolsheviks."[11]

Since the decisive defeats of the White Russians did not begin until October, it seems that the Allies might well have accepted this offer, however humiliating it might appear, in order to strengthen the White Russians whose cause they were still supporting. They were unable, however, to shake off what was almost a paralysis of will in regard to Soviet Russia. They were moving toward policies far removed from Poland's brash scheme: the French toward containment, the British (and the Italians) toward the liquidation of intervention, and the Americans toward withdrawal from all European affairs. What Clemenceau wanted was neither war nor peace with Soviet Russia. In Marshal Foch's presence, he agreed with Frank Polk, the American representative, that Poland's proposal would "set the whole of Russia against the Allies." In Foch's view, if Poland were a great and stable country, the situation would be different; as things were, it would be "very dangerous." Addressing himself directly to Paderewski, Clemenceau declared "that the Council did not desire that the Poles should march on Moscow." The decisive considerations, in Lloyd George's view, were, first, that no one was prepared to subsidize the Poles and, secondly, that no one knew what should be done once they reached Moscow as they were confident they would. Yet, the British Prime Minister was ready to use the Polish Army to force German General von der Goltz out of the Baltic States (and Paderewski was agreeable), only to abandon the idea when Paderewski revealed his thought that the Polish troops (and Polish political control) should remain there and when Polk, the American representative, objected that it would lead to a Polish-German war.[12]

On the question of increased shipments of military supplies, the Allies reacted more favorably, since this matter did not challenge so directly the trend of their Russian policies. General Weygand, on behalf of Marshal Foch, argued that the Polish army's shortages of clothing were so acute— one regiment had only two overcoats per company—that a danger of Bolshevist penetration might arise during the winter. In the end, the military authorities were commissioned to prepare the necessary plans.[13]

The discussion had shown, however, how little the Allies were thinking of encouraging an aggressive action by Poland. The American and Italian representatives both thought that her army was unnecessarily large and should be reduced. The Poles, it was clear, could not count upon the Italians for encouragement or support. Tittoni did not take the alleged perils of their position too seriously. His "immediate concern ... was not Bolshevism, for he felt that this was rapidly becoming less dangerous," a view from which the French strongly dissented. With Lloyd George's backing, the Marquis Imperiali secured the stipulation that aid sent to Poland "should be for the defense of her territories and not for other purposes."[14]

On the basis of Poland's actions during the remainder of the year, it is fair to conclude that the rebuff of Paderewski's proposal lowered the Pole's respect for the Allies' capacity for decision and action. Their reaction against France, despite her immense services, was especially acute, notwithstanding the general impression then and since the Poland was a French satellite. In reality, friction had accumulated from several sources, no one of which was perhaps of great significance but whose total effect made the approved treatment of Franco-Polish relations as an *affaire de coeur* somewhat absurd. Although the French had rendered them many services, the Poles accepted all as a matter of course and acted as if more was their rightful due. Their leaders whose background was Russian or Austrian were often rather Francophobe, and in elevating Jósef Pilsudski as Chief of State, they disregarded France's preference of the more conservative and pro-French Roman Dmowski. Wishing, like the United States, to conserve as much of the old Russia as possible for the future Russian government that would follow the Bolshevik regime, France had little liking for Pilsudski's federalist policy since it would mean the permanent separation of all of Russia's national minorities of the western borderlands.

Although General Henrys and the large French military mission doubtless contributed greatly to Poland's military revival, their activities in general produced perhaps more friction than good-will. A jaundiced eyewitness among the French officers questioned even the extent to which their professional advice was heeded. The lower ranks, he wrote, produced "endless notes, circulars, reports and instructions—without ... ever having found anyone to read them." At headquarters, the technical advisers were at best "merely tolerated ... as amiable but superfluous guests, who were rather in the way." There were officer-lecturers "whom the watchful hostility of the Polish Minister kept without students," and others supposedly attached to units wandered "about unoccupied and forlorn." In Warsaw, there were "some twenty [French] generals with no commands and no occupations, who for a long time past had maintained the prestige of the horizon blue uniform in the lounge of the hotel...."[15] Although this carping critic ignored the grateful friendliness of Poles whose number was doubtless large, it may be assumed that two nations, each profoundly conscious of its own worth, irritated each other in intimate contacts. This irritation, on Poland's part, was assuredly one of the reasons, if not the most important, why she was moved to assert her independence even of French leading strings.

In view of Clemenceau's turn toward the policy of containment and of his veto, as spokesman for the Supreme Council, of an offensive for the capture of Moscow under Allied auspices, the restless Poles, foreseeing the indefinite prolongation of the current indecisive hostilities began themselves to take the initiative in October, 1919. Without the resources of a great power, they, with characteristic romanticism, proposed to act like one, hoping perhaps to find somehow a substitute for solid strength. Since Lloyd George seemed to be calling the tune among the Allies, the first move was a naïve effort to enlist Britain behind France's back in a policy for the reorganization (and exploitation) of Russia. Count Skrzyński, Paderewski's successor as Foreign Minister, broached the matter with British Minister Sir Horace Rumbold in October. Geography and history, he thought, indicated Poland as the country to take Russia in hand, and the assistance Poland would need could only come from either Germany or Britain. Germany was impossible for her co-operation "would only mean that at the end of about fifty years there would be a fresh partition of Poland. It would, therefore, be advantageous if a confidential exchange of views were to take place between our two governments."[16] From conversations with other Polish leaders, private as well as official, Rumbold gained the impression of a firm determination to prevent a German penetration of Russia and of an understanding that Britain's aid would be necessary. The establishment of British firms in Poland was welcomed, for it was believed that they were to serve "as a stepping stone to Russia."[17] According to Rumbold, the Poles dismissed the French rather contemptuously as "concerned to obtain repayment of the large sum of money owing to her by Russia, and will not mind much the régime set up in that country provided she recovers the debt due her."[18]

Despite the fidelity with which Rumbold reported these advances, there was no response from London, but when Pilsudski took up the same refrain November 6, it was unmistakable evidence of Poland's seriousness and of a desire that the British government should declare itself. He began by speaking of the obstruction that the British government had offered to Polish interests in connection with Danzig, eastern Galicia, and other questions. In regard to Russia, he had no fears for Poland whatever the outcome, for his opinion of the military qualities of the Bolsheviks and the White Russians was equally low: "Poland had nothing to fear from a material point of view from Russia in the future, for she knew that Russia was bound to be very weak for a long time to come and would not have the strength to resist Poland." One thing was clear: "...whenever the Bolshevik régime was destroyed the régime that succeeded it would, for a long time to come, be quite incapable of organizing such an enormous country as Russia." The Russians would have to look abroad for assistance, and the Germans were ready at hand. While the Russians would be unable to resist Poland, she was too weak economically to organize Russia. "She could only do so in cooperation with another Power, meaning Great Britain." However, it would appear from the slowness with which Allied supplies were reaching

Poland that they were leaving her "to her own devices," both in dealing with Germany and in dealing with the Bolsheviks. That being the case, he drew the conclusion that it was for Poland to help herself and to make her own arrangements. Rumbold doubted Pilsudski's seriousness when he spoke of a possible agreement with either Germany[19] or the Bolsheviks, and these possibilities, equally distasteful to the British, were doubtless mentioned in order to induce the British to declare themselves, which, however, they continued to refrain from doing. When he spoke of "how useful it would be if he could know what the policy of His Majesty's Government was likely to be," Rumbold could only speak of his government's concentration upon domestic problems.[20] The attempted flight into the upper reaches of high policy had not even left the ground.

While these conversations coincided roughly with the turning point in the fortunes of the White Russians, this was not, of course, clear at the time. It still remained highly probable that a strong Polish offensive would have again turned the tide and have sealed the doom of the Bolsheviks. Nothing was further, at this time, from Pilsudski's intentions. As he saw the situation, he had less to fear from a victory of the Bolsheviks, which had no military terrors for him, than from the triumph of Denikin and Kolchak, which would imperil his federalist policy. Although the Poles doubtless exaggerated their shortages, lack of adequate clothing and munitions seem, nevertheless, to have been a real factor.

An agreement with the Bolsheviks, in these circumstances, was less improbable than Rumbold thought. Something like an unofficial truce was arranged in October, 1919, in connection with Red Cross conversations for an exchange of prisoners which was concluded on November 2.[21] According to a well-informed student of Pilsudski's policy, the Polish leader wrote to Lenin through a Polish Communist assuring him that Poland "will not be a gendarme of Europe," with the result that a "long" exchange of letters followed. In order to mislead his French ally, Pilsudski is said to have moved his troops about in simulated preparations for active operations,[22] and the affair seemed, indeed, to have resulted in the voluntary retreat of the Soviet forces at certain points and in Poland's offers of specific terms for an armistice.[23]

The Allies also had ample reason for irritation, and this irritation expressed itself in efforts to restrict Poland's freedom of action that, in turn, increased Polish grievances and feelings of frustration. The Supreme Council labored for months in 1919 to settle the status of eastern Galicia, where Poles and Ukrainians were in bitter conflict, in such a way as to satisfy Poland while protecting the rights of the non-Polish majority. Since the Poles were bent upon outright annexation, an acceptable accommodation seemed im-

possible, but the Allies turned hopefully to some sort of international super-
vision during a transitional period. Allied unity broke down at this point
with France and the United States backing a Polish mandate while the
British at first favored a League of Nations administration through a high
commissioner.

Lloyd George fought tooth and nail against what he regarded as a
serious threat to peace in the piling up of national minorities under Polish
rule, but he was forced into continuous retreat. First, he agreed to a
mandate for Poland, although he in effect vetoed a proposal that its tenure
should be indefinite.[24] In deference to American zeal on Poland's behalf,
he dropped his own proposal for a term of ten years and accepted one of
twenty-five years.[25] During the Anglo-French conversations in London,
December 11-12, 1919, Lloyd George expressed himself freely about the
Poles. They had always been, he told Clemenceau, "a very troublesome
people in Europe." He was not certain they had not already gone too far.
In Clemenceau's view, Lloyd George had never understood the importance
of Poland and her 500,000 good troops as a means of keeping Germany
down, and Clemenceau succeeded,[26] in private conversation during this
meeting, in persuading the prime minister to consent to the temporary suspension of the Supreme Council's decision for a twenty-five-year mandate.[27]
Eventually, Poland's *de facto* annexation was sanctioned by the Allies in
1923.[28] Since the Poles were certainly informed as to the source of the
opposition to their schemes in eastern Galicia, another grievance against
Lloyd George and the British had been added to their already considerable
list.

The crucial question of the location of Poland's eastern frontier, the
ultimate determination of which the Allies had reserved to themselves in
the Treaty of Versailles and in their treaty with Poland, June 28, 1919, had
been entrusted by the Peace Conference to a commission on Polish affairs
whose chairman was the veteran and able diplomat, Jules Cambon. The
Supreme Council unanimously accepted its Report No. 6 on September 25
with virtually no debate,[29] and it approved, December 2, the text of a
communication to Poland informing her of this decision.[30] Originally
drafted as a supplementary protocol to the treaty between the Allies and
Poland, June 28, it was changed to a simple declaration on the objection by
Polk, the American representative, that Poland's pride should not be
needlessly offended.

It was a bitter pill for the Poles. The line approximated the ethnographical frontier between the Polish and White Russian peoples, and was therefore far in the rear of that which was currently held by the Polish Army.
Anticipating this decision, Pilsudski (on November 6) warned Rumbold,

the British minister, against the harmful results if the Polish troops were to learn that the land they were defending was to be returned to Russia.[31] Thanks to Poland's French and American backers in the Supreme Council, an escape clause was included: "...the rights Poland may be able to establish over the territories situated to the East of the said line are expressly reserved."[32] The procedure by which she might acquire such rights was not, however, military conquest but by negotiations with a Russian government established after the overthrow of the Bolsheviks. It was not a pleasing prospect for convinced anti-Russians like Pilsudski who were certain that the White Russians, if they were victorious over the Bolsheviks, would yield no Russian soil unless compelled to do so. While it is doubtful that the Allies would ever have asked Poland to return any territory to Soviet rule, whatever the nationality of its population, Poland's title to the lands east of the frontier defined by the Supreme Council would, nevertheless, remain uncertain.

In attempting to unravel the main trends of international policies as they affected the Polish-Russian problem during the winter of 1919-20, the historian contends with a regrettable absence of adequate documentation. He must necessarily rely, in many instances, upon indirect evidence and upon inferences from what in fact happened. What the intentions of the Bolsheviks were as their victory in the Civil War became increasingly probable, it will, perhaps, never be possible to say with absolute certainty. Were their peaceful professions serious? Or did they intend to turn against Poland? In spite of the usual assumption that the French were constantly encouraging Polish aggression, the truth seems to have been more complex, but here again the evidence that might be decisive is so far lacking.

Nowhere is the situation more nebulous than in regard to Polish policy and its motives. There is little doubt of the restlessness and dissatisfaction of the Poles with the Allies' Russian policy, with its encouragement to Estonia and other Baltic States to make peace with the Soviets, and the restraints it attempted to impose upon Poland's freedom of action. Failing to arrange a partnership with Great Britain, the animus of the Poles became more and more concentrated against Lloyd George, especially after the Supreme Council lifted the blockade of Soviet Russia at his behest, January 16, 1920. Even Clemenceau's containment policy, the *cordon sanitaire*, was not to their liking since it imposed limits upon their dynamism, but the Millerand government seems to have taken a more accommodating attitude toward Poland's aspirations. Moreover, the Poles could at least count ultimately upon some supplies from the Allies since the Anglo-French conversations in London in December had envisaged Allied military assistance should Poland's existence be threatened by the Soviets, perhaps even if the Poles were the first to attack. In these circumstances, it was not surprising that the Poles decided to look after their own interests without too much regard for the wishes of the Allies.

It was apparently the Ukraine and Polish interests there that terminated Pilsudski's dealings with the Soviets. In spite of the fighting between the Poles and Ukrainians over eastern Galicia, he had reserved a place for an independent Ukraine in the federation which was his ultimate goal, and Polish landlords owned estates there. His negotiations with the Soviets apparently collapsed when, November 14, 1919, the Politburo rejected the demand for the cessation of hostilities against Petlyura.[33] Shortly thereafter the Red Army drove the Ukrainian chieftain into Poland where he was received so hospitably that the Bolsheviks must have drawn serious conclusions about Poland's intentions. On December 2, 1919, a preliminary agreement, later confirmed in a formal treaty April 21, 1920, was arranged in which Petlura abandoned the Ukraine's claim to eastern Galicia and Poland recognized him as the head of an autonomous Ukraine.[34]

The Soviets reacted by including Poland among the objectives of their peace campaign. As in their earlier proposals to Estonia, the other two Baltic States, and Finland, Chicherin's telegram to the Polish Foreign Minister of December 22 affirmed the Soviet government's sincere desire for peace as in the interest of the peoples of both countries and blamed foreign influences for such obstacles to its conclusion as existed. As in almost all such Soviet approaches, there was a clear effort to arouse pressure within Poland for peace, but there was no overt appeal for revolution. The Polish government was invited to "name the time and place" for the opening of negotiations.[35]

The Polish authorities, intending to prevent the note from arousing a demand for negotiations among the parties of the left, tried to prevent its publication,[36] but in vain for, according to American Minister Hugh Gibson, it became known with the anticipated result in the development of public pressure for peace.[37] The tone of reports from British press correspondents in Warsaw was, however, quite different. Writing under the date January 2, the *Times*'s (January 6) "Own Correspondent" wrote that the Polish Army would follow upon the heels of General Denikin's retreating army. The army staff had announced the occupation of two towns. "The distance to which the Poles advance depends on their success in policing the country, but if the strain on their resources is not too great, they may go on to Kieff." The *Morning Post*'s special correspondent (January 10, Warsaw, January 7) anticipated a Polish offensive but not the direction it eventually took. "The feeling grows that some decision must be reached immediately, and also that if this is at all possible an offensive which would have for its immediate objectives the relief of Moscow and Petrograd should be made ... it is definitely known that General Pilsudski is eager to embark on the offensive if proper support is forthcoming...." It will be recalled, however, that the same journals were printing scare articles on the danger of a Bolshevik attack from the same correspondents a few days later in mid-January. Rumbold was confident that the Poles would refuse the Soviet government's request for peace negotiations.[38]

Meanwhile, the Supreme Council had been meeting in Paris since January 10, and its decision on the sixteenth to resume trade with Soviet Russia, publicly announced on the same day, had immediate repercussions upon Poland's consideration of the Soviet government's peace offer. Foreign Minister Patek was then visiting London and Paris, but there is no evidence that his influence was felt during the council's deliberations. Engrossed by the presidential election and the impending transition from the Clemenceau to the Millerand government (January 18), French statesmen were in no position for the moment to do much for Patek. In Warsaw, however, the Polish government pressed its case upon the Allied ministers, emphasizing its need of munitions and its desire to know the views of the Allies. On January 17, Pilsudski spoke to Rumbold of an interim reply to the Bolsheviks saying that a definite answer would be sent after the Allies had been consulted as "a proof that the Poles wished to do nothing in this matter without consulting the Allies." While peace would only be made with greatest reluctance, Poland faced a choice between peace and "prosecuting war to a successful conclusion," and if the second course were chosen "war and railway" material would be required.[39]

Two days later, January 19, Rumbold summed up the situation and his conclusions as to policy for the benefit of his government. Only in conjunction with the Rumanian Army, which apparently was not a serious possibility, did he think that a Polish offensive would be successful. He, therefore, "deprecated" an offensive, but he believed that the Allies should furnish the "considerable support in the way of military equipment and railway" material a successful defense would require. If the "Polish barrier against Bolshevism goes," the barrier would be shifted much further west "thereby creating a very serious state of affairs for Central Europe and the Western Powers." In his view, however, the Poles wished to shift too much responsibility for the choice that faced them to the Allies, and Rumbold asked for authority to say that "this is a matter as to which the Poles should be principally guided by their own interests."[40] What he asked for was in substance a reaffirmation of the policy for Poland that was already being followed in regard to the Baltic States and which was in part responsible for the negotiations soon to result in the treaty of peace between Estonia and Soviet Russia, February 2.

Hoping perhaps to incite American pressure upon the Allies, Pilsudski emphasized the possibility that peace would be made with the Bolsheviks to Hugh Gibson, the American minister, on January 18. Although he had spoken only the day before of the folly of signing a treaty with them because of their bad faith and their inability to control their agents and Gibson had reminded him of it, he now felt that the shortages in all essential supplies would mean Poland's collapse if large-scale operations were undertaken. Unless the necessary aid were immediately forthcoming, the government was "seriously considering concluding peace with the Bolsheviks." There was, he thought, a "gambler's chance" that they themselves desired peace "long enough [for Poland] to get on her feet, that this chance was better than the certainty of being conquered and having conditions dictated to her if she persisted in continuing the struggle without necessary material."[41] Although the evidence is lacking, it is safe to assume that much the same thing was being said to the French government. Neither the French nor the Americans, however, brought any pressure to bear upon the British on Poland's behalf.

On January 26, Lloyd George minced few words in explaining personally the main lines of British policy to Patek, the Polish Foreign Minister. Pressed to say whether or not he spoke for the Allies, Lloyd George replied that he had not yet discussed the matter with Millerand, that Nitti, the Italian Prime Minister, was in complete accord, and, above all, that what he said was "the deliberate decision of the British Government." He declared "formally" that Poland must herself decide between peace and war in the light of her own interests but that "the British government certainly did not advise war," especially as Poland was alone. To advise war[42] would involve responsibilities Great Britain "could not discharge," and he then, departing from Rumbold's estimate, discounted the seriousness of the Bolshevik menace from the military point of view. He did not believe the Red Army to be an effective offensive force, and there were reasons for thinking that the Bolsheviks were becoming afraid of it. The principal obstacle to a Russo-Polish peace, the prime minister frankly said, was Poland's advance far beyond her ethnographical boundaries, and he warned that if the Soviet government attacked her in order to recover territory that was "indisputably" Russian according to the principle of self-determination, it would be difficult, perhaps impossible, to persuade British public opinion to support any military or financial assistance.

However, he did give Poland something like a formal guarantee, albeit upon a contingent basis unlike Neville Chamberlain's more fateful guarantee of March 31, 1939. If the Poles tried sincerely to make an equitable peace, "and if the Bolsheviks either refused peace or, having made peace, proceeded to repudiate it, Great Britain would feel bound to assist Poland to the best of its powers." In these circumstances, the British and French peoples could be aroused to fresh efforts but not otherwise. Yet he said that Britain could not guarantee any treaty that Poland might make or go beyond British obligations in the League of Nations.

He went on to explain that resumption of trade with Soviet Russia would be the best means of making peace "and of mitigating Bolshevism in Russia" and that Russian food was essential to the provisioning of Europe and to reducing prices. It was doubtless with some emphasis that he told the Polish Foreign Minister that the "British Government did not want Poland ...to maintain an economic barrier through warlike operations between itself and Russia while the Allies were themselves trading to the best of their abilities with the Russian peoples."[43]

Since the limited guarantee of which Lloyd George had spoken implied a Poland that would be content with her ethnographic boundaries, that is the eastern frontier designated by the Supreme Council on December 8, 1919, it could scarcely be satisfactory to Polish leaders who regarded the line then held by their troops as the minimum and who in all probability were already thinking of extending Polish control into the Ukraine. They were in no mood to accept these sacrifices passively, and henceforth until the Polish invasion of the Ukraine was launched on April 25 they attempted to induce a more positive attitude toward their view of Polish interests. Patek at once appealed to the British press and to the French and American governments. Interviewed by the Reuter's news agency, he denied the existence of a Russian state with which a treaty of peace could be made, and he clearly contradicted Lloyd George by speaking of the line held by the Polish army as "the inevitable result of events." Supported by an aroused national sentiment, Poland could hold her own; "neither Bolshevist menaces nor promises can rush her into a policy that has not been well considered."[44]

The *Daily Telegraph* (January 30) responded much as the Poles desired, for it depicted Poland as threatened "with invasion and conquest" unless the necessary weapons were at once placed in her hands. Those who believed that she should stand and defend a line acceptable to them did not understand the ruthlessness of her enemy. From Patek's statement it concluded that Paris and London had promised nothing more specific "than a general assurance that the Allies would not allow Poland to be crushed." That was not enough; "...time is flying, and the danger is imminent. Without assistance from her allies and guarantors Poland is exposed to destruction, and with Poland the whole of the barrier separating the forces of disruption in Germany from the armies of militant Bolshevism." From Warsaw, the press was informed, somewhat inaccurately, that Lloyd George had not promised Poland anything, and the prompt denials from the respective legations as usual failed to erase the first effect entirely.[45]

Radical opinion in Britain was less satisfactorily impressed. The London *Nation* (January 31) concluded from Patek's statement that he had been unable to secure an official decision from the Supreme Council and that Poland's aggressive designs had not been vetoed. "That is bad news... for Poland's proposal, if we are correctly informed, is not merely to hold the non-Polish territory she has already taken, but to advance in the South in order to occupy the Ukraine. That, of course, means a big and unlimited war...."

From Patek's inquiry of Lloyd George as to whether he spoke for the Supreme Council and the Polish Foreign Minister's statement to the press that he was returning to Warsaw without a clear decision of the council, it is evident that he had not secured a definite commitment from France. The Millerand government had apparently not yet clarified its foreign policy, although there was already strong support for encouraging Poland.[46]

More is known about Patek's attempt to sound out the attitude of the American government through its ambassador in London, John W. Davis. Lloyd George, he said, had made no real commitment. The League of Nations would doubtless go to Poland's aid if her ethnographic frontiers were violated, but the prime minister had given him to understand that she could expect no assistance in keeping the territory she held beyond those frontiers. In substance, Lloyd George had counselled Poland to make her peace with the Bolsheviks. The French, who were bitterly hostile to the recognition of the Soviet government, were undependable at the moment, and Italy was ready to do business with the Soviets. The Poles were therefore "particularly anxious to know whether American sentiment would be offended if they yielded to necessity and made the best terms possible." Davis could only reply, of course, that he would refer the question to his government.[47]

At the time of Patek's return to Warsaw on or about February 1, the international situation could scarcely have been less favorable for aggressive action by Poland. The French, of course, had little liking for Lloyd George's policy which seemed to oppose every move to increase Poland's ability to block Germany's *Drang nach Osten* and to defend Central Europe from bolshevism.[48] While the French government doubtless let the Poles know her opposition to peace negotiations with Soviet Russia, she was not prepared for an open break with Britain. France was in no position, as the nationalist publicist, Auguste Gauvain, pointed out, to support a Polish offensive against the Soviets without the co-operation of her allies,[49] and she agreed when the Supreme Council reaffirmed, February 25, its approval of trade with Soviet Russia. At the same time, she secured a more formal assurance that Poland would be protected against a Bolshevik attack, thus encouraging the Poles to feel that they would be protected from ultimate disaster although it might result from an adventure of their own.

It was even less likely that America's sympathies for Poland would result in the kind of support Poland desired. True, Hugh Gibson, the American minister, was her ardent advocate; he would have Washington sell Poland's case to the Allies. On the eve of Patek's return but after Rumbold had communicated the main lines of British policy to the Polish government, Gibson addressed, January 30, a series of questions to his government in the manifest hope of spurring it to action on Poland's behalf. Did it wish Poland to resist the Bolsheviks with force of arms, and, if so, would it send supplies and persuade the Allies to do likewise? If not, and if it advised her to make peace, "what measures does our government consider desirable to prevent the spread of Bolshevik doctrines to more western countries?"[50] Much as Lansing disliked Lloyd George's Russian policy and hated bolshevism, he could undertake no commitments that might mean active participation in European affairs. As a result, the British Prime Minister might almost have written his reply (which was also an answer to Davis' recent transmission of Patek's query from London): The American government was not in a position "to take any responsibility in advising Poland to adopt a specific policy toward Bolshevist Russia," and Gibson was told for his own information that it would be "most unfortunate if the Polish Government should conclude" that this silence implied "such military and economic assistance as might determine the Polish government in refusing to enter into armistice negotiations with Bolshevist Russia."[51]

On Patek's return to Warsaw, he was confronted with a new Soviet appeal for peace, this time in the form of a declaration by the Council of People's Commissars, January 28. It reaffirmed the Soviet government's acceptance of the self-determination of the Polish people and its unconditional recognition of "the independence and sovereignty of the Polish Republic," it pledged on behalf of the governments of Soviet Russia and Soviet Ukraine that the Red Army would not advance beyond the existing battle lines, and it denied the existence of agreements of any kind with Germany or any other country against Poland. There was no single question affecting Poland's or Russia's vital interests which could not be settled peacefully as the current negotiations with Estonia showed.[52] Unlike Chicherin's proposal of December 22, only a reference to the pressure of foreign imperialists—agents of Churchill and Clemenceau—for a war that had no connection with Poland's own interests testified to the Bolshevik origins of this document, for there was not even an appeal to Polish "workers and peasants" to demand peace.

At the same time, there was other evidence of a possibly serious desire for a period of peace or at least a "breathing spell." Speaking to the Executive Committee of the Soviets on the conclusion of peace with Estonia, February 2, Lenin spoke of their victory and their own renunciation of violence, although his "big lie" that the majority in all countries were on their side was scarcely reassuring.[53] On the same day, the All-Russian Central Executive Committee repudiated the use of force for the advancement of world revolution in an address to the Polish people signed by Kalinin and many others. "We are profoundly convinced that the workers of all countries will follow the example of the workers of Russia. But our enemies and yours mislead you in saying that the Soviet government wishes to establish Communism in Poland with Red Army bayonets. The Communist regime is only possible there where the overwhelming majority of the workers is profoundly penetrated by the determination to create Communism by themselves...."[54] The events of the summer of 1920, however, were to demonstrate the unreliability of this assurance when the "objective situation" seemed to promise much for the cause of world revolution through the use of these same Russian bayonets.

In spite of recurring talk in Poland and abroad of an impending Bolshevik offensive (especially on the eve of meetings of the Supreme Council at which the Russian problem would be considered),[55] the Soviets' desire for peace was taken seriously in unexpected Polish quarters. Pilsudski himself said as much in an interview with the London *Times*'s correspondent. "They have good reason," he said, "for wanting peace. They are at the end of their tether. Their people hunger for peace.... The Red Armies are sick and tired of war.... The whole thing is a hollow-shell which presents a hard exterior but has nothing inside."[56] L. Grabski, the leader of the National Democratic party, member of the Foreign Affairs Commission of the Diet, and soon to become the Prime Minister, professed confidence in the sincerity of the peace offer because the Bolsheviks doubted the outcome of an all-out war with Poland and the loyalty of the peasants,[57] while Daszyński, the head of the Socialist party, attributed the Soviet proposal, which he regarded as serious, to the fear of the Russian nationalism which a war with Poland would arouse as well as the subversive effect it might have upon the Soviet regime.[58]

Even American Minister Hugh Gibson, who had earlier reported a Bolshevik offensive as almost a certainty, finally admitted that the Bolsheviks probably did not intend to attack. "In view of the unexpected success which the Bolsheviks have had with their peace propaganda in England and Italy it seems hardly probable," he reported, March 3, "that they will compromise the situation by an unprovoked attack for the present. It seems increasingly clear the Russian railway situation is extremely bad and would hamper any aggressive movements at this time. While it does not seem that the Bolsheviks have abandoned their former aims, they probably realize that it would be well to secure a breathing spell and peace if possible."[59]

While it is doubtful that a reply was ever sent to Chicherin's offer of December 22, Patek speedily answered its renewal of January 28 in a wireless, February 4, laconically acknowledging its receipt and promising a reply after it had been studied.[60] It was Poland's obvious interest, as a demonstration that she had a choice of policies and to impress the Allies, to give the impression that the Soviet offer was being seriously considered.

Gauvain's reactions were perhaps representative of that part of French opinion which approximated the trend of official policy. He could not believe that peace would be made, even if the Soviets repeated their earlier offer of the frontiers of 1772. Since Pilsudski knew the Bolsheviks he understood that Polish independence could not be preserved unless good relations were maintained with a Russia reconstituted upon a democratic basis. He knew that the Red Army would attack sooner or later since the world revolution, the abolition of private property, and the dictatorship of the proletariat had not been abandoned. "They [the Poles] prefer therefore to prepare to defend themselves while they still have freedom of action and while their public opinion had not been contaminated."[61]

In contrast to later statements to the effect that the Soviet proposal was never seriously considered,[62] the Allies were given to understand the contrary at the time. On February 7, Patek told Gibson, the American minister, that he had almost completed the preliminary study of Poland's views on peace with Soviet Russia. He would, he said, submit the draft of his reply to the powers for their advice and suggestions.[63] A few days later, the Allied press was informed, probably with substantial accuracy, that the problem was being studied by a commission composed of Chief of State Pilsudski, the chief of staff, and the ministers of foreign affairs, war, finance, and interior.

There were early indications, however, that the Polish reply would probably be of such a nature as to assure its rejection. In the same interview that revealed the composition of the commission, the minister of war explained that it was not a question of just any peace, but of a "robust treaty in harmony with Polish and European interests." There was no need of undue haste. "Of what importance to us," he said in substance, "is the fact that the Bolsheviks have armies at their disposition near Irkutsk or even in the vicinity of Odessa? Given the enormous transport difficulties, these armies cannot reach our front for many long months."[64] The theme was taken up by Pilsudski, who told the *Matin*'s representative that the time had come not only for Poland but for the Entente to make peace with Russia. Support of Kolchak and Denikin should be abandoned. "It is," Pilsudski said, "impossible to revive the old Russia with the aid of these men of the old regime. We must seek new formulas. . . . We must have the courage to understand that a formidable change has occurred in Eastern Europe." When he spoke of the "moment for audacity" having arrived, of Poland's request for the Allies' support "in her crushing task," and of plans for restoring a system based upon law in Eastern Europe, his purposes could scarcely have been limited to peaceful negotiations. Admittedly, he conceded, risks were involved, but it was better to brave those risks "than to maintain indefinitely the existing absolutely disastrous state of affairs.... Fear of Bolshevism should not be the excuse for doing nothing."[65]

Elsewhere Pilsudski was, about the same time, discounting the danger of a showdown with Soviet Russia. To a representative of the London *Times*, he insisted that Poland had no reason to fear the Red Army. The Russians "were such bad soldiers. The Polish soldier is a far better man. We've alway beaten them.... My opinion is that it is impossible for Poland to be defeated in this war. She cannot lose."[66] He had never concealed his confidence, while talking with Western diplomats, in the ability of the Polish Army to capture Moscow at almost any time. Grabski also was confident of Poland's capacity, with Allied material assistance, to administer such a defeat to the "armies of barbarity" that the entire regime would collapse.[67]

In spite of the ominous implications in this rash of interviews, the Allies, for the most part, kept hands off, telling Poland that she should act in the light of her own interests. Gibson, however unwillingly, carried out Lansing's instructions of February 5, although he continued to stress Poland's desire to act according to the wishes of the Allies and his conviction that she should be given a definite lead even if Washington had to take the initiative.[68] He believed, however, that the French were "encouraging a decision to fight" while making "no definite promise to help...." The British minister was giving the Polish government to understand that "Lloyd George desires Poland to make peace,"[69] but this credited the British government with a more vigorous attitude that the facts warranted.

In the House of Commons, Lord Robert Cecil was deeply disturbed by multiplying signs of aggressive intentions on Poland's part, and he called upon the government to explain its attitude. Between Lloyd George and

Churchill, the two poles between which British policy had hitherto oscillated according to the ebb and flow of White Russian forces, Cecil's own choice fell upon Lloyd George and his reliance upon the beneficent influences of trade. The thought of Poland's going into Russia "to restore order is one of the most insane ideas that ever were conceived," for the ancient feud between Poles and Russians would inevitably rally Russian national sentiment behind the Bolsheviks. The Poles "would run the gravest risk of disaster." Replying for the government, Balfour described as "adjustment to circumstances" what Cecil had called oscillation, and, defending the interventionist policy in the past, he reaffirmed the refusal to have any political relations with the Bolshevik government. "We have never had formal relations with it. We have never recognized it in any sense yet, and perhaps never shall—I hope myself we never shall—as the Government of Russia." Nevertheless, the government had no intention of encouraging "any such folly" as Polish adventures.[70] Cecil's concern continued unabated. Later, on February 16, when Bonar Law repudiated on the government's behalf any responsibility for the decision between peace and war by the border states, including Poland, he inquired if Law thought "that we shall be able to maintain a condition of absolute detachment, whatever these powers do?" The reply was: "The future must take care of itself. We are only dealing with the present."[71]

Pilsudski indicated broadly Poland's reaction to the Allies' hands-off policy in a statement to a French press correspondent which was published on the same day, February 12, that Cecil addressed his first question to the Lloyd George government. "We are left alone," he said, "to face the eastern problems because Europe does not know what to do. France and England can afford to wait, watch events and procrastinate. We are immediate neighbors of Russia. We cannot afford to wait."[72]

The Poles were, in fact, nourishing the most ambitious designs, and not only in regard to their eastern frontiers and the Ukraine. Through an unofficial Hungarian agent, Count Csekonics, the highest Polish authorities, including Chief of State Pilsudski, were laying the foundation for future Polish-Hungarian friendship and co-operation by encouraging designs that could only be achieved by the partial partition of Czechoslovakia. For the time being, they could, of course, do nothing to establish a common frontier between the two countries (in Slovakia) in view of the attitude of the Allies to whom Poland was indebted, but they left no doubt of their interest at a more propitious moment.[73] When the Hungarians offered to collaborate in a joint military defense against bolshevism—their army, they said, had been founded for this mission—Patek evaded this explosive project (Hungary was still technically an enemy country). "Concerning joint defensive action against Bolshevism, Patek expressed the belief that this question is no longer of interest since Poland has entered into peace negotiations with the Soviet Government and since the Allies themselves are seeking peace with Russia."[74]

It would be a mistake, however, to accept this as a reliable indication of Polish policy; for one thing, Poland was not in fact engaged in negotiations with Soviet Russia, since the Soviet offer was still unanswered. On the same day, February 13, Patek revealed a completely different attitude in an interview with Hugh Gibson during which he allowed the American minister to read a note being sent to Millerand, the French Prime Minister. In it, Patek expressed himself, as the Polish Foreign Minister, as having no faith in the sincerity of the Bolsheviks' peace offer and as anticipating a large-scale Bolshevik offensive in view of what he alleged to be large concentrations on the Polish-Russian front. In connection with the enclosure—a long list of Polish requirements in munitions and supplies—it is significant that March 15 was mentioned as the date by which most of them should arrive if Poland's "defensive strength" were not to be seriously impaired.[75] A few days later, Foreign Minister Patek told Gibson that the Allies' failure to make "a coherent statement of the course Allied and Associated Powers desire Poland to follow" was hampering formulation of the reply to the Soviets' proposal.[76]

As spring and better conditions for military operations approached, tension inevitably increased. Signs multiplied of a general easing of Soviet Russia's international situation. The Treaty of Peace between Estonia and Soviet Russia, February 2, was followed by the conclusion of the Latvian-Soviet Russian Armistice on February 11 and the Anglo-Soviet agreement of February 12 at Copenhagen for the exchange and repatriation of prisoners; on February 25, the membership of the Soviet trade delegation was announced, and the Supreme Council in London reaffirmed the lifting of the blockade and the reopening of commercial relations. At the same time, the Supreme Council's public statement enabled Poland to count more firmly than ever upon being saved from the worst consequences of defeat at the hands of the Soviets. The Poles were clearly making up their minds to act independently of the Allies. In Prague, Eduard Beneš, the Czech Foreign Minister, told the American minister that Poland was going to demand her frontiers of 1772, "and this means hostilities, in which Poland could be crushed in six weeks."[77]

In Paris, where the Millerand government, increasingly irritated by Lloyd George's policy, was moving away from Clemenceau's containment policy to the support of more aggressive action, Marshal Foch and General Rozwadowski, the head of the Polish Military Mission to France, were reported to have agreed upon an armistice line to be presented to the Soviet government that included a part of the Ukraine down to Kiev. According to the Polish Mission (in Paris), Poland would be guided by the advice of France and the United States in the negotiations with the Soviet government. "In view of recent British policy, Polish officials feel that Poland is relieved from the obligation of further consulting with England."[78] By early March, Patek was telling Gibson that the idea of consulting the Allies in regard to the reply to the Soviet peace proposal had been almost abandoned.[79]

The Bolsheviks, it may safely be assumed, were under no illusions concerning Pilsudski's and Poland's intentions, however incomplete their information about the outside world may have been. Because of their ideological preconceptions, they were bound to believe that Poland—a government of landlords and capitalists—would at least try to seize as much territory as possible if not attempt to destroy the Bolshevik regime and that she would be abetted and aided by the imperialist Allies. Soviet appeals for peace were, accordingly, defensive in purpose even if the real aim was only a "breathing spell" of limited duration. As the prospects of a favorable response lessened, they brought other tactics into play while continuing the peace campaign. Even as early as January, 1920, Trotsky warned the Politburo that Pilsudski was preparing an offensive, and some small reinforcements were sent to the Polish front.[80] The tone of Lenin's speeches changed in significant respects. Speaking to the Congress of Cossack Workers, March 1, he revived the theme of world revolution instead of stressing, as in recent speeches, the need of concentrating upon economic reconstruction. "On our side," he declared, "we have never concealed the fact that our revolution is only a beginning, that it will succeed only when it embraces the entire world, and we thoroughly understand that the capitalists are exasperated enemies of the power of the Soviets."[81] Early in March, Chicherin forced the issue with Poland. In a wireless to Patek on the third, the Soviet Foreign Minister regretted the delay in replying to the Soviet government's offer to negotiate and warned that the serious threat to the Ukraine compelled it to withdraw its promise not to cross the existing battle line. Nevertheless, Russian and Ukranian troops would still "cross the mentioned line only where the necessities of defense against new aggressions" required them to do so.[82]

Shortly thereafter, on March 5, he tried to pressure the Allies (and the United States) into restraining Poland. While complaining that they had not responded to the Soviet Republic's peace appeals, Chicherin noted the first symptoms of revived trade as mutually desirable, but Poland's threats of aggression were serious obstacles to its development. The Soviets were frankly convinced that the Allied governments had the power to restrain Poland by clearer and more precise declarations of their attitude toward a Polish aggression. Should new military operations occur, it would be impossible to continue the current trade negotiations.[83] Though addressed to all Allied and associated governments, this wireless was obviously intended primarily for Lloyd George as the statesman most interested in the success of the trade negotiations, but it elicited no real effort on his part to restrain the Poles.

Relatively powerless as Germany was at this time, she was still a factor of some importance in anything having to do with Russia and Poland. Frenchmen, and others, were allergic to any indications of a rapprochement with Russia, even if existing power relationships seemed to put it in the realm of fantasy.[84] There was, however, support for this development at both extremes of German opinion. Spokesmen for the extreme left, strangely enough, evoked Bismarck's authority for a Russian orientation against the Allied policy of economic exploitation—the standard Bolshevik view of Allied policy in regard to Germany.[85] General von Seeckt's views, at nearly the opposite extreme, were especially important considering that he was soon to command the new Reichswehr. "Since I regard the future political and economic union with Great Russia as the immovable objective of our policy, we must at least try to avoid making an enemy of her," he wrote in a private letter, January 31, 1920. "I reject the support of Poland, even if it means her destruction. On the contrary, I count upon it, and if we do not now assist Russia to recover her old frontiers, we should at least not hinder her in this effort...."[86] During the early months of 1920, these long-term trends of opinion were greatly reinforced by the outburst of indignation against the Allies' demands for Germany's surrender of a long list of war criminals and for Holland's surrender of the Kaiser to stand trial in an Allied court. The effect upon the staff of the Foreign Ministry was especially significant, for its personnel began to give less attention to the White Russians and more to the establishment of contacts with the Soviets.[87] Karl Radek's version of the economic opportunities for Germany and German technicians in Russia attracted wide and favorable attention.[88] On March 3, 1920, representatives of all parties declared for the speedy resumption of economic relations at a meeting of the Reichstag's Foreign Affairs Commission.[89] So impressed was Eduard Beneš, the Czech Foreign Minister, by what he knew of these developments in Germany, that he confided his conviction to the American minister that a Russo-Polish war would result in Poland's conquest and a Russo-German union whether the left or right eventually won out in the two countries. Beneš hoped, therefore, that the Allies and the United States would restrain Poland from actions that would precipitate these dangers.[90]

While it is true that Poland's attitude and plans in regard to Russia were developing without any thought of Germany,[91] it is at least possible that the temporary seizure of power in Berlin by reactionary elements in the Kapp Putsch, March 12, helped to precipitate events. The immediate objectives of Kapp and his associates were restricted to domestic German politics, the overthrow of the Republic and its democratic institutions, and had little or no significance for Germany's foreign policy (von Seeckt and the army were neutral). It was obvious, especially in view of the anti-Polish sentiment and record of the Freikorps troops that supported the Putsch, that Poland must have foreseen more trouble than ever from Germany if the Putsch were successful. The situation made quick action advisable in order to attain Poland's objectives against Russia before serious difficulties developed on its western frontiers.

Coincidence or not, Patek communicated confidentially to Gibson, the American minister, on March 13, the terms Poland intended to demand of Russia during the negotiations that were envisaged for the end of the month. They included the frontiers of 1772 in order to "obliterate the consequences of the historical crime of which Poland was the victim" and in which Russia was one of the parties, Russia's recognition of the states formed from her former territory, the abandonment of all propaganda for social and political theories "beyond the frontiers of the Soviet State," and the ratification of the peace treaty by a representative assembly of the Russian people. Among other obligations, the Soviet government would be required to pay indemnities "for all destruction, requisitions and confiscations which have taken place during the war of 1914 and during the revolution of 1917." Poland would herself undertake to guide the destinies of the peoples living within the frontiers of 1772 in conformity with their wishes—a limited obeisance to self-determination but in reality promising some sort of autonomy at the most.[92] These terms soon became generally known in Poland and elsewhere,[93] including presumably in the Soviet Union. In Gibson's opinion, the reason why these terms exceeded anything that "Patek had led the representatives of the powers to believe and leave him open to the charge of imperialism which his moderate language has hitherto belied" was to be found "in the failure of the great powers to guide and counsel Poland. . . ." The result was "a new sense of independence and self-importance" and the "increased conviction that Poland had best get all advantages she can out of the present situation" regardless of the reactions of the powers.[94] According to Pilsudski's confidences to Gibson, he himself had been responsible for the inclusion of the demand for the frontiers of 1772, explaining that "Poland's hand had been forced by the action of England in renewing relations with the Bolsheviks and telling Poland she must make peace with the Bolsheviks. . . ."⁹⁵ This and later messages dealing with the crisis are stamped, "For the President."

In spite of information about Poland's intentions in the possession of the American and Allied governments, none of them, as far as is known, attempted to dissuade her from proceeding with her adventurous plans. The conclusion follows inevitably that, although skeptical as to the ultimate results, they would accommodate themselves to a Polish victory without too much trouble. Although there was no doubt about the State Department's displeasure, it took no action. Bainbridge Colby, the new Secretary of State, expressed its reserves to Gibson privately: "Many of the terms of peace . . . are manifestly impossible of execution and give this government the impression that Poland is not genuinely desirous of making peace." While the first draft of this telegram authorized Gibson at his discretion to inform Patek orally that "such is the impression on this Government by his note," this instruction was omitted from the final text.⁹⁶

Britain had no obvious ground for complaint; the Polish government had indeed, as Rumbold and Lloyd George advised, made up its mind on the basis of Poland's interests. Future events would show how solid were the assurances of British assistance if Poland's own existence were endangered—if that danger arose as the result of a Polish offensive.

The French, of course, were even less inclined to put on the brakes, and the Millerand government was testing the possibilities of a new direction in foreign policy which implied still greater reliance upon Poland. It was suspicious of British leniency toward Germany (nourished by Churchill's repeated pronouncements). A treaty between Great Britain and Persia in 1919 which advanced British interests at the expense of France's aspirations in the Middle East strengthened the reaction against Clemenceau's basic attachment to Anglo-French co-operation. At the same time, economic interests brought pressure to bear upon the new government to exploit the fluid situation in the Danube valley and France's military supremacy for their advantage.

These anti-British tendencies found a champion in Maurice Paléologue who at this time replaced Philippe Berthelot as Secretary General of the Quai d'Orsay. British contacts with the Russian liberals, especially the leaders of the Cadet party in 1916-1917, when Paléologue was Ambassador to Russia, had outraged his conviction that the Czarist regime was irreplacable, and anti-Bolshevism became a basic tenet with him. While Poland was moving toward a showdown with the Soviets, he encouraged the hopes of the Hungarian peace mission in Paris of a radical territorial and military revision of the terms communicated to it on January 15, attainably only at the expense of Czechoslovakia and Rumania, on the condition that sufficiently attractive economic advantages were offered France. These advantages gradually emerged as controlling shares in the Hungarian railways, transportation on the Danube, and banks. He went so far as to mention an alliance as a possibility. Although Paléologue had the grace always to stipulate negotiated agreements with Czechoslovakia and Rumania as prerequisites for the return of the territory desired by the Hungarians, these conversations carried the clear implication of a shift of French interest from Czechoslovakia and Rumania to a kind of Polish-Hungarian "axis."[97] Acting behind the backs of the British, as they had France's in Persia, but in a far more explosive context, France was unlikely to restrain the Poles from an adventure that might deal a mortal blow to bolshevism and at the same time give more substance to her assigned status as a great power.

On the very eve of the final Polish-Soviet exchange of messages, there was no reason to think that the Poles were going to wreck the negotiations on the question of the place where they should be held. Patek informed Gibson on March 26, the day before Patek's reply was finally sent to Moscow, that the negotiations would begin early in April. As to the place, "It is not yet decided where conference will be held but probably somewhere in the neighborhood of Warsaw."[98] Whose influence it was that at the last moment decided the Poles to insist upon a town directly on the battle-line is unknown, but it may reasonably be assumed that it was Pilsudski's, who presumably wished to go ahead with his offensive into the Ukraine. On March 27, Patek informed Chicherin that his government was ready to begin negotiations on April 10 at Borisov (Chicherin's message of December 22, 1919, had invited Poland to name the time and place), a town on the line between the two armies, and that it would order the suspension of hostilities "in the sector of the Borisov bridgehead twenty-four hours in advance of the time the Soviet government would set for the arrival of its plenipotentiaries."[99]

In his speeches at this time, Lenin was speaking more confidently than ever of the Soviets' prospects if the Poles attacked. To the Moscow Soviet, he declared, March 6, if the Polish landlords and capitalists, supported by France, should attack, "they must and will receive such a blow that their fragile capitalism and their imperialism will collapse forever."[100] On March 29, the day after Chicherin's reply, he spoke enthusiastically to the Congress of the Russian Bolshevik party of the prospects of the revolution in Germany as a result of the Kapp Putsch. "From the international point of view, our situation has never been as good as now. The news we receive daily from Germany especially fills us with joy and strength; it shows that however painful its infancy has been, the proletarian Soviet revolution is maturing irresistibly in that country. The German Kornilovs have exactly the same role as the Russian Kornilov. After their coup d'état, a turn favorable to the proletariat power has begun, among the rural as well as the urban proletariat. It confirms our confidence in our cause and gives us the certainty that the time is not distant when we will march hand in hand with a Soviet German government."[101] Trotsky, moreover, advocated strong-arm methods against Poland in the place of Chicherin's soft words and diplomatic roles.[102]

The immediate problem, from the Soviets' point of view, was the apparently impending Polish attack against which the German Communists could be of no possible assistance. Since the truce mentioned in Patek's note was limited to Borisov and the immediate vicinity, it offered no guarantee that an offensive would not be launched elsewhere during the negotiations. On the contrary, such was quite possibly Pilsudski's purpose. The preparations—the troop movements and concentration of supplies—must have already started. On March 28, within twenty-four hours of the receipt of the Polish note, Chicherin replied, protesting vigorously against the rigorously restricted truce area, rejecting Borisov as the place of meeting but suggesting a neutral country such as Estonia. He welcomed, however, April 10 as the date for the beginning of the negotiations.[103] In further notes, Chicherin underplayed the demand for a general truce, strenuously objected to Borisov but mentioned London and Paris as acceptable places, while Patek stood immovably upon Borisov.[104]

At this point, there again appeared a concordance between the German crisis and Polish decisions. After co-operating with the trade unions and the Social Democrats to defeat the reactionaries in the Kapp Putsch, the Communists, encouraged from Moscow, again tried to exploit the momentary confusion for the seizure of power. They were soon routed in Saxony, Hamburg, and the Ruhr, for General von Seeckt and the Reichswehr, who had been neutral while Kapp's forces tried to overthrow the Republic, acted immediately and efficiently against the Communists when they attempted to do the same thing. On April 3, army units pursued fleeing Communist bands into the demilitarized zone on the right bank of the Rhine in the Ruhr area in violation of the Treaty of Versailles, thus giving France a plausible ground for sanctions against Germany. Without consulting its allies, the Millerand government ordered French troops into Frankfort and Duisburg on April 6. Within hours on April 7, the Poles virtually killed all hope that negotiations with the Soviets might still avert full-scale war when Patek demanded a final reply (meaning the acceptance of Borisov), although he seemed to leave the door slightly ajar by mentioning April 17 as a possible new date for the meeting. There is no known evidence that these actions had been arranged between the French and the Poles, but the close relations between their military authorities more than suggests the co-ordination of efforts to impose their respective wills upon their opponents.

In his reply to Poland's curt note, Chicherin declared, April 9, it had the appearance of an ultimatum and thus shattered the negotiations "on a question of locality, a fact without precedent in the history of [diplomatic] relations."[105] The importance attributed to Borisov by both parties requires some consideration. While it was understandable that the Soviets should insist upon a cease-fire for the entire Polish front since it would prevent a Polish offensive for the duration of the truce, their refusal to go to Borisov is much less comprehensible.[106] The Bolsheviks were appreciably less bent upon peace at almost any price than they had earlier been, but it seems more likely that they saw in Poland's willingness to break on the issue of Borisov a chance to discredit her in world opinion. On receiving Poland's note, Chicherin immediately, April 7, appealed to the Allies to restrain her in part because of this irresponsible conduct. Since their concern, and especially Lloyd George's, for European economic recovery was well known, Chicherin began by blaming Poland for Soviet Russia's inability to concentrate upon economic reconstruction and for interfering with the resumption of trade, but he stressed even more the unprecedented insistence upon Borisov and the willingness of the Soviet government to go to Estonia, Petrograd, Warsaw, London, or Paris. "The many decisions of the Entente powers regarding the states bordering upon Russia show sufficiently that these governments regard their influence there as decisive. . . ." The responsibility for the consequences of Poland's obstinacy would be theirs.[107] In a statement on April 9 that appeared in the *Manchester Guardian* (April 15), Chicherin suggested that Poland had perhaps objected to Estonia because that country had been the first to make peace with Soviet Russia. The Poles might also feel that to go to Petrograd or Moscow would give the impression of a Polish defeat. "We, knowing our strength, have no such fears, and are willing to go to Warsaw. But perhaps they are afraid our presence in Warsaw would excite the Polish working masses to demonstrations. We are ready to negotiate with them anywhere else [Paris or London] outside the military zone."[108]

Poland's insistence upon Borisov was defended at the time by its official spokesmen as motivated by the determination not to permit any contacts between the Soviet representatives and local Communists, the inevitable result of the choice of a site outside the military zone.[109] In later years, after the victory had finally been won, they were franker and more candid, if also boastful. According to Count Skrzyński, earlier Polish Foreign Minister, the question of Borisov "was raised in such an offensive spirit that the whole question stopped at that point,"[110] and when Hugh Gibson met Patek in Tokyo in the 1930's the former Polish Foreign Minister related "with considerable satisfaction his part in having persuaded the Polish Government to launch this 'preventive attack.' "[111]

On the whole, the Allies continued their hands-off policy to the end, at least on the diplomatic level. The flow of military supplies almost certainly increased, mostly from France, judging by the ado about it a few weeks later based upon the fact that the preliminary preparations could not have been accomplished overnight. While Lloyd George persisted in his drive for trade negotiations and carried an unwilling Millerand government along with him at the San Remo Conference, the Soviets had been irritatingly obstructive.

They did not break off the negotiations as Chicherin threatened in his note to the Allies of March 5, but the Soviet delegation stayed indefinitely in Copenhagen rather than complying with Britain's refusal to admit Litvinov who was its head.[112] At the end of March, 1920, when the British finally stopped shipping supplies to Denikin's forces in South Russia, the British attempted to assure at least the personal safety of Denikin's troops by asking the Soviet government to grant a general amnesty in return for a cessation of hostilities on the Crimean front and the disbandment of the volunteer army. Otherwise, there would be little hope for the success of the commercial negotiations.[113] Chicherin's reply showed that the Soviets were not in a yielding mood. Since the British had made the broad problem of Anglo-Soviet relations dependent upon the welfare of General Wrangel's followers (he had replaced Denikin), Soviet Russia would follow their example, bringing in Poland's much more extensive hostilities and demanding free transit for the survivors of Béla Kun's Communist regime in Hungary to Soviet Russia.[114] The Soviets' pressure for the exercise of restraint in Warsaw was, nevertheless, echoed by many in Britain, where Laborites, many Liberals, and others like Lord Robert Cecil felt that Poland should not be allowed to ignite a fire whose consequences no one could foresee.[115]

For Lloyd George to have acted as they wished would have meant, however, a dangerous challenge to the French in addition to the serious differences that had rapidly accumulated between the two countries. Nothing was done in response to the Soviets' appeal of April 7 which was not even acknowledged, and later when the fortunes of war turned against Poland and he was pressed in the Commons to explain the government's inaction, he said that the only obstacle to peace negotiations between the Polish and Soviet governments seemed at the time to be the choice of the meeting place: ". . . it did not seem likely that the renewed intervention at this stage of His Majesty's Government, who had already advised the Polish Government to come to terms, would be attended with practical results."[116] He did not, of course, admit that the advice to make peace had been offset to some extent by what the Poles felt to be a promise not to permit the destruction of their country under any circumstances.

Meanwhile, Paléologue at the Quai d'Orsay continued, behind Britain's back, his dubious dealings with the Hungarians. In response, finally, to their insistence upon a political commitment in favor of their revisionist aims as the price for the economic concessions he expected, he signed a memorandum on April 15 to be communicated to Admiral Horthy, the Hungarian Regent. It contained the essentials of accords Hungary was to arrange directly with Czechoslovakia and Rumania (presumably with the assistance of French pressure upon these countries) for the return of areas of predominantly Magyar population and for autonomy in other instances.[117]

But Paléologue's intense anti-bolshevism and pro-Hungarian and Polish predilections did not determine French policy toward Great Britain. In fact, the Anglo-Soviet agreement for the exchange of prisoners of February 12 was followed by a similar Franco-Soviet agreement on April 21, which is said to have contained reciprocal promises of non-interference in domestic affairs and France's specific pledge that she "would participate in no aggressive measures against the Soviet Republics of Russia and the Ukraine."[118] If made, this promise was of exceedingly doubtful sincerity, for in a matter of days a Polish army, largely equipped by the French, was to invade the Ukraine with at least France's best wishes. It is, however, an established fact that Millerand, however unwillingly, agreed when Lloyd George, with Italy's support, proposed during the Conference of San Remo (April 24) the final authorization of negotiations with the Soviet trade delegation. Millerand's approval was given notwithstanding the additional provisions, which was a notable departure from earlier decisions, that other means than the Russian co-operatives might be used for the re-opening of trade.

Since the Allies, and especially France, had military missions as well as diplomatic representatives in Poland, it seems almost incredible that at least their governments were not aware of the impending offensive into the Ukraine that was launched on April 25. The public's lack of information is explained by the fact that for the preceding ten days Polish censors had forbidden the press and foreign correspondents to report anything about military preparations.[119] However, the governments apparently had no adequate warning.[120] On April 22, the American chargé d'affaires reported on a visit to the front without indicating any unusual developments.[121] When Churchill was questioned later in the House of Commons, he said that the British Military Mission had speculated on the possibility of an offensive in telegrams dated April 22, 23, and 24, the last arriving after the attack had begun, but most reports had "dwelt, rather, on the Soviet Government's preparations for a revival of the Bolshevik attack, which was delivered in great force in March and finally checked in April."[122] The Poles had waited until almost the last moment before concluding the final agreement with the Ukrainian pretender, Petlyura, on April 21 and announcing it publicly on April 23. It was the prelude to immediate action. Poland [Pilsudski signed it] promised to liberate the Ukraine west of the Dnieper River (including Kiev) and Petlyura confirmed his earlier renunciation of all claims to eastern Galicia.[123] Two days later, April 25, Pilsudski launched his offensive on the southern front in the direction of Kiev.

IV

The Polish Offensive
April and May, 1920,
and Its Repercussions

The adventure into which Pilsudski led his country, April 25, was not a crusade against bolshevism, although he never doubted Poland's military superiority or his ability to capture Moscow at his pleasure. It was a calculated move in power politics, the use of war to attain an important objective of his federalist policy. While he had not promised Petlyura Poland's direct participation for more than the liberation of Ukrainian territory west of the Dnieper River and had promptly announced his intention to withdraw from that limited area in a proclamation to the Ukrainian people,[1] he apparently counted upon a popular rising, with secondary Polish support, to drive the Bolsheviks out of the entire Ukraine. Under Polish guidance and influence, that vast region, organized as an independent or autonomous state, would become the southern anchor of a federation of the former Russian borderlands whose survival would require a permanently weakened Russia.[2] For this reason, he had marked time during the advance of the White Russian armies toward Moscow in 1919, and he was perhaps almost as suspicious of what the Allies would do for Russia if he should capture Moscow and overthrow the Bolshevik regime himself—assuming that he could have accomplished what no invader of Russia since Napoleon has so far done.

From the strictly military point of view, Pilsudski's plans were well laid, at least in the first phase of the campaign. Despite numerous indications that Kiev was his objective, the Soviet authorities took a "calculated risk" in that direction in order to strengthen the White Russian front which covered the direct route to Moscow where it was fairly certain that the decisive battles would be fought. The first relatively small reinforcements were sent there.[3] The result was a three to one numerical superiority in Poland's favor at the point of attack, and Pilsudski was able to occupy Kiev on May 6 against comparatively light resistance.[4] Except for presumably secondary operations in support of the expected rising of the Ukrainians, it was his intention to remain upon the defensive on the lower Dnieper and to concentrate the bulk of the Polish forces north of the impassable marshes where the war would presumably be won or lost.[5] There, however, on May 15, the Red Army seized the initiative, near the northern extremity of the front, in an attack, which the Poles were able to repel only with considerable difficulty.[6] It was a warning that the Polish victory was not as decisive as it seemed. That warning was renewed with greater force when Budënny's cavalry army, after a forced march across the Ukraine, outflanked Kiev from the north and compelled its evacuation on June 12.

From the political point of view as well, Pilsudski's plans were based upon mistaken calculations. The rising of the Ukrainians, upon which he had relied to wrest the entire Ukraine from the Bolsheviks, did not take place; the hatred of the peasants for the Polish Pans approached their detestation of the Bolsheviks. Most fateful of all, however, was the effect of the Polish invasion upon the Bolsheviks and the Russian people. Without the coal and iron as well as the food resources of the Ukraine, the future was bleak, indeed, for the Soviet regime. The Bolsheviks immediately accepted the challenge. Trotsky warned the party's Central Committee that it would be "a life-or-death struggle" and the central problem not only for the Red Army but "of all Worker-Peasant Russia."[7] On May 1, he ordered the Red Army to strike a "blow which would resound in the streets of Warsaw and throughout the world."[8] On the next day, May 2, he predicted, in a press interview, that the war "will end with a worker's revolution in Poland," not, however, that this revolution would occur at once, a testimonial to the greater appreciation of realities that sometimes distinguished him from other Bolshevik leaders, Lenin included.[9] Trotsky doubtless agreed with Radek that the Poles would at first be dominated by "the blind nationalism of the masses for whom a Red General or a White General always remains a Russian General."[10]

In Lenin's immediate reaction to the Polish invasion, first place was given to the necessity of defense and the second to the interests of world revolution. Speaking on April 29, he called upon everyone to rise as one man in defense of the Ukraine, and if as usual he referred to the international proletariat, it was to express confidence that the workers of England and France would not support intervention on the part of their governments, that the attack had been undertaken against the will of the Polish workers, and that the workers and peasants should be shown that the invasion was the result of the pressure of the Entente powers. Adding that the Entente's purpose was "to fortify the obstacle between us and the German proletariat," he betrayed the direction his thought was taking in the event of a favorable turn in the fortunes of the war.[11] Another such indication was the satisfaction with which he hailed what he claimed to be giant strides of the international revolution in a speech, May 5, to the All-Russian Central Executive Committee.[12] The loss of Kiev was promptly followed by a forthright call for a Bolshevik revolution in Poland in a manifesto, May 9, by the Central Executive Committee in which Lenin's was, of course, the dominant voice. The Polish workers, peasants and soldiers were assured that they would be able freely to choose their form of government, "even the existing regime." They were told, however, that the "Soviet power will crush your seigneurs." The manifesto ended with the cry, "Down with the Polish government of landlords and capitalists! Down with this criminal and fratricidal war! Long live peace between the laboring masses of Poland and Russia! Long live the free workers' and peasants' Poland!"[13] In the event of a victory of the Red Army, the freedom of choice on the part of the Polish people would have been, to say the least, extremely doubtful, judging by the tone of this pronouncement!

While Lenin played the theme of world revolution, the Bolsheviks at home took advantage of the upsurge of Russian national sentiment incited by the Polish invasion to enlist the services of many domestic enemies of the Soviet regime, especially those of General A. Brusilov, one of the more successful Tsarist chiefs of the General Staff.[14] In the end, Trotsky enrolled some thousands of former Tsarist officers who apparently contributed in no small degree to the Red Army's increasing effectiveness. Many had already fought on the Bolshevik side in the Civil War, including the youthful M. Tukhachevsky who at twenty-seven commanded the Red Army on the northern Polish front and his superior, S. Kamenev, the commander-in-chief of the entire western front.

The Polish offensive and its temporary success at once changed the conditions affecting the still pending trade negotiations in London.[15] It need scarcely be said that Lenin's interest in the matter had always been determined by the service it might render the cause of world revolution and by Russia's economic need. Always alert to the hostility which he regarded as the natural and inevitable attitude of capitalist powers, his suspicions were immensely strengthened by the Polish invasion which he believed, not without reason, would have been impossible without the moral and material support of the Allies.[16] It boded no good for the rapid progress of the trade negotiations that he blamed the British in particular. He lost no time in speaking, April 29, of the change for the worse in the hitherto well-disposed attitude of the British government as shown by its failure even to reply to the offer to guarantee the lives of General Wrangel and his followers (Chicherin's note of April 14 on this matter did not, in fact, contain such an offer, except by implication)[17] in return for the safe transit for the Hungarian Communist leaders from Austria to Soviet Russia.[18] While these exchanges regarding Wrangel's status never produced anything definite, the Soviets, their attention concentrated upon Poland, did agree to negotiations for an unofficial suspension of hostilities on the Crimean front.[19] The *de facto* truce enabled the Red Army to hold the line there with second-rate troops, but it was perhaps a greater boon to Wrangel in giving him time to build up his forces and to revive their weakened morale.

What Wrangel's future should be became one of the multiplying differences between Great Britain and France. Persuaded that the White Russian cause was irretrievably lost and anxious to avoid unnecessary bloodshed, the British tried to restrain him from aggressive action, the British High Commissioner in Constantinople warning, June 3, that an offensive would result in the loss of British interest in the fate of his army. The French, however, seem to have incited him with promises of material aid and of the participation of French warships. The counsel of General Mangin, France's military representative, may have decided Wrangel to launch the last White Russian offensive of any significance on June 6, and it is not unlikely that the French hoped to help the Poles who were in trouble on their Ukrainian front by this diversion.[20] Since the British had assisted in the unofficial suspension of hostilities, Lenin drew the unjustified but, in the circumstances, the not unnatural conclusion that it was another instance of British perfidy—which he, of course, regarded as the normal attitude of all capitalist countries.

Three developments during this period underscored Soviet Russia's more defiant attitude. On May 5, the League of Nations' request for the admission of its Commission of Enquiry for the purpose of investigating conditions was brusquely rejected on that ground that the members represented states that were supporting Poland's invasion of the Soviet Republics.[21] The second was another of Lenin's appeals for the world revolution. Replying to the request from British Laborites for his views as to whether violence would be necessary for a successful British revolution, he called upon the workers to use the Bolshevik Revolution as their model and to seize power in a letter that was published early in June.[22] Of much greater effect upon British policy was the Soviets' diplomatic and military intervention in the Near and Middle East. On April 26, the day after Pilsudski invaded the Ukraine, Mustapha Kemal, the Turkish nationalist leader, proposed the establishment of regular relations and co-operation against "foreign imperialism" from the Turkish National Assembly in Angora. Drawn together by a community of interest against the influence of European powers in the small Caucasus states, Georgia, Armenia, and Azerbaijan, diplomatic relations were re-established by July 11, a gesture of defiance toward Britain which at that time and for the next two years opposed the Turkish national movement with all the means at its command. Since the Bolsheviks drew back from firm commitments with the essentially bourgeois Kemal, their military advance in the Caucasus was a graver and more immediate threat to British imperial interests. On May 18, their occupation of the Caspian port of Enzeli at once rendered the entire British position in the Caucasus untenable, overthrew the Azerbaijan Republic and substituted an organization on the Soviet model, and destroyed whatever chance there had been that the Persian parliament would ratify the Anglo-Persian Treaty of 1919.[23] The advance into the Caucasus was, according to evidence in Trotsky's private papers, at least partly intended as retaliation for Britain's alleged support of the Poles.[24]

With the exception of percipient individuals such as Lord Robert Cecil and of those who, like George Lansbury, editor of the Labor *Daily Herald*, took their cue from Soviet sources, the Polish offensive took Western opinion —and perhaps the governments as well—by surprise. Its reactions were largely conditioned by prevailing attitudes toward bolshevism and Soviet Russia, but the problem cannot be said to have been a major preoccupation as long as things went well for the Poles.[25] In the conservative, anti-Bolshevik press of Great Britain and France, the Poles had many ardent partisans who did not hesitate to misrepresent the facts in order to exonerate them from blame. According to the *Times* (May 1), the Soviet government had responded to Poland's offer to meet in Borisov with "an audacious demand for a meeting in Warsaw," whereas it had, in fact, suggested alternatives in neutral countries as well as in Soviet Russia. The *Temps* (May 6) was more scrupulous on this point—it mentioned the Soviets' proposal of London or Paris—but it was guilty of an even more serious distortion in declaring that the Poles "had promised to undertake no offensive action in any other sector [than Borisov] as long as the conversations lasted."[26] In any event, the bad faith of the Bolsheviks made negotiations impossible. One and all agreed that the Polish offensive was a justifiable anticipation of the attack which the Bolsheviks were planning.[27] The *Temps* (May 6) seized upon this plausible thesis, which in view of the almost complete lack of data about the Red Army and its operations was difficult to contradict, as a convenient stick with which to belabor Lloyd George and his policy of trade with Russia. Before mounting their offensive, the Bolsheviks wanted to secure locomotives and rolling stock from the Allies along with material for repair of tracks for the rehabilitation of the Russian railway system; such was the mission assigned to Litvinov and Krassin in Copenhagen. The French could also be counted upon to bring the German peril into the picture, the *Temps* (May 6) suggesting that the Bolsheviks were also playing for time in the hope of a successful reactionary coup in Germany and a subsequent attack upon Poland from the West. In the *Soir* (May 8), Gaston Doumergue wrote of the "important German forces in Silesia" as giving substance to Polish fears of a joint Soviet-German offensive.

If this school of thought on both sides of the Channel had any doubts, they were not at first because of fear of an eventual Polish disaster. On the eve of the occupation of Kiev, the *Temps* (May 4) reported that the Bolshevik defeat was taking on the dimensions of a rout, and when Patek, the Polish Foreign Minister, told the press in Rome that the Poles had captured 160 locomotives and 2,000 cannons, no one seems to have raised a skeptical voice.[28] In London, the weekly *Spectator* (May 8) seems to have trusted the ability of the Poles to go about as far as they pleased. Indeed, the British press printed communiqués on the progress of the fighting based upon information from the Polish legation. Both the *Times* (May 1) and the *Temps* (May 6) were manifestly alarmed that the Poles might bite off more Russian territory than they could absorb. Some of their announced peace aims were "fantastic" even to as ardent a friend as the *Times*. But the French, after some original qualms and in considerable contradiction to their support of General Wrangel's offensive on June 8, were not alone in adjusting themselves to Pilsudski's projects in the Ukraine.[29] Winston Churchill thought well of them. In a memorandum, May 21, he foresaw a possible general peace during the approaching summer if Petlyura were able to organize a "civilized type [of government] capable of liberating the corn supplies of the Ukraine, and with that territory sheltered and assisted by a strong Poland...."[30] But the thought that loomed largest among the conservatives everywhere, and it was to influence others as well, was that Poland stood in the first line of defense of Western security and civilization, with the inference that she should be forgiven much and supported in her arduous task.

The picture of Poland as the indispensable bulwark of Western civilization did not carry universal conviction. Critical opinion estimated Poland's strength in comparison with Russia's (and Germany's) potential in more realistic terms. It feared the consequences of a nationalist conflict between Poland and Russia, not only for the direct participants but for the rest of Europe. In its view, the Poles were guilty of a secretly planned aggression for outrageously imperialistic purposes, and the Allies of a failure to restrain them. The excuse that the Soviets would have attacked carried no conviction in view of what was known about the internal weaknesses of Soviet Russia. Because of the almost complete lack of news from Russia, Lenin's ominous emphasis upon world revolution, especially in Germany, largely escaped the attention it deserved.

The feeling that the Allies, belatedly, should restrain Poland overshadowed the long-pending trade negotiations with the Russians. It was expressed by Lord Robert Cecil, writing as the Chairman of the League of Nations Union, to Lord Curzon, the Foreign Minister, on May 3. Cecil hoped that Great Britain would initiate a meeting of the League's Council to deal with the problem since "For months past Poland has been notoriously preparing to attack Russia...." Curzon replied with a similarly open letter, May 11, in which he denied the existence of grounds for the intervention of the council. Poland's alleged preparations for an aggression were not confirmed by available information and "until quite recently" there had been "no evidence to show that the Poles had been contemplating an offensive." In any event, that offensive had not precipitated a new war; it was a phase of a war that had been going on for some time. "We told them that His Majesty's government could offer them no advice and that they must choose peace or war on their own responsibility. Having left them free to choose, I hardly think it is open to us to attempt to repress their action when they have made their choice. Such an attempt would certainly be regarded as intervention in favour of the Bolshevists and against our Allies—a result which it would be difficult to defend."[31] While Lloyd George did not often see eye-to-eye with his foreign secretary about Russia and Poland, it was, nevertheless, clear that he was not going to exert his influence in the Supreme Council for the purpose of restraining Poland.

Signs of restlessness in Labor party circles appeared that developed into a storm in August. Lansbury's journal, as Lenin had done at the same time, at once placed the major responsibility squarely upon the Allies and called the forces of Labor into action. "Without Allied approval, without Allied help in finance and in munitions, the conspirators would be powerless, dared not have moved. The marionettes are in Warsaw, but the strings are pulled from London and Paris. One word from here, and the whole mad adventure must end. It is for British Labour to insist that that word shall be spoken, and spoken at once. If Europe is to be saved, Labour must speak—and if need be act—decisively and now."[32] This sentiment was fully shared by the radical weeklies, except for Lansbury's permature summons of Labor to direct action. Because of recent experience, the *Nation* (May 22) declared, Labor "is so convinced that every ministerial statement about our Russian policy is false, that it would be sceptical if Downing Street were for once to tell the truth." The *New Statesman* (May 8) found nothing at all to approve in Poland's cause. She was not even engaged in an effort "to upset the Bolshevik regime and to establish a strong and efficient government in Moscow. That is the very last thing they desire. They are simply seeking territory—which one day a reorganized Russia will certainly recover. It is impossible, therefore, for anyone who is concerned for the future peace of Europe to hope for anything but an early disaster for the Polish armies. The Supreme Council seems determined to make us all pro-Bolsheviks." Even the less biased expert on Eastern European affairs, R. W. Seton-Watson, wrote scathingly of Pilsudski's arrangements with Petlyura: "They strike a more serious blow at the principles of the League of Nations than at the military power of Soviet Russia."[33]

For a Frenchman, even a Socialist, to have thus expressed himself publicly, given the atmosphere of emotional attachment to Poland, would have been almost impossible. A Socialist member of the Chamber had been thrice howled down when he as much as suggested that Poland might, like Estonia, find it to her interest to make peace with the Soviets.[34] If in these circumstances there were non-Socialists who still ventured, however circumspectly, to criticize Poland's conduct, it was symptomatic of widespread doubt. One who defended her offensive admitted that the seizure of Kiev was a mistake since it enabled the Bolsheviks to enlist the services of patriotic Russians.[35]

Philippe Millet, foreign affairs expert on an important Parisian daily newspaper, the *Petit Parisien,* and editor of the weekly *Europe nouvelle,* endorsed the universal warmth with which French opinion regarded Poland, the support that France would always give her *"quoi qu'il arrivera,"* and denied to the Allies, after their lack of firmness, the right to cast stones at Poland. France's friendship, nevertheless, justified some plain words. Not only was the invasion of the Ukraine a menace to the economy of Poland

and of Eastern Europe in general, but Poland's federalist policy threatened to degenerate into the crassest imperialism. Millet asked how it was that an independent or autonomous Ukraine for which Poland had denied any real claim to existence in 1919 could become possible and an article of faith in 1920? His real feeling emerged in his denunciation of the provocation of Russian national feeling; Poland was herself making a Russia that would be its "eternal and implacable adversary. She is cheerfully preparing the Russo-German reconciliation at a time when impartial observers ask themselves if this great Poland which the war has exhumed from a sepulchre is a living being or merely a ghost." Poland had best withdraw immediately within her frontiers, for otherwise it was doubtful that even France's assistance could protect her from the consequences of her actions.[36]

Some thoughtful Frenchmen were uneasy for the future and the part they thought Poland should play between Germany and Russia. One of them, who witnessed in Poland the entire crisis, from the occupation of Kiev to the Polish victory on the Vistula, was convinced that she could not survive if both were her enemies. She must inevitably reach an understanding with one in order to defend herself successfully against the other. "Her choice is not a matter of indifference: the balance of power and peace of Europe depends upon it." If an agreement with Soviet Russia was out of the question, it was possible and necessary to "keep the door open (*ménager*) for a durable understanding with the Russian people" and therefore carefully to avoid "anything calculated to provoke an irreconcilable antagonism."[37] Millerand's failure, as President of the Council, to fix a time for the discussion of Jean Hennessy's interpellation of the government's policy "on the subject of the Russo-Polish military operations and on the failure to apply Article 17 of the Covenant of the League of Nations" did not augur well for the government's receptivity to these ideas.[38]

Just as Lloyd George had never shared the instinctive and implacable hostility toward Soviet Russia of the anti-Bolshevik, the prime minister's attitude during the crisis precipitated by the Polish invasion of the Ukraine closely resembled that of Liberal and Labor opinion, except in regard to the practical steps that should be taken. He had expected serious trouble from its political inexperience and the imperialist ambitions which the French had encouraged. That Poland would be able alone to save itself from the consequences of its own folly, he did not believe, and he feared that the Allies, including Great Britain, would eventually have to go to the rescue as, indeed, they had given the Poles reason to expect. In a private conversation during a weekend in the country, May 9, he mentioned the Poles with the French as "two nations in Europe who have gone rather mad.... Unless the Poles are careful they will revive and intensify the spirit of Russian nationality. Nothing can do this more effectively than arrogance on the part of the foreigners. The Poles are inclined to be arrogant and they will have to take care that they don't get their heads punched."[39] Two weeks later, the same confidant reported Lloyd George's prediction, after a conference with the Polish Ambassador, Prince Sapieha, that "the Poles would suffer a severe defeat."[40] On May 19, another appeal from the Soviets to the Allied and Associated Powers must have reminded Lloyd George that the means of restraining Poland was at hand, as the press reminded him repeatedly, since it was dependent upon outside assistance.[41] Although perhaps the preponderance of British opinion—but not of its expression in the House of Commons—had already reached the same conclusion, Lloyd George neither replied nor did he do anything to restrain the Poles.

In the exceedingly complex situation that confronted him, he was impelled even more than was his usual wont to play both sides of the street. At home he had to contend with vociferous partisans of Poland in the press and with her sympathizers in his government. There was, of course, Winston Churchill, the Secretary of State for War, whose semi-conversion to the prime minister's Russian policy was suddenly dropped when Poland's aggression again opened the prospect of a serious blow at bolshevism.[42] According to the American Embassy, the Foreign Office was friendly to the Poles,[43] and the exchange of letters between Curzon, the Foreign Secretary, and Cecil suggests that its chief shared this feeling. Abroad, Lloyd George could count upon Italy's support but he had to reckon with the stiffening resistance of France, especially in the Polish question, and with America's carping criticism.

What throws the most questionable light upon his purposes at this time is the fact that his government was morally and materially assisting Poland in what he had called her "madness," although not on anywhere near France's scale. He himself must have sanctioned King George V's message, May 3, "of greetings and congratulations" to Marshal Pilsudski on the anniversary of the adoption of the Polish Constitution of 1791. Since it followed the first reports of Polish victories, it was understandable that the king's words that his country "has watched with the greatest sympathy the resurrection of Poland" could be misrepresented as an implied approval of the Polish offensive.[44] More significantly considerable shipments of munitions from British stores were leaving British ports for Poland, although Churchill denied in the House of Commons as late as May 11 that the War Office had given any "assistance to the Poles in this enterprise [Polish offensive]...."[45] When the facts were revealed as a result of Labor's first direct action when dock workers refused to load the S. S. "Jolly George" with munitions for Poland, it became evident that Churchill had been less than candid. Bonar Law, the government leader in the Commons, replying to questions in the Commons, May 20, revealed that the government had agreed the preceding October to give Poland "a certain quantity of surplus stores on condition that the cost of transport should be undertaken by the Polish Government . . . the material in question became the property of the Polish Government, and part of it is now being shipped by that Government."[46] According to the information in the possession of the American Embassy, these munitions attained respectable totals: 25,000 rifles, 50 million cartridges, 400 machine guns, 48 field guns, 96,000 rounds of artillery ammunition, and complete equipment for 40,000 men.[47] No wonder otherwise friendly critics could make neither head nor tail of Lloyd George's policy. In the *Nation's* (May 15) view, it was purely opportunistic.[48]

While the Bolsheviks' illusion that Lloyd George's interest in trade was great enough to enable them to pressure him into restraining Poland may have contributed to the Trade Delegation's marking time in Copenhagen, even Lloyd George was apparently in no great hurry for it to proceed to London. A Foreign Office note of April 29—four days after the Polish offensive began—to the American Embassy, belatedly replying to the American government's statement of its intention to remove all restrictions upon trade relations with Russia, spoke of the "momentarily expected arrival of the Krassin delegation" as a reason why the United States should not act immediately.[49] Almost another month passed, however, before the Russians at last arrived in London on May 27, and it seems to have been political questions, especially the dangerous situation of British imperial interests in Persia and the Middle East, more than trade that removed the last difficulties.

The views of J. L. Garvin's Sunday *Observer*, which were followed closely in Paris for light on the direction of Lloyd George's policy, were significant. Moved especially by the advance already won by the Soviets in the Caucasus area, the *Observer* underscored on May 2 the need of peace with Russia, "and the sooner negotiations are opened on the subject the better."[50] The Soviets' occupation of Enzeli on the Caspian Sea (May 18) gave greater urgency to its demand for peace. "Those who countenance the wild Polish ambitions and aggressions," it declared, May 23, "know not what they do. They are encouraging Poland to its doom with an inevitable sequel for which Britain above all will pay in blood and expense. That madness must be stopped at any price, or Britain and France above all will rue it," and Poland will be crushed "utterly as a prevailing elephant kneads a tiger to death."[51] The question as to what action the loss of Enzeli required was considered at a meeting of the Cabinet on May 21. After an exchange of recriminations between Curzon, who reproached Sir Henry Wilson, the Chief of the Imperial General Staff, for having exaggerated the defensive capabilities of that position, and Wilson, who pointed out that the Caucasus states had in the end joined the Bolsheviks instead of fighting to the death as Curzon had said they would, it was decided that the order to concentrate on a more southern line should be tentative, "i.e. until Lloyd George had had a talk with the Bolshevik, Krassin, who is coming here on the 30th...."[52]

On May 27, Krassin and his four associates (the Soviets had finally withdrawn Litvinov) finally arrived in London. They came with the purpose, it may safely be assumed, of exploiting every favorable opportunity for the interests of Soviet Russia whether in trade, the attainment of equality and recognition in political matters, or the fostering of differences between the anti-Bolshevik powers and Poland. While George Lansbury's pro-Bolshevik sympathies placed the *Daily Herald* at the Krassin delegation's disposal for the communication of diplomatic notes and views to the British public, the direct propaganda for world revolution seems to have proceeded from Moscow, presumably in view of the risk that such activity on the part of Krassin's delegation might cause its expulsion.[53] Its presence in the capital of the British Empire was bitter medicine for anti-Bolsheviks everywhere; since no one any longer took seriously the pretense that it represented the Russian co-operatives, it could only mean a step toward the official recognition of the Soviet regime, whose leaders Churchill compared "to a snake creeping along on its slimy stomach and then suddenly striking at its prey."[54] Krassin, said the *Times* (May 28), might not have blood on his own hands, but he was the colleague of those who had sacrificed more innocent lives than the wildest of Jacobins.

Since Lloyd George happened to have talked freely in private conversation at this time, it is fairly definitely established that he was restrained by few scruples about Bolshevik ethics. He thought that bolshevism had failed as it was bound to do since "it ignored some of the most important qualities of human nature." Nevertheless, Lenin's "great economic experiment... had to be tried and he [Lloyd George] did not object to the experiment so long as it was not tried here!" He had no fear of the infection of the British working-classes but they "did not wish it to be interfered with.... The innate feeling of the Briton is that foreigners, and especially Russians, are queer devils who engage in all sorts of strange practices." Lloyd George confidently expected changes in the direction of moderation. Since, in his view, Lenin was "the biggest man in politics... he would modify his plans and govern Russia by other methods."[55] It was doubtless with this thought of the future Russia, as well as the practical problems of trade and of Middle Eastern politics, in mind that Lloyd George and members of his cabinet personally welcomed Krassin at No. 10 Downing Street.

The mandate Lloyd George had received from the Supreme Council was strictly limited to the resumption of trade, although the Conference of San Remo had approved a certain liberalization in the sense that the negotiations were not necessarily restricted to representatives of the Russian co-operatives. In view of the opportunity to safeguard British imperial interests and of advancing his larger purposes in regard to Russia, he paid little heed to this restriction. It was significant that he chose Sir Robert Horne, President of the Board of Trade, rather than Curzon, or another Foreign Office official, as the chief British spokesman in dealing with Krassin. At an early point in the conversations, Horne proposed a general political agreement as the condition for a commercial accord. There would be a mutual renunciation of hostility and propaganda against the institutions of the British Empire and the Soviet Republic, but specific pledges as well. The Soviet government would refrain "from any attempt by military or diplomatic or any other form of action or propaganda to encourage any of the peoples of Asia in any form of hostile action against British interests or the British Empire, especially in India and in the independent State of Afghanistan." For its part, the British government would similarly pledge itself "in respect of the countries which formed part of the former Russian Empire and which now have become independent."[56]

If the Soviet leaders had at this moment seriously feared for the survival of the Bolshevik regime, their failure to snap up this offer would seem almost incredible, considering the advantages it offered them. The British were offering to divorce themselves from the Polish cause in such a way as probably to submit the Anglo-French Entente to an intolerable strain. The price, to be sure, would have been the renunciation of the world revolution in Asia. Gathering the Soviet forces for a counterattack, the first phase of which took the form of Budënny's piercing of the Polish line north of Kiev on June 8 and banking mistakenly upon a German revolution in the near future, the Bolsheviks regarded this price as too high. However, Krassin seems to have played for time, while responding with the obvious proposal for the broadening of the scope of the negotiations.

Until more is known about Anglo-French relations at this time, it is impossible to be certain that Lloyd George had given the French any inkling of his intentions. The Paris press claimed that he had addressed some sort of a question to Millerand, presumably after Krassin's first mention of a general conference and that the British Prime Minister then received Krassin at No. 10 Downing Street without waiting for a reply.[57] Writing to his son, French Ambassador Paul Cambon said that he had delivered "our refusal to the English Government" on May 30, and his claiming that Krassin "wishes a conference which would quickly turn into a search for political understandings" clearly suggested that Lloyd George had asked Millerand if France would attend such a conference.[58] French opinion regarded Lloyd George's direct contacts with alarm. It felt that "when Mr. Lloyd George went forward with extended hand in the hall of No. 10 Downing Street to greet the eminently capable and respectable M. Krassin, he was in reality indulging in an official handshake with Lenin and Trotsky."[59] Except for a few discordant voices that reproached the government for not following Lloyd George's example,[60] one and all agreed that Krassin's presence in London was the result of the Bolshevik occupation of Enzeli and the Poles' capture of Kiev. The inevitable implication was that Lloyd George was prepared to sacrifice the Poles in order to ease the British situation in the Middle East. He was advised that the proper way to defend Persia and the approaches to India was not to deal with the Bolsheviks but to tear up the Anglo-Persian Treaty of 1919.[61]

Lloyd George, nevertheless, refused to give up the difficult task of coming to terms with the Russians. Replying to questioners in the House of Commons, June 3, he made clear his intention to settle such questions as the exchange of prisoners and to secure a guarantee against attacks on British interests in the East and at home in direct negotiations. "These things we must clear out of the way ourselves. The negotiations as to trade with them will be conducted by representatives of the Governments."[62] Nor did he surrender to the anti-bolshevism of Conservative back-benchers during the debate on June 7. He reviewed the decisions of the Supreme Council at Paris (Clemenceau was no Bolshevik sympathizer) and London and of the San Remo Conference for the revival of trade. While Lloyd George loyally quoted the decision against any change in political policy, he did not again speak of the political questions that were to be settled directly with the Russians, but he insisted that the form of government, even the matter of atrocities, should not be decisive. Had not Britain continued to trade with Turkey during the Armenian massacres? "It is really new doctrine that you must approve of the habits, the customs, the government, the religion, or the manners of the people before you start trading with them." That he still had more than trade in mind was evident in his possibly exaggerated estimate of the sacrifices that the destruction of the Soviet regime would require of Britain. "If you say you are going to crush Bolshevism because it is an evil thing, put your might into it, and put your manhood into it. We have lost hundreds of thousands of lives. Are you prepared to lose hundreds of thousands more? We have £8,000,000,000 of debt, are we going to pile up £3,000,000,000 or £4,000,000,000 more? If you are not prepared to do that, what is the good of talking like that?" When a member suggested "let Poland do it," Lloyd George was doubtful of her capacity. "I think," he said, "they were badly advised."[63]

In regard to the details of the intermittent conversations that followed during the next three weeks, little is known. It is clear, however, that pressure at home, the situation in Eastern Europe, and the increasing confidence of the Soviet leaders all contributed to obstruct progress. According to Soviet sources, the British added the demand for the recognition in principle of the liability for private commercial claims to the conditions required for a trading agreement at a meeting on June 7,[64] the day on which Lloyd George defended his policy of a peaceful settlement with Soviet Russia in the House of Commons. Krassin is said to have replied two days later with a long statement giving priority to the Soviet's claims for damages arising from the Allied intervention and calling for a general peace conference to consider these and all other political problems in which Soviet Russia would be an equal.[65]

At the same time, Budënny's cavalry attack began auspiciously, resulting in the Polish evacuation of Kiev in a few days (June 12), and General Wrangel's offensive, June 8, from the Crimean front added new venom to Anglo-Soviet relations. On June 11, Chicherin accepted Curzon's disavowal of British responsibility for Wrangel's violation of the unofficial truce with offensive skepticism, citing the protection Britain had given him and the aid he had received from the Allies. The Soviet government expected the British government to take the same unspecified action against him with which it had threatened the Soviets when they had not at once granted him an amnesty.[66]

On the same day, the *Times* (June 11) further increased Lloyd George's difficulties by printing Lenin's letter to Tom Shaw and other left-wing Laborites on the proper revolutionary tactics in Great Britain. Although Lenin wrote as an "ordinary Communist" and not in his capacity as a member of the Soviet government, it was a serious error, understandable only when his belief in the fundamental hostility of the British government and in the rosy future of world revolution is remembered. The parliamentary and trade union leaders of British Labor had deserted the workers for the bourgeoisie in the "revolutionary struggle of the proletariat," a desertion that had been covered by "reformist and pacifist phrases about peaceful evolution, about democracy...." Whether it would be more useful to work for peace with Soviet Russia or to join the Third International was, he wrote evasively, a matter of conviction, but the proletariat's cause would only be injured if those workers who persisted in intellectual slavery joined the Third International. What outraged British opinion most was Lenin's advice to the British workers to seize power and reveal the imperialist treaties between the Allies for the plunder of other countries whose existence must be known to every literate in those countries. It was an incitement to violent revolution in a country with which an official Soviet delegation was supposedly seeking a political understanding. Even leftist opinion could find little or nothing to say in extenuation.

Although the *Nation* (June 17) glossed over the most offensive passages, it did say that there was not the slightest chance "that any but a negligible fringe of British Labor will believe in the eventual success [of bolshevism] and become revolutionaries." The *New Statesman* (June 19) described the letter as "an almost incredibly inept piece of work. Its crude violence, its tone of contemptuous condescension, its doctrinaire shibboleths...in short, nearly every one of its features, might have been expressly designed by some subtle enemy to discredit its writer in the sight not only of the ordinary British workingman but even of those enthusiastic left-wingers who have hitherto been proud to dub themselves 'Bolsheviks.'" It was doubtful that any sympathy would survive in the ranks of Labor "unless Mr. Churchill will oblige with a new anti-Bolshevik war."[67]

Lloyd George spoke of the letter as "an insane document" which, he feared, might make the already stumbling negotiations with Krassin still "more difficult." There is, however, no evidence that the prime minister was thinking of breaking off,[68] although Cambon, the French Ambassador, noted the lack of progress with much satisfaction. The participants reminded him of the clown entangled in fly-paper from which he was unable to extricate himself. "The more they maneuver and confer, the more inextricable the situation becomes."[69]

By the end of June, Lloyd George had evidently decided to bring the conversations to a head. Time was passing, and the defeat he expected the Soviets to administer to the Poles might make them still more intractable. Even the slight evidence that is available testifies to his irritation at Krassin's delays and evasiveness, which he attributed to Krassin's fear of Moscow. "'He is always looking over his shoulder,'" Lloyd George said in private conversation, "'as if he expected to be shot.'"[70] Moreover, a settlement with Soviet Russia might strengthen the prime minister's hand at the forthcoming conference for the consideration of German disarmament and coal deliveries, in Spa (Belgium) early in July, in which for the first time since the war Germany was to be represented.

Lloyd George took the first step toward a possible showdown on June 29. The only evidence by a participant so far available, concerning what he told the Russian delegation, is Krassin's brief summary in a note to Curzon on October 6, 1920, after Poland's victory on the Vistula in August and just before the preliminary peace of Riga, in which Lloyd George's offers were almost certainly exaggerated in order to establish the best possible conditions for the renewal of the suspended Anglo-Soviet negotiations. According to Krassin, the prime minister stated what he required from the Soviet government for an agreement. If he received an affirmative reply at Spa by July 9 at the latest, he would make a public declaration of England's intention to resume relations with Soviet Russia regardless of the attitude of the other Allies, including that of France. The acceptance of his conditions would, moreover, amount to a truce and the British government would then be ready immediately to begin negotiations for the conclusion of a general peace.[71]

Krassin then handed Lloyd George a memorandum, written before the meeting on the basis of the British statements during the sessions on May 31 and June 7, of which two versions exist in print: a summary contained in the Soviet Commissariat of Foreign Affairs' statement of July 9[72] and what purports to be the full text.[73] While the latter shows Krassin's awareness of the prime minister's irritation by complaints about the poor telegraphic communication with Moscow, which was responsible for the failure of 20 to 30 per cent of the messages getting through at all or arriving in garbled form, and about Litvinov's absence in view of the political character of the conversations, both versions attest to the Soviet government's willingness to pledge itself to abandon hostile propaganda in return for a similar promise, to settle all property claims on a reciprocal basis, and to revise its general foreign policy under the same condition. In neither, however, was there a specific acceptance of the British conditions and of a trade agreement as the next step, but rather both parties insisted upon negotiations ending in a formal state treaty, especially since some of Britain's allies were directly or indirectly engaged in hostile actions against Soviet Russia.

On the next day, June 30, the British government handed an important note to Krassin for transmission to his government in reply to the latter's memorandum. Again there are two versions in print: a summary in the Narkomindel's (Soviet Foreign Commissariat) statement on the Anglo-Soviet negotiations,[74] and the supposedly full text circulated by Bonar Law, the government's leader in the House of Commons.[75] Except for one significant difference in the statement of the British conditions for a trade agreement, there is substantial agreement between them, but both show that Chicherin's version of October 6 of Lloyd George's oral promises of June 28 was unreliable. In the Narkomindel's summary, the specific undertaking in regard to British interests in Asia was phrased as a Soviet pledge "not to join in military activities or propaganda conducted by Asiatic peoples against British interests or the British Empire," whereas the text as communicated to the House of Commons reads as follows: "...that the Soviet Government will refrain from any attempt by military action or propaganda to encourage any of the peoples of Asia in any form of hostile action against British interests or the British Empire." The difference, of course, arose from the Soviets' desire to score the propaganda point that they were being required to keep hands off the spontaneous anti-British agitation on the part of Asiatic peoples and not to renounce the effort to stimulate such manifestations. Aside from this distortion, the British demands—a mutual renunciation of hostile action and propaganda, a general and immediate exchange of nationals of the two countries, a mutual recognition in principle for the property claims of individuals, the reserved right to refuse admission to Great Britain of Soviet representatives on the *persona non grata* basis—were stated accurately enough. The first of these demands, including the specific pledge about Asia, was designated as "the fundamental condition of any trading agreement" not only between Soviet Russia and Great Britain but of "any Western Power."[76]

The inducement offered in the British note, while it carried far-reaching implications, was not nearly as positive as Chicherin's version of what Lloyd George had said suggests. According to the latter, a favorable reply would be followed by an announcement of Britain's intention to resume "relations with the Soviet Government" (i.e., granting of diplomatic recognition), regardless of the other Allies, including France. The British note of June 30 stated: "The British Government propose what is tantamount to a general armistice, as a condition for the resumption of trade relations, in the hope that this armistice may lead ere long to a general peace."[77] In other words, Lloyd George was telling the Soviet government that its acceptance might lead to a general cessation of hostilities against it and, in the not too distant future, to a general peace which by implication meant a general peace conference with Soviet Russia as an equal participant. He thus ignored Krassin's stipulation of a separate Anglo-Soviet state treaty.

The note closed with a threat. "Should, however, no affirmative reply be obtained within one week of the presentation of this note, the British Government will regard these negotiations as at an end, and, in view of the declared unwillingness of the Soviet Government to cease its attacks upon the British Empire, will take council with its Allies as to the measures to deal with the situation."[78] It was doubtless to provide for the worst eventuality that the British government at this very moment offered no opposition in the Council of Ambassadors to the reinforcement of General Wrangel's offensive. On June 30, the day that Krassin was given the above note, Lord Derby, the British Ambassador in Paris, told the council that his government "does not in any way oppose the return of this Bredow Corps to the Crimea,[79] but does not wish to have anything to do with it, it does not wish to afford any help towards that end."[80]

Considering the strong aversion to the direction Lloyd George's policy was taking on the part of the American and French governments, it seems highly improbable that he would have been able to make good his vague promises, if he had been called upon to do so. Officially, the American attitude on the eve of Pilsudski's offensive had been substantially the same as Lloyd George's, and, because of the negligible attention to that operation in the press as long as things went well for the Poles, there was little or no pressure from public opinion. Such as developed came from the left which, as in Britain, was alert to the slightest evidence of material assistance to the Polish aggressors. Lincoln Colcord, the radical journalist, drew the worst conclusions when Newton Baker and the Navy Department refused to confirm or to deny that supplies were being sold to the Poles on long-term credit.[81] For the time being, the problem of trading with Soviet Russia was of greater official concern, for the demands of certain industrial interests clashed with the administration's firm stand against any move that would strengthen the Bolsheviks or open the door to official recognition. Great Britain had been informed that the removal of all restrictions was under consideration to take effect at an early date, but, on the basis of what happened later, it is a justifiable inference that the State Department intended to set an example for other governments to follow that would take away with the left hand what the right hand had apparently given. It agreed with the French government on almost all points: the need of safeguarding the commercial and financial claims of governments and individuals against payments for imports by the export of gold and by economic concessions.

The attitude of the British government soon became a sore point. As a result of its note of April 29, in which American action at an early date was deprecated in view of the impending conversations with the Russians,[82] the suggested dates were allowed to pass without a decision. On May 26, Washington learned that Britain had rejected the suggestion that legislation be enacted to provide for the return to its rightful owners of any gold the Soviets might ship in payment for imports. The only recourse such claimants would have would be to the normal procedure of the courts.[83] The British, it was evident, had no intention of making the renewal of trade a purely formal matter. Nowhere were Lloyd George's conversations with Krassin more bitterly resented and regarded more suspiciously than in Washington. That the Soviet government's agent had been received by the prime minister and members of his Cabinet astounded everyone, according to the correspondent of the *New York Times* (June 6), especially since the Soviet system was reported on the best authority to be in complete disintegration.[84] The possibility that Britain and other countries were stealing a march on America and actually doing some trading was a matter of some concern even to the Cabinet.[85] Evidently reassured, Colby, the new Secretary of State, authorized Consul General Skinner in London to attend the meetings of the Wise Committee of the Supreme Economic Council as an unofficial observer when Russian trade was under consideration.[86] This co-operative spirit was of short duration, because of suspicions of Lloyd George's intentions. Without spelling it out, the American government let it be known that it wished to be consulted before any agreement was concluded, for Colby asked if it was intended to submit the terms to the Allied and United States governments.[87]

Lloyd George himself found an occasion to reply in the House of Commons, obviously in part for the purpose of allaying alarm that he was alienating the United States. In any event, what he said increased rather than diminished American irritation. The Americans, he said, had been given prior notice of the decisions on trade with Russia at San Remo and earlier, and they were being informed of the current negotiations. By misrepresenting the American decision to have an observer at the meetings of Wise Committee during the discussion of Russian trade as the appointment of an expert to participate "in the economic negotiations," he made matters worse.[88]

Incensed by press reports of the prime minister's statement, Colby promptly called for the full text and countermanded the earlier instructions to Consul General Skinner "for the time being."[89] Ambassador John W. Davis was unable to confirm the prime minister's statement that the United States was being informed of current negotiations. While Davis and members of the embassy had had conversations with Lloyd George and Curzon and the minutes of the Wise Committee had been communicated to the embassy, there had been "no continued or spontaneous effort ... either by the Prime Minister or by Foreign Office to furnish me with details concerning the progress of the negotiations...."[90]

Davis' not entirely accurate estimate of British public opinion as in the main opposed to Lloyd George's Russian policy probably influenced the next step.[91] On June 22, the question of trading with Russia was again discussed in the Cabinet with the result that President Wilson informed the Acting Secretary of State, Norman Davis, that he had been convinced of the desirability of resuming that trade. Although he did not develop his conception of the extent of the trade in this brief note, the phraseology suggests the expectation of a real exchange of goods such as might have been expected from his earlier hopes, despite the statement that no official assistance could be expected "inasmuch as there would be no official Russia with whom we could deal in such matters."[92] Such, in any event, was not the intention of the State Department which was to give a purely formal satisfaction to those industries that were clamoring for trade, to anticipate and forestall Lloyd George, and to make sure that there would result little or no exchange of goods. No time was lost in communicating the decision to the Allied governments. On June 24, within twenty-four hours of the president's note, the Allied ambassadors were informed (and the American embassies in the Allied capitals were instructed to communicate the same to these governments) that the president had decided the "restrictions now existing on trade with Russia shall soon be removed," with such probable exceptions as war materials and railway equipment. For the rest, this preliminary notice underscored the intention of avoiding anything like the recognition of the Soviet regime or of any other Russian faction. No economic concession would be accepted as valid and no protection would be given American nationals who might engage in the Russian trade. A word of warning to Lloyd George was included for communication to all of the Allied governments. While the United States government understood Britain's desire to protect her Near Eastern interests and, for this purpose, to conclude political arrangements "with those elements which at present control Russia," it could not see "how such arrangements could be entered into without involving at least a constructive political recognition." Such a course was not what it had in mind in March when it proposed the planning of common action "for dealing with the problem of trading with Russia...."[93]

The speed with which the decision of the American government was reached and carried out was a sign that events were moving toward a crisis. On July 2, shortly after the British note of June 30 holding out the prospect of diplomatic recognition was handed to Krassin in London, the State Department submitted the draft of a proposed official statement to the president who promptly approved it, suggesting only that the term "Bolshevist Russia" should be replaced by "Russia."[94] This statement, which was given to the press on July 7, was the basis for the instructions sent on the same day to the embassy in Paris for repetition to the other Allied capitals. In addition to the points made in the instruction of July 2, it added others which were bound to give the impression that no real trade with Russia was desired. The legal title to "commodities and other values" taken in payment for exports to Russia might be challenged. No passports would be valid for travel to Russia, there would be no change in the visa regulations, and the post office would accept no mail for Russia.[95] In other words, the announced removal of restraints upon trade with Russia was largely nullified by administrative measures. The *New York Times* (July 9) regarded the prospect of little or no trade as fortunate for "the cause of peace and good-will on earth." Large exports "would bolster up the Bolshevist cause, postpone its collapse and prolong the period of danger for Russia's neighbors, for all countries where Bolshevist propaganda is active." To make certain that there should be no misunderstanding, "well-informed" sources in Washington told the press that the important thing was not the removal of restrictions upon this trade, but rather the statement of basic policy against the recognition of the Soviet government. It was regarded in diplomatic circles as "the strongest and most definitely anti-Bolshevist attitude yet taken by any of the great Powers."[96]

It can scarcely be doubted that the purpose of the American government was, if possible, to prevent the success of Lloyd George's policy. Norman Davis' instructions of July 2 closed in this sense when he wrote confidentially that "...the American Government feels that there can be no constructive result from the present negotiations with the Russian agents...."[97] That the American point of view appreciably diverted Lloyd George from his purposes there is no evidence. He may have felt about it as did the Washington correspondent of the London *Times* (June 7) who wrote that there was only one certainty about the attitude of America; it was "that the country would impose a veto upon American participation in any considerable degree in any show of force, direct or indirect, that may be needed against Russia...." That having been substantially true, it was not surprising that the American position had no great effect upon either Lloyd George or British public opinion.

Up to a certain point, the American attitude toward Soviet Russia and the problem of trade was most satisfactory to the French. It was practically identical with their own in regard to anything that might lead to normal political relations and diplomatic recognition and therefore to Lloyd George's conversations with Krassin. On June 24, Millerand, breaking his silence on French policy in Eastern Europe, took sharp issue with a Socialist deputy on the inevitability of political relations with the Soviet government and declared that such relations depended upon that government, not France. Of the premier's two concrete reasons why Soviet Russia could not be treated as a real government, one had largely colored France's reactions since the Bolsheviks' original repudiation of the foreign debts of earlier Russian governments—the Soviet government's failure to assume responsibility for the international obligations of its predecessors—and the other (a reminder to Lloyd George as to what his attitude should be) was indicated by Lenin's letter calling for revolution "against the British government while seeming to desire conversations with it." Until these things changed "we have nothing to do with a government that is not a government," Millerand declared to loud applause.[98] This approximate identity of Franco-American views was, however, ideological in character, since the French had no reason to believe that American arms would again intervene in Europe, and it did not include the German problem, still France's major preoccupation, as the American government's unfavorable reaction to the occupation of Frankfort had recently shown. It would, therefore, have been foolhardy to provoke the British, who could count upon Italy's support, too far in view of the decisions on German disarmament and coal deliveries that were to be taken at the approaching Spa Conference. Millerand never allowed a debate on Hennessy's interpellation of the government's policy in regard to the Polish-Soviet conflict,[99] but it was clear that France had finally decided to gamble on the Poles.[100]

In Central Europe, France was developing a policy that threw a curious light upon her complaint that Lloyd George had not consulted her views before engaging upon political conversations with Krassin. For months, Paléologue, the Secretary General of the Quai d'Orsay, had been secretly talking with the Hungarian government through its peace delegation in Paris, without the knowledge of the British, for purposes that would have revolutionized the situation in a large part of Central Europe and have destroyed the peace settlement there. The formal communication of the terms of what became the Treaty of the Trianon and of Millerand's accompanying letter (*lettre d'envoie*), May 6, was followed by the successful conclusion of Paléologue's efforts on behalf of French financial and industrial groups to secure controlling interests in the Hungarian railways, banks, and transportation on the Danube. In return, the French government promised in an official, written declaration its support "in correcting the ethnical and economic injustices of the terms of peace" through satisfactory agreements with Hungary's neighbors.[101] There were, of course, the usual affirmations of loyalty to treaties in this and later statements, but the meaning was clear that the French, for the moment under the leadership of Millerand and Paléologue, were backing Hungarian revisionism, at the expense of the territorial integrity of Czechoslovakia and Rumania. Not until or if the French documents become available will it be possible to assess their motives and purposes more accurately, but what Paléologue told the Hungarians is now known. They must have gained the impression from him that only considerations of expediency restrained him from advising immediate action. On May 4, he told the Hungarian peace delegation: "...the Franco-Hungarian rapprochement should be regarded as a long term affair which will sooner or later lead, however, to the results desired by Hungary. He repeatedly emphasized that France is firmly determined to base her policy in Eastern Europe on Hungary."[102] Through his *chef de cabinet,* Montille, he was much more explicit. France could not be ex-

Soviet Communism and Western Opinion, 1919-1921

pected to invite the accusation of "secretly assisting in the overthrow of a treaty [Trianon] which they had forced Hungary to sign only a few days ago [June 2]. At the same time, he said we might rest assured that we could tear this treaty to pieces whenever we felt sufficiently strong to do so and that when that time came, we could rely on the whole-hearted support of France."[103] As to Hungary's desire for compulsory instead of voluntary service as the basis of the small army permitted her, Laroche, the specialist for Hungary in the Quai d'Orsay, imparted Paléologue's "final reply," June 24. It was that Hungary should not act until after Germany had been disarmed; she would otherwise prejudice her case since the Peace Conference had decided in favor of the voluntary system which Britain had championed and the Supreme Council had rejected Bulgaria's request for compulsory service.[104]

In due course, the British became aware of these intrigues, at first through the economic concessions France was to receive which were publicly discussed in Budapest. Hohler, their high commissioner, protested to the Hungarian Foreign Minister, Teleki, that they would violate the terms of peace which provided that the total income of the Hungarian state should be treated as security for the claims of the Allied and Associated Powers.[105] They seem thereafter to have learned the general nature of the Hungarian *quid pro quo*. On June 26, Athelstan-Johnson, the Secretary of Legation, told Teleki, who had assured Hohler on June 5 that he had assumed Britain's approval of the negotiations, that "no responsible French statesman had discussed the matter with the British . . ." and, four days later, he read a letter from Lord Curzon to the effect that "such promises [for territorial concessions] cannot be in conformity with the real intentions of the French Government and, in his view, the French have played a shady game with the Hungarians."[106]

The game was, indeed, shady—and shabby, too, in its economic aspects —but it did not lack all merit if, as seems probable, Paléologue's purposes included the creation of an anti-Bolshevik bloc whose axis would be Poland and Hungary. He was obviously not a partisan of the later diplomatic grouping, the Little Entente, which his rival, Philippe Berthelot, helped to create as a check upon Hungarian revisionism, although he seems to have been under the illusion that Czechoslovakia and Rumania could have been persuaded to turn over the territory Hungary desired and to be content with the role of satellites to the Budapest-Warsaw axis. As an immediate threat to the peace of Europe, his schemes were far more dangerous than Lloyd George's political conversations with Krassin. They probably help to explain why Lloyd George continued to pay France no great heed in the crisis that was soon to break in Eastern Europe.

102

V

The Red Counteroffensive
and Lloyd George's Mediation,
July and August, 1920

T he respective contributions of Pilsudski and Lenin to the rapidly developing crisis are far from easy to assess. Their ultimate purposes were similarly dangerous to the precarious stability of postwar Europe and also out of proportion to the effective resources at their disposal. Both men disregarded realistic warnings, those of Poland's Western friends and allies is the case of Pilsudski, and those of Trotsky, Radek, and others in that of Lenin. Reduced to its simplest terms, the problem apparently ceased to exist, since the Bolshevik leader's eagerness to set off the chain reaction leading to world revolution was, of course, potentially more dangerous than the Poles' far-reaching nationalist ambitions—the frontiers of 1772 and a federation of the border states (including the Ukraine) under Poland's leadership. It was, in these terms, a case of unlimited against relatively limited objectives, but this analysis oversimplifies a complex situation. Since conditions in Poland and Germany, not to speak of the more Western countries, by no means justified Lenin's expectations, the Bolshevik program of world revolution was more of an irritating nuisance than a serious menace unless he should try to impose it with the aid of a victorious Red Army. On the other hand, Pilsudski's success would plant the seeds of new wars, not only with Russia, under whatever form of government and social system, but also with Germany. His first move, the invasion of the Ukraine, without having the strength to strike a decisive blow, shifted Lenin's attention from the desperate economic situation at home to a gamble for world revolution, as Carr and Deutscher so well point out.[1] It invited not only retaliation, but also an effort to revolutionize Poland as insurance against renewed attack and as an approach to the frontiers of Germany.

After the recovery of Kiev (June 12), thanks to the bold operations of Budënny's cavalry army, the Red Army launched its counteroffensive in full force under Tukhachevsky on the northern front during the first days of July. Three days of fighting along the Berezina River (July 4-7) resulted in a deep penetration of the Polish lines that compelled the Polish Army, threatened with being rolled up and driven into the Polesian marshes, to retreat at top speed, losing heavily in matériel but remaining in being. Advancing at an extraordinary rate for infantry, the Red Army outflanked each successive defense line. On July 11, Minsk was taken, Vilna fell on the fourteenth, and on the twelfth the first diplomatic fruits were plucked in the Treaty of Peace with Lithuania, which assured the safety of the Red Army's right flank during its further advance. Before the end of the month, it was approaching the Russo-Polish boundary drawn by the Allied Supreme Council, December 8, 1919,[2] when decisions of great moment faced all concerned, the Allied as well as the Soviet and Polish governments. As far as Tukhachevsky was concerned, there was no doubt as to his intention to take Warsaw and to sovietize the Polish government, if his order of the day, dated July 2, picked up by the Poles was authentic. Its tone, in any event, accorded well with the ambitions of this youthful general who, though a former officer of the Imperial Guards, used revolution like Napoleon for the glory of his country and perhaps of his own.[3] "The destiny of the world revolution," it proclaimed, "is being determined to the West—the route of the world conflagration passes over Poland's corpse. Forward against Vilna, Minsk, Warsaw!"[4]

Lenin's would be, however, the final decision to stop at Poland's ethnographic frontier or, by crossing it, to announce to the world that his purpose was to take Warsaw and to impose communism. Despite repeated assertions of respect for the right of the Poles to self-determination, Bolsheviks had already talked of destroying that government of "capitalists and landlords," and Lenin himself had said that his sole concern was with the Polish workers and peasants. On the news of the recovery of Kiev, he told a conference in Moscow, June 12, that the Bolsheviks, as always, were willing to talk peace; they had even offered the existing Polish government Lithuanian and White Russian territory to which it had no claim. "We reckon only with the Polish workers and the Polish peasants, but not with you, landlords and bourgeois of Poland . . . and we shall see what will result from these conversations."[5]

The arrogant self-confidence of the Poles in their military superiority suffered rude blows in June and July. They at once extended and intensified the search for aid which had earlier been restricted to the Allies. As a consequence of Poland's lust for territory regardless of the wishes of the peoples concerned, none of her immediate neighbors showed any willingness to assist her. The Germans, savoring the not entirely praiseworthy joys of *Schadenfreude* at her distress, were not disposed to lift a finger; indeed, they declared their neutrality and used it as an excuse to forbid the transit of war supplies across their territory. Lithuania, antagonized by Polish claims to Vilna and Polish arrogance, chose rather to assist the Red Army after the Peace Treaty of July 12. Since Rumania and Czechoslovakia, like Poland, owed either their national existence or territorial enlargement to the Allies, it would seem that these countries would be sufficiently interested in Poland's survival to assure their assistance, for a decisive Soviet victory would probably mean a serious threat to their own existence and to the entire peace settlement in Eastern Europe. Although the Red Army was understandably concerned about the attitude of Rumania,[6] the latter, having already seized Bessarabia earlier in the Russian Revolution, cherished no unfulfilled aspirations for more Russian territory and was fearful of Hungarian revisionist designs on Transylvania. Rumania's assistance did not go beyond the permission to use her railroads and roads for the transport of war supplies,[7] even if, as is likely, the French and British governments later joined in representations at Bucharest in Poland's behalf.[8]

Because of the Czech-Polish quarrel over Teschen, the Allies had even less success in Prague, where Soviet Russia's strength, at least in comparison with Poland's, was highly rated. For weeks Czech railway workers, reacting against the Polish invasion of the Ukraine and occupation of Kiev, refused to operate the trains carrying French war supplies to Poland. In the hope of assuring their arrival, the Polish government turned to the United States, whose chargé d'affaires—Gibson was home on leave—was wholeheartedly sympathetic, and probably turned to France, although the evidence in the latter instance is not available. If the State Department shared his view that "the Poles are fighting the battle of civilization against the Bolsheviks," wrote the American chargé, it would be desirable "in view of the credit which the American nation enjoys with the Czechs, for the Department to address pointed inquiries to Prague."[9] After the State Department checked Warsaw for more information,[10] Beneš, the Czech Foreign Minister, was asked about the matter with disappointing results. He confirmed the reports but gave no indication that he was willing to do anything. He had told Patek, the Polish Foreign Minister, that the Czech government would not intervene "because Foreign Affairs Committee of Polish Parliament's resolution favoring break of relations with Czechoslovakia and because Polish Press says continually Teschen question could only be solved by force of arms. If Poland could control hostile attitude of press and parliament he would then take up the matter."[11] Thanks no doubt to French and British pressure (there is no evidence of American participation), Beneš and Grabski, the new Polish Foreign Minister, submitted a joint statement to the Allies during the first days of the Spa Conference explaining the difficulties of a plebiscite as a solution of the Teschen problem and agreeing to accept an adjudication of the frontier by the Supreme Council.[12] Poland may have profited by the release of some troops on the Czech frontier and by the eventual resumption of the traffic in military supplies across Czechoslovakia, but she received neither arms nor supplies from the Czechs, not to speak of troops.

Poland could count upon Hungary, though she had been a tower of strength to Germany during the war and was not an immediate neighbor, for a more sympathetic understanding. She had recently experienced, and, with the assistance of the Allies, had disposed of, Béla Kun's Communist regime. On the basis of common hostility to Soviet Russia, the Hungarians hoped to enlist Poland's assistance in changing the disarmament terms of the Treaty of Trianon they had just signed, June 2. For their part, the Poles also had other reasons than military necessities to regard Hungary with sympathetic interest. As far as political forms went, Poland was more democratic than the Horthy regime, but, in terms of real power, the political, social, and economic position of the Polish aristocracy and the Magyar magnates was much alike. The two countries shared, too, a common hostility to Czechoslovakia.

Encouraged by Poland's sympathetic response to earlier approaches, Admiral Horthy, the Hungarian regent, addressed himself directly to Field Marshal Pilsudski in a letter dated June 6, expressing the hope that *la justice réparatrice* would remove the artificial barrier (Slovakia) between the two countries. Since Poland's reliance upon the Allies made it impossible to countenance the despoiling of Czechoslovakia, Pilsudski was of necessity silent on this point, but his response in other respects was so friendly that the Hungarian representative expressed Hungary's willingness "to extend assistance as far as our inadequate armament permits."[13]

On Pilsudski's instructions, the Polish War Minister, General Sosnkowski, told the Hungarians that Poland was prepared "to help as much as possible Hungary's rearmament" (which in practice meant her good offices in France), and he even mentioned a military agreement as desirable.[14] In response to Polish appeals after the fortunes of war turned in favor of the Bolsheviks, Hungary put at the disposition of the Poles her entire reserve of ammunition at the Weiss factory, the principal munitions works, and that factory was instructed to turn over to them its entire output during the next fortnight.[15] When, however, Csekonics, acting upon "a hint received from a very competent [Polish] authority," asked his government for "twenty or thirty thousand cavalry troops," which might be moved through Rumania,[16] Budapest cooled off rapidly.

Hungary, according to Teleki, simply had no cavalry, but if Poland could induce the Allies to change the terms of the peace treaty (Trianon) "we should be willing to assist Poland against the Bolsheviks within a short time." However, other troops of "considerable strategic value" might be sent.[17] Hungary's representative in Paris was promptly instructed to ascertain from Paléologue whether or not France would agree to a change in the military terms of peace in view of the Bolshevik danger. Specifically, Hungary wanted seven infantry and one cavalry divisions—requirements that pointed to Hungary's own needs rather than Poland's—and the necessary arms and equipment, especially in heavy artillery, which France should furnish.[18] Paléologue was sympathetic, but he pleaded the necessity of delaying the reply until Millerand's return (from the Spa Conference).[19] In view of France's determination to enforce the disarmament of Germany, it was inconceivable that she would openly approve the rearmament of another defeated country. For a week, the embarrassing question was evaded. When Millerand's reply was finally relayed through Paléologue, it was still evasive: he was not averse in principle, but the time, in his opinion, was not ripe for action.[20] In the end, no Hungarian troops went to Poland's assistance, although there was talk to the end of a volunteer legion that would be armed by the Poles. By that time, however, the decisive battle of the Vistula had been won and Poland was no longer in danger.

It was, of course, to the Allies that Poland chiefly turned for aid. Had they not furnished a large part of the arms and equipment that made Pilsudski's offensive possible and had they not repeatedly promised to save it from destruction at the hands of the Bolsheviks? It was also true, of course, that the Polish government had paid scant heed to their counsels, at least Great Britain's, although that counsel had fallen short of complete clarity and was susceptible, in some instances, of more than one interpretation. As if the Poles were anticipating a catastrophe before the issue of the opening battle of the Red Army's offensive on the Berezina had been decided, Premier Ladislas Grabski and Foreign Minister Patek appeared at Spa, July 6, the day after the beginning of the conference (July 5-16). The Russian problem and the Soviet-Polish War were not on the agenda, but the Poles used the opportunity to put their case for aid to the Allied statesmen. Since the Poles were doubtless sure of France—and perhaps because France saw a chance to prevent the resumption of Lloyd George's negotiations with the Soviets—the Polish statesmen addressed themselves primarily to the British Prime Minister. According to the well-informed American press correspondent, Edwin L. James, Patek was the first to try his hand with Lloyd George, July 6; he was told that the Poles "had made war against his [Lloyd George's] advice and now they should make peace on [the] best terms they could get." James understood that Millerand had failed to change Lloyd George's mind, reporting that "no aid would be forthcoming" as the prevailing view.[21]

Between Patek's first effort on July 6 and July 10, when Grabski made the second and more important effort, there were two developments, the net effect of which was to make Lloyd George more responsive to the Polish plea. The first was the arrival at Spa, presumably on July 9, of the Narkomindel's reply to the British note of June 30 which had been dispatched from Moscow on July 7. After reviewing the recent Anglo-Soviet negotiations in such a way as to blame the British government for the failure to achieve positive results, the Soviet note concluded with a succinct and apparently unconditional acceptance of the British demands. In order "to meet the wish of the British Government for the speedy conclusion of peace between Russia and Great Britain, the Russian Government accepts the principles laid down in the British Government's aide mémoire as the basis for an agreement between Russia and Great Britain, which will form the subject of negotiations between the two to be started immediately. It agrees that the plan proposed by the British Government is equivalent to an armistice between the two countries, and it shares the expectation that it prepared the way for a definitive peace. . . ."[22] While the Russian reply did narrow the vague wording of the British note of June 30 to an Anglo-Russian armistice and peace, its effect upon Lloyd George, other things being equal, would almost certainly have been wholly favorable. However, it was more than neutralized by the news of the Polish defeat on the Berezina and of the Polish retreat, for the thought may well have suggested itself that what appeared to be a sincere acceptance was a maneuver designed to tie Britain's hands during the Red Army's advance.

The first reports of the defeat of the Polish Army had, moreover, a significant effect upon liberal and radical opinion in Britain, for part of British opinion which had been bitterly critical of Poland's aggressiveness agreed at once that the independence of ethnographic Poland must be defended. "The Poles," declared the Liberal *Daily Chronicle* (July 8), "have played for high stakes and lost, and there can be no question of the Allies recovering the stakes for them. On the other hand, since a free and strong Poland is a key-feature in the Allies' scheme of a new Europe, they cannot afford to see the Polish Republic crushed too far—least of all by a victorious Bolshevism." Labor was not to see the issue as clearly, but the radical *Nation* (July 10) drew the worst conclusions for the peace of Europe should Poland be entirely overrun. The result would be the contact of "the two races [German and Russian] whom our Western capitalist civilization has schemed to bring under a crushing tribute to itself" and "in a position to help each other." It did not regard revolution in Germany or Western Europe as probable or near, but it did expect Ludendorff to offer his sword to Lenin just "as Brusilov did the other day," especially if the French were to be permitted to have their way in Germany.

The situation had therefore changed when Lloyd George talked with Grabski on July 10. Speaking in what was described as "curt, peremptory tones," he declared: "'Your army is at present on territory which does not appear to be Polish,'" and he indicated a line that followed, in the main, that which the Supreme Council had laid down, December 8, 1919, for Poland's eastern frontier. When Grabski objected, he reminded him that Poland was still dependent upon the good-will of the Allies in Upper Silesia, eastern Galicia, and Danzig, but in the end he promised the aid of the Allies, including Britain's, if the Bolsheviks continued to attack after the Polish Army had retreated to the line he had indicated.[23]

That the next step was largely of Lloyd George's own contrivance and not, in at least its initial stage, that of the Foreign Office seems almost certain. He had bypassed it to a large extent in his Russian policy. It was probably not a coincidence that Philip Kerr, his private secretary who is better known under his later title Lord Lothian, chose this moment to complain to Lloyd George's confidant that the Foreign Office was incapable of comprehending the magnitude of the prime minister's efforts on behalf of European recovery and, in this connection, "the necessity for achieving a Russian settlement."[24] To Lloyd George's fertile imagination, Soviet Russia's acceptance of the conditions stated in the British note of June 30 and Poland's defeat furnished an opportunity for a comprehensive solution of the Eastern European problem: a settlement of the Russo-Polish War on the basis of Poland's ethnographic frontier, and a conference to negotiate a peace treaty and to consider other questions such as eastern Galicia and General Wrangel's future.

Whatever doubts Lord Curzon may have felt, he lent his name to the note that was dispatched to Moscow, July 11, from Spa. It proposed as the first step a Russo-Polish armistice that would require the withdrawal by the Polish Army of almost one hundred kilometers at some points to what became known as the Curzon Line (generally the same as the line drawn by the Supreme Council, December 8, 1919, and indicated by the prime minister to Grabski on July 10) and the halting of the advance of the Red Army fifty kilometers east of that line. As soon thereafter as possible, a peace conference comprising representatives of Soviet Russia, Poland, Lithuania, Latvia, and Finland would meet in London. Spokesmen for eastern Galicia and General Wrangel would be given an opportunity to state their cases but would not be members. Poland, Moscow was informed, was prepared to initiate an armistice and to make peace with Soviet Russia on this basis. The note closed with a menace. Just as the British government had pledged itself "to give no assistance to Poland for any purpose hostile to Russia and to take no action itself hostile to Russia," it was bound under the Covenant of the League of Nations to defend "the integrity and independence of Poland within its ethnographic frontiers." If Soviet Russia was dissatisfied with Poland's withdrawal from Russian soil and attacked Poland's own territory, "the British Government and its Allies would feel bound to assist the Polish nation to defend its existence with all the means at their disposal." A time limit of a week for Soviet Russia's reply was mentioned, although the tone employed was not as brusque as the similar stipulation in the note of June 30.[25]

In view of the encouragement they almost certainly had given Pilsudski's offensive, the French were astonishingly content to remain in the background. It is not too much to credit Millerand with the limitation of the proposed London conference to the delegates of Eastern European countries, in view of Lloyd George's predilection for a general conference that might, in the French view, revise the Treaty of Versailles. Given the apparently desperate situation in Poland, Millerand could not object to an armistice on Poland's ethnographic frontier, but there is no possible doubt of his whole-hearted approval of the pledge of all possible aid should the Red Army cross that line. In any event, he had accepted Lloyd George's leadership of Allied policy in this crisis. Speaking on the Spa Conference in the Chamber of Deputies, July 20, Millerand could only say in regard to the Russo-Polish war that the Soviet government's failure to heed his admonition to respect the customs of nations had forced him to abstain from signing the Curzon note. He had, however, "declared to the British government that I much appreciated, in the given circumstances, its initiative and that I hoped very much for its success. . . ."[26]

As if aware of their own government's unimpressive part in these events, most Frenchmen, as always primarily concerned with Germany and the signs of her recalcitrance, awaited the outcome in comparative silence. The gravest danger seemed to be Germany's reaction to the advance of the Red Army, for the demeanor of Hugo Stinnes, the powerful industrialist, and of General von Seeckt, the commander of the new Reichswehr, at the Spa Conference was regarded as meaning that the spirit of "blood and iron" still prevailed.[27] In the decisions made at Spa—the adjournment of the reduction of the German armed forces to the treaty limit of 100,000 men by some six months and a relatively modest reduction in coal deliveries—was scented the dreaded beginning of treaty revision. It was not the voice of Georg Bernhard, the editor of the *Vossische Zeitung,* in welcoming (July 18) the results of Spa as proof that gradual concessions could be expected from the victorious Allies that was accepted as typical; it was rather the views of the partisans of an Eastern orientation that were taken most seriously.[28] "Between the two comrades [Lenin and Trotsky] and Simons (the German Foreign Minister)," wrote Louis Barthou, "I suspect a terrible game will soon be played." The Spa Conference had given Simons six months leeway when it delayed the enforcement of the treaty limitations upon the German Army.[29]

In regard to Poland, the dangerous consequences of her aggressive policy did not destroy the illusions of the most respected spokesmen for French traditional interest in a large Poland. René Pinon still insisted that her vast territorial claims were justified by the "radiation of Polish civilisation" and were in the higher interest of Europe.[30] As for measures that were more within the range of practical politics given Poland's apparent defeat, the most influential leaders of French opinion seized upon the promise of aid in the Curzon note. If Poland were told to make the best terms she could, asked the *Temps* (July 14), how could the Allies expect to make Germany respect their authority? It was the opinion of the *Journal des débats* (July 13) that the best hope lay in the Bolsheviks' refusal of the British "ultimatum." In that case, the situation, while not good, would be clear, for then "the Allies will find themselves in open war with the Soviet government, and there would be no alternative to seeking the best means of giving military support to Poland." There is, however, little evidence that the French people were prepared to back up these brave words with troops.

When Bonar Law read the Curzon note in the House of Commons, July 14, there was complete silence except for one member's objection that Parliament had not been consulted. "Mr. Stanton," according to the *Times* (July 14), "cried 'Disgraceful' in his buzzing bass."[31] To Conservative opinion, which had never reconciled itself to the negotiations with Krassin, the note's most objectionable feature was the proposed conference in London for it looked like another step toward the recognition of the Soviet government.[32] The pledge to defend Poland's independence sufficed to moderate the denunciation of any dealings with the Bolsheviks that was normal to this section of British opinion. Indeed, the proposed Russo-Polish armistice must have seemed at the moment the most practicable way to preserve Poland as a barrier to a union between the Russians and Germans.[33] On July 13, the *Times* stressed the menace of a Russo-German alliance with a report whose inaccuracies exceeded the norm for news about Russia. After noting the departure from Stettin on February 28 for Soviet Russia of a group of forty German army officers to join the "hundreds" already there to help train the Red Army, this "correspondent" went on to say that the German Army would itself attack the Poles at the proper moment in the Soviet advance on the excuse that the Allies were doing nothing and that it would then join forces with the Red Army "and, Poland being already in their grasp, together they would turn West."[34]

For the rest of British opinion, except Labor, the only serious doubt arose from the note's somewhat dictatorial tone, especially in the mention of a week as the time limit for the reply. In comparison with earlier communications to the Soviet government, the *Nation* (July 17) felt that the note was "polite and even friendly in tone," but J. L. Garvin's *Observer* (July 18) was so anxious for a favorable reply that it detected in the mention of a time limit "just a touch of summary dictation" which Russia, flushed with victory, would resent. The obvious advantages to Russia seemed an assurance of the note's acceptance, according to the Liberal *Westminster Gazette* (July 12). In the *New Statesman's* (July 17) opinion, her need of peace and the implied diplomatic recognition would be decisive,[35] but if the answer were negative "we certainly shall not oppose—and we hope that British Liberals and Labourists will not oppose—any measures which the British Government may decide to take in support of Poland." The Poles had undoubtedly "provoked reprisals," but "Russian armies have no legitimate business in Warsaw." The significance of Russia's decision was nowhere more clearly stated than in the radical weekly, the London *Nation*. It sympathized with her desire "for some better guarantees against a renewed attack than this note offers," but a leading article showed why this consideration should not determine her response. Lloyd George had brushed the French aside, although their entire diplomatic system was collapsing with Poland's defeat, and he offered conditions that assured the safety of the Soviet regime. The Russian decision would probably depend "on whether Lenin and Trotsky care at this moment chiefly to consolidate the Russian Revolution, or whether they think the time has come to carry revolution into Central Europe."[36]

It is safe to say that Western opinion hoped overwhelmingly that Soviet Russia would accept the British proposals. However, those who were confident that she would should have read the *Daily Herald* more carefully, for its editor, George Lansbury, seems to have had excellent sources for the intentions of the Soviets. At first, it published a warning from the Socialist, H. N. Brailsford, who had recently returned from Russia, to the Russians not to expect a revolution in Poland while the war continued and against a bold stroke in behalf of revolution in Central Europe in view of Russia's shortages in transport, fuel, and food.[37] In the same number, the "diplomatic correspondent" rejected this cautious attitude. He said that Lloyd George was not proposing a fair peace but one that would be "dictated by the governments which encouraged and abetted" Poland's "wanton and treacherous aggression." The prime minister had no right to intervene "now that the Polish oligarchy is faced with the consequences of defeat," because he had refused to act "while he hoped that Poland might win." He was not an honest mediator but "a truculent ally of the aggressors. Russia will refuse."[38] For Labor opinion in general, which was not unsympathetic to Poland's right to independence within her ethnographic frontiers, the most important part of the Curzon note was the promised support of Poland. Labor foresaw Britain's involvement in war by a government that retained the services of Winston Churchill. The miners were already calling for a general strike against aid to Poland and the dockers were refusing to load ships with munitions bound for her army.[39]

The Curzon note (July 11) confronted the Soviet leaders with a choice. They could accept an armistice that would confine Poland within her ethnographic frontier (while preserving its existing government and social order) and a conference which, while implying the diplomatic recognition of the Soviet government, would write the definitive treaty of peace with Poland as well as other border states; or they could violate the Curzon Line in an effort to overrun all of Poland and to sovietize her government and social order as a preliminary to the extension of the revolution to Germany. The continuation of the anti-British and anti-Lloyd George propaganda seemed to foreshadow the refusal of Britain's offers. On July 10, the Moscow wireless station sent out an indictment of British policy. The British government was using the negotiations as a cover to hide the "use of its ally, the French Government," in the pursuit of the "policy of strangling Russia and finally to present the Soviet Government with a series of demands and conditions." An armistice with England would be no guarantee against "the future dispatch by French marshals of arms and ammunition, made in the works of the Entente (even in England itself) to the Poles and the White Russians in the Crimea."[40] The gravity of the choice was, however, equaled by the tension it created in the inner leadership of the Soviet government where the debate rivalled that which had preceded the Treaty of Brest-Litovsk. In the end, the issue was settled between Lenin and Trotsky.

On July 13, Lenin sent Trotsky, then on the Polish front, a copy of the Curzon note.[41] Trotsky's reactions were determined to a large extent by his disbelief in the imminence of revolution in Poland. Instead of welcoming the Red Army as deliverers and of fighting with it, the Polish workers and peasants would, he was convinced, resist it under their traditional leaders as representing Russia, Poland's historic enemy. This conclusion confirmed and strengthened what was, in all probability, his unfavorable estimate of the prospects of an all-out revolutionary war. Although Tukhachevsky, the commander on the main Polish front, seems then and always to have insisted that the prospects were excellent from the revolutionary as well as the military point of view,[42] his immediate superior, S. Kamenev, who commanded the entire western front, at first took a position similar to that of Trotsky. In a report dated July 16 to the Revolutionary War Council, of which Trotsky was President, Kamenev advised that regroupings would be necessary to meet the danger that Finland, Latvia, and Rumania would enter in war, that an extension of the war would be dangerous, and that the line indicated in the Curzon note should be the limit of the Red Army's advance.[43] Trotsky, therefore, was able to assess the Curzon note and the negotiations with Britain from the broader point of view of the advantages that it might offer Russia. He saw two trends in Lloyd George's policy: one of support of France and intervention, the other in favor of arrangements with the Soviet government. The second tendency should be encouraged. Trotsky, therefore, at once advised Chicherin and the Politburo that Lloyd George's mediation should be accepted and that an armistice and peace on the basis of the so-called Curzon Line should be the objectives of Soviet policy.

Counter to Trotsky's advice, Lenin chose to follow the lead of his own wishful thinking. A prisoner of his own assumptions that the capitalist governments, and the British especially, were bound to be implacably hostile, his confidence in the existence of a revolutionary situation that the approach of the Red Army would precipitate was unshakable. The favorable moment for the launching of world revolution must therefore not be lost, and those who, like Radek[44] and perhaps Trotsky, thought otherwise, were disregarded as defeatists.

As usual, Lenin's voice prevailed; by the time that the reply to the

Curzon note was dispatched, it was certain that the Red Army would not halt at the Curzon Line and that Poland would, if possible, be sovietized whether the expected rising of the Polish workers and peasants occurred or not. In the government's chief press organ, *Izvestia,* Radek, contradicting his own views as to the proper course, revealed the direction that Soviet policy was about to take. He advised the diplomats of London and Paris "not to trouble themselves over the issue of the Russo-Polish War." The independence of Poland was assured by the principles of "proletarian policy" which did not vary with the fortunes of war "even should the last soldier of the White Polish Army be a prisoner of the Russian Soviet." That this was an early example of "double-talk" in which words do not mean what they seem to mean was revealed by Radek's remark that what really counted were the interests of the Russian and Polish workers "which are identical and conform with the interests of world revolution."[45]

In accordance with party discipline, Trotsky as President of the Revolutionary War Council was called upon to justify the decision for a revolutionary war and to dispatch the appropriate directives, against his own better judgment. This he did in a report to the Council of War on July 17. The Curzon note "itself constitutes the best proof that the Soviets' victories threaten to the highest degree the international relations and internal situations resulting from the shaky peace of Versailles." While the Entente exerted itself to the utmost to bring Rumania into the war and to aid the Poles and Wrangel at top speed, the note and its offer of Britain's mediation were intended to conceal from the workers of the Allied and other countries these preparations for a new attack upon the Soviets and to gain time to reorganize and reinforce Pilsudski's and Wrangel's troops. "We cannot allow them to gain this time." The offer of mediation has been rejected, and the high command must assure an energetic and rapid pursuit of the routed White Polish forces. Soviet troops from the interior would guard against flanking attacks from the Baltic area and Rumania to which S. Kamenev had called attention. The western and southwestern commanders were, however, "to receive strict orders to continue operations against Poland without the slightest interruption beyond as well as up to the limits assigned by the Entente [the Curzon Line]."[46]

Meanwhile, Lloyd George awaited the reply to the Curzon note with lively interest but no great optimism. At Spa, he had given serious thought to special military moves after hearing that the Bolsheviks were going to overrun all of Poland. At a meeting with Millerand, Foch, and Field Marshal Sir Henry Wilson, the prime minister asked if Marshal Foch might not go to Warsaw "to steady the situation," a suggestion that met with general disapproval as risking the sacrifice of Foch's prestige in trying to redeem what was thought to be Poland's hopeless situation. Foch and Wilson were both opposed to the pouring into Poland of more arms "unless, and until, the Poles had a good national government, fully representative of a united people determined to stand against invasion."[47] There is no evidence, however, of an interruption in the flow of supplies, and on July 20, the Poles formed a national government under Witos, the leader of the Peasant party. Back in England, Lloyd George spent Sunday, July 18, in the country at Cobden with Lord Riddell in eager anticipation of the Soviet reply. Two or three times Lloyd George called London about it. "The conduct of international affairs," Riddell noted in his diary, "is a great game. L. G. was just as eager about this message as a lover awaiting a telegram." That evening, about 9:30, he was given the gist of Chicherin's reply over the telephone.[48]

The Soviet reply began with a sarcastic comparison between Britain's indifference at the time of Poland's attack and Britain's present desire, which the Soviet government noted with "great satisfaction," to assist the restoration of peace in Eastern Europe. Not a word was said about the proposed conference in London, and the claims that the League of Nations should sit in judgment were roundly dismissed. Britain's mediation on behalf of a Russo-Polish armistice was indirectly but firmly rejected on the ground that her attitude in the past did not qualify her for that role. While the Soviet government desired peace with Poland in spite of her unjustified aggression, the failure of the Polish government to address the Soviet government directly stood in the way of a cessation of hostilities. It would not, however, reject direct Polish representations "for the opening of peace negotiations"; indeed, prospects for a more generous frontier than the Curzon Line were held out, and proposals regarding the lesser matter of an armistice would be studied. Pressure for a revolutionary overturn in Poland was applied in the promise of more considerate treatment if her internal organization were harmonized with that of Soviet Russia and in the emphatic statement that concern for the interests of the Polish as well as those of Russian workers was paramount in Soviet policy.[49]

Lloyd George was in general pleased although he would not permit Krassin to return until a Polish armistice had been concluded. After reading the notes he had taken to Riddell, the prime minister remarked: "I don't call that unreasonable."[50] His later actions showed that he regarded the note as a basis for further efforts for peace, notwithstanding his public criticism of specific passages.

France was the first to express herself officially, hoping no doubt to compel Lloyd George to follow her lead. What her attitude would be was clearly foreshadowed on the evening of July 19 by the editorial comments of the *Temps* (July 20). The time had come to fulfill the pledge to Poland in the Curzon note (July 11); otherwise, the peoples of Eastern and Central Europe would conclude that Britain never lived up to her word and that the vaunted support and aid of the Allies were worth nothing (*ne vaut rien*). Even more significant, it condemned the Curzon note's patronizing tone in regard to General Wrangel and its failure to admit him to the proposed London conference, and it raised the question of his diplomatic recognition. In what respects did he and the territory he controlled differ from Latvia, Lithuania, or Georgia whose *de facto* recognition the Allies had granted? By a timely coincidence, the premier's reply to the interpellation on France's policy at the Spa Conference gave him an opportunity, July 20, to state the government's position on these matters. He described the Soviet note, on the basis of the French Ambassador's report that morning, as composed "with rare impertinence," and Millerand did not hesitate to give a somewhat exaggerated version of Britain's pledge in the Curzon note when he said that it had promised to "unite with her allies to defend Poland with all their strength and in every way (*sous toutes les formes*)."[51] His silence on the substance of the Soviet note—the necessary conditions for a Russo-Polish armistice—signified by no means his desire for a settlement, for France under his direction was about to gamble on another reversal of the fortunes of that war. What he said about Wrangel tends to confirm this inference. Like the *Temps,* Millerand suggested that the White Russian general deserved diplomatic recognition; he had organized *un véritable gouvernement de fait,* had won the support of the peoples of the Crimea and the Taurida, and was fighting the Bolsheviks successfully. Wrangel, however, would have to accept the international obligations of preceding Russian governments, surely a hint that for the moment at least Millerand was once more contemplating the overthrow of the Bolshevik régime.[52]

Although the complete text of the Soviet note was not published in London until July 22 and until then was known only to the government,[53] such information about it as was leaked to the public moved the Conservative press to claim that "it rejects the British proposals" and that "it flouts the British Government."[54] Further reflection, and perhaps these expressions of critical opinion, caused Lloyd George to modify his originally favorable impression when he addressed the House of Commons, July 21, during the protracted debate on the situation. He would, he said, describe the note as "incoherent" and not as "impertinent" as the French Premier had. If it meant that the Soviet government would deal only with a proletarian Polish government, that would be intolerable. "We want to save the life of Poland. We cannot allow it to perish. It would be a disaster to the world; it would be a crime. Whether Poland has made mistakes or not, that is no reason why we should destroy a nation." It was Britain's business, Lloyd George said, "to see that the Poles are properly equipped. We can do that." He was convinced that the Bolsheviks would regret it if they continued to advance (across the Curzon Line), but "it is our business to prepare for [that] contingency. . . . The time may never come, and I hope it never will come." If it did, he would put the whole matter to the House.[55]

More seriously than ever before in questions relating to Soviet Russia, he took issue with Labor members when one of them declared for peace even if it meant the establishment of the Soviet system in Warsaw.[56] "Has Poland," he asked, "the sympathy of that Party in its struggle for its national existence?" Speaking for the Labor party, J. H. Thomas affirmed its support of Polish independence, but he stated that it regarded the danger of war, to which the prime minister had twice referred, as paramount. "There can be no mistake, whatever this House might think, about the feeling of this country about another war. I feel that there is nothing the people of this country are so sick of as war." The prime minister would be held to his word that he would consult the House before making an irretrievable decision.[57]

There is little doubt, however, that British public opinion continued for the most part to favor negotiations and a peaceful solution, even if the agitation for direct action against material assistance to the Poles was largely restricted to Labor and the trade unions.[58] A significant straw in the wind was the support that a fundamental change of attitude toward Soviet Russia was finding in unexpected quarters. J. L. Garvin's weekly, the *Observer*, had already affirmed its necessity. "The Western Governments," it declared, "have been distinctly inclined to assume a superior air and to get on their high horses in their dealings with Russia." They "will have to get off that high horse. They will have to deal firmly but courteously as equals with equals. The Russia of today, totally changed in some ways from what it was even a year ago, is once more a Great Power."[59] Even the Conservative *Daily Telegraph* (July 20) broke with its past. "These people," it wrote, "are the *de facto* Government of Great Russia, the only Government that seems able to maintain itself in that immense tract of Europe and Asia; and, much as we may dislike both their principles and their methods, we cannot do away with the uncomfortable facts." Less surprising was the Liberal *Westminster Gazette's* (July 20) appeal to put "away all prejudices against dealing frankly with her *de facto* Government." It offered the one hope that the Bolshevik government would "become what we should prefer it to be. . . ." The Liberal *Manchester Guardian* (July 22) went much further in regretting that "many people seem to think that because the Bolsheviks are so unlike ourselves we need not observe towards them the common standards of honourable conduct." Liberal opinion, especially, rejected Millerand's and Lloyd George's evaluation of Chicherin's note. For the *Guardian* (July 21), it was neither "insolent" nor "incoherent," but "basically satisfactory," and the *New Statesman* (July 24) thought "its meaning is not in the least ambiguous . . . on almost all counts its arguments and representations are unanswerable." The London *Nation* (July 24) spoke of it as a "brilliantly pointed reply" and as a "masterpiece," while the less radical *Observer* (July 25) felt that it was "most uncomfortably to the point."

Liberal and Labor opinion remembered the Allies' tolerance of Poland's aggression too well and feared involvement in a war too much to assess correctly the implications of the Soviet note. Its pacifistic predilections forced Labor into a thoroughly unrealistic and inconsistent attitude that was only resolved by the complete triumph of pacifism. Its parliamentary leader, J. H. Thomas, stated the dilemma well without being aware of its self-contradictory implications. We are, he declared, "going to do all we can to maintain the independence of Poland, but ... we are also going to avail ourselves of every opportunity of reaching a complete understanding with Russia."[60] The radical *Nation* (July 24) continued to be more realistic; if the Soviets decided to march on Warsaw, there would be no choice but to break off the negotiations, "reopen formal hostilities" and give Poland all possible assistance.[61]

As a result of his rejection of Trotsky's counsel, Lenin's intentions at this juncture were beyond dispute. He was gambling upon the swift overrunning of all Poland, a rising of the Polish workers and peasants, the sovietizing of that country, and the establishment of a position from which he might precipitate the revolutionary situation in Germany. He demanded a furious "speeding up of the offensive on Warsaw," for his plan was "to probe Europe with the bayonets of the Red Army." At a later meeting of the Revolutionary War Council, he passed a note to Trotsky: "Warsaw must be taken within three to five days."[62] Obviously, not even Poland's immediate and abject compliance with the terms of Chicherin's note (July 17) to Curzon would divert Lenin and the Red Army. "We can envisage," reported S. Kamenev to the Revolutionary War Council, July 21, "the possibility of completing our mission within three weeks." If the Poles asked for an armistice, it "would prove that they cannot count upon serious support from any direction" and would "open for us a period of liberty of action conducive to an energetic offensive in the interior of

Poland." If the Poles failed to act, or if Allied support became probable, it would then be necessary to safeguard the Bolsheviks against these dangers "without renouncing the offensive against Poland," for he was confident that the three armies on the western front could crush it if the support the Allies gave the Poles were limited to the entrance of Latvia and Rumania into the war.[63] A provisional Polish Revolutionary Committee, comprised of Polish Communists more familiar with Moscow than with the climate of opinion in Poland, followed the Red Army across the Curzon Line during the last of July to meet only disappointment in efforts to arouse the Polish peasants.[64]

While these evidences of the Bolshevik purposes were mostly unknown to the British government and its chief, they were aware of the apparently hopeless state of the Polish defenses between the advancing Red Army and Warsaw. On July 19, the Cabinet had learned, "There is now nothing but disorderly rabble between Warsaw and the Bolsheviks, and if they continue their advances at the present rate, they will be in front of Warsaw in ten days time."[65] In this crisis, Lloyd George co-operated with Millerand to stiffen the Polish resistance from the political and military points of view, while the prime minister himself continued the diplomatic campaign.

After a Council of National Defense took over the Polish Diet's legislative functions, a government of national union was formed on July 20 under W. Witos, the leader of the Peasant party, as Prime Minister, I. Daszyński as Vice-Premier, and Prince Sapieha, formerly Minister in London, as Foreign Minister.[66] In order, presumably, to convince even the landless peasants that they had a material stake in the defense of the nation and to weaken the effectiveness of the Bolshevik propaganda, a liberal agrarian law was at once enacted whose enforcement, however, did not fail to lag and then almost to disappear once the victory on the Vistula was won.

On the day that the Witos government was formed, there was appointed on Britain's initiative a joint Franco-British military and diplomatic mission including General Weygand, Foch's collaborator during the war, as the principal military member, and two diplomats, Lord d'Abernon, newly appointed British Ambassador to Germany, and Jules Jusserand, home on leave from his post as French Ambassador in Washington. According to Millerand's announcement in the French Senate, July 23, it would go to Warsaw to support Poland "with all its strength," to report upon the situation, and "to tell us what aid in material, munitions, and instructors the Polish army desires from us." An objection from the floor that it was too late led him to speak in general terms of what France had already done for Poland. The Poles expected more than reproaches from France, "and I assure them that their expectations will not be in vain."[67]

Meanwhile, Lloyd George continued to seek an end to the war and a peaceful settlement by diplomatic methods. In view of what is now known of the bad faith of the Soviet government, especially in the armistice negotiations with Poland, the question arises as to the usefulness of an effort to unravel the complexities of what followed. The difficulties are considerable. While almost every important communication between Great Britain, Poland, and Soviet Russia was apparently given or leaked to the press, none of these governments has since printed a systematic collection of these documents and they can now only be located, widely scattered, in the contemporary press.[68] No doubt the textual accuracy of this material, much of which is in translation, leaves much to be desired, but the story, nevertheless, emerges from it with reasonable certainty. That it deserves telling follows from the support it gives to the conclusion that the good faith of the Polish government was only less suspect than that of Soviet Russia; it also throws light on Soviet Russia's diplomatic technique in this early crisis with the West, and gives an indication of the policies of the Western powers.

According to information received by the American Embassy, the British Cabinet decided, July 19, "to assume [in spite of the vagueness of Chicherin's note of July 17] that the Bolsheviks were willing to conclude [an] armistice," but instructions were also sent to Revel that the Russian trade delegation would not be allowed to return to London until the conclusion of an armistice.[69] Curzon, thereupon, instructed Rumbold, the British Minister in Warsaw, "to ask the Polish government to send a formal message to the Soviet Headquarters as well as to Moscow requesting an immediate armistice and proposing peace," thus endorsing Chicherin's specifications in regard to a Polish approach.[70] On the following day, July 20, Curzon, replying to the Soviet note of July 17, spoke of this step as intended to end the hostilities with the least possible delay notwithstanding the controversial problems that note had raised. The British government did not insist upon the limited international conference it had proposed with the thought that "it would bring Russia into relations with the Peace Conference and so pave the way to a better understanding between Russia and the outer world." As in the case of the Curzon note of July 11, this one also ended with a menace which was conditioned upon the Soviet government's response to the Polish approach. If the Soviet armies continued to advance after Poland's request for an armistice, the British government and its allies "must necessarily assume that it is the intention of the Soviet Government to make war upon the Polish people, and will, in conjunction with their Allies, give Poland the assistance and support they have promised in that event." Moreover, the trade negotiations could not be resumed "if Soviet Russia invades Poland," and Kamenev (recently designated as the Russian delegation's new chief and political expert) and Krassin were to delay their return until an armistice had been concluded.[71]

In view of their apparently desperate military situation, the Poles had little choice but to accept Britain's counsel. There can be little doubt, in the circumstances, of the sincerity of their desire for an armistice. Without undue delay, Prince Sapieha, the new Foreign Minister, addressed himself to Moscow and to the Headquarters of the Red Army on July 23 in notes that were couched in the form Chicherin had laid down and Curzon had recommended. In contrast to the Borisov negotiations in April, not a word was said about a cease-fire, since the Soviets would certainly have used it as an excuse to reject the entire approach. Taking note of the Soviet government's expressed willingness to accept an official Polish peace proposal and desiring to halt the loss of life as quickly as possible, these messages continued: "...the Polish government propose to the Soviet government an immediate armistice and the opening of peace negotiations."[72] Although the die had been cast for the capture of Warsaw, the fact remains that the Soviets lost no time in replying to the Poles. On July 24, Chicherin informed Sapieha that the Soviet government had ordered the Supreme Command of the Red Army to begin "immediate pourparlers with the Polish military command leading to the conclusion of an armistice and to prepare for the future peace between the two countries." The Red Army Command would advise the Polish Command of the time and place for the military conversations.[73] On the same day, July 24, the Polish Army Headquarters received a similarly worded wireless from the Red Army High Command that contained, however, the instruction that the "Polish representatives, furnished with full powers" (the first appearance of this key phrase) were to go to a rendezvous that the Russian Command would designate later.[74] The Soviet still did not delay in furnishing this information. On July 25, a wireless signed by Tukhachevsky informed the Poles that their representatives were to present themselves at the most advanced Red Army post on the Baranowicze-Brest road at 8:00 P.M. on July 30. The Polish delegation would be expected to conform "to the rules of [the] Red Army for the reception and passage of parliamentaries," rules that were unspecified but which presumably differed from normal usage.[75] This unnecessary delay of at least five days, which Tukhachevsky justified on the flimsy ground that the hatred aroused by the conduct of the Polish troops in White Russia required special security precautions, and the puzzling reference to unknown Red Army rules revealed clearly for the first time that the Soviet government's real aim was to win time for the completion of the Red Army's victory if not to prevent the conclusion of an armistice.[76]

The Soviets had thus set the example, if indeed any were needed, for similar chicaneries by the Poles. At first, General Rozwadowski, the Chief of the Polish General Staff, inquired, quite legitimately, what exactly the Red Army's regulations were for the reception of parliamentaries and suggested as an alternative the generally recognized usages of international law as stated in the Hague Convention of 1899.[77]

The Poles, meanwhile, were slowly recovering from the near panic that had apparently caused them to conform exactly to Curzon's advice in their first approach to the Soviet government and the Red Army. While the military situation was seemingly as bleak as ever, something like a national awakening had occurred in response to the Russian danger, the reorganization of the government under Witos, and the evidence of Allied concern in the arrival in Warsaw on or about July 25 of the Allied mission and General Weygand. The new spirit of resistance expressed itself in the government's failure to give adequate powers to the Polish delegation. In every Soviet message beginning with Chicherin's note to Curzon of July 17, it was clear that Poland would be expected to discuss more than an armistice, although the exact nature of the additional topics relating to peace had been left extremely vague. The Red Army's Supreme Command had stipulated that the Polish delegation should be given "full powers" in its wireless of July 24, and the Polish government seems to have been fully aware of this requirement. On the morning of July 29, Prime Minister Witos informed the American chargé confidentially that the military mission that would cross the lines the next evening would be given "full powers," but he at once mentioned as reservations, "One, the independence of Poland, which means that a Soviet Government cannot be agreed to. Two, no line west of that either at present held or indicated by Lloyd George in his armistice proposal is acceptable. Three, no disarmament."[78] Justified or not, these reservations meant that the powers of the delegation would be scarcely "full," and no victorious government, no matter what its coloration, would have granted an armistice without military provisions, such as disarmament or arms limitation, that would give an assurance against renewed attack. In any event, the Polish delegation apparently was instructed to discuss only an armistice when it crossed the battle line on August 1, instead of July 30, and in view of this limitation the Russians refused to discuss even an armistice.[79]

On August 2, the head of the Polish delegation informed Warsaw over the Russian wireless that the Soviet authorities were asking that the delegation's powers be enlarged or that a new commission empowered to discuss questions relating to peace as well as an armistice should be appointed to meet the Russians again at Minsk on August 4.[80] The fact that the Polish delegates returned to Warsaw without specific instructions strongly suggests that their original instructions had included the discretionary authority to do this if the Soviets insisted upon discussing questions relating to peace as well as an armistice. According to Moscow's version, the real cause of the collapse of these negotiations was Poland's failure to implement its own promises to consider "the principal conditions of peace as well as those of an armistice."[81] The armistice negotiations were at an end for the time being, to the probable satisfaction of both the Russians and Poles, for neither made a serious effort to bring about the meeting on the date fixed by the Russians (August 4).[82]

If, as seems probable, the part played by Chicherin at this juncture was intended to reduce the danger of effective Allied intervention while the Red Army thrust continued toward Warsaw, the results paid off handsomely. The armistice negotiations convinced many that the end of the war was near. Lloyd George was as bent as ever upon a general settlement through negotiation, despite his stiffer stand on Poland's independence. He received the news of Soviet Russia's professed willingness to grant an armistice to Poland "in [a] high state of glee."[83]

At the same time that the Poles had been instructed to send their delegation across the battle-lines on July 30 (note of July 24), Chicherin's note of July 24 with an apparently far-reaching proposal was in Lloyd George's hands. There were recriminations at Britain's suspension of the trade negotiations after the Soviet government had accepted all of her demands (the Soviet reply, July 7). The Soviet government, however, was willing to accept the proposal "to convene a conference with the purpose of establishing a definite agreement between Russia and other Powers which participate in hostile actions against her or [which] support such, and is of the opinion that the said Conference ought to be composed of representatives of Russia and the leading Powers of the Entente." Less seductive, however, must have been the firm stipulation that "the surrender of ex-general Wrangel and of his military forces will be carried out on the condition of securing personal safety to him, his adherents and the fugitives under his protectives, and of the transfer to the Soviet Powers of all the war materials, stores, means of communication, and vessels now in his hands," must precede the conference, but it does not seem to have given Lloyd George pause, despite Millerand's talk in the Chamber of Deputies, July 20, of Wrangel's *de facto* recognition.[84]

The prime minister was enthusiastic. "This is a great occasion," he told Riddell. Lloyd George was "very pleased" at the prospect of a general discussion on peace.[85] In his oral summary of the note in the House of Commons, he, nevertheless, carefully suppressed the demand for General Wrangel's surrender, emphasizing the proposed conference with evident approval. Lloyd George was, he said, in communication with the Allies about it, and he hoped to see Millerand on the following day. The prime minister did not at this point object to the silence of the Soviet note concerning the conference's competence to conclude a Russo-Polish peace treaty. Noting the Soviet complaint that the British had raised new demands after the original conditions for the continuation of the trade negotiations (in the British note of June 30) had been accepted (Narkomindel statement of July 7), he explained that the Soviet's invasion of Poland's rightful territory had been the reason for the suspension of the trade conversations. "Now that the Russian Government have agreed to the Armistice we can withdraw our objection."[86]

This speech foreshadowed the contents of the note sent to Moscow on the same day (July 26) over Curzon's name. It noted the armistice negotiations "with satisfaction," expressed Britain's willingness to agree to a conference in London "for the purpose of establishing a definite agreement between Russia and the Powers which were engaging in hostile actions against her or supporting such action," and mentioned that contacts with the Allies had been made in regard to the proposed conference. Denying that the suspension of the trade negotiations after the acceptance of Britain's conditions was an act of bad faith, it pointed out that no trade agreement could have produced results "if Soviet Russia had refused an armistice and invaded Poland, and had thus forced Great Britain and her Allies to give active support to the Polish people in defending their liberties and independence." In view of Soviet Russia's favorable reply to the Polish request for an armistice, the British government was sending a destroyer immediately to bring L. B. Kamenev and Krassin to England. To save time, they should be empowered to make arrangements regarding the conference.[87]

Rarely had Lloyd George's policy, which was essentially personal despite Curzon's signature on these notes, more clearly demonstrated its shortcomings in the prime minister's apparently easy assumption that public opinion and the Allies would go along with his acceptance of a general international conference. He could count, it is true, upon the almost solid support of Liberal-Labor opinion at home, but the thought of the visible elevation of Soviet Russia to equality with the great powers as a member of an international conference meeting in the capital of the British Empire was more than the anti-Bolshevik sentiment of the conservatives could tolerate. Although J. L. Garvin's *Observer* (July 25) insisted, "we must meet Russia face to face at the Council Table or face to face in war," there was an immediate outraged protest on both sides of the Channel. "The linked battalions of the *'Temps'* and the *'Times'* and *'Matin'* and the *'Débats'* were all heavily engaged within twelve hours of the receipt of the Soviet note."[88] The Soviet government and its Bolshevik leaders themselves placed effective weapons in the hands of the enemies of the proposed conference. Many members of the House had doubtless read the leading editorial of the *Times* (July 26) before Lloyd George spoke that morning and indicated his acceptance of the conference. It called attention to Trotsky's speech as transmitted by the Moscow wireless station in which the War Commissar had boasted that Poland would soon cease to be a buffer (between Germany and Russia) and "would become a Red bridge of Social Revolution for the whole of Western Europe." As the *Times* said, it could not easily be reconciled with Chicherin's notes.

Since the idea of an international conference was anathema to the French government and to the dominant trends of French opinion, because of the German as well as the Russian problem, the French were more disgruntled than ever. They were convinced that a close kinship existed between British Labor, whose influence upon Lloyd George's policy they suspected, and the Bolsheviks. As a result of British reactions to the Spa Conference, the French feared that the proposed conference would attempt to revise the Treaty of Versailles for Germany's benefit. Had not Herbert Asquith, the former prime minister, spoken in this sense of the Spa Conference in the House of Commons even in the face of Lloyd George's disapproval? "Whatever the form of language you may employ," Asquith had said, "it has been really, and in effect, a conference for the revision of the terms of the Treaty."[89] From Soviet Russia's victories in Poland, J. L. Garvin's *Observer* (July 25) concluded that "Nothing in connection with the Treaty of Versailles will ever again be the same," and without a timely revision by a large conference "there will be total collapse involving the loss of many of the results of the war."

Because of this fear of a revision of Versailles and other considerations, including the Polish problem and the Soviets' demand for the surrender of General Wrangel whose *de facto* recognition he had manifestly in mind, Millerand went to meet Lloyd George at Boulogne, July 27, determined to scuttle the proposed conference by one means or another. What was said there on the Russian and Polish problems is still unknown, but not the result. Lloyd George was forced to back water. On July 29, Curzon sent another note to Chicherin revising and stiffening the British position on the conference with the implication that the changes were the result of the consultation with Millerand. This time, care was taken to require the conclusion of a Russo-Polish armistice and the reference to the conference of the problem of peace between Russia and other border states, with whom no treaties had as yet been concluded, as well as with Poland as conditions for Britain's acceptance. The other border states would have to be represented along with Poland if the Allies were to meet Soviet Russia with any prospect of success. The conference's tasks would therefore be: (1) the conclusion of peace between Poland and Soviet Russia, (2) peaceful settlements with such other border states as had not signed peace treaties with Soviet Russia, and (3) the settlement of the relations between Soviet Russia and the Allies. Because of the phrasing of the third point, it is questionable that it was seriously meant. "After the settlement of these questions [points (1) and (2)] the Conference could proceed to deal with the matters in dispute between the government of Soviet Russia and the Allies, and the re-establishment of normal relations between them."[90]

Had Lenin's aims been those of Russia's national interests rather than of world revolution, he might well have accepted these conditions in order to gain the advantages that full membership—and Lloyd George's policy—would almost certainly have assured. There was every prospect that the Soviet-Polish frontier would have been fixed on the Curzon Line, and, if the sovietizing of Poland would have had to be abandoned, Lenin could have counted without much doubt upon Lloyd George's support for some limitation of her armed forces as a guarantee against another attack. Besides the probability of a trading agreement with Britain and doubtless other countries, diplomatic recognition and the establishment of normal relations would have followed almost inevitably from membership as an equal in the conference.

This attractive prospect caused many to expect and some to fear the Soviet government's acceptance. Curzon himself anticipated a favorable response, because of its "eagerness for some form of recognition by the principal powers," as he told the American Ambassador.[91] In Lloyd George's view, the fate of France when her revolutionists forced Pitt's England into war should have assured the Bolsheviks' acceptance.[92] Raymond Poincaré, the former premier and president of France, who began his brief career as a political commentator at this time, obviously assumed as a matter of course that the Bolsheviks would seize the opportunity to become an accepted member of the international community. He complimented the "powerful logic" of Chicherin's notes and expected them to exploit the advantages they had won. "They can now affect a generous attitude [*de se montrer bon prince*], offer to resume the economic negotiations, smile upon those whom they disdain, claim the surrender of General Wrangel, and install themselves, elbows on the table, in the midst of European conferences."[93] Engrossed by his dream of world revolution, Lenin was not at all impressed, as Western statesmen thought he would be, by the prospect of being treated as their equals. He chose rather to urge the Red Army onward toward Warsaw and the German frontier, while Chicherin and Kamenev tried (as will be shown in a later chapter) to keep the negotiations going.

On the other hand, the French government was perhaps even less interested than Lenin in the proposed conference, although it could not afford a complete break with Lloyd George in view of the overriding importance of British co-operation in the enforcement of the Treaty of Versailles and the potential value of his promise to help defend Poland's independence. Millerand proposed to escape from this dilemma, and at the same time to make sure that the conference would never meet, by imposing ever more difficult conditions for France's participation. Refusing to sign Curzon's note of July 29, the premier retained his freedom of action. Far from making a secret of his intention, he told Edwin L. James, of the *New York Times,* during the meeting with Lloyd George in Boulogne, that "he [Millerand] had committed himself in no way, and that even if Moscow accepted the conditions imposed in the Lloyd George note today the way was free to advance other conditions, such as recognition of the Russian foreign debt and good peace terms for General Wrangel."[94] The French Foreign Ministry was devising still more drastic demands to be held in reserve. According to a high official of the Quai d'Orsay, who told the sympathetic American chargé d'affaires, Leland Harrison, about them, they included the requirement "that the Soviet Government should hold elections, thus making itself a regular government," as well as others for the representation of the United States and General Wrangel in the conference.[95] It was, of course, fantastic to suppose that the Soviet government would agree to the more drastic of these demands, and this, of course, was France's reason for thinking of them.

As usual, the Italians could be counted upon to follow Lloyd George's lead, but the French turned with more confidence to the United States for at least moral support. American press correspondents reported this maneuver in a somewhat exaggerated form. The French government, it was claimed, was awaiting action by the United States before "clearly shaping its own policy."[96] As indicated by Millerand's favorable mention of General Wrangel's claims to *de facto* recognition in the Chamber of Deputies, July 20, and his stand on the proposed conference during the conversations with Lloyd George at Boulogne, a week later, there is little doubt that French policy had already taken form and that what France wanted from Washington was support. On the evening of July 27, the date of the Boulogne meeting, the *Temps* (July 28) confidently predicted France's choice of America's as against Britain's Russian policy and urged the Allies to make an agreement with the American government before reaching a decision in regard to the proposed conference.[97]

In Washington, official opinion not only sympathized with France's intransigence but there was a disposition to make at least a gesture in its support. "Washington sees in the developments of the world tragedy now in the limelight, a crucial battle for life or death between the two systems of philosophy, collective and individual modes of existence."[98] At the same time, the State Department was preparing to freeze American policy in an attitude of unyielding hostility to a conference in which Soviet Russia would be represented and to anything like the diplomatic recognition of the Soviet government. On July 30, it had received from the ambassador in London the following analysis of British and French intentions: "The British government clearly contemplates in accord with Italy the *de facto* recognition of the Soviet government. France is willing to treat with reference to peace for Poland and the border states and to enter a conference with this end in view but is not willing to go further unless the Soviet agrees to acknowledge the obligations of pre-existing government. Failing this France will probably withdraw."[99]

The first American move was the secretary of state's confidential circular of August 2, to the Allied capitals, London, Paris, Rome, and also to Warsaw, and the second on August 10 (which will be discussed in a later chapter) was the more famous Colby note, which was, at the same time, a public pronouncement of American policy. The time had not yet arrived, according to the first of these notes, to give full publicity to the views of the American government, and the contents were to be used with "discretion and restraint." While sympathizing with the efforts to save Poland's integrity by the arrangement of a Russo-Polish armistice, the American government could not agree "to take part in plans to extend the armistice negotiations so as to bring about a general European conference involving the recognition of the Bolshevik government" in a way that would almost certainly involve the partitioning of Russia. The United States was "opposed to any relations [with the Soviet government] in excess of the narrowest limits within which the arrangement of an armistice can be kept." In the recognition of the Soviet government or dealings with it was seen the sacrifice of moral strength for temporary material advantage that would not be worth the price. Short of the establishment of a representative government, no solution of the Russian problem seemed possible.[100] Although this note does not seem to have been brought to the attention of either the French or British governments, the former, had it been so informed, would have almost certainly been pleased. It was a declaration for the French and against Lloyd George's position on the proposed conference. For America's Russian policy, its stress on morality as the decisive consideration was most significant for the future.

Meanwhile, Kamenev and Krassin returned to London on August 2, the date of Colby's circular. Of Kamenev's reception, Radek was to write ironically: "Lloyd George received him with as much cordiality as if he had been an envoy of the bloodiest of the Tsars and not of proletarian, democratic Russia."[101]   Nevertheless, the prime minister's confidence was being subjected to severe tests.   Riddell, who had hitherto shared his feeling about the proper policy in regard to Russia, now warned him that the Bolsheviks were "trying to trick us. . . . Being fanatics, they think the end justifies the means. . . .   There is no doubt that they are out to smash Western civilization as we know it. . . .   No doubt Lenin is thinking of the day when he will string you up to a lamp post in Whitehall!"[102]   From Poland came the news of the collapse of the armistice negotiations because of the Soviets' insistence upon taking up the peace conditions as well.   In due course, the Liberal and Labor press were to make the valid point that the Soviets' demand was in accord with the language of the preliminary correspondence, but the situation did not augur well for a favorable reply to Curzon's note of July 29.

On the other hand, Lloyd George still hoped to bring the conference into being by increasing the pressure on the Soviet government.   The *Observer* expressed a point of view that was probably close to his own.   "Either we go forward to a full peace with Russia and its corollary of economic reconstruction and a general convalescence of the body politic, or we go back to renewed war."   The issue was simple, and Lloyd George "was going to try for general peace. . . .   He has carried the Allies solidly with him. . . .   He has offered the Bolsheviks a straight, fair road to peace.   It remains to be seen whether they will take it."   If the fanatics were in power in Moscow, it would be war; if the politicians were in control, it meant peace.[103]   On August 3, Lloyd George tried to save the conference by exerting additional pressure in a new note which he justified by the Soviet government's delay in replying to the note of July 29.   According to a press report from Moscow, the insistence upon the discussion of "the fundamental conditions of peace" had caused the failure of the armistice negotiations.   The Soviet government should realize, it pointed out, that "the project of a Conference falls to the ground" if it demanded the settlement of the peace conditions by direct Polish-Russian negotiations "to the exclusion of other Powers."   Moreover, the Soviet Army seemed to have "advanced far into ethnographic Poland"; if it continued during the interruption of the armistice negotiations, the British government "will be driven to the conclusion that it is not the intention of the Soviet government to respect the liberty and independence of Poland, and the situation contemplated in their telegram to M. Tchicherin [*sic*] of 20th July will have arisen."[104]

The absence of a firm deadline for a reply gave the Soviet government every opportunity to halt the Red Army without appearing to yield to an ultimatum, but, within twenty four hours, the prime minister was speaking with a firmer tone. In the presence of Bonar Law, the government's leader of the House of Commons, Kamenev and Krassin were told by Lloyd George (August 4) that if his warning was not heeded, the blockade would be reimposed, the British fleet would be ready to sail into the Baltic in a matter of days, and supplies would be poured into Poland through Danzig.[105] According to the Soviet version, he fixed three days as the period within which the Soviet government must reply.[106]

It soon became standard practice for Soviet publicists and historians to boast that the reply was a prompt and unequivocal negative. Radek's contemporary account stressed Lloyd George's conciliatory attitude while it implied its fundamental insincerity. Hoping doubtless to sow a few seeds of discord between France and Britain, Radek claimed that the prime minister had told Kamenev and Krassin in confidence of differences with Millerand, although those differences were known to "every street urchin." Soviet Russia had, nevertheless, rejected Lloyd George's offer to liquidate the Allies' entire anti-Bolshevik policy and also his threats: "neither the whip nor the gingerbread stopped the Russian advance. Soviet Russia was ready for peace, but it should be a peace between the Russian and Polish peoples which would make it impossible once and for all for the Entente to wield Poland's sword against her."[107] According to a recent Soviet history of this crisis, the Soviet reply of August 5, which can only have been Kamenev's letter to Lloyd George of this date, yielded nothing.[108]

Kamenev's letter, however, was in fact conciliatory in tone, although it insisted upon the continuation of the Russo-Polish bilateral negotiations. Lloyd George's threat to renew the blockade had been referred to the Soviet government, but Kamenev was authorized to reply to the note of August 3. The diplomatic correspondence between the Soviet, British, and Polish governments had always associated the armistice and peace preliminaries as subjects to be considered between Soviet Russia and Poland. "It goes without saying that the Russian Soviet government has not, and never has had, any desire to combine the negotiations for an armistice with negotiations for a definite peace treaty between Poland and Russia." In view, however, of the danger that a suspension of hostilities would be used for the reorganization and reinforcement of the Polish armies, a risk that Poland's recent actions, France's support, and Wrangel's situation demonstrated, "certain conditions and guaranties over and above the strictly military" conditions must be required. The Soviet government was, therefore, still of the opinion that direct negotiations would serve the best interests of the two peoples, but its earlier assurances concerning Poland's independence and its eastern frontier were still valid. At the same time, Soviet Russia was still

interested in the conference with the Allied powers which Britain's repudiation of any interest in the participation of other governments in the Russo-
Polish negotiations had inspired. The conference alone could assure the
peace of Europe since other states could not wage war without the support
of its members. "Such a conference in London between the leading Powers
of the Entente and Russia would have for its object the regularization of
the international position of Russia, and the settlement of all outstanding
questions between her and the Allies for the benefit of the general peace."[109]
While yielding nothing on the vital questions of the advance of the Red
Army and of the inclusion of at least the preliminary peace terms in the
subjects to be discussed between Soviet Russia and Poland, the Soviet note
seems to have shaken Lloyd George's firmer stand in defense of Poland.
He seems to have been favorably impressed by the evidence Kamenev
presented that everyone had agreed that more than purely military questions
should be discussed. These things exerted, in any event, an important influence upon Liberal and Labor opinion, turning it more than ever against
the Poles.

That Lloyd George had not abandoned hope for an armistice, a conference, and a general settlement is certain from the fact that, like France,
he turned to the United States in a secret letter to President Wilson on
August 5, almost certainly after reading Kamenev's communication. It was
a *tour d'horizon* of the world's danger spots in twenty-two typewritten pages
concluding with the Russian problem and the Russo-Polish war and requesting Wilson's "confidential advice" and "opinions from the more detached standpoint which you at present occupy." In general, the "outlook"
as to Russia was "baffling as ever" and "we are by no means out of the
woods." The Allies were "reaping the inevitable reward" of Poland's folly,
but, since "the advance of the Soviet armies to the German and Czecho-
Slovak borders would be a very serious thing for Europe," the best efforts
were being made "to make the Soviet armies stop outside its [Poland's]
ethnographic boundaries." (The Red Army had in fact crossed the Curzon
Line some days earlier.) The issue was still in doubt. In Lloyd George's
opinion, the threat to break off the trade negotiations was evidently a more
effective defense of Poland's independence than military resistance. "The
Poles are the embodiment of perverse inefficiency. It is like trying to save
a drowning man who does all the silly things he is wanted not to do and
does nothing he is begged to do." Although the French government had
insisted from the beginning that it would enter into no relations with the
Soviet government unless it recognized the Tsarist debts, it had agreed to
attend the conference provided the Polish question was given first place on
its agenda. If Soviet Russia was interested in a "fair armistice" with Poland

and agreed to the London conference, "there ought to be real peace, in a military sense, from one [end] of Europe to the other," but if the Soviet government decided to overwhelm Poland, "then we are in for a new period of revolutionary unrest which will have consequences ... which no one can foretell." Lloyd George wished to know, if a conference between Russia and the Allies actually met in the autumn, "whether it will be possible for the United States to be represented at it" and by someone in real authority. He would also like to know "what part you think we can expect America to play after the election is over."[110]

By the time this letter was in the ailing president's hands, American policy had been frozen in an attitude of uncompromising hostility in the famous Colby note and public manifesto of August 10 that made an immediate reply pointless. Not until November 3, 1920, on the eve of the presidential election in which the Republican candidate, Senator Warren Harding, decisively defeated his Democratic opponent, Governor James Cox, did Wilson reply. In any event, the president and prime minister had ceased to see eye-to-eye on the Russian problem since the Peace Conference, in considerable part because Wilson, like most Americans and unlike an increasing fraction of the British people, refused to accept the Soviet government as an accomplished fact. He felt that "Bolshevism would have burned itself out long ago if let alone," but he also felt that nothing was to be gained and much to be lost, by the proposed conference since it might strengthen the Bolsheviks and prolong their control of Russia. He "could not conscientiously enter into the proposed negotiations."[111] Whatever expectations Lloyd George may have had when he wrote to Wilson, there is no reason to think that they materially influenced the prime minister's actions during the critical fortnight that followed August 5. In any event, the battle of the Vistula had been engaged and the victory of the Poles was assured by the time, August 18, his letter reached Wilson.

VI

Germany:
Temptations and Realities

Weakened by defeat and seriously discredited in world opinion, Germany seemed destined to the passive role of an onlooker during the East-West conflict in 1920. There was no lack of unofficial proposals in Great Britain (some of which have been noticed and one of greater significance will be examined in this chapter) that Germany should be enlisted in the cause of the West, but, in general, the Allied governments desired nothing more from her than the fulfillment of the terms of peace. While the Soviet government was showing early signs of the interest in co-operating with the bourgeois German government that was to result in the Treaty of Rapallo in April, 1922, the Bolsheviks' chief concern at this time, under Lenin's lead, was with the supposedly imminent revolution that would take Germany into the Bolshevik camp. Otherwise, Soviet Russia desired only neutrality from her. Momentarily deprived of the elements of power and hence of prestige, Germany was in no position to thrust herself into the center of the international stage, no matter how tempting the situation might seem. Her diplomatic eclipse (even her diplomatic missions abroad were not fully re-established since the ratification of the Treaty of Versailles had not been completed until January 10, 1920) was recorded for all to see in the fact that her name scarcely appeared in the correspondence concerning the Russo-Polish armistice and the London conference. Not even the Soviet government proposed her as a member. Behind the curtain of official policy and diplomacy, where the fears, hopes, and temptations aroused by the knowledge that German weakness would not last forever had full play, the situation was very different. What her decisions would be in view of Poland's defeat and the approach of the Red Army was a matter of agonizing speculation in France and elsewhere. Prussia's weakness in 1812, greater than Germany's in 1920, had not prevented General Yorck from making a military agreement with the Russian Army against Napoleon. Frenchmen feared a similar deal between a nationalist or a revolutionary Germany and the Red Army.

Circumstances forced an attitude of cautious reserve, for the most part, upon the German government, but the general public was far less restrained. Among the influences that contributed to the confusion of counsels, Germany's geographic situation in the heart of Europe among Poland and Soviet Russia and the Allies (whose armies were encamped on the Rhine), the bitterness of defeat, a burning sense of injustice, and ideological preferences were among the most important. As *das Land der Mitte,* a concept that has never been far from the center of German thoughts and emotions, Germany and the Germans were pulled in three directions: toward an eastern, a western, and a neutral orientation. Substantial unanimity existed, however, on certain matters. Except for the extreme left wing that soon became the German Communist party, there was little dissent from the view that Germany's cultural ties were with the West.[1] So firm was the commitment to Western democratic and humanitarian ideas that some of the Independent Social Democrats who attended the Second Congress of the Third International refused to swallow the formulas of class dictatorship and terror as suitable for the German scene.[2] Fewer still were those who questioned Russia's long-range importance for the economic recovery of Germany, as a market for German products, an outlet for German skills, and as a source for raw materials, although many were justifiably skeptical of Russian trade as a source of immediate advantages.

The key to most German reactions was undoubtedly the attitude of the Allies toward the enforcement of the Treaty of Versailles, at least until the Red Army's victories awakened even profounder fears in certain quarters and opened new perspectives in others. The opportunity to present Germany's case face-to-face for the first time on the questions of the coal deliveries and the reduction of her armed forces at the Spa Conference (July 5-16) failed in the end to change the intensified animosity caused by the demands for the surrender of the alleged war criminals and for Holland's extradition of the Kaiser. The immediately ensuing events showed that the worst fears, that France would purchase British support for her pound-of-flesh German policy by yielding to Lloyd George in the Russian problem, were not well-founded,[3] for the Franco-British differences in regard to Poland and Russia were plain for all to see. That the French did agree at Spa to the concessions which caused Asquith to speak of Spa as the beginning of the revision of the Versailles Treaty was attributable to their fear of bolshevism and to the willingness moderately to encourage the Germans to defend themselves should the Red Army reach their frontiers. These concessions, the lowering of the monthly coal deliveries from 3.4 million tons to 2 million tons and the adjournment from July 1, 1920, to January 1, 1921, as the deadline for the reduction of the armed forces to 100,000 men, did little to strengthen the support of a Western orientation. While Georg Bernhard, editor of the liberal *Vossische Zeitung*, depicted them as proof that revisionism could be attained through negotiation,[4] not many were impressed by his argument. German opinion was far from satisfied, thus giving the French some cause for claiming that the Germans would never be content with moderate concessions. The new figure for the coal deliveries was still double the actual deliveries and the delay in the reduction of the armed forces was not a permanent gain. If the German government accepted these changes, which even a liberal like Theodor Wolff thought should be met by passive resistance and the protest of coal miners throughout the world,[5] the reason was generally attributed to France's alleged intention to occupy the Ruhr in the event of Germany's refusal.[6]

The Spa Conference was already in session when the Red Army broke through the Polish lines and commenced its astonishing advance that was to take it to the gates of Warsaw in early August. At once the French drew the conclusion that Germany's respect for Versailles and the Spa terms would depend upon the outcome in Poland. "Whatever they sign at Spa," declared the *Temps*, "the real value will depend on what happens tomorrow on the Polish front."[7] It seemed useless to compel Germany's observance of the Versailles terms if "thanks to the Russians, the hope of recovering what the Treaty took from her in the East is reborn."[8] The French were unable to decide which of two specters was the more dangerous: a Russo-German union for revenge and the destruction of the peace settlement, or German blackmail of the Allies through the exploitation of the menace of bolshevism. Both involved the loss of the fruits of victory, the only difference being one of time, for the second might require a little longer to achieve the same result. The conclusion drawn from these considerations and from the impossibility of sending troops to Poland was that France could most effectively defend Poland (by preventing Germany from stabbing her in the back) and protect herself by restraining Germany through the threat of the occupation of the Ruhr. The threat was not often spelled out, perhaps out of consideration for British and American reactions, but the Germans were in no doubt about its reality.

In the early days of the Red Army's advance German opinion was in a state of almost unalloyed satisfaction. Soviet Russia was doing to Poland what most Germans doubtless would like to be doing themselves, and the Allies, moreover, could not call them to account for it. The untranslatable German word *Schadenfreude* best expressed this malicious satisfaction. Of the territorial losses imposed in the Treaty of Versailles, none caused nearly as much bitterness as those of Danzig, Posen, and the Polish Corridor, and a still undefined part of Upper Silesia, for they meant not only the surrender of cherished territory and valuable economic resources but of some two million Germans to the Poles, whom many Germans regarded with hatred and contempt. In the larger view, it meant a serious reversal for the German cause in the age-old struggle between Teuton and Slav in Eastern Europe. Even leftist opinion, normally free of excessive nationalism, shared these emotions. A Social Democrat, for example, applauded the overwhelming victory for union with Germany in the plebiscite (July 11) under the League of Nations' auspices in Allenstein and Marienwerder, a success to which the victories of the Red Army may have contributed to some extent, and declared his support of the recovery of the Polish Corridor.[9] No one wrote more contemptuously of Poland than Theodor Wolff and his liberal *Berliner Tageblatt*. Nothing would bring a Soviet German rapprochement into existence more quickly than "this artificial Polish state, whose national existence had been unearned" and which betrayed delusions of grandeur in its conduct toward its neighbors. Again, this journal spoke of an "artificial Polish structure," and Wolff himself wrote, "It is premature to predict the complete collapse of this product of the Parisian salons, but this Poland is dead even if it continues to exist."[10] Along with other moderate journals such as the *Frankfurter Zeitung*, the *Kölnische Zeitung*, and even a nationalist newspaper like the *Deutsche Allgemeine Zeitung*, the *Berliner Tageblatt*, nevertheless, warned against the illusion that Germany's salvation was to be found in Soviet Russia, but of course no one was averse to such advantages as might result automatically from Poland's defeat. The *Deutsche Allgemeine Zeitung* threatened that the results of Spa might drive Germany in a direction more alien to her than an understanding with the Western powers.[11]

Among the consequences of Germany's defeat in internal politics, the increased attention to a union of nationalism and socialism, in one form or another,[12] was one of the most significant for future developments. The circumstances of post-Versailles Germany, the disorientation resulting from the national collapse, naturally fostered extremes, a tendency that was shortly to produce Adolf Hitler's national socialism, a combination in which a perverted nationalism was overwhelmingly dominant. It was preceded by a temporary merging of disoriented individuals from the extremes of the political spectrum in national bolshevism. It envisaged a union between Soviet Russia and Germany in preparation for which Germany would proceed further along the road of the nationalization of the means of production. The appearance of national bolshevism among extremists and the youth was noticed by early July, 1920.[13]

More important in numbers and influence than those who expected the Red Army to overrun Germany were those who saw in its victories an opportunity to pressure advantages for Germany from the Allies. When Hugo Stinnes, the powerful German industrialist, defied the Allies during the Spa Conference, Samuel Hoare, speaking in the House of Commons, July 21, declared that Stinnes "was thinking much more of the advance of the Bolsheviks upon Warsaw than...of the details of the German coal supply."[14] If Stinnes had had his way, according to Walther Rathenau, the future German Foreign Minister and victim of nationalist bullets, Germany would have rejected the Allies' terms at Spa even at the price of the occupation of more German territory and of the bolshevization of the rest, for they would eventually yield what was Germany's rightful due when they saw the Bolshevik danger at their own threshold.[15] This was what the French meant when they spoke of German blackmail.

While it is true that a great many Germans undoubtedly looked forward to a decisive improvement in Germany's position, perhaps a revision of her eastern frontier, they were for the most part not naive enough to expect the Allies to offer these concessions freely. The French were not the only foreign observers who took the possibility of a Russo-German alliance seriously. According to a responsible British press correspondent, the nationalists hoped for "an eventual alliance with the new Russian State, which in their opinion differs little save in form from that of the Tsars and is essentially military in character."[16] The conclusions of an American expatriate living in Holland whose views on Germany had been solicited by the State Department during the war were essentially the same after a visit to Berlin where he talked with Foreign Minister Walter Simons and other leaders. Because of increasing hatred of France the American thought an invitation possible to "the Bolshevist armies to enter Germany and bring about a military demonstration against France."[17] In the United States, Colonel House was quoted in the press as predicting that "Germany will be the next to go" if Poland succumbed, "largely for the reason that Germany will elect to go. There may be passive resistance, but a majority of Germans will welcome the Russians as deliverers."[18]

Ludendorff was telling foreigners in Germany much the same thing. Through a go-between, he confided (to a British press correspondent) that he expected the Bolshevik avalanche to submerge Germany, that half of the German people were Socialists "or even pro-Soviet," and that France, though she might occupy western Germany, was unequal to the task of halting the Red Army since she dared not risk a general mobilization. The correspondent sensed an element of calculated hope in his pessimism. "Certainly many of the younger officers are eager to draw their swords again in a fighting alliance with Russia, heedless of the colour of the banner, and there is a perfectly frank intrigue between them and the small group of so-called national communists."[19] Ludendorff spoke in the same vein to Ellis Dresel, the American diplomatic agent in Berlin, on August 1. In Ludendorff's view, something like the ancient migration of peoples was taking place which the German people would be unable to resist. "It is," he said, "a great mistake to assume that German soil was not favorable to the spirit of Bolshevism. The people were like putty and would not resist." Many of his army friends "had turned to Bolshevism in order to be fully prepared for the inevitable," and he himself "had debated seriously whether he would not come out in favor of Bolshevism, and if the situation became much worse, it was quite likely that he would do so."[20] However, Ludendorff's estimate of the strength of pro-bolshevism was about as far from the truth as Lenin's reliance upon the revolutionary dynamism of the rank and file of German labor. "A plague on both your houses" was almost certainly more representative of German opinion than a pronounced partiality for either Soviet Russia or the Allies, except in regard to the Poles whose misfortunes virtually all Germans regarded with satisfaction.

According to an undocumented Soviet version, which finds no confirmation elsewhere, the effect of the situation in Poland upon Germany, or at least her military authorities, was quite different from what the French had expected it to be. During the Spa Conference, German military authorities were supposed to have approached the Allies, not the Red Army's High Command as the French feared, with an offer of common action against bolshevism which Foch rejected because he feared the Germans would destroy Poland and then turn against France. But this unsupported allegation must be regarded with the greatest reserve especially in view of what is known of General von Seeckt's attitude before and after the crisis of 1920.[21]

What the Germans did ask the Allies in the form of military concessions when the Red Army approached the German frontier was far less sensational. On July 21, they requested permission to organize volunteer frontier defense units from the local population and to send them through Allenstein and Marienwerder, the plebescite area still under Allied control, to the frontier.[22] Nine days later, July 30, they called attention to the presence of German security police alone in the eastern part of the plebescite area from which the Allies had removed their troops and asked the Allies to authorize the International Commission to summon "whatever Reichswehr troops may be necessary in accordance with the circumstances" and to permit the replacement of Allied by German troops wherever the former might be withdrawn.[23]

While the French reluctantly acquiesced, their press continued to anticipate more ambitious efforts to blackmail the Allies or even the use of the German troops in the plebescite area to cut Poland's communications with Danzig. Léon Daudet, the monarchist, was sure that the Germans were ready to fight or to co-operate with the Bolsheviks, whichever offered the more advantages.[24] These suspicions created a receptive and credulous audience for fantastic reports of Russo-German agreements for a common front against the imperialist Entente powers and the destruction of Poland.[25]

Such combinations, though they became realities in the future, were scarcely within the range of practical politics in 1920, but in less spectacular and less dangerous ways the German government did seek to improve its position by using the Polish defeat to approach the Soviet government. On July 20, President Ebert proclaimed Germany's neutrality in the Russo-Polish War and called upon all German nationals at home and abroad to refrain from all actions in the contrary sense.[26] Six days later, the Fehrenbach Cabinet forbade the export from and transit through Germany of arms, ammunition, explosives, and other war materials to Poland or to Soviet Russia, the effect of which, of course, favored the Russians since the shipment of supplies to Poland was seriously hampered and since Soviet Russia received nothing from abroad in any case.[27] So determined were the Germans not to contribute anything, even indirectly, to the Polish war against Soviet Russia or to Poland's survival that the government insisted that the arms surrendered to the Allies could not be turned over to the Poles since their destruction was required by the Treaty of Versailles.[28]

The government's official neutrality undoubtedly enjoyed the overwhelming support of public opinion, and the disadvantages it brought to the Poles by no means diminished popular approval. While the *Rote Fahne,* the Communist voice in the Berlin press, openly agitated for an alliance with Soviet Russia,[29] Rudolf Breitscheid, the Independent Social Democratic leader in the Reichstag, endorsed it despite his emotional response to the revolutionary implications of the Red Army's victorious offensive.[30] The Majority Social Democrats, dominated by the fear that Germany would become the battleground between Soviet Russia and the Allies or that the French would occupy western Germany, were among the staunchest supporters of neutrality.[31] Overcoming their profound aversion and contempt for the Communists, the Social Democratic party and the principal trade union organization with which it was associated joined the German Communist party in a public manifesto. It pledged the united efforts of German workers to prevent, by direct action if necessary, the shipment of arms from or through Germany to Poland, and the railway workers did in fact block the effort to send such shipments by the Allied occupation authorities in the Rhineland.[32] Distasteful as this self-assured authority of the workers was from the point of view of moderate and conservative opinion, the latter saw no real alternative to neutrality, a view that was shared, as will be seen, by the leading partisan of a Western orientation, Gustav Stresemann.

Despite its official neutrality, the German government did not hesitate to do certain favors for Soviet Russia, to explore through secret channels the possibilities of practical arrangements and the re-establishment of full diplomatic relations, and even to make a dramatic public demonstration of good-will. The Béla Kun affair offered the Fehrenbach government a timely opportunity for a friendly service, at little or no disadvantage to itself, to Soviet Russia, whereas the British government had ignored Chicherin's request for assistance in securing a safe-conduct for Kun to go to Russia. Released by the Austrians in connection with an exchange of prisoners with Soviet Russia, the former Communist dictator of Hungary was arrested in Germany. The Hungarians immediately requested that he should be detained until a formal demand for his extradition "on charges of murder, robbery, theft and counterfeiting" could be prepared and presented.[33] The German authorities at first gave their loyal wartime ally reason to think that their wishes would be respected, despite the clamor on Béla Kun's behalf by the *Freiheit,* the Independent Social Democratic organ in the Berlin press, and other left-wing newspapers,[34] but Walter Simons, the Foreign Minister, finally told the Hungarian representatives that Kun would, as an undesirable alien, be allowed to leave the country across the frontier of his choice. He naturally chose a route that took him to Moscow. Although the Germans talked of Hungary's delays and of the danger to social peace arising from the agitation for Kun's release, the Hungarians rightly concluded that the real reason was Simons' desire to foster friendly relations with the Soviet government.[35]

By this time, the Foreign Ministry's earlier and zealous fostering of contacts with White Russian leaders had declined, and Victor Kopp, the Soviets' representative in Berlin for the affairs of the prisoners of war, became something of the man of the hour. The star of anti-Soviet Ministerial Director Behren, the former grain merchant who was supposed to introduce the common sense and efficiency of the business world into the aristocratic atmosphere of the Foreign Ministry, declined in the formulation of policy in Russian affairs. The influence of the famous "Red Baron" Ago von Maltzan correspondingly increased. Foreign Minister Simons gave him his personal permission for conversations with Kopp when the Red Army's offensive began.[36] In the course of these talks, Maltzan presented a request for an assurance that the Red Army would respect Germany's frontiers during its advance into Poland, which was manifestly Germany's immediate interest.

After consulting Moscow, Kopp gave the desired assurance for what it was worth,[37] and, indeed, there is evidence that S. Kamenev, the commander-in-chief on the western front, intended at first to halt the offensive on the German frontier of 1914, an indication that he perhaps anticipated a deal that would return the lost provinces to Germany.[38] In any event, Kopp and other Soviet agents firmed up this confidential assurance with statements to the German press. Soviet Russia's overriding interest was in commercial relations with Germany—an argument that was well calculated to impress in view of the practically unanimous interest of the German public in trade—an interest that would not be served by the reactionary coup d'état that a violation of her frontier by the Red Army would precipitate.[39]

The German Communists also tried to allay alarm, denying in their principal newspaper that they counted upon the Soviets' Red Army to carry the day for them in Germany. "We German Communists have always said and we say today: that the German proletarian revolution is the sole concern of the German worker, and that it cannot be led to victory with the aid of Soviet Russia's Red Army. We know that our victorious Russian brothers agree. The Russians will not cross the German frontier."[40] While anything the German Communists said normally carried little weight with the German public, the hopes placed by so many Germans in the economic development of Russia perhaps assured some influence to Kopp's statements in quieting the most extreme fears. In any event, the Red Army found no occasion to violate the frontier of East Prussia as it advanced along it toward the Corridor.

These official contacts were not limited to Maltzan's comparatively low level. Presumably acting on instructions from Moscow, Kopp suggested Germany's *de jure* recognition of the Soviet government as the basis for further negotiations,[41] a question that could only be settled by the highest authorities. The Legal Division of the Foreign Ministry, however, at once argued that legal satisfaction must first be secured for Count von Mirbach's unexpiated murder. Unpublished German documents anonymously communicated to E. H. Carr, the British historian of the Bolshevik Revolution, fit into the picture at this point. On July 22, Foreign Minister Simons himself handed Kopp a letter for Chicherin proposing negotiations for the resumption of normal diplomatic relations—thus suggesting that the question of *de jure* recognition did not arise since it already existed—and stipulating a ceremonial raising of the German flag over the embassy building in Moscow in the presence of a company of Red Army troops as Germany's satisfaction for the murder of her ambassador. He hoped that trade would be resumed and asked that a German military representative be allowed to accompany the Red Army as it approached "the old German frontier" in order to avoid "undesirable incidents."[42] Even this comparatively mild expiation was eventually rejected, but its moderation bespoke Germany's anxious interest in normalizing her relations with Soviet Russia. The inference is warranted, even though the evidence is incomplete, that Simons was preparing the foundations for a claim to be heard in the settlement of the Eastern European and Russian problems and perhaps for an effort to revise Germany's eastern frontier should events offer a favorable opportunity. From the Soviets' practice of open (and propagandistic) diplomacy at this time, he must soon have become aware that these questions might be settled without Germany's being heard by an international conference or by direct Russo-Polish negotiations.

These matters and official confidential exchanges constitute the background of Simons' speech in the Reichstag, July 26, on the Spa Conference, in which Soviet Russia and Germany's relations with her were by all odds the most significant themes. What he said was clearly addressed as much to the Soviet government as to the Reichstag and the German people, and it was in part to be understood in connection with his note to Chicherin of July 22 and the latter's note, July 24, to Curzon proposing an international conference without reference to Germany. In view of Germany's neutrality, Simons could not, of course, offer the Soviets any direct support. Instead, he took the opportunity to deny flatly Allied press reports of a Russo-German agreement. The Allies' moral condemnation of bolshevism and the Soviet regime, their rejection of official relations, and their defense of Poland's independence and of her territorial integrity suggested ways of influencing Soviet policy in Germany's interest by friendlier professions in all these respects. This is what he proceeded to do. His appreciative references to Lloyd George, inspired no doubt by the hope that he would restrain France from extending the zone of occupation to the Ruhr, were less significant than a surprisingly cordial attitude toward Soviet Russia.

Simons may have surprised the Soviet government nearly as much as the Allies when he took the legally sound position that the question of *de jure* recognition did not arise for Germany, since it had been granted in the signing of the Treaty of Brest-Litovsk and had since never been withdrawn even when diplomatic relations were severed after the assassination of Mirbach. In Simons' view, as he pointed out later in the debate, the Soviets were in effective control of Russia; they were therefore a national power like any other. To restore normal diplomatic relations, all that the Soviet government had to do would be to perform the required but modest ceremonial satisfaction for the murder of Mirbach. Germany shared Soviet Russia's desire for a commercial treaty, and, later in the discussion, Simons made a point of defining Germany's attitude to political treaties. They would interest her only if Soviet Russia would be prepared to defend them against the Allies, a remark that betrayed his suspicion that the Soviet government might yield to the pressure of the Allies. It was much too soon for this left-handed and premature anticipation of the policy of Rapallo to have practical significance, except as an indication of Simons' own thinking.

While this small straw in the wind passed virtually unnoticed, what Simons said about the Soviet regime itself and his own reactions to it created a sensation. "I am not," he said, "as worried about Eastern developments as perhaps many of you are. I came to know Chicherin at Brest-Litovsk and I regard him as an unusually clever man. I do not believe it is in the interest of the Soviet Republic to overrun Germany with murdering and burning hordes. What the Soviet Republic needs is economic aid. It had robbed itself of a large part of its economic strength by an excessive emphasis of the Soviet idea (*durch Überspannung der Räte-Idee*) which would have made the reconstruction of the ruined economic system possible. I do not belong among those who see nothing but chaos in Russia. I know from reports of independent and knowledgeable men that a truly enormous creative work has been accomplished, a work which in many respects we would do well to take as an example. [...*dass in Sowjetrussland eine geradezu enorme aufbauende Wirtschaft geleistet wird, eine Arbeit, bie der wir gut täten, uns nach mancher Richtung ein Muster zu nehmen.*] I am prepared and willing to give you the evidence."

Concerning Poland, the foreign minister went on to say that Germany would neither aid her nor assist in wiping her from the map. The extraordinary vitality of Polish nationalism made it necessary for Germany to live in peace with some sort of a Polish state, but his real thought as to what was likely to happen emerged when he added, "even if, in the long run, the international-legal conditions of the Polish State may take such forms that it is no longer entirely sovereign." This, he suggested, was only a possibility. "Even if Soviet Russia succeeds in the negotiations with Poland in placing Poland again under some form of Russian suzerainty, it would then still be important to us to maintain good relations with Poland." Although phrased indirectly, this was tantamount to saying that Germany would accept, even welcome, the restoration of some degree of Russian control in Poland, perhaps even if it meant the introduction of Soviet institutions, while the Allies would halt Russian influence at the Curzon Line. Simons knew, of course, that the Russians would not take offense when he added that Poland "will have a very troubled, uncertain, and unhappy future if she regards it as her mission to act as a barrier between Russia and Germany." Poland's future would be the happier if she could reconcile herself to serving as a bridge between them.

Toward the end of his opening speech, he took note of the proposed conference (Chicherin's note of July 24) between the Entente powers and Soviet Russia "on which we received telegraphic reports today (July 26)" and then warned the Entente powers not to repeat their mistake in not allowing Germany a voice in the settlement of Western and Central European problems. "If they do, then the peace in the East will be a still . . . feebler and more uncertain house of cards than the Treaty of Versailles."[43]

Considered as a whole, Simons' speech was a remarkable performance. "It seemed," according to Dresel, the American diplomatic agent, "that a constructive statesman of unconventional views and enlightened statesmanship had at last been found who might lead Germany out of the wilderness."[44] In the best tradition of old-fashioned power politics, he tried to wring advantages for Germany from every favorable circumstance. If he failed, the reasons were the weakness of Germany, the temporary collapse of her prestige, and his failure to assess correctly the revolutionary nature of the war that Lenin was waging in Poland and to foresee Poland's eventual victory.

Simons' friendly gestures did not have their expected effect upon the Soviet government which apparently had complete victory within its grasp. Why deal with the bourgeois German government at a moment when a German revolution was in prospect? On July 31, the Moscow wireless sent out an article by *Izvestia*'s editor, Y. Steklov, flaying the German along with the other "bourgeois" governments for its hostility, although the author concentrated his venom against France for trying to purchase Hungary's military assistance for Poland with promises of "extensive territories." Germany's neutrality was the result of the workers' pressure, not of the government's free decision. "Whatever declarations are made by the bourgeois [German] government, we do not doubt for a moment that on the first possible pretext it will do all in its power to harm the Soviet Republic."[45] Even after World War II, Soviet historians were still charging Germany with unneutral conduct at this time.[46] On August 2, Chicherin dealt a deadly blow to Simons' hopes. Replying most courteously to the latter's letter of July 22, Chicherin flatly rejected the apparently modest satisfaction for Mirbach's assassination, although the hope was expressed that Russo-German co-operation would continue.[47] Simons immediately but inaccurately blamed Soviet Russia's strange obedience to Allied pressure against her negotiations with Germany.[48] The furor that would have followed similarly complimentary references to the Soviet regime by a responsible minister of an Allied country or of the United States may easily be imagined.

Otto Hoetzsch, the historian and nationalist deputy, stood alone in the Reichstag debate in expressing the bitter anti-bolshevism of Western opinion. However, he accepted Poland's apparent fate and even the prospect of a common Russo-German frontier with equanimity, while bitterly protesting against any political relations with the Soviet government. On Simons' acknowledgement of its positive economic achievements, Hoetzsch commented caustically: we are "supposed to have a bourgeois cabinet, and a bourgeois Foreign Minister speaks to us as its spokesman. He finds no stronger criticism to make than an 'overemphasis of the Soviet dictatorship' in regard to the terror and brutality of the working class against the other classes of Russian society. . . . It is a notably restrained judgment . . . considering this ocean of blood and tears and ruins. . . ."

While the skepticism that Gustav Stresemann expressed in the Reichstag debate in regard to the Soviet government's alleged achievements was shared by many, there was a minimum of moral indignation and general approval of the foreign minister's views in most other respects.[49] According to the *Kölnische Zeitung* (July 28), what the German Foreign Minister had said would be worth an army to Chicherin—a somewhat inflated evaluation. Yet the *Allgemeine Zeitung* of Munich, a more venerable if not as widely read nationalist journal, saw (August 1) nothing to object to in Simons' speech from the point of view of German interest. It refused to be frightened by Trotsky's statement that Poland must become a Red bridge for the Revolution to the West, since the German people were immune to bolshevism. In regard to Poland, "the terrible prospect . . . could elicit only satisfaction from the entire German People. Even if *Schadenfreude* is not an especially admirable emotion from the moral point of view, Paderewski and others like him have created nothing but hatred and contempt in Germany." Hoetzsch's moral protest was not loudly echoed by liberal opinion, although the *Vossische Zeitung* (July 27) questioned Simons' assumption that the Bolsheviks had established a viable regime. The *Frankfurter Zeitung* (July 27) agreed that Germany and Russia needed each other despite their different social systems. Speaking during the Reichstag debate, Martin Spahn, the leader of the Catholic Center party, was chiefly concerned with the danger that Britain might acquire a monopolistic economic position in Russia which, he declared, would have to be prevented at all costs. He was convinced that Lenin's views were evolving toward bourgeois concepts, in regard to factory management in particular.[50]

Given their general hostility toward bolshevism, the Majority Social Democrats found much that was objectionable in the foreign minister's case. Friedrich Stampfer, the editor of the party's principal newspaper, *Vorwärts,* doubted that the Bolsheviks would ever make much of Russia's resources and repudiated the Bolshevik terror, the destruction of democratic and humanitarian principles as completely alien to the German situation. Passing over Poland in silence, he fully endorsed the government's policy of neutrality and called upon Germany to act as the mediator between bolshevism and Western capitalism, to neither of which she in reality belonged.[51] On Russia and Poland the affinity between Simons and the views of the Independent Social Democrats was so clear that the former told the Reichstag that he agreed completely with Rudolf Breitscheid's speech. Breitscheid, for his part, found the minister's position so much in accord with the Independent Social Democratic party's position that Breitscheid inquired, with not wholly mock solicitude, if Simons did not experience premonitions of death at the hands of the extreme right.[52]

In general, therefore, there was no serious dissent anywhere, in the Reichstag or press, in regard to neutrality, Simons' stand on the question of *de jure* recognition, and his attitude toward Poland and to Germany's right to a voice in the settlement of Eastern European problems. The foreign minister found it advisable, however, after making his friendly gestures in the direction of Moscow, to add a warning. To the displeasure of his admirers among the Independent Social Democrats, he declared that Germany would join the Allies and Poland if the Soviets violated Germany's neutrality by crossing her frontier.[53]

While the triumphal advance of the Red Army undoubtedly caused many to hope that the day of Germany's emancipation from the Treaty of Versailles was near, others kept their feet on the ground. They believed that the best hope lay in an honest effort to comply with the terms of peace and in general to show that Germany's sympathies at least were on the side of the Allies. Since they also were wholeheartedly in favor of neutrality, there was, however, virtually no support for any sort of direct or indirect material assistance to Poland.

A small group, which had scarcely any following in public opinion, worked behind the scenes for a deal with the Allies in which Germany would co-operate against Soviet Russia and bolshevism in return for the revision of the Treaty of Versailles. Essentially an intrigue that operated in the twilight zone between official and private affairs, the evidence is too scanty and indirect for the full story to be told. The participants seem for the most part to have been sincere partisans of a Western orientation, while anxious to serve the cause of German recovery. However, Baron Ago von Maltzan, of the Foreign Ministry, who was apparently the first to approach the Allied representatives in Berlin early in 1920, was apparently an easterner at heart even then. Since the hopelessness of the White Russian cause had not yet been demonstrated with finality, Maltzan was doubtless moved by the same considerations that led him to establish contacts with Russian refugee circles in view of an eventual restoration in Russia. General Malcolm, the British military representative, was apparently the most receptive, and since his immediate responsibility was to the War Office in London, its chief, Winston Churchill, must have known and approved of these contacts. According to General Max Hoffmann, the most active anti-Bolshevik among the military personalities in Germany, Churchill let it be known indirectly that he would gladly discuss with him the possibilities of a campaign against Soviet Russia.[54] The French and British (if Blücher's account is to be believed), finally broke these contacts, the French because they decided to rely upon the threat of occupying the Ruhr to restrain Germany from joining Russia and the British because they regarded Lenin as a lesser evil than Ludendorff.[55]

While Maltzan shifted permanently to an Eastern orientation, others continued to work secretly for an anti-Bolshevik agreement with the Allies. Dresel, the American diplomatic agent, thought that the government itself was perhaps considering this course until Simons' speech of July 26 showed Dresel's mistake. Because the Allies had committed themselves to defend Poland without the means of doing so effectively, Germany, he cabled, was in a strong bargaining position. The Germans felt themselves to be "the key to the situation as there is war material in this country, trained men, officers who have beaten the Russians before, and many elements in society which would consider a war against [the] Soviets a valuable means of solidifying labor conditions. I submit as a possibility the hypothesis that neutrality has been declared to make it impossible for relief to be dispatched quickly through Germany to Poland thus putting Allies where they must beg gravely of German government."[56] If Dresel was mistaken in regard to the government's attitude his analysis applied to those individuals who continued to work for an anti-Bolshevik union with the Allies.

Among the most zealous was the industrialist and amateur politician without a following, Arnold Rechberg, who was just beginning his long career as an impresario of anti-Bolshevik enterprises. From Stresemann's unpublished private papers, it is now clear that Rechberg was perceptive enough to see Stresemann as a rising star in German politics and to try to attach himself and his cause to him. Rechberg was also in contact with General Hoffmann, the reactionary Minister President Gustav von Kahr of Bavaria, and the British General Malcolm. Because of the lack of unimpeachable evidence of Stresemann's own views, his attitude, though obviously friendly, remains uncertain, but there is no doubt at all that his private secretary, Fritz Rauch, who at this time answered much of his private correspondence, was an ardent advocate of Rechberg's plans.

As the days of the last government based upon the Weimar coalition of Social Democrats and moderate parties ran out in June, Rechberg tried to plant a man who shared his views in the reorganized government and for this purpose he appealed to Stresemann. Reminding him of his recent remark that an energetic general was needed as minister of defense in view of the danger of a leftist coup d'état, Rechberg urged the merits of General Hoffmann because of his expert knowledge of bolshevism and of the Russian style of warfare.[57] There is no evidence that Stresemann exerted himself in Hoffmann's behalf, and when the Centrist Konstantin Fehrenbach announced his cabinet, June 20, Otto Karl Gessler was carried over from the Müller government as Minister of Defense.[58]

Undiscouraged, Rechberg continued his efforts. Writing from Munich, July 10, he announced von Kahr's agreement with Rechberg's view that the time for action would come "when England finally sees that she cannot escape the decisive conflict with the Moscow Soviet government and that she is unable to fight this struggle to the end without Germany."[59] On July 24, as the international crisis became more acute, Rechberg brought the draft of an Anglo-Franco-German alliance, which he ascribed to himself and a certain Hamilton whom he described as the unofficial representative of Lord Kilmarnock, the British chargé d'affaires, to Rauch. For the duration of the struggle against bolshevism, the Treaty of Versailles would be suspended, and a new European settlement would be worked out with Germany at its conclusion by which she would recover her 1914 frontiers, plus Austria, with the exception of Alsace-Lorraine and northern Schleswig. Germany would be obligated to raise an army of 1,500,000 men which Ludendorff and Hoffmann would command and which the Allies would equip.[60]

As it must be assumed that Stresemann knew in general the contents of his files, it is reasonable to conclude that he was willing at least to keep in touch with Rechberg's intrigues, fantastic and unrealistic as they were, and also that Stresemann's sympathies lay in this general direction. He could not, however, have thought for a moment that an alliance like the above was within the range of practical politics. The letters that his secretary, Rauch, wrote in his stead doubtless reflect, however, the general direction of his thinking. Stresemann regretted the failure of the Allies to understand the true meaning of Poland's collapse, foresaw the overrunning of Germany unless they awoke at the last moment to the solidarity of all civilized peoples against bolshevism and gave Germany the means of fulfilling her mission to defend the West. No accommodation with the Bolsheviks was possible, for they were doomed unless they achieved their purpose of world revolution.[61] Undated notes which Stresemann apparently dictated about this time (July, 1920) show that he saw in the crisis the means of a thorough revision of the Treaty of Versailles (*dass der Vertrag von Versailles gründlich revidiert werden kann*), except that the conflict in England between those who desired peace with Russia at any price and Churchill's view that Germany should be permitted to recover as a defense against bolshevism tied Germany's hands.[62] From information furnished by Vice Chancellor Heinze, that the Cabinet had discussed the Red Army's break-through of the Polish lines for three hours on July 5,[63] Stresemann seems to have concluded that the government would exploit the Bolshevik danger at the Spa Conference, and it seemed to him that neither the Chancellor, Fehrenbach, nor Foreign Minister Simons had made effective use of the crisis there.

On July 23, Stresemann's secretary, Fritz Rauch, tried to spur him to action. Writing to him at Bansin, Rauch enclosed clippings from the *Temps* and *Matin* which, he claimed, showed that France would welcome German aid against the Bolsheviks and advised Stresemann to act along Rechberg's lines before the Allies themselves demanded a decision from Germany. The time had come for Stresemann to assume the responsibilities of government.[64] Stresemann himself knew, however, that his hour had not yet struck, perhaps because the days when he was "Ludendorff's young man" in the Reichstag were too fresh in people's memories.[65] On July 26, after the foreign minister's speech, when Stresemann addressed the secret caucus of the German People's party of which he was the leader, he advised against an effort to overthrow the government and said nothing about his own political plans. His criticism of Simons' views on foreign policy deserves attention. Stresemann regretted the avoidance of the Bolshevik question at Spa: "Only by placing the Eastern question in the forefront of the debate could Germany achieve something in the disarmament question. We should have squarely confronted the Entente with the question: what did it think of the situation created by the advance of Bolshevism toward Germany? I regarded this as possible, because in the Entente countries, in England perhaps more than in France, there is a movement of opinion which takes the position that there exists something like a common bourgeois-cultural interest against Asiatic Bolshevism, and because Lloyd George has had to fight hard against this movement. An Englishman [Churchill?] has telegraphed to Berlin: why don't the Germans bring the Eastern question into the debate, so that I can second them? How much could have been changed if this had been done, I am unable to say, but I regret that the effort was not made. If nothing resulted, then we could at least have placed the Entente before world opinion in a position of the greatest moral disadvantage."[66]

In the briefing of his party associates on his proposed reply to Simons, there was not a word on the anti-Bolshevik union with the Allies for which Rechberg and Stresemann's own secretary were working. Stresemann would, he said, reach very different conclusions about the situation in Russia from the foreign minister's but he would also say that Germany had no reason to sympathize with the Poles.[67] When he took the floor in the Reichstag it was to attack Simons on several grounds. Stresemann called attention to Trotsky's prediction that Poland would become a bridge for the export of bolshevism to Germany in reply to the view that she would be a bridge for commercial exchanges. Stresemann doubted the availability of goods in Russia for the revival of trade, and he questioned Breitscheid's assurance that the Red Army would respect the German frontier. Above all, Stresemann denied the validity of the foreign minister's tribute to the productive achievements of the Soviet regime, citing Soviet statistics on the numbers of locomotives in use and out of action to show the collapse of the railway system. Speaking for his party, Stresemann, nevertheless, approved the minister's position that for Germany the *de facto* recognition of the Soviet government was an accomplished fact and, by implication, the government's neutral policy. "The Russian state exists. What its form is, is its own affair. We must therefore recognize it and also draw the necessary conclusions." Stresemann betrayed nothing of his interest in an agreement with the Allies against Soviet Russia, nor was there so much as a hint of approval of a crusade against bolshevism. The only positive action he asked for was defensive measures against Bolshevik propaganda.[68] As a practical politician, he was not prepared to identify himself with a cause as devoid of popular appeal as Rechberg's and with one, moreover, that might limit his freedom of action when and if he attained power himself.[69]

Where Rechberg, and even Stresemann, went astray in estimating British opinion and the opposition to Lloyd George's Russian policy was in equating anti-bolshevism with pro-Germanism. The true anti-Bolshevik was usually also extremely hostile to Germany, as was the case of most of the Tory press. Although rumors circulated of contacts between British agents and German leaders in Berlin for combined military operations against Soviet Russia, they were mostly ignored as incredible. The *Manchester Guardian* (July 27) dismissed them as "malicious gossip from Berlin."[70]

Winston Churchill, of course, knew better. As Secretary of State for War, he certainly must have been familiar with and he may have even initiated General Malcolm's contacts, whose significance he seems to have exaggerated. Lloyd George's eager pursuit of an international congress and the plight of the Poles strained Churchill's acquiescence in the prime minister's policy to the breaking point. On July 22, after Lloyd George had agreed to the direct Soviet-Polish armistice negotiations, Churchill expressed himself with considerable frankness to Riddell who presumably informed the prime minister. Churchill agreed with Riddell that Great Britain and France had undertaken a mission, "the management of Europe," that was beyond their strength. "They have not got the money and they have not got the men." Churchill, like Riddell, felt that the indifference of the United States, after President Wilson's great contribution to the revival of Poland, was "one of the greatest historical scandals." However, the United States, in Churchill's opinion, was not alone to blame; Lloyd George and Philip Kerr should return the management of foreign policy to the Foreign Office. Churchill then addressed himself to the current crisis and hinted at a possible initiative of his own. "The Bolsheviks," he said, "are fanatics. Nothing will induce them to give up their propaganda and endeavour to create a communist world." They would try to set up a Soviet government in Poland "and later on endeavour to accomplish their purpose in Germany. It may well be that Great Britain and France will have to call upon the Germans for their assistance."[71]

On Monday morning, July 26, after Chicherin's proposal (July 24) of a conference in London between Soviet Russia and the Allies for a general peace and just before Lloyd George's speech on the same day in the House of Commons accepting it, Lord Northcliffe's *Daily Mail* carried on four-line announcement in italics that the *Evening News* would print "an important article" by Winston Churchill on the following Wednesday. This signed article turned out to be a sensational appeal to Germany to earn her way back into European esteem by joining the Allies against Soviet Russia. Poland's conquest would bring Soviet Russia and Germany into direct contact and then "an awful, yet in some ways a wonderful choice will be presented to Germany." Weak as the Germans were in many respects, they would have it in their power to "redouble the miseries of Europe, or to render a service to civilization of the highest order."

The choice was presented in true Churchillian style: "It will be open to the Germans to sink their own social structure in the general Bolshevist welter and spread the reign of chaos far and wide throughout the continent; or, on the other hand, by a supreme effort of sobriety, of firmness, or self-restraint, and of courage—undertaken, as most great exploits have to be, under conditions of peculiar difficulty and discouragement—to build a dyke of peaceful, lawful, patient strength and virtue against the flood of red barbarism flowing from the East, and thus safeguard their own interests and the interests of their principal antagonists in the West."

Should the Germans render this service, "not by reckless military adventure or with ulterior motives, they would unquestionably have taken a giant step upon the path of self-redemption which would lead them surely and swiftly as the years pass to their own great place in the councils of Christendom, and would render easier the sincere cooperation between Britain, France, and Germany on which the very salvation of Europe depends." An accommodation with the Bolsheviks, he warned perhaps on account of Simons' speech of July 26, would be useless since their purpose would be world revolution in peace as in war. "In fact a Bolshevist peace is only another form of war." As to Poland, she was, Churchill said, "the linchpin of Versailles" with the implication that its loss would cause the collapse of the peace settlement—a view that possessed little persuasive power for a German audience![72]

In view of the stiffening in Lloyd George's attitude toward Russia following his Boulogne meeting with Millerand, the apparent contradiction between the prime minister's policy and Churchill's views may not have been as real as it seemed on the surface, since they might conceivably impress the Soviet government or, if not, serve as the basis of an alternate policy to that of an international conference. Such was the tentative conclusion of an official of the American State Department in an analysis prepared for the secretary of state. Reading Churchill's article along with Ellis Dresel's telegram of July 24, he thought that if Churchill were retained in the Cabinet it would seem that "Lloyd George thought him a good counterpoise to his own (official) policy regarding Russia." He might be using Churchill "to put ideas into the Germans' heads and simultaneously to awe the Bolshevists into a less recalcitrant attitude," or the article might be "a *'ballon d'essai'* to see how the British public would feel about using a German club to impress Moscow."[73] Churchill's earlier challenges of his chief's Russian policy and his known disapproval of the prime minister's personal control of foreign policy makes it more probable, however, that he had acted independently. At any rate, Lloyd George was visibly embarrassed when he faced a barrage of questions in the House of Commons, August 2, on Churchill's authority to write as he had. Thrice, the prime minister replied evasively. The article, he said at first, "does not bear the interpretation sought to be placed upon it." Then: "I only read it this morning. I do not think it so much an expression of policy as a hankering." And finally: "I really cannot control my colleague's desires."[74] If the public reaction to Churchill's article had been less critical than it was, Lloyd George's responses might not perhaps have approached so closely to a brusque repudiation.

Churchill's trial balloon, although momentarily a world sensation, was a complete fiasco, and not less so in Great Britain than in Germany. One British commentator of Russian origin was one of the few who agreed. Germany was of "paramount importance." She had only two choices, Moscow or the Western democracies, for "neutrality cannot be considered an alternative," since a neutral Germany would create an impossible barrier between Poland and her friends. "For the Allies the moment has arrived to put a straight question to Berlin: 'Are you with us or against us? *Tertium non datur.*'" Where Churchill was silent on the price the Allies would have to pay, this writer at least made clear that it would be high if Germany declared herself "against the hideous Thing on her eastern marches. You cannot buy something for nothing." Germany's price would be "the highest which her diplomats and statesmen can possibly obtain...."[75] In the British press, Churchill's article was usually either given the silent treatment, which was the case of Conservative journals whose anti-Germanism rivalled their anti-bolshevism, or roundly denounced. The proposed alliance with Prussian militarism moved an extreme nationalist editor, who expressed hesitation to criticize a minister who was the *bête noir* of British Bolsheviks, to condemn it as "a monstrous suggestion."[76] R. W. Seton-Watson, the historian and Eastern European expert, had earlier sided with Churchill on the Russian problem, but he later went over to Lloyd George. Of Churchill, the *New Europe,* the short-lived but well-informed weekly of which he was the proprietor and editor, wrote: this "Prince of Bourbons," convinced that war was the cure of bolshevism, "goes from failure to failure, still nursing the delusion that he can find some valiant nation or general to fight his Russian battle for him.... His essay ... is a warning to his fellow-countrymen that a brilliant intellect unguided by judgment is the most perilous of all equipment for a public man."[77]   The Liberal and radical press refused to take Churchill seriously.   The effect of his article, declared the weekly *Nation* (July 31), was negligible, but the gravest danger was that Moscow might doubt Lloyd George's sincerity.   The *Manchester Guardian* (August 3) wrote of Churchill's "rather harum-scarum piece of amateur journalism" and suggested that the prime minister might not like to be stabbed in the back.   Under the ironical caption, "Awful and wonderful," the *Westminster Gazette* (July 29) found "these irresponsible excursions" to be "mortifying and humiliating" to the entire country.   "We have suffered enough in credit and reputation in the vain search of the Allies for somebody else to do to Bolshevik Russia what they are unwilling to do themselves, and that a British Minister should now, finally, after all he has learnt, or should have learnt, during the last two months, go cap in hand to Germany passes the limits."   To the Labor *Daily Herald* (July 29) for whose naive editor, Lansbury, Soviet Russia could do no wrong, Churchill was bent upon sabotaging all chances of an agreement.   Churchill had issued his own version of the Communist Manifesto: "Capitalists of the world unite.   You have nothing to lose but your souls."

In Italy, the recently organized Giolitti government (June 16, 1920) was perhaps less inclined than Nitti's to follow Lloyd George's lead unquestioningly.   It was, however, even less receptive to the anti-Bolshevik crusade implied in Churchill's appeal.   Count Carlo Sforza, its Foreign Minister, evaded the historian Gaetano Salvemini's interpellation on the significance of Churchill's article and on Italy's attitude toward the Lloyd George–Millerand meeting at Boulogne (July 27).[78]   According to Sforza, he was approached at this time in an effort to secure Italy's collaboration in an anti-Bolshevik enterprise, but what he told Parliament, August 2, amounted to a refusal.   "Attacks from the outside will never be a solution. I believe in liberty and that is why I am against Bolshevism.   But the Bolshevist experiment must evolve freely to the end; that is, as long as the Russians will continue it."[79]   Four days later, Sforza announced the impending arrival of Vatzlav Vorovsky, the Soviet government's agent, and promised him the most liberal hospitality while affirming Italy's support of Poland's independence.[80]

On the other hand, Churchill's uncompromising hatred of bolshevism, his intuitive sense of the tragic consequences of the solid establishment of Soviet power for Western civilization, and his readiness to use force to destroy communism commended him to the prevailing trend of French opinion and presumably to the French government.   But his desire to enlist the Germans in a kind of crusade, according to the London correspondent of the *Temps* (July 30), with the Germans in the vanguard like the Teutonic knights of old, was definitely another matter. Since the French Parliament adjourned before the end of July, unlike those of Great Britain, Italy, and Germany, there was no opportunity to elicit the government's views, but the attitude of the leading journals left little doubt as to what they were. The *Temps* (July 31) agreed completely with Churchill's diagnosis of the problem and his estimate of its consequences, but what a cure! ("Quel remède!"). Because his heart was in the right place, it gave him a lesson from history from the time of the French Revolution (1794-95) when the Empress Catherine was advancing upon Warsaw and when France supported Prussia in order to strengthen her as a bulwark against Russia. Just as the Prussians had then joined the Russians and partitioned Poland, another experiment in using the Germans to stop the Russians would end in another partition of Poland. In the *Écho de Paris* (July 31), Pertinax wrote of "Churchill's madness" and of his efforts during the past year, aided by General Malcolm in Berlin, to use bolshevism as the basis of co-operation between Germany and the Allies. "To act on these counsels would mean that nothing would remain of the Treaty of Versailles." The effect in France was to confirm the determination to enforce the terms of that treaty and to threaten Germany from the Rhine in order to restrain her from making common cause with Soviet Russia against Poland. "The farther the Reds advance in Poland," Pertinax affirmed, "the more firmly must we keep our adversary in the harness of the treaty and redouble our vigilance on the Rhine." The *Temps* (August 6) read into Simons' statement in the Reichstag on August 2 an offer of an alliance to the Soviets in order to impose his will upon the Allies. "Bolshevism is our enemy and what would Bolshevism be without Berlin?"[81] More explicit was the *Journal des débats* (August 6). The Allies must be prepared for the immediate employment of the two weapons at their disposal against Russo-German co-operation: the British fleet in the Baltic, and the Allied armies of occupation on the Rhine. There should be no more delays in the disarmament of Germany. The Berlin government must be warned "that any form of cooperation, occult or public, with the Bolshevik armies, will be considered as a threat to the security of the Allies and will be followed by the necessary measures on land and sea to safeguard that security...." Instead of asking for German cooperation as Churchill had proposed, all anti-German forces should be aligned against the Bolshevik irruption and Germany herself should be kept under strict surveillance. With some justification a German nationalist journal noted the unanimity of the demand in the French press for action upon the Rhine, a unanimity "which betrayed a common inspiration."[82]

In view of the extreme rarity of friendly gestures from abroad for a good many years and the not unpleasing sensation of being courted again, Churchill's article undoubtedly made pleasant reading to many Germans. The liberal *Frankfurter Zeitung* (July 31) summarized his article fairly, only to note, however, the unfavorable reaction of the British press. His vagueness as to what gains Germany might expect doubtless discouraged those who hoped for a serious revision of the Treaty of Versailles. In any event, German opinion shortly turned decisively against any *Landsknecht* service for the Allies and against any participation in an anti-Bolshevik crusade. Foreign Minister Simons chose to use a press article by a White Russian refugee favoring some sort of a crusade as the text for a forthright repudiation. Already he had declared that the Bolshevik danger could not be overcome by a crusade or a *cordon sanitaire,* but only by spiritual work at home.[83] He warned the German youth, after having made so many sacrifices for the greatness of the Fatherland, not to throw Germany's last reserves of strength against bolshevism. They would learn too late that they were defending the creditors of Russia, not Western civilization. In the history of Islam, he found reasons for thinking that Bolshevik dynamism would in time find its natural limits.[84] He had, therefore, already taken his stand when Rudolf Breitscheid, the leader of the Independent Social Democrats in the Reichstag, called upon him, August 2, to reject Churchill's invitation to serve as "the gendarme of Europe and Western capitalism." In approving Breitscheid's speech "from beginning to end" at the risk, he said, of being taken as an inscribed member of his party, he specifically warned that Germany would serve as no one's *Landsknecht.*[85] In the *Kölnische Zeitung's* view (August 7), for Germany to follow the counsels of either the National Bolsheviks or Churchill would mean invasion by France or Soviet Russia and civil war. "The overwhelming majority in Germany knows very well that any departure from neutrality must lead us into civil war." Since the Bolsheviks ignored Simons' advances just as the Germans rejected Churchill's, the remote chance that Germany might play a decisive part in the crisis passed into oblivion.

VII

Western Dissension
and
Poland's Victory, August, 1920

1. Lloyd George and Poland's Peril

When Warsaw's fall seemed most certain, the military situation changed in Poland's favor largely as the result of errors on the part of the Red Army command. It allowed itself to be diverted from the main task of destroying the bulk of the Polish army as it retreated to the Warsaw area. To the south, Budënny's cavalry army struck at the fortified stronghold of Lvov instead of closing up in support of Tukhachevsky's left flank.[1] Tukhachevsky was still more seriously at fault in sending his overbalanced northern flank across the Polish Corridor toward the German frontier.[2] Despite fairly heavy losses, the Polish army was able to concentrate its major strength close to its base in Warsaw with all of the advantages that implied.[3] The Red Army had outdistanced its inadequate supply services and, contrary to Lenin's expectations, it was operating in the midst of a sullen peasantry which, far from welcoming the invaders as liberators, turned against them as traditional enemies. From the strictly military point of view, the classic requirements for a successful Polish counteroffensive were taking shape, as Marshal Pilsudski and General Weygand were both aware. They differed as to where and when it should be launched, but it matters little for present purposes which of them was the principal architect of the final victory.[4]

The military experts were not alone in sensing the possibility of a sudden reversal in the fortunes of war. "The Russian swing of the pendulum," wrote a British press correspondent, "is losing its impetus. If and when it starts to swing back it is calculated to gather equal or greater momentum than the Polish repulse, and the demoralization of the Red Army will probably prove just as great."[5] Except in Warsaw, few, however, would have given much for Poland's chance of survival, and even the Poles could not count with certainty upon the success of the counteroffensive. In Prague, Eduard Beneš, the Czech Foreign Minister, told the American minister that Warsaw would be taken "tomorrow [August 8] or Monday," and a Polish Soviet would be established "from inside and outside. Patriotic spirit in Poland has died out and a terrible catastrophe has taken place."[6]

Poland's pleas for aid, despite the sympathy her plight aroused, had disappointing results. Of the Central European countries, only Hungary was willing, and she could not possibly send assistance on a scale commensurate with Poland's needs. The Allies responded, not with troops, but with increased shipments of war supplies, but the German dockworkers made Danzig, the best port of entry, useless at the height of the crisis.[7] Germany's strict neutrality forbade the use of the direct land route and forced the resort to roundabout communications, one of which was also blocked by railway strikes in Czechoslovakia. No wonder the Poles felt abandoned! At a joint meeting between the Allied Mission and the Polish Council of National Defense on August 5, Prince Sapieha, the Foreign Minister, declared that the Soviets were flouting the Entente and that "the only fitting response would be a declaration of war."[8] Knowing only the Polish version of the negotiations with Soviet Russia, D'Abernon, the British envoy, was convinced that Poland was doing her best to secure an armistice and that there would be no real negotiations until the Red Army had experienced a serious defeat. He joined his French colleague, Jules Jusserand, in telegraphing their governments that they should send not less than two infantry and two cavalry divisions to Poland, a move that would have meant open war. If this proved impossible, as they no doubt anticipated, Danzig should be occupied to guarantee the free flow of war matériel. On his own, D'Abernon urged the importance of Germany's cooperation upon the Cabinet through its secretary, Sir Maurice Hankey, although he expected France's attitude and the Germans' contempt for the Poles to present insuperable obstacles.[9]

From the available information the only possible conclusion was that Poland's days were numbered. Only a miracle, it seemed, could save her, and miracles, warned the political analyst of a French Catholic review, could not be counted upon.[10] There was no disputing the importance of what was at stake; Poland, wrote the *Temps* (August 4), was the keystone of the entire peace settlement. The circles frequented by the most influential foreign correspondents in Paris buzzed with talk of war. "There is," reported Walter Duranty of the *New York Times,* "a strong feeling... that what is needed now, and needed quickly, is an allied ultimatum to Moscow. It is not anything in the way of notes that is suggested, but a real old-style ultimatum, such as was flying about Europe exactly this time six years ago."[11] Actually, there was no prospect of such drastic action, not only because of war-weariness but also because French nationalists themselves were not satisfied with the Polish case. None could doubt Jacques Bardoux's patriotism, yet the Soviets' insistence upon associating the preliminary terms of peace with the armistice seemed entirely legitimate to him. Ignorance alone accounted for the Allies' failure to do the same at the time of the German Armistice.[12] An observer more to the left deplored the folly of relying upon an irresponsibly nationalist Poland, ravaged by typhus and burdened with a worthless currency, as a bulwark against both Germany and Russia. "Are we powerful enough," he asked, "to fight both the bourgeois German Republic and the Russian Workers' and Peasants' Republic?" There should be a choice. "In a word are we more bourgeois than germanophobe?"[13] Neither the French people nor their government faced this issue squarely, for they clung tenaciously to their anti-Bolshevik and anti-German views. There was little or no thought of giving Poland more than material aid. The *Temps* (August 4) was more concerned with blocking Lloyd George's schemes for an international conference than with war. Lacombe of the Catholic *Correspondant* cherished few illusions about Poland. The Polish General Staff, he wrote, "has neither skill nor prudence, and when advice is offered, it plays deaf." The utmost aid should be sent and Poland should be protected against a stab in the back by a firm word in Berlin. Nevertheless, "the Allies evidently cannot go to war with Russia. England, like France, has too much to do elsewhere."[14]

In Britain, the threat to Poland's independence momentarily overshadowed her faults in the eyes of the Liberals, although they still felt that she was largely responsible for the failure of the armistice negotiations. The *Manchester Guardian* (August 5) pointed to her "dilatory and apparently evasive proceedings," but a new situation would arise if the Red Army's advance menaced her legitimate territorial integrity or her political independence. "We might not be able to save the Polish State from military disaster," but "all possibility of opening up trade or establishing stable peaceful relations with Russia would have disappeared." These views were echoed by the *Westminster Gazette* (August 4). While it was right that Poland should be penalized for her blunders, Kamenev and Krassin, who seemed to think that their mission and the Red Army operated in different worlds, should be warned that Britain was pledged to support Poland's "independence within her ethnical" limits. And independence, as Britain understood it "includes the right of the independent State to choose its own form of government." No agreement would be possible if Soviet Russia attempted to force upon "the Polish people a form of government which they would not accept of their own free will." In these comments there was the same implied hope that could be read between the lines of Lloyd George's letter to President Wilson of August 5—that the Soviet government might still place a higher value upon trade and eventual diplomatic recognition than upon Poland's conquest.

The Tory press took a firmer stand, as was to be expected. The *Daily Telegraph* (August 6) warned the Bolsheviks not to be misled "once again by the noisy little band of their sympathisers abroad." True, the British and the French "do not want to fight the Russians, or with anybody else; but if honour and duty are at stake they will answer to such reasonable calls as their Governments may make upon them. We did not beat Germany in order to be bullied by Russia or by the gang of cosmopolitan adventurers who have their claws into that country." Yet Lord Northcliffe's *Daily Mail* (August 5), an equally conservative journal, drew back from war, perhaps because its mass circulation made it more sensitive to popular sentiment. In its view, the "means of applying pressure to the treacherous and inhuman tyrants of Russia" should be the blockade of every Russian port and the seizure of all leading Bolsheviks within reach (Kamenev and Krassin were obviously meant) as hostages for the fair treatment of British subjects in Soviet Russia.

Apparently assured of the public's acceptance of Poland's right to independence (even Labor agreed in principle), Lloyd George increased the pressure upon the Soviet government from August 4. He began by warning Kamenev and Krassin that the refusal to conclude an armistice unless it included the fundamental terms of peace and the Red Army's continued advance on Warsaw made Soviet Russia's motives suspect. In the absence of satisfactory assurances in Kamenev's reply to the British note of July 29, Lloyd George tightened the screws the next day (August 5) in a statement to the House of Commons in which he hinted, with immediate and disturbing consequences for public opinion, that Britain might resort to force. Only "the immediate conclusion of an Armistice on fair terms" would dispel suspicion, and if Russia's reply proved unsatisfactory, "I will make a full statement to the House on Monday [August 9] as to such naval or military action which it may be necessary to take."[15]   In view of his confidential appeal on the same day (August 5) to President Wilson on behalf of an international conference, it may reasonably be concluded that Lloyd George hoped stronger language would bring the Soviets to their senses. So, at least, the Liberal *Manchester Guardian* (August 7) suspected; yet it dubbed his statement "a plain enough threat of war."

Labor was in no mood for diplomatic subtleties. Lloyd George's statement was the signal for an impressive, nation-wide demonstration of mass opinion against the government's supposed war policy and military aid to Poland.[16]   While this campaign was getting under way, Lloyd George continued his feverish efforts to get the Russians' approval of an armistice through diplomacy.

Despite his ominous gesture in the House of Commons, Lloyd George was still impressed by the Soviets' case against Poland's evasions and by their need of more guarantees than a simple ceasefire, as his attitude during the following negotiations clearly showed. On August 6, he and Bonar Law discussed the terms of an armistice with Kamenev and Krassin in the presence of the Chief of the Imperial General Staff, Field Marshal Sir Henry Wilson, for more than four hours. According to Wilson's jaundiced eye—he was no admirer of Lloyd George's policies—he was "almost servile" in the way he "looked after Russian interests." Wilson's impression was that Lloyd George "is in company with friends and kindred spirits when with Bolsheviks," but Wilson had mistaken the natural technique of a charmer in a poor bargaining position for ideological sympathy. This was not all that the irascible Wilson, with his friendly feelings toward France, had to endure, for "Lloyd George went on to say that if the French did not agree to the peace terms, then he would not support Poland nor make war on the Bolsheviks. Whew!"[17] He was, indeed, prepared to pay a high price— at the expense of others—if only the advance of the Red Army could be halted. That price induced the Russian delegation to agree, subject of course to Moscow's final decision, that the armistice should begin at midnight, August 9-10, but Lloyd George accepted the extraordinarily brief period of ten days for its duration. In order to convince the suspicious Russians of the Allies' good faith, they were to have the right to post observers at designated places (including Danzig) behind the Polish lines to make sure that the armistice was not used to rush munitions into Poland, and the Polish Army was not to regroup its forces. There were no comparable provisions for a Polish inspection of the Red Army's rear areas, but it was to halt at its existing lines and apparently not to bring more troops into Poland.[18]

There was little prospect that either Moscow or Warsaw would accept an armistice on these terms. The absence of any provision for the immediate reduction of the Polish Army would have damned it in the eyes of any government similarly in sight of complete victory. In any event, Lenin was not interested in an armistice on any terms other than those that would enable him to sovietize Poland by one means or another and to strengthen the forces of revolution in Germany. For Poland, even in her apparently desperate situation, the presence of Soviet observers behind her lines made the terms equally unacceptable, especially as the counteroffensive was in course of preparation.

Rather than entrusting her interests to Lloyd George's none too friendly hands, Poland had already acted to resume direct negotiations with the Soviet government. On August 5, Prince Sapieha informed Chicherin that he was prepared to send a Polish delegation to Minsk to negotiate the preliminary terms of peace along with those of an armistice, naturally stipulating a general cease-fire at the beginning of the negotiations and refusing to discuss the "internal affairs of Poland."[19] Although the Moscow wireless station claimed that it never received this message, it seems more likely that the Soviets chose to ignore it, presumably on account of the conditions it stated regarding the Minsk negotiations. In any event, Sapieha at once exploited the incident for all it was worth for propaganda purposes.[20] In a wireless to Sapieha of August 6, Chicherin ignored it, complaining that no word had been received since the Polish delegation had left Baranowicze a week earlier as to the date when it would again arrive at the Russian front. With tongue in cheek, he added: "Fearing that some wireless communication may have been lost, we inform you that . . . all our preceding arrangements remain in force."[21] The Poles now dropped their conditions, doubtless in view of the obvious advantages of direct contact with the Soviet government at the time of their approaching counteroffensive. On August 7, Sapieha informed Chicherin without qualification that the Polish government was "ready to accept the proposal to send its delegates to Minsk for conclusion of armistice and for adoption of peace preliminaries,"[22] and Chicherin promptly replied on the same day that this decision "corresponds fully to the Russian government's proposal of July 23." The Russian delegates would arrive in Minsk on August 11.[23] There was, however, to be further delay, for the Polish delegation did not in fact appear there until August 16.

What influence the French exerted upon Poland at this time, if any, is unknown, but they went to England in full force on August 8. During most of that day, Millerand, assisted by Philippe Berthelot of the Quai d'Orsay (not Maurice Paléologue, who was still its Secretary General) and Marshal Foch, conferred with Lloyd George, who had Field Marshal Wilson and

Lord Beatty of the navy with him, at Lympne near Hythe. Lloyd George began by reading the terms of the armistice he and Kamenev had agreed upon. From Wilson's brief account—which, so far, is the only available source—Millerand made it clear that he would have nothing to do with the Bolsheviks, "that their word and signature meant nothing, and that they had neither honour nor laws." The impasse was broken, according to Wilson, by the arrival of messages showing that the Bolsheviks were insisting "for all practical purposes" upon a Polish Soviet, the demobilization of the Polish Army, and Poland's disarmament.[24] It is impossible to identify these "messages" with complete assurance, but they almost certainly included a paper prepared by the Soviet delegation for the British Prime Minister. On the condition that the Allies, and France especially, renounced all direct and indirect hostilities against Soviet Russia, withdrew General Wrangel's army from the Crimea, and that Poland accepted the Soviets' armistice terms "which deal principally with the reduction of her armed strength," the Soviet government, it promised, would pull its troops back to the Curzon Line and even reduce them.[25] Chicherin's wireless to Lloyd George of August 8 also may have reached him before the conference adjourned for the day. The British government should be satisfied with the arrangement for the Polish delegation to cross the battlelines, August 9, to begin the negotiation of an armistice and the preliminaries of peace at Minsk on the eleventh.[26]

Nothing more, it was clear, was to be heard of the Lloyd George–Kamenev agreement on the terms of an armistice, and there was ample evidence that the Soviet government was not interested at this time in an armistice of any kind. On August 7, Trotsky announced at the closing session of the Congress of the Third International in Moscow that Russia was about to fulfill her great mission of returning "martyred and brutalized Poland to the Polish worker and peasant" and Chicherin declared publicly the next day (August 8) that the British "ultimatum" of August 4 and the threat to use the British fleet had made agreement impossible.[27]

While Lloyd George would not agree to such drastic action as the expulsion of Kamenev from England, the prime minister did go along with the French in a statement to the press that evening (August 8): "The Moscow Government has definitely refused to agree to the British proposals. The Hythe [Lympne] Conference has referred the matter to its naval and military advisers, who will report to the Conference tomorrow." A few hours later a Reuter agency dispatch reported that the conference would consider "what action should be taken under the circumstances" at a meeting on the morning of August 9.[28]

The "very warlike aspect" of the conference, as the Associated Press described it for its American subscribers, was somewhat deceptive. There was "no talk of officially declaring war," but the Allies, according to the same source, were ready to reimpose the blockade and "to give Poland all possible military, naval, and economic assistance without delay."[29] According to Field Marshal Wilson, aid to General Wrangel was also discussed, but the final official statement at 4:00 P.M., August 9, merely affirmed the existence of complete agreement "regarding the action to be taken in reference to the Polish situation." In view of Lloyd George's earlier promise not to commit the country to war without consulting the House of Commons, the concluding reservation, "subject, however, to the approval of Parliament in the case of Great Britain" had a most ominous sound to pacifist opinion. An unofficial statement attempted to allay the worst alarm by denying any intention "of employing Allied troops" but it hinted that Poland might be aided "by certain naval measures."[30]

News that the Polish-Soviet negotiations were about to resume and that Poland had agreed to discuss the preliminary terms of peace as well as an armistice seems to have occasioned concern in official circles about her attitude. On August 10, the day after the close of the Lympne Conference, the French and British governments sent a joint note to Warsaw, which urged the Poles to do their best to secure an armistice, even a preliminary peace if necessary. But, at the same time, it prescribed such conditions for Allied aid as practically to assure the failure of the Minsk negotiations as may indeed have been the Allies' intention or at least France's. They included the demand that Poland refuse to disarm and, indeed, maintain an army of twenty-two divisions, although it was known that her disarmament was a *sine qua non* of an armistice from the Soviet point of view. Poland was also to agree to a preliminary peace only if her ethnographic frontier and her independence were assured, to declare her intention of defending that independence to the end, to appoint a commander-in-chief with powers limited to military matters (a gesture against Pilsudski's status combining the functions of military command and those of the chief of state), to reject any demand for her disarmament, and to heed the advice of the Allied military missions. On these conditions, the Allies would do everything in their power to cut Russia off from the outside world, furnish the requisites for the twenty-two divisions, and do their best to keep communications open to Poland. There was, however, a warning (it was at the same time a reply to D'Abernon's and Jusserand's appeal for Allied divisions) that "they cannot in any circumstances send Allied troops over and above [the] missions already there."[31]

This curious and self-contradictory note registered the price that Lloyd George had to pay for France's signature. It was exorbitant and to little or no avail in the end. However meager the chances for an armistice were in view of Lenin's purposes, they were nullified by the requirement that Poland should refuse any demand for her disarmament. The limits placed upon the Allies' support represented no real concession on France's part, since it was as impossible for her as for Britain to commit troops on any considerable scale. The conditions relating to the diminishing of Pilsudski's powers and to the ineffectual status of the Allied military advisers were obviously inserted to satisfy France's long-standing grievances. In regard to the larger Russian question, the French kept in reserve other and more drastic demands to present if, contrary to all reasonable prospects, the Polish war should be ended on acceptable terms. According to Maurice Paléologue's confidential remarks to Leland Harrison, the American chargé d'affaires, France intended to insist even more strongly upon the holding of general elections in Russia than upon the recognition of the Tsarist debts.[32] France was evidently in the mood to part company with Lloyd George should he weaken again.

2. *British Labor and the Crisis*

For once, Lloyd George's stand on the Polish-Soviet war won the approval of the Conservative and implacably anti-Bolshevik press. Strongly pro-Entente and sympathetic with France's uncompromising attitude toward bolshevism, it was pleased by the apparent accord.[33] It had no doubt whatever of the unqualified justice of the Polish case. The Labor *Daily Herald* warned the workers that the Tory press (and the government) would reiterate the sincerity of Poland's peace efforts and talk of the Bolsheviks' "policy of imperialist aggression which will carry them through a heroically resisting Poland to join hands with the militarists of Germany and overthrow the western world. It will be all lies."[34] This warning was well-founded, although it betrayed a fatal misapprehension of Soviet intentions. The Polish version of the abortive efforts to arrange an armistice was accepted without question,[35] but the Conservatives were less concerned with history than with the advance of the Red Army. Whatever the Soviet government might say, they were certain that the occupation of Warsaw would be followed by the establishment of a Polish Soviet regime, which, the *Daily Telegraph* (August 9) pointed out, would doubtless be represented as the fulfillment of the people's "yearning for a 'Workmen's and Peasants' Council.'" Just as the Labor party's journal had predicted, the chief danger was said to be that Soviet Russia and Germany would join hands. "Across the quivering body of the martyred nation," the *Daily Telegraph* (August 10) declared, "they will join with Germany, their old patron...." The *Times* (August 9) wrote of "the deadliest scheme of the German 'militarists' and of the Russian Bolshevists" that must be foiled by the closest harmony between Great Britain and France. What was feared, however, was not an immediate military onslaught against the West. Once Warsaw was taken and "perhaps sacked," the *Times* (August 7) expected the Soviet government to announce its willingness to attend an international conference "on condition that German delegates take part in it for the purpose of a general revision of the Treaty of Versailles."

As to what should be done, the bitterest enemies of the Soviets hastened to assure a war-weary and pacific nation that war was unnecessary. The *Times* (August 9) rejected the need of "great armaments" or of "the invasion of distant lands." The *Morning Post* (August 10) insisted that "now no one wants war with Russia," but it added "as such." The Allies, according to the *Daily Telegraph* (August 7), had not the slightest interest in plunging into "warlike operations for ambitious or aggressive objects."

Nevertheless, Labor's charge that the Tory press and those for whom it spoke were leading the nation into war and that the government was moving in the same direction was not without foundation. There is little doubt that even Lloyd George was momentarily convinced that everything possible should be done to save Poland, although he, unlike the militant anti-Bolsheviks, probably never really conceived open war as within the range of the "possible." Despite its denials, the Tory press recognized no such limitations and did its best to win support for whatever action Poland's salvation might require. The greatest issues—the future of Western civilization and the security of the British Empire—were at stake just as in August, 1914. Then France and Belgium had to be rescued, and the *Morning Post* (August 9) insisted that "the maintenance of that civilization saved from the German depends upon the salvation of Poland." It was not a question "of war with Russia, which, as such, no one desires." The real issue was "peace or war with Bolshevism"—as if the two could in practice be separated! Bolshevism's objective, while Warsaw for the moment, was "ultimately London and Paris." The *Daily Telegraph* (August 5) agreed that the situation was much the same as in 1914. "We fought in 1914 to keep the Huns out of Paris. And now, in 1920, another horde of Hunnish people from the steppes and plains is closing upon a European capital, which also stands for the ideals and culture of Latin Christendom." Soon "the invaders may be in possession right up to the German frontier, and once again Poland may be wiped off the map of Europe. *Finis Poloniae!* Must that shameful phrase be placed on record once more—with the Great Powers who won the Great War looking on in indignant impotence?" As in 1914, "the country," it warned, "may have to learn that we are committed to 'naval and military action' against one of the great armed Powers of the European continent."[36]

"Once more," it proclaimed, "the nation stands at one of the turning points in its history."[37] Once more, cried the *Times* (August 6), the "terrible truth" was "that we stand upon the edge of a crisis fraught with possibilities only less tragic than those that lowered over us in the first week of August six years ago.... We must face it with the same equanimity and courage with which we faced the crisis of 1914."

The fault, of course, was not Britain's or the Allies' for their attitude was entirely defensive. "If, unhappily," wrote the *Daily Telegraph,* "they are forced to take action, it will be done purely to help the Poles to defend themselves...no countenance will be given to any aggressive designs or ambitions. Russia, we are agreed, is to decide her own destiny."[38] Winston Churchill brought this argument home to Labor in replying to its attacks upon his interventionist record. Like his critics, he was also sick and tired of war. "We have had enough of war, and more than enough. It is not, however, the British who are making war, but the Russian Bolsheviks." They were invading Poland and "trampling down its freedom. They were doing their best to light the flames of war in Persia, Afghanistan, and if possible, in India. Their avowed intention is to procure a revolution in every country."[39]

The claim that a united nation, or a great majority, would support any action Lloyd George might recommend to Parliament was ill-founded. The embarrassed vagueness concerning the kind and extent of force required, the evasiveness on the issue of war with Russia, and the exaggeration of a long-range into an immediate menace implicitly testified to the depth and strength of the desire for peace. What concerned the greater part of British opinion was not so much the justice of either the Polish or the Russian cause as it was the danger of involvement in any war. The masses, declared the evangelical *British Weekly* (August 12) whose opinion on such matters Lloyd George respected, "were simply stunned by the tocsin sounding to arms Friday morning [August 6]." When the *Times* and the *Daily Telegraph* compared the crisis with that of 1914, it protested that "such language found no echo among the people...war with Russia would be hateful to the working classes, and not to them alone." The Liberal press promptly hedged its recognition of the need to defend the independence of Poland. After the publication of Kamenev's letter of August 5, it was less convinced of the justice of Poland's case and, therefore, of the moral justification of serious risks in her behalf. In the *Manchester Guardian*'s (August 9) view, the Soviet government had affirmed its respect for her independence and territorial integrity. Until its actions disproved these professions, where, then, was the cause for war? The uneasiness of Liberal opinion was perhaps best expressed by the *Westminster Gazette*. How much better it would be, it wrote (August 9), if "the passion and resentment" against the Bolsheviks were eliminated and if it were possible to "imagine ourselves dealing with Russia as a Power among Powers." If reason were to prevail, "we must do that, and quickly." Poland's invasion of the Ukraine had been an "outrage," unless it was true "that Russia was outside the pale and entitled to no respect from her neighbours or benefit from the law of nations...." She was justified in repelling that attack, in taking "her own measures with the aggressor," and in dealing "directly with him, at all events in the armistice proposals." For two years, the Allies' treatment of Russia had been one "of half-war, half-peace, and incessant underground scheming" and it had been "utterly disastrous." They had involved themselves "in a network of duplicity, and [had] exposed themselves to the charge of abandoning and betraying those whom they had incited to do what they were unwilling or unable to do themselves." The Russians should be told "plainly that we will deal with them fairly and openly, and respect their institutions if they will respect ours." The *Westminster Gazette* warned the government of the grave difficulties it would encounter at home if it declared a state of war. It would be "grossly misled if it imagined that it could carry a united nation into a conflict with Russia."[40]

As an indictment of Poland and the Allies, the Liberal attitude owed its effectiveness to the complete neglect of Soviet Russia's revolutionary purposes, which, of course, should have suggested the gravest doubts as to the sincerity of its assurances. It was an illusion to think that a more business-like, above-board treatment of Russia would elicit a similar response from fanatical Bolsheviks, especially at a moment when the world revolution seemed within their grasp. If the Liberals were closer than the Conservatives to the truth in refusing to regard the menace as immediate, the Liberals were right for the wrong reasons, since the decisive defeat and swift recession of the Red Army, which were to follow in a matter of days, resulted from technical military factors and the failure of Lenin's calculations based upon the existence of revolutionary situations in Poland and Germany and not from any intentions of the Soviet government. In any case, Liberal opinion was content to express itself in accordance with tradition and constitutional practice in the press and in parliament.

The powerful Labor movement was, however, prepared to resort to unprecedented measures, even to "direct action," to prevent the country's involvement in war and also effective assistance to Poland. Although the Conservative press blamed its left-wing leaders, calling them British Bolsheviks—a charge that in some instances was not without foundation—and traitors to their country,[41] and complimented the sober leaders and the rank and file as loyal subjects, there was little room for doubt that Labor in general was prepared for unorthodox procedures. Pacifism was the compelling motive, but there were other reasons. Labor had emerged from the war with a mission to enhance the place of the working classes in the life and government of the country, a feeling of dedication, intensified by postwar economic problems, that was shortly to make it one of Britain's two most powerful political parties.

The situation was such as to impress upon Labor the apparent hopelessness of its aspirations under the coalition government.[42] The Commons, as constituted by the election of December 12, 1918, when wartime passions ran high, was profoundly Conservative as well as intensely nationalist. Harold Laski's low opinion, expressed in a letter to Justice O. W. Holmes of the United States Supreme Court, probably was typical of the attitude of the young intellectuals among the left-wing leaders. "I went," he wrote, "to a full dress debate in the House of Commons with the final impression that it was the worst legislature England has ever known. I suppose academic people like myself don't appreciate the business man as he should be appreciated, but there they were *en masse,* and they talked, as I thought, on a plane utterly unconnected with the world about us."[43] Labor had expressed distrust of its willingness or capacity to prevent adventurous decisions in imperial and foreign affairs well before the crisis in the Polish-Soviet war.[44] A group of Labor leaders had gone to Ireland to take evidence on the affairs of that unhappy land as a basis for the party's policy, and others made the famous visit to Soviet Russia, enterprises that must have convinced many that these problems were more complex than they had supposed. Wide apart as the members of the second delegation were in their assessment of the Bolshevik experiment, they agreed in a fervent endorsement of the Russian cause in the war with Poland and in urging the need of peace with Soviet Russia.[45]

In view of the strength of the peace sentiment in the country at large, it would have been strange if some Labor leaders had not seen in it a chance to enhance the party's fortunes, but this political motive in no way diminished the obvious sincerity of their desire of peace. When, however, George Lansbury's *Daily Herald* extended the purpose of the agitation to the blocking of all aid to Poland, it served the interests of Lenin's revolutionary foreign policy as much as, if not more than, the cause of peace. Lansbury, whose naive idealism and rejection of the imperfect social structure of the West had blinded him to the harsh realities of the Bolshevik regime, believed that Poland had sinned against humanity's best hope. The Russians, according to the *Daily Herald* (July 24) had "shown themselves conciliatory and generous to a fault." The government should warn the Poles "that they will get from the Allies not a single cartridge and not a single uniform." An effort to go to Poland's aid would paralyze the country and bring the government down within a week. If the Baranowicze meeting had not materialized the fault was exclusively the Poles.[46]

The *Daily Herald*'s appeal for organized resistance, however, does not seem to have brought much response until the first hint that the use of force might be necessary during Lloyd George's meeting with the Soviet representatives on August 4, and in the prime minister's promise the next day to consult Parliament before making any decision that might involve the country in war. On August 5, the *Herald* appealed to the workers to organize against the movement for war. It was their responsibility "to stop this insensate crime. . . . Get to work then. Pour in your resolutions. Let the Prime Minister know that you will not have this war—that you will down tools from one end of the country to the other rather than to fight a wanton war or allow one to be fought."[47] For the next five days, it sounded the call to passive resistance, even while Lloyd George was conferring with Millerand at Lympne. On August 7, a manifesto to the same effect appeared above the signature of Arthur Henderson, the Secretary of the Labor party, of nine Labor members of Parliament, and of seven other Labor leaders, including Ernest Bevin, of the Union of Dock Workers, and George Lansbury. Warning the public against "the possibility of drifting into war," it expressed the reasoned conclusion that there would be "no possibility of any wholehearted co-operation between the organized working people and the Government if and when any effort is made to involve us in another calamitous war."[48] Resolutions by the hundreds calling for "down tools" poured into Labor headquarters in London from trade union and Labor party meetings all over the country during the weekend of August 7-8.

An emergency meeting of the Parliamentary Committee of the Trade Union Congress, the National Executive of the Labor party, and the Parliamentary Labor party was held in the House of Commons on the evening of Monday, August 9. It resolved that the war in the process of manufacture was "an intolerable crime against humanity" to defeat which the entire industrial power of organized labor should be mobilized, that the affiliated executive committees should come to London when summoned to a national conference and that they should be empowered to give the signal to "down tools." These decisions should be carried out by a Council of Action to be organized at once, and a minority called for an immediate stoppage of work. A delegation that promptly became the Council of Action was named to present Labor's views to the prime minister the following day (August 10) before he made his statement to the House of Commons.[49] It comprised nineteen members, representing the Parliamentary Labor party, the

Parliamentary Committee of the Trade Union Congress, and the Executive Committee of the Labor party.

Although the *Morning Post* (August 9) had damned the Labor leaders who called for "down tools" as "British Bolsheviks," "traitors to their country," and their cause as "a call to revolution in this country," Lloyd George received the delegation at No. 10 Downing Street at noon, August 10. It included the left-wing Robert Williams and Margaret Bondfield, whose pro-Bolshevik sympathies had survived the visit to Russia, but they played no part in the proceedings. Rejecting a suggestion by William Adamson, the chairman, that an official record might be made of Lloyd George's remarks, the prime minister immediately blocked this effort to give the meeting the appearance of formal negotiations. The British government, he objected, was not yet a Soviet and his statement would be made that afternoon to the House of Commons.

Ernest Bevin, who spoke for the delegation, refused to be diverted, presenting Labor's views at length with something of the feeling for realities that distinguished his later career. He took no stock in the claim that the undeclared wars against Russia were caused by "the fear that Russia would overrun the world, because she did not have the power to do so." The principal responsibility rested in Paris and, more generally, in "an antipathy to a political policy or an economic system to which the other Powers had objections." Twice he mentioned the feeling of Labor and of British democracy that the Russians had not received "fair play" since the Bolshevik Revolution. Their treatment was "unparalleled in history." Bevin took particular pains to explain that the resolution adopted by the Joint Labor Conference was directed against measures short of open war, such as a blockade and the supplying of munitions, as well as "direct military action . . . the actual use of soldiers and sailors in actual fighting." An "enormous number" of resolutions, letters, etc., proved that Labor's stand expressed the views of the overwhelming majority of six million trade unionists. It was not against the government that Labor would act but against the reactionary forces that influenced its decisions. As to what it would do, Bevin would put his cards on the table and say that "if war with Russia is carried on directly in support of Poland or indirectly in support of General Wrangel there will be a match set to an explosive material the result of which none of us can foresee today."

From the questions that the prime minister pressed upon the Labor spokesman, it was clear that Lloyd George wished to pin Labor down in regard to Poland's independence and to ascertain whether it would strike against the sending "of a single pair of shoes" if the Soviet government did reveal the intention of destroying it. At first, Bevin replied that the question had not arisen, that "the independence of Poland," which Labor supported, "is not at stake," but when pressed further, he conceded that "Labour will consider its position when the occasion arises." When Lloyd George remarked, "Very well. That is quite good enough for me," Bevin insisted upon being understood as saying that Labor did not consider Polish independence as actually endangered. The prime minister agreed: "You need not make it clear to me, because I agree with you. I do not think it has arisen, but it will arise in one way or the other when the [Soviet government's] terms are known."[50]

If the Council of Action had hoped to convert the prime minister, his speech to the House of Commons later that day revealed its miscalculation. The council had blamed the Poles for the failure to arrange an armistice, but he said nothing about their calculated evasions and placed the whole responsibility upon the Soviet government. Of its designation of August 11 as the date for the Minsk negotiations, he said, "I cannot imagine that if there was a real desire to have an armistice, to stop fighting and to negotiate peace that the Soviet Government . . . would not have fixed a date a week or ten days earlier." The continued advance of the Red Army, betraying a preference for conquest to the guarantees that could be secured through negotiations, would imperil not only Poland's rights but the security of the Allies, since it would mean that Germany and Soviet Russia would be coterminous and that Soviet Russia was "an aggressive Imperialist State which is a menace to the freedom of the whole world." If the Poles were presented at Minsk with terms that were "absolutely inconsistent with the independence and existence of Poland as a free nation," "a very serious situation" would then arise. The Covenant of the League of Nations would be reduced to a scrap of paper if its members did not act under Article 10.

The steps the Allies would take were those he and Millerand had agreed upon at Lympne, including an economic squeeze "by naval action [by the British Navy] or international action or both" and material aid to Poland. Britain, Lloyd George added, would feel free to equip General Wrangel's forces, despite the earlier withdrawal of support. No troops would be sent, and the measures that might be taken would not mean war. Nevertheless, Lloyd George gave the House to understand that he was prepared even for war in circumstances which he defined in such a way as to make it difficult for the Laborites to object. "If they have a real desire for peace they can get it, but if they are out to challenge the institutions upon which the liberties of Europe and civilization depend, we shall meet them in the gate." A warning to the Poles showed, however, that he had not signed a "blank check" to cover anything they chose to do.

If they rejected the terms, which the Russians, as the victims of Poland's aggression, were entitled to exact, the Allies would not support the Poles.[51]

Lloyd George did his best to disillusion Labor about the Soviet regime. He quoted the reports of members of the Labor delegation that had visited Russia (and Bertrand Russell's) to show that the Soviets, instead of being a workers' government as Labor mistakenly believed, constituted an iron dictatorship in which the status of workingmen was not far from slavery. He found it difficult to reconcile Labor's attitude with its support of the self-determination of nations.

In the main, Labor's spokesmen stood their ground. If Tom Shaw and others had criticized bolshevism, that testified to the party's efforts to get at the truth, but the matter, in any event, was irrelevant to its case against the government's "intervention between Poland and Russia. Who had advised Poland? Who had armed her?" John R. Clynes agreed that the "independence of Poland" was "essential to the continued peace of the world," but he thought that "fine distinctions" existed as to the exact meaning of independence, although it would admittedly cease to exist if a form of government were forced upon Poland from the outside. No one would defend the delays for which Russia was responsible, but the Allies had also delayed the armistice with Germany for six weeks. "When Britain is the victor we assert our right, when the victor is Russia we cannot deny it."

In exploiting the weaker points in Labor's position, Lloyd George failed to deal with questions that bothered the Liberals as was evident when Herbert Asquith, the former prime minister, spoke. Poland, after all, had attacked first, and, though a member of the League of Nations, it had not thought of appealing to it as long as it was winning. The goal had been Poland's frontiers of 1772 even if it meant the conquest of immense territories with only a small minority of Poles. As for the Soviet regime, he doubted the consistency and wisdom of damning it "as an accursed thing" when in fact its representatives had been "for weeks and months in frequent and almost daily official or semi-official contact with His Majesty's Government." Moreover, he questioned the constitutionality of Lloyd George's procedure. Asquith had never heard of the House of Commons being asked to sanction "belligerent measures, for such they are or such they are about to be . . . upon a hypothesis which is not realized. . . ."[52]

Thanks to the government's overwhelming majority, a test would doubtless have been favorable to Lloyd George though with less support than usual, but a vote was never taken. Sometime during the day a message containing the terms the Soviet government claimed it intended to present to the Poles reached Kamenev. Although addressed to the British government, it was first given to the *Daily Herald* early enough for it to print a special edition that appeared on the floor of the House of Commons before the end of the debate. Meanwhile, Kamenev sent the message to Lloyd George who was perhaps called from the House to receive it.

The Soviet terms, as Lloyd George read them to the House, seemed to have been framed for the purpose of making it impossible for Poland to launch another offensive and of courting the friendship of a future Polish government if it would renounce imperialist adventures. Her troops —not Soviet Russia's as in Curzon's note of July 10—were to withdraw immediately fifty versts westward from the battle line at the time of the armistice or from the Curzon Line wherever they had not yet fallen back that far, and they were not to be reinforced or to receive war matériel from abroad during the period of the armistice. After Poland's complete demobilization within one month, her permanent army was to be limited "to one annual contingent of 50,000 men," plus 10,000 supplementary troops, and all arms and equipment were to be surrendered except such as were required for the needs of the above forces "as well as of the civic militia"—the sleeper phrase that was to play a decisive part later. Soviet Russia was to be given the control and use of a railroad running from her frontier to the Baltic, which of course meant an access to Danzig if not to the German frontier. On the other hand, an undefined number of Soviet troops would be withdrawn simultaneously with Poland's demobilization, and, on the assumption of a friendly Polish government, the number permanently stationed on the new frontier would be "considerably reduced and fixed at a figure to be agreed upon."

As for the political terms, the Russo-Polish frontier would, for the most part, follow the Curzon Line, but at certain specified points it would be extended further east giving Poland more territory than the Allies themselves had ever offered. Within these boundaries Poland would presumably be sovereign and independent. Nevertheless, some of the terms could evidently be used to influence her internal structure. In addition to the "friendliness" mentioned in connection with the possible reduction of the Soviet troops on the new frontier, there was also the railway under Soviet control, the provision that land should be given to the "families of all Polish citizens killed, wounded, or incapacitated by the war," and the statement in Kamenev's accompanying note that additional details might be added later. At first, nobody paid any attention to the apparently innocuous reference to a "civic militia."

In Lloyd George's view, these terms were not unduly severe in the existing circumstances and, as far as he could see immediately, did not threaten Poland's independence. After reading them to the House along with Kamenev's note, and after remarking that certain phrases would doubtless require closer definition, he explained that a telegram had been sent to the Polish, French, and, he thought, the Italian governments giving "our preliminary expression," and he agreed "that this created a new situation."[53] What he meant was, of course, that Poland should accept them as a basis for negotiation. According to an allegedly inspired statement to the Press Association, it was clearly intimated that, if the terms were *bona fide* "the British Government was of the opinion that the British people would not approve a declaration of war in order to obtain better terms for Poland."[54]

As both the Russian and the Polish authorities knew, in advance, these terms were not presented at Minsk, August 11, for the good reason that the Polish emissaries had not crossed the battle line. The strange actions of the Moscow wireless station on August 5 and 6 in failing to accept Sapieha's messages helped to place the responsibility upon the Soviet government, though in reality the Polish government was probably no more eager than the Soviets for the negotiations to begin as scheduled.

Meanwhile, important changes occurred in British opinion and policy in connection with Lloyd George's indirect approval of the Russian peace terms and Labor's program of "direct action." Even though somewhat reserved, the Conservatives joined in the general chorus of approval, adding to the weight of evidence for the general longing for peace. The worst that the *Times* (August 11) could say of the Soviets' peace terms was that they were "in some respects ambiguous and in others dangerously vague," and it reported a rumor "of a demand to be presented at Minsk for the establishment of a Soviet in Poland." The *Pall Mall Gazette* declared that the country was determined that peace should be made with Russia, provided that she renounced the aggressiveness that threatened all Europe.[55] Liberals anticipated no further difficulties in making peace. In the opinion of the *Manchester Guardian* (August 11), the Soviet government's record of "straightforwardness in its communications" was an assurance that the terms reflected its real intentions. The *Daily Chronicle* (August 11) captioned its editorial comments "Peace in Sight"; it welcomed the terms since they accepted the Curzon Line and did not threaten Poland's independence. Although the *Westminster Gazette* (August 11) deplored Lloyd George's moral indignation at Soviet methods as untimely in view of his efforts to "get on civil terms with the Bolsheviks," it discounted it as a sop to "the Churchillian wing of his own party."

The Russian terms of peace enjoyed, of course, the wholehearted approval of Labor's *Daily Herald* (August 11) which naturally credited itself with a victory. Fearing the worst from a government that retained the services of its favorite villain, Winston Churchill, from Lloyd George's threats of action, and from the way the Soviet government was immediately blamed for the failure of the Polish delegation to appear at Minsk on August 11, Labor continued its campaign for "direct action." The radical *Nation* (August 14) wrote enthusiastically of the "wonderful and spontaneous uprising of Labor against a new war" as "much the most significant event in our post-war history. . . ."[56] Thousands of meetings, including great open-air demonstrations, had taken place throughout the country, all inspired by a determination to defeat the "Churchill Putsch." The entire nation, it concluded with some exaggeration, "is ferociously opposed" to the war which the prime minister had talked about and that "Labor will not allow him to carry out. To do him justice, there is no reason to think that he himself desires it."

On the morning of August 13, more than a thousand delegates from all over Britain met as a National Labor Conference in Central Hall, Westminster, not far from Whitehall. They sang the "Red Flag," cheered the "new [Labor] diplomacy," and the solidarity of Labor. Its first resolution, adopted unanimously, approved the creation of the Council of Action. The motion to "down tools," if the Council of Action deemed it necessary, passed with an emotional unanimity that, so it seemed to Harold Laski, was "almost unexampled in Labor Congresses. For a moment after its unanimous passage, there was deadly silence. Then, as its significance became apparent, a cheer went up which might have penetrated into Downing Street, not five hundred yards away. . . ."[57] To some of the leaders, carried away by the emotionalism of these days, the possibilities apparently went far beyond the immediate crisis. J. H. Thomas, though he was not generally regarded as a member of the left-wing, allowed himself to say: "This resolution doesn't mean a mere strike. . . . It means a challenge to the whole constitution of the country."[58] This challenge to the constitution, if such it was, resulted from the fact, according to Laski, "that men have ceased to look to the present House of Commons either for common sense or courage."[59]

While the threat of direct action in the form of a general strike probably did not have the undivided support even of Labor, notwithstanding the Labor Convention's unanimity,[60] there is little doubt where the mass of opinion stood as between war and peace. The *Westminster Gazette* (August 14) suspected that "some very astute men" among the Labor extremists had seen an "opportunity of leading a movement in which public opinion is behind them," but it warned that "our politicians had better be alive to the fact that it [opinion] will accept Labour leadership in default of other leadership. What we are concerned with is no ordinary political movement. . . . Behind it is a deep distrust of Governments and Foreign Offices, and a prevailing sense of the helplessness of Parliaments."

Labor's action caused the Conservatives to permit the fear of revolution at home to overshadow their concern for the fate of Poland. The *Morning Post* expressed the views of the extremists with a pronounced anti-Semitic accent. The Council of Action was "the outpost of Russian Bolshevism in this country taking its orders from the Jews in Moscow. It is the London Soviet." The situation was intolerable. "To dally and to compromise is to lose all. And to lose it to whom? To a gang of foreign Jews, whose motive and inspiration are a mortal hatred of the British Empire and a fierce desire to destroy it."[61] To the supposedly better balanced weekly *Spectator* (August 14), the name "Council of Action" had a "sinister sound." It was an "impertinence" as well as "a challenge to representative government." Further reflection did not change the *Spectator*'s estimate of the danger. On August 21, it charged Labor with using the Polish-Russian War as a mere excuse for "getting the various sections of the Labour party to agree to a campaign of revolution." Field Marshal Sir Henry Wilson, for months a prophet of doom, advised Churchill, still the head of the War Office, that stern measures were necessary. In a note on the military problem arising from the Council of Action's challenge "in close touch and collaboration with the Bolsheviks," Wilson urged that it was a military necessity "to uncover the whole of this nefarious plot" and to explain "to the troops what it was that they were going to be called upon to fight . . . , otherwise I could not guarantee what would happen." Churchill, according to Wilson, wrote a minute "of uncompromising character," but, instead of sanctioning the psychological preparations for civil war that Wilson desired, the only concrete action the war minister urged was the expulsion of Kamenev and Krassin. At Churchill's request, Wilson then prepared a memorandum, in collaboration with Sir Basil Thomson and the director of Naval Intelligence on the connection between Kamenev and "some extremist members" of the Labor party.[62]

Meanwhile, the government launched a counteroffensive against Labor on two fronts. One purpose was to take the wind out of its sails by assuming an attitude of shocked innocence, another was to discredit the *Daily Herald*. There was really no occasion for Labor's excitement for everyone wanted peace. In his statement to the Commons, August 16, on the motion to adjourn, Bonar Law, the government's leader of the House, denied that the outburst of public opinion had "forced a change of policy." It was "not antagonistic to, but in support of our policy."[63] A sanely Conservative journal, the *Daily Telegraph* (August 16) had expressed substantially the same point of view. Labor was attacking a "bogey of their own creation." As for a war against Soviet Russia, "nobody in England is prepared to recommend that monstrous enterprise." Indeed, the press furnished the prime minister an effective figure of speech with which to drive home the government's innocence. Already on August 14, after J. H. Thomas' challenge to the constitution, Northcliffe's *Daily Mail* declared that "it challenges nothing and nobody. The Labor Conference is battering at an open door." It still saw no reason for concern on the morning of the sixteenth. A free people was not annoyed, it reasoned, "by threats of 'direct action' when we are ordered to take a course which we had already decided upon. If there is ever to be a clash with the 'revolutionists' in this kingdom, it will be time enough to set about it when they command us to do something which we are determined not to do." Later that day, replying to a Tory back-bencher, Lloyd George minimized the importance of Labor's action. "The swinging of a sledge hammer against an open door," he said, "is merely made for purposes of display." However, efforts to dictate the government's policy by industrial pressure struck "at the root of the democratic constitution of this country, and will be resisted by all of the resources at the Government's command."[64]

Neither stern warning nor lavish application of salve reassured an aroused Labor opinion, which was enjoying the feeling of popular support. Claiming to speak for all Labor members of the House, Captain James O'Grady declared that "we are not going to adopt any different policy until that suspicion has been absolutely removed. We are going to make sure, as far as we are concerned, that there is going to be no war with Russia on any pretext whatever, indirect or direct."[65]

Since the military threat to Warsaw seemed as acute as ever, for the Polish counteroffensive only began on August 16, Labor's threat of direct action almost certainly contributed to Lloyd George's change of heart and to the general repudiation of anything like intentions of war. The danger of civil disturbances, if it had ever existed, was probably over before the meeting of the National Labor Conference. When moderate leaders such as Clynes and Thomas professed a willingness to use unconstitutional methods, the sense of shock that ensued cost Labor much Liberal sympathy. The *Westminster Gazette* (August 19) remembered too well Churchill's questionable procedures in furthering the interventionist cause in Russia, the none too meticulous respect for the powers of Parliament on the part of Lloyd George's coalition government and of its majority in the House of Commons to be unduly critical, but it reminded Labor that if its threats had "apparent success at the present moment, it is because it has behind it a solid opinion to which the Government must defer." Other Liberal journals, appalled at the prospect of civil violence, were far less considerate.

There was, in the *Daily Chronicle*'s view (August 17), never any justification for action as if "a desperate situation required a desperate remedy." While it suspected that Clynes and Thomas never believed it would be necessary to make good their threats of unconstitutional action, they had forgotten that "sane and practical leaders in a period of change open sluices that sweep them away" by surrendering principles in order to obtain some immediately practical advantage. The *Manchester Guardian* (August 17, 18) went further and, forgetting its own recent charges of belligerent intentions, affirmed its full confidence in the government's peaceful purposes. In the country's unanimity for peace, Labor was an important factor but not the cause. "We are," it declared, "no friends of 'direct action,' or the threat of it, for political ends."

Meanwhile, the uncritical Bolshevist sympathies of George Lansbury, the editor of the *Daily Herald,* and of other left-wing Labor leaders rendered them extremely vulnerable to the charge of serving the interests of the Soviet government's revolutionary foreign policy. The Tory press, especially the *Morning Post,* called them "British Bolsheviks," charged them with treason, and dubbed the *Daily Herald* a Soviet organ, without, however, an appreciable effect upon Liberal opinion. Unwilling to widen the already dangerous social and political divisions within the nation, the government refrained from open measures against the left-wing Labor leaders, but it had been secretly accumulating evidence that might be used against them at a decisive moment. The *Daily Herald*'s shaky financial situation, the result of the failure on the part of the Labor party and the trade unions to provide it with sufficient working capital, resulted in Lansbury's dealings with the Soviet government for the purpose of securing money for the purchase of paper.[66] Over a period of months, Chicherin had exchanged a series of wireless messages with Litvinov relating to this matter, which, intercepted, came into the hands of the British Intelligence.[67] One that was especially damning was sent by Chicherin on July 11: "If we do not support the *Daily Herald,* which is now passing through a fresh crisis, paper will have to turn 'Right' Trade Union. In Russian questions it acts as if it were our organ."

After the meeting of the National Labor Conference, August 13, and its approval of a general strike on the call of the Council of Action, it was decided to give the incriminating documents to the press, and word to this effect was passed to the American and, presumably, the French embassies. On the following day, the former cabled Washington: "I am informed that on Tuesday [August 17] the British authorities intend to publish disclosures of subsidizing of *Daily Herald* by Bolshevik Government."[68] There was apparently a last minute delay, for, on the morning of August 18, Sir Basil Thomson told Field Marshal Sir Henry Wilson that "he was publishing this morning in America and in the *Temps* [Paris] certain wireless messages which showed the connection between the *Daily Herald* and the Bolsheviks." According to Wilson, the Cabinet had approved after references to Kamenev, which might have aroused a demand for his expulsion, had been eliminated.[69] These documents, preceded by a brief, factual statement, were printed by every important British newspaper on August 19 and, of course, were grist to the anti-Bolshevik and Tory press. That the Liberal newspapers refrained from editorial comment resulted, it may reasonably be supposed, from the fact that their disapproval of Lansbury's actions was neutralized by the government's obvious desire to discredit the Labor journal.[70] The *Daily Herald* (August 19) printed them too, along with Lansbury's statement describing the affair as a straight business transaction made necessary by a boycott of the *Daily Herald* by the dealers in newsprint. The pertinent documents, he said, were available to all in the *Daily Herald*'s office.

An even more flagrant "indiscretion," since it involved an illegal action, on the part of Francis Meynell, an associate editor, threw a curious light upon this "straight business transaction." He smuggled jewels of Russian provenance into Britain from Stockholm, but again, according to Lloyd George's letter to Ernest Bevin, the authorities, in this case the police, traced the payment of £75,000 to Meynell and Lansbury's son Edgar.[71] Despite this unfavorable publicity, and the government's efforts to discredit Labor's left-wing leadership, the Council of Action continued its activity, and if its effectiveness rapidly declined, the chief reason was the Polish victory on the Vistula.

3. *France's Recognition of General Wrangel*

In France, panic prevailed, for it seemed that the fruits of victory in the Great War and civilization itself were menaced as never before. An hysterical press conjured up the spectre of a fusion between the Red peril and the German danger at a time when France could no longer count upon its wartime allies. Fear that the Bolsheviks would advance to the Rhine and beyond spread throughout France.[72] "France," declared a columnist in an influential journal, "sees the Bolshevik danger for what it is, a revitalized and perfected Pan-Germanism. Germany is again preparing to use '*la révolution*' in her game."[73] Confidence in the determination of the Polish government to stand firm weakened, partly no doubt because Premier Witos was the head of the Peasant party and some of his associates were Socialists.[74] In any event, it was regarded as certain that the occupation of Warsaw would be followed immediately by the proclamation of a Soviet regime.[75] No one doubted that the Bolsheviks would eagerly enter into Germany's schemes. Foch was heard to say at Lympne that he expected them, once Poland was under their control, to offer Germany Danzig, the Corridor, and Upper Silesia.[76] The Red Army was reported to be fraternizing with the German frontier guards as it passed along the East Prussian frontier and to be including Germans in the formation of provisional local administrations, while in Berlin, *"le docteur Simons"* had rallied everyone "to his game and it is the *red card that is trump."*[77]

The realities were, in fact, quite different from what the frightened French thought. No doubt they did not exaggerate the Bolsheviks' designs, but it was with a "Red" Germany, not the existing bourgeois or a possible nationalist regime, that the Bolsheviks wished to work for they still cherished the illusion of an imminent world revolution. Moreover, blinded by traditional suspicions and wartime passions, the French were unable to assess the German attitude accurately. They were, as Theodor Wolff, the editor of the liberal *Berliner Tageblatt* (August 13), observed in connection with the review of the provincial press in the *Temps* (August 17), deceived by "frightening nightmares" into thinking that the Bolsheviks would be able to enlist the Germans in their cause, unless the latter were driven to the extremes of despair. There were extreme nationalists, like Reventlow, whose program of repression of Communists at home and co-operation with the Soviets abroad attracted considerable but, for the most part, unfavorable attention[78] and the handful of National Bolsheviks which even Moscow viewed askance. While the economic ties that were publicly advocated by Victor Kopp, the Soviet agent in Berlin, which as the *Berliner Tageblatt* (August 13) agreeably conceded might in time acquire political significance, had a more favorable reception, German policy and opinion were firmly neutral except in regard to Poland. "But we are convinced," wrote Wolff for his British readers, "that Poland, in the form which has been given it, is strangling our life without living herself, and therefore it must be reasonably organized."[79]

Oppressed by a sense of the gravest danger, French opinion awaited the results of Millerand's conversations with Lloyd George at Lympne with exaggerated expectations. Surely the decisions would be equal to the needs of the crisis. The firebrand, Gustave Hervé, supposed that Millerand would show how a division of troops from each of the Allies would have assured a solution a year earlier, how the necessary quota had since risen to an army corps, and how a complete army might be required from each in the future if the Allies' hesitation continued.[80] Few, however, went so far in openly approving direct military intervention. In the *Matin's* view (August 8), the conference's task would be to devise an adequate defense for the major areas threatened by the Red Army—Poland, Czechoslovakia, Rumania, and the Near East—and to agree upon a common policy as to an acceptable settlement with Soviet Russia as well as to the ultimate form, unitary or federal, of a future Russia.

In comparison with these French expectations, the actual results, as Lloyd George explained them to the House of Commons, August 10, were disappointing. "This program," wrote the *Journal des débats* (August 11), "is certainly far from brilliant and its efficacy is doubtful." Criticism was, however, pointless, since active measures should have been decided upon some six or seven weeks earlier. Even the most authoritative journals conceded that there could be no question of the commitment of Allied troops. Armed intervention, the *Temps* acknowledged, "would be impossible and would add the obstacles of 1813 [German nationalism] to those of 1812 [Russian nationalism]."[81] Pertinax's substitute denied in the *Écho de Paris* (August 12) that Lloyd George had spoken for France; his manner of applying the Lympne agreements was not at all what she had envisaged. His speech proved that he had not understood the menace that civilization faced as France did and he had passed over the German peril in "disdainful silence." Pierre Bernus felt that Lloyd George's mind had not changed in regard to Russia since the beginning of 1919 and the Prinkipo affair.[82]

This regretful acceptance changed, for the most part, to embittered rejection of the armistice terms as Lloyd George read them to the House of Commons.[83] It is true that advanced leftist opinion did not share this negative reaction. Already, Marcel Sembat, L. Frossard, and others had signed a manifesto in the Socialist *humanité* (August 12) hailing the victorious advance of the Red Army "which carried with it the emblem of the regeneration of the world" and declaring that the Entente had recoiled before the power of the proletariat at Lympne.[84] But for all who believed that France's interests required a strong Poland, there was little good that could be said for these terms, even before the Russians spelled out what they meant by a "civic militia," and least of all for Lloyd George's advice to Poland. Pierre Bernus expressed the general feeling when he wrote that they meant "nothing less than the submission of a disarmed Poland to the permanent domination of her neighbors."[85] No more than the Poles were the French, who counted upon them to check both Soviet Russia and Germany and to keep them divided, prepared to accept the limitation of the Polish Army.[86] Moreover, the requirements for the distribution of free land and the Russian control of a Polish railway seemed effective means of Bolshveik subversion should, by any chance, the Russians decide to respect the forms of Polish sovereignty. Still more objectionable, because it seemed to foreshadow Lloyd George's return to his favorite scheme for an international conference, was his communication of the terms to Poland with the scarcely veiled advice to accept them, and French pride resented his acting without prior consultation. From the talk in Britain that the conference should seek a firmer basis for the general peace of Europe and that Germany should be represented,[87] arose the spectre of the revision of the Treaty of Versailles,[88] a development that the French government was determined to prevent at all costs.

In the panicky atmosphere of Paris, the danger was real that an ill-considered decision would be made to get back at Lloyd George immediately. Such a decision had in fact been held in reserve since the British had first formally proposed a conference in Curzon's note of July 19 to Chicherin. Two days later, Millerand replied by telling the Chamber of Deputies that the French government was considering the *de facto* recognition of General Wrangel, but in fact nothing was done about it during the next three weeks. At 10:00 A.M. on the morning of August 11, the day after Lloyd George's speech in the House of Commons, the French Cabinet decided to announce publicly and immediately Wrangel's recognition as the chief of the *de facto* government of south Russia. The reasons, according to the official communiqué, were his effective control of the territory under his control and his acknowledgment of responsibility for Russia's international debts. In order to avoid the appearance of a direct challenge to Lloyd George, it was explained that his communication to Poland and his conditional endorsement of Russia's terms were not officially known to the French government until more than two hours after the Cabinet had approved Wrangel's recognition.[89] But even the communiqué, in saying that France's commercial representative in London had been instructed to have no contact with Kamenev and Krassin, registered openly the divergence between French and British policies.[90] Moreover, it is likely that action was taken in Warsaw to neutralize the effect of Lloyd George's advice. According to a well-informed American press correspondent, the French government "has sent to the Polish Government a note advising it not to accept the Bolshevist peace terms as endangering the independence and life of Poland."[91] This assertion of France's independence was no doubt gratifying to French pride and especially so to the many critics of Lloyd George and his alleged submission to Labor pressure. "Must the Entente Cordiale," asked Henry de Jouvenel, "be subordinated to Lloyd George's electoral policy?"[92]

In reality, Wrangel's recognition turned out to be little more than an empty gesture, whatever prestige the presence of a French diplomatic agent might imply. The French made it perfectly plain that it meant, in terms of active assistance, nothing more than increased shipments of arms which in the end proved insufficient to save him. There was never any question of the commitment of French troops. The *Temps* (August 11) had already ruled it out of the realm of practical politics. A few days later (August 15), it dismissed *"une expédition de Russie"* as an "absurd legend." If it became "necessary to defend Poland, it will be done in the West, not in the East." The nationalist *Écho de Paris* (August 17) denied that France, any more than Britain, was going "to send our troops to fight on distant soil."

Besides those who expressed only the prevalent war weariness, there were many who doubted the wisdom of what the Millerand government had done. Its independence looked too much like isolation, even for some who perhaps shrugged off Anatole France's lament at the loss of France's wartime allies as the opinion of a Socialist and a *littérateur*.[93] André Tardieu, Clemenceau's disciple and spokesman, had probably already completed a blistering attack upon Millerand's encouragement of Poland's imperialism (which Clemenceau had restrained) and Millerand's failure to retain the leadership of Allied policy (which Clemenceau had maintained) until the Lympne Conference, by which time he had lost many trump cards.[94]

Some were foresighted enough to doubt that Wrangel's recognition would accomplish any practical results. According to Phillippe Millet, the foreign affairs expert of the *Petit Parisien* and editor of the weekly *Europe nouvelle,* it might well throw Soviet Russia into the arms of Germany. "But who are the Soviets today? Russia herself."[95] Jacques Bainville, the nationalist publicist and historian, attacked the basic principles of French policy since the end of the Great War. In his view, it was a delusion to think that the border states could be built up as an effective bulwark against both Germany and Russia. As the strongest of them, Poland's experience was decisive: "The barrier is a joke. The 'rampart' is made of flowers. Attacked from one side alone, Poland could not defend herself. Suppose she had been attacked simultaneously by Russia and Germany." He agreed, however, that the Soviet threat could only be countered by moving into Germany from the Rhine. "The Bolsheviks strike at us through the Poles. We will strike at them through the Germans."[96] The French were serious about Germany, but not in their support of Wrangel. His recognition had no appreciable effect upon events in Poland or in Russia, since it did not enable him even to defend himself successfully. It meant, however, a continued irreconcilable hostility toward Soviet Russia and the repudiation of Lloyd George's policy.

So surprised and astounded were official British circles, including Lloyd George, at the first news of the French recognition of Wrangel, that its authenticity was doubted.[97] Doubt was soon dispelled, but scarcely a voice was raised in favor of following France's example. In the Tory press, only the *Morning Post* (August 12) approved her action and urged that Britain should do likewise, thereby earning the accolade of the *Temps* for defending French policy.[98] Ardently pro-French as the *Times* was, it nevertheless regarded Wrangel's recognition as a regrettable mistake.[99] The *Daily Telegraph* (August 14) feared that Millerand had helped the Soviet regime to pose as the champion of Russian nationalism against foreign intervention, and later (August 16) it aligned itself with Lloyd George. "If the Russians are content to lie passive under the communist régime, that is their affair; if they wish to get rid of it they must do so by their own exertions. We could, indeed, only help them effectually by going to war with the Soviet, and nobody in England is prepared to recommend that monstrous enterprise." The *Evening Standard* addressed some plain words to "our friends across the Channel." Not only did Britain lack the men and money for a war, but France was worse off than she was. "Does she feel able to assume alone the large burdens of a war with the Soviet government?" On the condition that Soviet Russia renounced the aggressiveness that threatened all Europe, Britain, declared the *Pall Mall Gazette,* was determined "to make peace with Russia."[100]

With the exception of Labor, British opinion appreciated the importance of maintaining the Entente with France, but not, according to the Liberal press, at the price of yielding in regard to Russia. If all went well at Minsk, Britain intended, wrote the *Manchester Guardian* (August 12), to open trade with Russia and to refer all outstanding differences with her to an international conference. Everything possible should be done to heal the breach "but we cannot go back on decisions already made." Later, the *Guardian* put the matter more definitely: "France has gone her way in this great business. We shall go ours."[101] The *Daily Chronicle* (August 13)—under the caption "A Policy which is not Britain's"—also regretted the differences that divided the Entente, but the British people were united as never before in opposition "not merely to a war with Russia, but to the continuation of the old illogical policy of a war which was not a war." If France supported one Russian party against another, she would do so alone.

As was to be expected, the reactions of radical opinion were still more unpalatable from the French point of view. There was, in the weekly *New Statesmen's* opinion (August 14), a real cleavage, a profound difference rooted in principle between the two nations on policy toward Russia, "due to different aims and a fundamentally different outlook." While co-operation was possible in other matters, it was pointless to manufacture an artificial reconciliation on this issue. To the *Nation* (August 14), the situation simplified the prime minister's problem: "We are now free to go our [way]," but it was by no means certain of his steadfastness (after all, he had not dismissed Churchill) since his opposition to armed intervention had always been based upon doubts as to its success and not upon principle.[102]

The Labor *Daily Herald* (August 12) at once sensed "the sinister figure of Foch" who "thirsts for more bloodshed. If the Poles will not serve his purpose, there is still Wrangel." In view of its campaign for "direct action," it would never do to allow France's action to unite opinion behind Lloyd George. It therefore asked "where does Mr. Lloyd George stand in reference" to the war "his French accomplice" was waging "for the restoration of capitalism in Russia." He would have to choose between France and peace with Soviet Russia. "He will trick us, this Premier, if we allow him. He will trick us, if he can into war, at the bidding of the Paris politicians."[103]

If British Labor suspected Lloyd George of belligerent purposes, the French drew the opposite conclusion from pretty much the same evidence. The peace he sought, most of them were convinced, could only be attained by sacrifices vital to France's interests.[104] This, in the prevailing mood of semi-panic, they were determined to prevent at any price. In recognizing General Wrangel without the will or the means of assuring his success or even survival, they ignored the obvious lesson of the Allies' intervention on behalf of his predecessors as R. W. Seton-Watson pointed out most clearly. "It does not seem to occur to the French Government or to the irresponsible backers of General Wrangel in England that the sole condition on which they have any right to 'recognize' him is their unquestionable ability—and will—to see him through his difficulties without flinching. Such ability they do not possess; nor have they ever possessed it."[105]

If the French gambled on events to rally Great Britain—and they dreamed also of American support—even Poland's surprising last-minute victory on the Vistula was to have quite different results, and the immediate effect was to solidify British opinion behind that peace policy which the French regarded as most dangerous. A London weekly, hitherto sympathetic to France and firmly anti-Bolshevik, insisted that the essence of the agreement between Lloyd George and Millerand was "that military and semi-military enterprises should be abandoned and that we should try round a conference table to achieve a general peace."[106] What Lloyd George's views were in detail are still unknown, but the French press usually turned to J. L. Garvin's *Observer* for indications of British policy.

What it read in its columns of August 15 must have confirmed its worst fears. Britain, Garvin wrote, did not wish "to constrain our neighbor," who had just declared "theoretical war" against Russia; "Neither shall we be constrained"; and "Our unalterable aim is the restoration of full world-peace by definite constructive steps. The Russian peace is only the first. . . ." France must accept as a fact "the status of Russia as a Great Power and as the paramount factor in the affairs of all Eastern Europe. That is the rather mighty truth which the Quai d'Orsay will have to recognize if French policy desires that a single scrap of the Treaty of Versailles shall remain. Much of it will have to go in any case, but something might still be permanently saved by a ruthless return to sanity."[107] Since Italy could be expected to follow the British lead, it was difficult to see how the recognition of Wrangel had improved France's position.

4. *America Takes Her Stand: The Colby Note, August 10, 1920*

Among the reasons why Europe seemed unable to cope with an apparently mortal danger, the inability of the anti-Bolshevik countries to co-operate effectively against it, as Lenin asserted, was undoubtedly decisive. Each had what it considered to be more vital interests. Germany would not lift a finger to save Poland or to aid the victors; the Allies, war-weary and exhausted, carefully rationed their aid to the White Russians and the Poles and finally differed sharply among themselves as to the proper policy toward Russia and Poland. In these circumstances, it was natural that the protagonists of these divergent views turned to the United States for assistance in one form or another, in spite of its well-known reversion into isolationism. Poland sought, to no avail, a double advantage, a measure of military assistance from Britain and a concrete financial tie with the United States by offering to take over a small part of the British war debts in order to facilitate the payment of a prospective British volunteer force. The reply was a flat refusal on the ground that the proposal involved what amounted to a loan which Congress would reject.[108] As the policy differences between Great Britain and France over Poland and Russia became increasingly acute, each turned to Washington for support against the other and perhaps, in the case of France, for more concrete aid against Russia.

In Britain, where the public was far better informed about the American scene than in France, there were few illusions about America's return to active participation in European affairs. Nevertheless, on August 5 (as noted in an earlier chapter) Lloyd George appealed to President Wilson in a private letter for his support of, and America's participation in, an international conference in which Soviet Russia would be represented, not so much in connection with the forthcoming conversations with Millerand as in the longer view.[109] There is no reason, however, for thinking that calculations regarding the United States seriously affected British policy or opinion during the hectic fortnight that followed. In the case of France, while there was apparently no similarly direct appeal, greater hopes were placed in the president and in the United States, and not without reason, despite the ailing president's dislike of France's German policy.

Since the Paris Peace Conference, Wilson had become more definitely anti-Bolshevik, and American opinion, as shown in the recent Red Scare and by the major newspapers, notably the *New York Times,* had been among the first to sense the potential danger of bolshevism. While there was a certain amount of criticism of Poland's conduct and also of the Allies' toward Soviet Russia, the prospect of a decisive Bolshevik victory aroused grave concern. For example, Frederic Wile, in the Republican *Public Ledger* of Philadelphia, attributed the appearance of Soviet Russia as a military menace to the "Polish aggression against Russian territory, aided and abetted by the Allies" with the consequence that even anti-Bolshevik Russians had rallied to the defense of the fatherland, and a southern Democratic journal, the Knoxville (Tennessee) *Sentinel* reported the feeling of many that "Poland does not come into the court of conscience with clean hands."[110] Like the British Liberals, the *New Republic* (August 11) blamed the Poles for the failure to end the war. They regarded an armistice with extreme aversion, "hoping against hope that the British and the French might . . . send armies to check the Russian advance," but it admitted the probable existence in Russia of "a party that would welcome the declaration of a holy war." Despite these doubts about Poland's case, the prospect of a decisive Bolshevik victory excited grave concern. "Until Lenine [*sic*] and Trotsky are shorn of military power," wrote Wile after his criticism of Poland, "Western civilization will sit enthroned on a powder-barrel." Cartoonists pictured a valiant but weak Poland defending the Western world against the onslaught of oriental hordes.[111] In the *Literary Digest*'s probably well-founded opinion, most newspaper editors, however, did not favor more than the moral support of Poland on the ground that her defense was a European problem which Europeans should solve.

So great was the apparent need that Frenchmen concentrated upon the abundant evidence that Americans felt like themselves about bolshevism and Soviet Russia. The *Matin* (August 4) insisted that President Wilson's views on bolshevism had completely changed and that "America will not be indifferent if the Bolsheviks threaten Europe." It also noted the concern of her bankers and businessmen about the loans advanced to the Russian provisional government in 1917 as an interest that united the two countries. In fact, the authoritative *Temps,* since the last days of July, more than once advocated co-operation with the United States as a desirable and feasible alternative to further involvement in Lloyd George's policies.

More recently, however, the French Embassy, in the absence of distinguished and respected Ambassador Jules Jusserand, then in France (he served as France's diplomatic representative on the special Allied Mission to Warsaw) was responsible for an incident that diminished any inclination of the president and the Department of State to do France a favor of any kind. Its new counsellor, Count de Galard de Béarn, acting as chargé d'affaires, went to the White House instead of the Department of State, as was the recognized diplomatic procedure, to transact business, the purport of which cannot now be determined, but presumably to establish direct communication with the president.[112] At any rate, the ill and sensitive president took offense, although Under-Secretary of State Norman Davis discounted it as the result of inexperience or pure ignorance and wrote in reply of "our very deep resentment."[113] It was France's ill fortune to have as its chief spokesman in Washington at the peak of the crisis a man so poorly regarded in the highest circles.

As in western Europe, the capture of Warsaw and the establishment of a Soviet government there were regarded as imminent in Washington during the early days of August.[114] There was even a hint of panic in the press report (or were they trial balloons?) of sentiment in official quarters in favor of a military assistance to Poland, and some senators were said to favor a special session of Congress.[115] In the *Washington Post* (August 6), Albert M. Fox, a columnist, attributed to Secretary of State Colby the statement that the situation was fully as serious as the press was reporting it to be, but there was, of course, no chance at all for the calling of Congress into special session on the Polish question. Nevertheless, something like a crisis atmosphere prevailed in official circles, one indication of which was President Wilson's conversion to the desirability of at least a gesture on the part of the American government. Hugh Gibson, home on leave from his post in Warsaw, had urged (in a memorandum that Secretary of State Colby sent to the White House on July 18) that the president should make a brief statement showing where he stood on bolshevism, Russia, and Poland. In a personal note, Colby seconded this recommendation, arguing that "it could not fail to exert a beneficial effect upon public opinion in Poland, and would tend to steady a situation which at the moment is disturbed and perilous."[116] The president replied two days later that he "would be glad to do anything that I thought would be effective in assisting her [Poland]" but he sadly added that he hesitated to act "because I think the time has passed when personal intervention on my part or suggestion in regard to foreign politics would be of service."[117]

During the following weeks, as the Red Army crossed the Curzon Line and penetrated into the heart of Poland, the State Department inundated the White House with telegrams having any significance in regard to the crisis. On August 6, Secretary of State Colby and Under-Secretary Norman H. Davis conferred with the president in the White House for more than an hour. Although no official statement was published as to the subjects discussed or the decisions reached, the press revealed that some sort of intervention had been decided upon. The correspondents were told that they had taken earlier declarations of inability to act too literally. "Today," wrote one, "it is assumed that a way may be found of helping Poland in her straits and at the same time checking the spread of Bolshevism."[118] Whatever the results of the White House conference may have been, the State Department suddenly awoke to the fact that its knowledge of the diplomatic background was incomplete, for Colby, on the following day, August 7, called upon the embassy in London to cable "the full text of all exchanges between London and Moscow regarding the Polish situation." Actually, however, Colby acted before this information arrived.[119]

Meanwhile, De Béarn, at the French Embassy, watched for evidence of the State Department's intentions after the White House conference. He apparently made no direct inquiries; he seems to have searched Albert M. Fox's columns in the *Washington Post* for clues. They were unpleasant reading, for if they were true, France could expect little that was good. In view of France's fears of Lloyd George's projects for an international conference, Fox's column of August 5 must have been hair-raising: ". . . the question has arisen of revising the Versailles Treaty and removing the unreal and academic features which have been the constant source of trouble," and the United States would, according to administrative officials, "attend a conference for this purpose."[120]

Although it is not known that De Béarn reported this certain inaccurate item to the Quai d'Orsay, he did so in connection with Fox's more sensational copyrighted article of August 7. It contained a mishmash of sound information and rumor. In summarizing the results of the White House conference, it was doubtless correct in saying that American policy "toward the Russian conflict and the Bolshevik menace" had been decided and that an important declaration by the Allies and the United States or by the United States alone could be expected "in the near future." Fox then indicated, in general terms, what in fact were to be the main points of the Colby note of August 10: an assurance of America's friendship for the Russian nation, a declaration against the partition of its prewar territorial possessions, and a statement in "unmistakable opposition" to the recognition of "the Soviet government and all that bolshevism implies." But in discussing the immediate problem of the Russo-Polish war, Fox attributed views of a decidedly different complexion to State Department officials. The original Polish aggression had rallied the Russians to the defense of their country at a time when the Bolshevik military machine had been rapidly approaching complete disintegration. The Red Army, now "a real and tremendous power, . . . is Bolshevik in name but Russian national in composition." In conclusion, Fox quoted a former Tsarist army officer who had been a member of an Imperial Russian Mission to the United States: "The spirit of the Russian Army today is the spirit of the American Army of 1776 and Brussilov is its Chief of Staff [*sic*]."

Count de Béarn's telegram on this article, which apparently reached the Quai d'Orsay during the night of August 9-10 (that is on the eve of Lloyd George's speech), had a staggering effect upon "French official circles."[121] This reaction was a symptom of the prevailing panic caused by the apparently impending fall of Warsaw, increasing tension in Anglo-French relations, and Italy's acceptance of Lloyd George's policy.[122] It must therefore have seemed that France's isolation at this dangerous moment was about to be sealed by an unfriendly American declaration. As an American newspaper published in Paris put it, "tension in France over the fate of Poland and its attendant possibilities for France has been growing almost hourly. The French are perceiving a new peril, greater than any since 1918, and they are becoming sensitive to any outside influence tending to aid the forces that constitute their danger."[123]

Taking their cue from a possibly misplaced emphasis in De Béarn's dispatch upon the nationalist and patriotic reaction in Russia to the war with Poland as foreshadowing in part the content of the American declaration, officials of the Quai d'Orsay resorted to an overly clever maneuver to smoke out Washington's true intentions. They gave the press a much abbreviated and distorted version of Fox's article for publication in the morning newspapers of August 10, representing it as a communiqué from the American government. While the *New York Herald* (Paris edition) covered itself by saying, "The summary given out by the Foreign Office follows,"[124] a number of Paris journals carried it as a Washington dispatch, dated August 9.[125] The English version, which was a substantially accurate translation of the French text announced, "The American Press publishes a communiqué concerning the policy of the United States in the Russo-Polish conflict, according to which declaration the Russian Army of the present moment is Bolshevist because Lenin is at the head of the Moscow Government, but it is really and essentially a Russian Army." By identifying General Brusilov as the Chief of Staff of the Red Army, it copied Fox's error, but it added something that his article had not contained in saying, "It can be admitted that they have no wish to sacrifice the sovereignty of Poland." It faithfully described, as Fox had, American policy as desirous of preserving Russia's territorial integrity until the Russian people were able to settle their own problems, but it ignored completely the forecast of a sharp declaration against bolshevism.[126]

Apparently informed at once by the press corps in Washington, the State Department immediately issued a denial which, however, failed to allay the outraged reaction of French opinion, although it reached Paris in time to be published that evening (*Temps*, August 11).[127] The *Matin* (August 10) detected the president's style (!) in the communiqué and tied it up with the White House conference on August 6. The American chargé at once reported the *Matin*'s reaction and also the *Figaro*'s (August 10): "Are we dreaming? Has Mr. Wilson forgotten [that the] Versailles treaty is his work?" In the *Journal* (August 10), Saint Brice wrote: "Mr. Wilson has just issued a communiqué which goes even further than the British plea by acknowledging that the Russian offensive against Poland was justified. This is fine support for Lloyd George but what a disappointment for the Poles and the champions of European peace."[128] As for the State Department's denial, even the sober *Temps* (August 11) noted that it did not cover the White House and the president.

Needless to say, this piece of sharp practice was not well received in Washington. The next day, August 11, Secretary of State Colby, protested to the Paris embassy that the press statement was "wholly unfounded," that De Béarn's dispatch had been based upon "an erroneous and irresponsible press item," the text of which he had misread "without verifying it at the Department." The French Foreign Ministry, however, was also at fault, and Harrison was to "express to the Foreign Office the feeling of surprise on the part of this Government that the Foreign Office should venture to issue any statement, whether authentic or not, declaratory of this Government's policy."[129] By the time Harrison saw Maurice Paléologue, the Secretary General of the Quai d'Orsay, to carry out this instruction, the famous Colby note had transformed the atmosphere in official circles toward the American government. Paléologue was apologetic, yet he was less than candid when he explained that the trouble was entirely the result of a mistake of De Béarn in Washington and the press section of the Foreign Ministry in Paris in omitting quotation marks from a Washington news item.[130] Only the statement of the Tsarist officer about the spirit of the Russian Army had in fact been set off from the rest of Fox's article by quotation marks.[131] For a while it seemed that De Béarn would suffer for the folly for which he was perhaps not chiefly responsible. His "callow, irresponsible conduct" made him, according to a permanent official of the State Department, A. A. Adee, "clearly *persona non grata*," but in the end nothing was done to secure his removal from Washington.[132]

As far as the American attitude toward bolshevism and the Soviet government was concerned, France's alarm was needless. Since the White House conference of August 6, at least, the Department of State had been working on a formal policy declaration in regard to which the French action had no other effect than, perhaps, to eliminate France as its primary recipient and to hasten its delivery and publication. Despite the fact that the point of view of his own government was almost its complete opposite, Italian Ambassador Avezzana was the obvious choice after his convenient inquiry concerning the attitude of the American government, of which the papers of the State Department apparently have no direct record.[133] If August 10 was chosen as the time to announce American policy, the reason was perhaps as much the danger that Lloyd George's accommodating attitude toward Soviet Russia might prevail as a desire to correct the unfortunate impressions arising from France's ill-conceived stratagem. In any event, on this date Secretary of State Colby answered Avezzana in a note that was also sent as a circular to all American diplomatic missions in the major countries involved in the Russian and Polish problems, and the full text was then communicated to the press in Washington and other capitals.

Colby's note was a hard-hitting, comprehensive statement that followed the Bolshevik precedent in jettisoning the customary restraint of the language of diplomacy. On the question of Soviet Russia's international standing, it minced no words. The United States government could not recognize "the present rulers of Russia as a Government with which the relations common to friendly governments can be maintained. . . ." The United States was convinced, "against its will, . . . that the existing regime in Russia is based upon the negation of every principle of honor and good faith, and every usage and convention, underlying the whole structure of international law. . . ." Its leaders had boasted of their willingness to sign treaties without the least intention of carrying them out, and those that might be concluded with non-Bolshevik governments had no moral force. Moreover, the Third International, heavily subsidized by the Soviet government, aimed at "the promotion of Bolshevik revolutions throughout the world," and the Soviets' diplomatic agencies would undoubtedly devote themselves to their preparation.

Concerning immediate problems, the note declared in effect for the French rather than the British position. After affirming the American people's earnest solicitude for "Poland's political independence and territorial integrity," the government's intention to employ "all possible means" to preserve them, and the absence of objections to an armistice, it aimed a heavy blow at Lloyd George by declaring that the United States would not "at least for the present, participate in any plan for the expansion of the Armistice negotiations into a general European conference," which would almost certainly lead to the recognition of the Bolshevik regime and the dismemberment of Russia from which "this country strongly recoils." These points, opposition to a conference with Soviet Russia represented and support of Russia's territorial integrity, merely repeated the earlier confidential note of August 2, but now they were announced to the world. Except for Finland, Poland, and Armenia, the determination of Russia's frontiers should be adjourned until the Russian people regained control of their own affairs. From the French point of view, it was a most satisfactory pronouncement, except for its silence in regard to General Wrangel and, above all, in regard to what America would do to assure the triumph of its excellent principles.[134]

As in France's *de facto* recognition of General Wrangel, there was nothing in the Colby note itself and little in the reactions of American opinion to encourage the hope of concrete action. In practice, the reference to "all possible means" to assure Poland's independence and integrity meant little. While surplus war and other supplies worth some millions of dollars had been sold at a discount and on easy credit terms to the Polish government, its request for indirect financial assistance had been rejected, and the American government wisely discouraged any effort to send war material to Poland across Germany. There was, as the *New York Times* was informed, little prospect that the blockade of Soviet Russia would be reimposed or that the United States would furnish Poland either munitions or loans. The administration felt that the note was far as it could go. It was not a trial balloon; it was "the last word of this government with reference to the manner in which it will participate in the handling of the serious questions involving Polish independence and Bolshevist rule in Russia."[135]

Those who drafted the Colby note were obviously even more concerned about Russia than with Poland, and it was this aspect which made it one of the most important papers in the history of American foreign policy. Despite the efforts of mavericks like Raymond Robins and Senator Borah on behalf of recognition, it set American policy on a non-recognition course until Franklin D. Roosevelt reversed it in 1933, and it undoubtedly expressed an always important, although not always dominant, trend of American opinion since 1920. By a curious paradox, some of those who most ardently cherished the moral approach to politics implicitly denied its applicability, at least in Colby's version, to relations with Soviet Russia.

The radical *Nation* (August 21), for example, declared that the note "serves to perpetuate strife on earth and ill-will among men . . . it is for us to do business with them and to stop the moral posing which has already done us and Russia so much harm." The isolationist view was expressed in the hard-shell Republican press; the government was meddling in matters that were not its proper concern.[136] While some hoped, on the basis of a possibly exaggerated estimate of the influence of President Wilson's pronouncements in bringing about the German Revolution and the downfall of the imperial regime, that the note would act as a signal for the Russian people to rise and overthrow the Bolshevik despotism,[137] the Associated Press was doubtless justified in seeing another and more attainable purpose. The proposed London conference "which was to have dealt with the Soviet delegates with the possibility of the political recognition of the Bolsheviki has faded into improbability."[138]

There was, in addition to the freezing of American foreign policy in regard to Russia, a larger objective, which in fact was not attained; the note, according to a well-informed press correspondent, was expected "to serve as a rallying point of sound and determined principle." In other words, it was in considerable part an attempt to enlist peoples and governments in a sort of moral blockade of Soviet Russia, a tacit non-intercourse pact that would put the Bolsheviks under the moral ban of Western civilization. From this position to a call for a new crusade was no great step which this correspondent, inspired perhaps by some indiscreet official's loose talk, was ready to take but which was certainly not to the taste of the great majority of Americans. "It is," he wrote, "the first time that Communism, as an active world danger . . . has been denounced and repudiated." The note had "the same impress of treating the greatest world issues as the historic challenge to German Kaiserism which President Wilson voiced in the famous utterance of 1917. Now America has come out as the champion of democracy, warning the world of the mortal danger which threatens it in the form of militant Communism. There can be no understanding between Sovietism and democracy, and there can be no conciliation between military autocracy and Americanism."[139]

Having launched his thunderbolt, it was good practice for Colby to assess its effect abroad, and the diplomatic missions were instructed to report the reactions of press and opinion. A unanimous acceptance of America's lead, or even a strongly favorable response might, despite isolationist tendencies, have encouraged the State Department to risk a further step as Hugh Gibson was to advise from Warsaw a few weeks later, but on the whole, except in France, the reaction was not encouraging.

Only in France did the press publish the note promptly and in full, and without pressure from American officials; from Paris alone, "which with a feeling of bitterness has been accepting the rather humiliating position of drifting in the back waters of British politics,"[140] there was a positive, public and official response. Agreeably surprised after the fears occasioned by the statement falsely attributed to President Wilson, the Paris press lost no time in proclaiming the solidarity of the two republics.[141] Nor was the government slow to act. On August 14, De Béarn handed a note to the Department of State above the signature of Millerand as foreign minister, although the original Colby note had been addressed to the Italian, not the French government. The French note was likewise at once given to the press. It affirmed France's complete agreement with Colby's views, plainly hinting, however, that the United States might follow France's example in recognizing General Wrangel's government "which declares that it accepts these principles."[142]

While approval and gratification were general in the two countries, sour notes were heard on both sides of the Atlantic. The American authorities made it plain that their endorsement of French policy was not without reservation. Under-Secretary Norman Davis told De Béarn that the accord between the views of the two governments was "most gratifying," but Davis had unpleasant counsel for France in regard to General Wrangel and to her German policy. The under-secretary doubted the wisdom of Wrangel's recognition since his success seemed uncertain in the light of the American government's information. What Davis said of Germany must have been a serious blow to the French government. He was frankly skeptical about France's fear that she would go Bolshevik, provided that she was not driven "to take such a course by desperation. . . ." He would, therefore, advise France "at this juncture to make a public statement regarding her aims *vis-à-vis* Germany, stating perhaps that there was no intention of taking any steps in regard to Germany other than to secure an enforcement of the treaty, and that France was prepared to take a liberal attitude in regard to the terms of the treaty and to agree to a definitive and reasonable sum for reparations payments."[143] In France, the Americans' disapproving attitude about the recognition of Wrangel was tactfully ignored and, of course, not a word was said by the press about the advice in regard to Germany. Indeed, *Figaro* (August 12) promptly misrepresented the views of the American government, declaring that "it sympathized with France's recognition of Wrangel," and Edwin L. James of the *New York Times* was informed that the French Cabinet had the Colby note before it when the decision was made.[144] It did not escape the attention of the French press, however, that little was to be expected from the United States in the form of positive action. The *Journal des débats* (August 14) regretted, for example, that America "acts so little when she talks so well." A publicist remarked that the condemnation "of Bolshevist morality and the formulation of the principle of Russia's territorial integrity would not suffice to halt the march on Warsaw and to dispose of the [Russo-German] plot in West Prussia."[145] Philippe Millet doubted the practical value of the "distant approbation of the United States which doesn't like Bolshevism but which neither recognizes Wrangel nor subsidizes Poland."[146]

In other countries, the reception accorded Colby's implicit appeal to follow America's moral lead varied from cool to cold. They would long continue to struggle with problems without her aid which they conveniently, but not without justification, attributed in part to President Wilson's tendency to oversimplify them as conflicts between the forces of good and evil. For a repetition of the crusade against Germany, few had any zest. Germany's reaction can be disposed of briefly: there was practically none, for the Germans, hypnotized by what they regarded as President Wilson's betrayal of the Fourteen Points, saw no advantage in playing up to the United States at this time. Moreover, the moralistic view was at most a secondary factor in the German attitude toward Soviet Russia. Despite the distribution of the note to all important Berlin newspapers, including the organ of the Independent Social Democrats (*Die Freiheit*), not one printed its full text, and, according to Ellis Dresel, the American diplomatic agent, even the extracts they did carry were "exceedingly brief and comment sparing." He correctly concluded "that the widespread hostility in Germany toward all that is Polish or French, together with the hope of establishing a basis for the exchange [of] products between Germany and Russia, no matter what the political direction of the latter country, predestined the American note to unfavorable comment."[147]

The greatest disappointment awaited the State Department in Italy, since the note had been addressed to its ambassador. From the speech of Foreign Minister Count Carlo Sforza to the Chamber of Deputies on August 6, it was evident that the Giolitti government, like that of Nitti, had gone too far in following Lloyd George's policy toward trade relations with Soviet Russia to reverse itself. There was, in fact, apparently no formal reply. The publicity given the Colby note was reluctant, incomplete, and tardy, and it was accompanied, for the most part, by unfavorable comment. The respected *Corriere della Sera* (August 12) first noted it on its back page in a brief summary from Washington, then (August 13) it quoted one paragraph on America's refusal to recognize the Soviet government in a first page dispatch from Paris, and it was not until August 17 that it printed, not the full text, but extensive extracts, all without editorial comment. Between August 12 and 20, the *Giornale d'Italia* did not even mention the note, at least prominently. In the *Messagero's* opinion (August 17), there was a choice between only two policies toward Russia: "open war to the last drop of blood with a million men in the field . . . or peace," while the "American doctrine ends in theoretical negation and stiffens into immobility." It concluded, "To perpetuate the Russian agony will contribute nothing to the solution of the European crisis." The *Tribune* regarded the note as "vague and inexplicable. . . . To search for another Russian Government today is like looking for another chair of agreement as full of thorns as that on which we are already sitting." The *Popolo Romano* doubted that the Italian Ambassador had acted upon the government's instructions in querying the State Department: "If the American note responds to a request from the *Consulta* it places Italy in great embarrassment."[148] In fact, the American Ambassador bluntly cabled on August 30: "Avezzana acted without instructions in making inquiry concerning our position and Italian government is accordingly much embarrassed."[149]

As for Great Britain, the State Department could only hope to ignite a backfire in public opinion, starting with the anti-Bolshevik Tory press, against Lloyd George's policy of an accommodation with Soviet Russia. The more important newspapers printed the Colby note in full, but only after the embassy gave them copies on August 12. In a final summary of British reactions, the American chargé, J. Butler Wright, claimed that the American position though "directly opposed" to avowed British policy, "reflects the views of the majority of thinking men in England. . . ."[150] Certainly British opinion, thinking or otherwise, had no use for bolshevism as a philosophy and as a program of action, but it was quite a different matter when it came to deciding what British policy should be in the international and also the domestic situation. It had reached along with Lloyd George quite different conclusions than those of the American government, and America's obvious refusal to act in support of her high principles was not calculated to change them. Indeed, the Colby note made a comparatively slight impression. France's recognition of Wrangel, reported American Ambassador Davis, "more or less overshadowed the American attitude."[151]

British press correspondents in Washington made it clear that the administration's words would not be supported with deeds. While the *Morning Post's* representative attributed the Colby note to "the official belief that England, France, and Italy attach too little importance to the danger of Bolshevism overrunning the whole of Europe," he concluded that the United States had been reduced to "the role of an impotent spectator."[152]

Much the same estimate was reported to the Conservative *Daily Telegraph*. Pending a mandate in the November election, the government felt unable to make "any pledge regarding the European situation," and by that time "presumably the crisis will be over."[153] Its diplomatic correspondent saw nothing in the American attitude to "warrant an alteration by the British Government of its present policy towards Soviet Russia" since the proposed conference would not be concerned with *de jure* recognition.

Torn between its friendliness toward America and admiration for President Wilson on the one hand and its conviction that peace with Soviet Russia was needed on the other, the Liberal press was understandably embarrassed. The *Westminster Gazette* (August 12) felt that judgment should be withheld for the clarification that would probably follow, but it at least found satisfaction in the fact that the note said nothing of a military attack upon Soviet Russia. According to the *Manchester Guardian* (August 16), President Wilson's attitude toward the Russia of the Tsars as "a sort of sacred heritage for an unnamed and unknown future Russian Government" was "a curious idealistic policy" which hardly corresponded "with the facts and possibilities of today...." The *New Statesman* (August 21) regarded the note as a "production so odd as to seem inexplicable" at a time when "all Europe," except a small party in France, was clinging to "agonized hope of peace at last." But it was the Conservative *Daily Telegraph* (August 12) that perhaps best expressed the general British reaction to America's dramatic intervention. From her position on the far side of the Atlantic, the United States might be able to "afford to ostracize Russia as long as Lenin and Trotsky are in control of her destinies," but Europe meanwhile "is kept on the rack."

In comparison with its importance in American policy, the effect of the Colby note upon the European and Asiatic governments and upon opinion abroad is difficult to assess. The Italian government did not even reply, and of the others, only that of France—and of Czechoslovakia—took formal notice of it. In both France and Czechoslovakia, Colby preached to a converted audience, and the Czech response paid chiefly lip service to its sentiments, for it stressed the importance of trade with Russia to the peace of Europe.[154] The refusal of the American government to attend an international conference would undoubtedly have been a serious obstacle to Lloyd George's policy, yet France's recognition of Wrangel consolidated much of British opinion behind it. Moreover, two years later a conference including a Soviet delegation did meet in Genoa, although the policy of the United States on recognition had not changed. So completely did the Polish victory over the Red Army change the terms of the problem that the immediate and practical influence of Colby's pronouncement must be discounted. It was, nonetheless, the most extreme official and public indictment thus far of the Soviet regime and policy by a government speaking for a country which the Soviets regarded as the most powerful representative of the capitalist world.

If the Soviets replied, as they did at great length, it was perhaps not so much, as Louis Fischer suggests, that "Bolsheviks love an argument" as it was an implicit acknowledgment of the influence that the United States still exerted. Ludwig Martens, the unofficial Soviet agent in the United States, who was shortly to be deported to Russia, promptly and skillfully depicted the note as perpetuating "war and poverty" at a time when certain European countries, under working class pressure, were moving toward an accommodation. The problem of recognition, he contended, had nothing to do with morality, and, in any event, the note constituted an unwarranted interference in the domestic affairs of Russia.[155] The official reply was reserved for Chicherin who addressed it first to the Russians themselves in the government's principal newspaper, *Izvestia* (September 10),[156] then to the world (September 17),[157] and finally to Avezzana, the Italian Ambassador in Washington. Martens saw that the Department of State received a copy on October 4.

The official Soviet reply was at the same time a denial that Colby's indictment had any foundation in fact, an attack upon American policy, and an implicit invitation for at least a *modus vivendi* with the United States. In comparison with the venal institutions of bourgeois governments, the Soviet system assured, other things being equal, the rule of the workers from the smallest locality upward. Chicherin admitted, however, the existence of a dictatorship, but if practice did not conform to theory, the responsibility belonged to the capitalist countries whose intervention forced upon the workers the acceptance of a strong government for the defense of the revolution. Colby's failure to include the Caucasus republics and the Ukraine with Finland, Poland, and Armenia as independent states demonstrated his ignorance of Russian affairs and of the Soviet government's respect for and practice of self-determination on the part "of the workers" (in practice, however, the republics of the Caucasus were soon to receive short shrift and, of course, the Ukraine enjoyed only nominal independence). His refusal to recognize the Soviet government meant, Chicherin said, a preference for a government that foreign financial interests, the strongest of which were American, could dominate. There was, he continued, no validity to the claim that Soviet Russia's pledged word could not be relied upon or that her agents abroad had the mission of preparing the world revolution. On the contrary, she scrupulously respected her treaty obligations, even in the case of the unjust Treaty of Brest-Litovsk, and revolution, in her view, was exclusively the concern of the workers of each country (a glaring contradiction to the proceedings to the Congress of the Peoples of the East that convened at Baku, September 1, 1920, and to the calculations behind the Red Army's offensive into Poland). Chicherin, nevertheless, was confident that the pressure of the workers and also the long-range interests of businessmen would soon bring about working arrangements between the two countries.[158] Chicherin's comparative moderation reflected, of course, the sudden change of fortunes in the Polish war.

5. *The Minsk Negotiations, August 16-23, 1920*

On August 12, Marshal Pilsudski left Warsaw to command the Polish counteroffensive that was launched southeast of the capital four days later.[159] The strategic situation was favorable as a result of the weakening of the Red Army's center because of the operations of its extreme northern and southern flanks. In Paris, where the Polish plans were doubtless known, the government, encouraged by America's moral support and having ventured the recognition of Wrangel, gambled upon a reversal of the fortunes of war,[160] yet a last-minute Polish victory could not, of course, be counted upon as certain. It was advisable, in either eventuality, that Poland should be in direct contact with the Soviet government, an interest that the latter obviously reciprocated. In spite of past evasions and delays on both sides, the date, August 16, which the Soviet government had finally set for the meeting at Minsk, was observed without a hitch. At 8:15 on the evening of August 13, Sapieha, the Polish Foreign Minister, informed Chicherin that the Polish delegation of thirty officials, accompanied by numerous representatives of the Polish and foreign press, would cross the battle line the next day.[161] Earlier the Soviets might have seized upon the size of the press delegation as an excuse for further delay, but at 8:30 on the morning of August 14, Chicherin informed Sapieha that the Polish delegation would be met at the time and place mentioned.[162] The Poles arrived in Minsk in time to hold the first formal meeting with the Soviet delegation on August 16, the day when Pilsudski launched the Polish counteroffensive. Thanks to the weakness of the enemy's line at the point attacked, the operation was immediately successful. The rapidity of the advance, threatening to cut off Tukhachevsky's forces operating in the Corridor, forced the Red Army to retreat as swiftly as it had advanced.

Although apparently in the dark as to the details of the victory as the result of actual or, as was more likely, contrived communication difficulties, the Polish delegation was doubtless aware that the battle was going well; it was, therefore, to Poland's interest to mark time so that the full weight of the Soviet defeat could make itself felt. "The Poles," according to Chicherin, "seek to gain time and seize every pretext to create delays.... It is clear that the military situation dominates the situation."[163] On the other hand, Soviet Russia's interest, in view of the military situation and of the failure of the revolution to materialize in Poland, manifestly lay in a prompt settlement at Minsk, despite the persistence of confidence, or the profession of it, in the strength of her position, well beyond the confirmation of the military defeat. Writing in *Pravda* (August 15), on the very eve of the catastrophe, Y. Steklov declared that Russia's "international significance" had never been as great. "We are a first-rate power before which capitalist drones are beginning to tremble." The reason was that "our country" was a "State of the proletariat," not because it was "the Russian State." With more than a little exaggeration, he vaunted the "hundreds of millions of hands of workmen" that were on all sides "stretched towards us to uphold us."[164] When, a few days later, the defeat could not be ignored, Chicherin minimized its significance for Kamenev's benefit in London, but tacitly conceded the need of peace. "The army is now regrouping; its fighting power is not lost. A new offensive is to be expected, if peace is not concluded."[165]

At the first business session on August 17, N. Danilevski, the president of the Soviet delegation, accordingly read the complete list of Soviet Russia's terms, seemingly leaving it up to the Poles to decide whether it was intended as a basis for discussion or as an ultimatum. Kamenev, while admitting that there might be additions (and changes) in details, had assured Lloyd George in writing, August 10, and again as recently as August 15,[166] that the Soviet government's terms remained unchanged. In fact, there were notable differences, one of which struck a blow at the remarkable amount of good-will that Soviet Russia's case enjoyed in the West. Another change, obviously intended as sugar-coating for others that were less palatable since it was placed first among the fifteen points, pledged the unconditional acceptance of the independence of the Polish Republic and solemnly affirmed "the unconditional right of the Polish people to order their life and to establish the form of government at their own discretion." The provision for the free distribution of land was to apply to the entire population and not merely to the families of Polish casualties of the war who, however, were to receive preferential consideration. From this provision and the general military and political amnesty that meant the return of the Communist exiles in Russia, the Soviets evidently expected the end of the dominant role of the landed aristocracy as well as other changes in Poland's social and economic structure. Less significant was the new demand for the publication of "all material and documents relating to the war between the Polish Republic and the Russian and the Ukrainian Soviet Republics." With one exception, the other terms were substantially the same as those on

Kamenev's list, but that exception was of crucial importance, for it defined what was meant by the "civic militia," which Kamenev had merely mentioned. It was to be "constituted of workers and destined to preserve order and the security of the population," but the details were reserved for the definitive treaty.[167] This was clearly the chosen agency for the subversion of the Polish state.

In Moscow, there seems to have been little or no effort to conceal the intention of foisting a working-class military force upon Poland, although its function was misrepresented as exclusively a guarantee against another Polish attack. On or about August 11, Chicherin gave this explanation in writing in reply to questions presented by Frank Mason of the International News Service. While Soviet Russia did not have the slightest intention of destroying Poland, she did desire effective guarantees against new Polish attacks. She demanded, in addition to the reduction of the Polish Army to fifty thousand men, the arming of "the Polish workers in Trade Unions... in order to maintain peace and order. This workers' militia will be the counter-weight to the imperialist Polish landlords."[168] It was, Chicherin asserted, "an entirely new idea in international politics"—as, indeed, it was, although his reason for its newness was less than candid! "Instead of a Russian occupation, the Soviet government relies upon the armed workers for the maintenance of peace." This effort on the part of the Soviet Commisar for Foreign Affairs to moderate the West's unfavorable reaction, which he evidently anticipated, misfired, because his statement strangely passed almost unnoticed. Kamenev's version of these terms concealed the Soviets' true intention by a passing mention of a "civic militia," and when its significance escaped attention, Chicherin quietly dropped the matter.[169]

On the very eve of the Minsk negotiations, Danilevski gave the British press correspondents there—they included H. N. Brailsford who represented the *Daily Herald*—another reason why a Polish militia should cause no concern. It was, he said, really a concession since it would augment Poland's armed forces, although its usefulness, he admitted, would be limited to defensive operations.[170] The Soviets' true intentions were, however, too self-evident for these diversionary efforts to fool anyone but their blindest partisans.

Since the French, for the most part, had expected Soviet Russia's final terms to be harsher than Kamenev's version, they hailed her demand for a working-class militia as confirmation of what they had been saying. The effect in Great Britain was more significant. It played into the hands of the Tory press, disillusioned Liberal opinion to a degree and probably shook the confidence of moderate Laborites in the justice of the Soviet cause. The *Manchester Guardian* (August 19) regarded the arming of the Polish workers as "a disturbing suggestion," for "it clearly would constitute an interference in the internal affairs of Poland and a very serious one, since it might not impossibly lead to civil war in Poland." In addition to the Soviet government's failure to heed the advice not to try to take Warsaw, it was another reason why the *Westminster Gazette* (August 19) was "heartily glad that the Poles have succeeded for the time being at all events in throwing them back," as Poland's hands would now be strengthened at Minsk. The *Daily Chronicle* (August 25) described the demand as "the well-worn and well-recognized avenue to the forcible establishment of a Bolshevik regime."

Whatever the feeling among the moderate elements of Labor may have been, the *Daily Herald* was too committed to be visibly shaken. It had, as early as August 3, shown its understanding and approval of moves to change the control of the Polish armed forces. The instinct of the Russian workers, it asserted, would avoid the same blunder that the Allies had made in Germany. "It is that the control of the armed forces left to Poland should be taken out of the hands of the class that has proved itself unfit to hold such power, and that it should be placed in the hands of the aroused workers themselves." Had its columns been read more assiduously for hints as to Soviet Russia's intentions, the meaning of the term "civic militia" would have been clearer, but no one supposed that the *Daily Herald* possessed the confidence of the Soviet government to this extent. The Labor organ was able, August 12, to claim, by citing its article of August 3, that there was nothing new in the demand at Minsk. There was only "a slight amplification of the terms"; the Soviet government had displayed "the same generosity, the same genuine desire for peace and respect for principles, with no imposition of any form of government from outside. It is made clear that the civic militia would not be a revolutionary force, but purely for the maintenance of order." It noted—few others did—what it described as the understandable consternation in Paris and Whitehall at the demand for Poland's publication of her documents relating to the war. By and large, however, British opinion accepted the proposed workers' militia as proof of the Soviet government's bad faith, a fact that might well have influenced British policy had the Battle of the Vistula ended in Poland's final defeat.

The Polish victory, of course, reversed the situation. When, on August 23, the Soviet delegation at Minsk insisted that the Poles take a definite stand on the Russian terms, the military victory enabled the Poles to reject them flatly. At the same time, they revived the problem of Polish imperialism by condemning the Curzon Line, which the Russian terms had in general accepted, as "arbitrary and not based upon anything"—in fact, as meaning another partition.[171] The Poles had acted without consulting the Allies, and, indeed, in defiance of their known views, but they had no intention of breaking contact with the Russians.

Whatever problems Poland's intransigence and imperialism were to pose for the future, her victory on the Vistula rescued the Allies from an almost impossible situation. Even the apparent certainty of the Red Army's capture of Warsaw had failed to unite them behind an effective policy. Everywhere there were those who saw (and exaggerated) the danger and who accepted the need of whatever sacrifices its defeat might require. After another World War had established Soviet power not only in Poland but also on the Elbe River and throughout East Central Europe from the Baltic to the Black Seas, the Allies were then to speak for the great majority and to determine policy, but not in 1920. The Cassandras were not generally believed. From the point of view of liberal opinion everywhere, Poland's invasion of the Ukraine overshadowed Soviet Russia's advance into ethnographic Poland, for the latter seemed to be doing merely what many other countries had done in retaliation against aggression and in order to secure legitimate guarantees for the future. Still more decisive was the universal weariness of war, which those who, like Churchill, were oppressed by forebodings, if the danger was not immediately scotched, had to accept. It forced arch-interventionist France to draw the line short of the commitment of her own troops, and it paralyzed Lloyd George when, for a moment, he considered the use of force, for it undoubtedly contributed greatly to the weight of opinion behind Labor's Council of Action and its threat of "direct action."

From the Great War two great nations had drawn conclusions that also limited or blocked united action; isolationism in America meant that the administration could not go beyond the moral denunciation and the negative attitudes in the Colby note, while Germany, nourishing her hatreds, dreamed of using Russia for her recovery and, meanwhile, entrenched herself behind a policy of complete neutrality. Against these obstacles, those who advocated effective, even forceful measures, could not prevail, nor, on the other hand, could Lloyd George and the partisans of an accommodation with Soviet Russia. They, too, met immovable resistance, especially from France and the United States.

Nor is it entirely certain that the West would have been galvanized into agreement and action if Soviet Russia and not Poland had won the battle of the Vistula. While France would have been sorely tempted to send her troops further into Germany, she would have invited by this move the result she feared most—Germany's throwing herself into the arms of the Soviets—and the *entente cordiale* would have been strained to the breaking point. Lloyd George had pledged British support to the defense of Poland's independence with all possible means and soon events were to show that he regarded the demand for a workers' militia as a menace to that independence. Although Liberal opinion parted company with Labor on this issue, it is doubtful that he could have resorted to force against the powerful pacifist tendencies of Liberal opinion and Labor's determined resistance. After all, the demand for a workers' militia probably meant that a Polish Soviet would not have been the immediate consequence of the fall of Warsaw and that the process of subversion would have required a considerable period of time. While there would have been little doubt as to the ultimate result, the prospects of effective action against this contingent danger were not wholly reassuring. In any event, Poland's victory saved the Western powers from the decision that they were perhaps incapable of making.

VIII

Peace and Trade

1. The Preliminary Peace of Riga, October 12, 1920

The victory on the Vistula and the rapid retreat of the Red Army opened dazzling vistas, including the overthrow of the Bolshevik regime, to Polish leaders. Marshal Pilsudski made no secret of his belief that the enemy's total destruction was within his grasp. The Red Army's losses, which he estimated at 100,000 men, would, he explained to the press, require a long period of reorganization and he doubted "whether they [the Bolshevik forces] will even then be of great military value." Unless Russia was thoroughly crushed, the defense of Poland's long frontier would be beyond her capacity.[1] The Witos government was, however, concerned with the country's wretched social and economic conditions as well as with the strictly military situation. In the Soviets' willingness to sacrifice territory, it saw a chance to conclude a more favorable peace treaty than any that a White Russian government would be likely to approve. Prince Sapieha, therefore, demanded a high price for Poland's continuation of the war, a price which he frankly defined to the American chargé, August 20. After inquiring whether the United States would regard a peace with Soviet Russia as a betrayal of the Allies, Sapieha explained: "On the other hand, were Poland to continue, the war assurances of Allied help would have to be more categorical than in the past and an agreement would have to be reached as to Poland's boundaries in order that a future Russian Government would not accord less favorable terms in this respect that might be obtained from the Soviets."[2]

There were at first indications of a firmer anti-Bolshevik stand on the part of the Allies. The effect upon Lloyd George was immediate. When he left London for Switzerland on the adjournment of Parliament, August 16, his main purpose was, according to Riddell, aside from enjoyment of mountains, to meet Giolitti, the Italian Prime Minister. Because the British premier was unaware of the Minsk terms during the Lucerne conversations on August 22, the communiqué he and Sir Maurice Hankey drafted seems to have been unfriendly to the Poles. It was promptly scrapped that evening as likely to embitter the French after Riddell showed Lloyd George a newspaper containing the text of Russia's demands. He was especially incensed by the explanation of the "civic militia" and also by the demand for the publication of the papers relating to the war.[3] In its final form, the Lloyd George–Giolitti statement to the press was an indictment and a warning so pleasing to the French that they overlooked the intro- ductory appeal for moderation in the enforcement of the Treaty of Ver- sailles.[4] The British and Italian governments regretted the violence that the Soviets contemplated to Polish independence in view of their efforts to bring Soviet Russia into contact with the outside world. Coming after Kamenev's guarantee that his version of the Russian terms omitted nothing but matters of secondary importance, the demand for a workers' militia was "a serious breach of faith, and negotiations of whatever character, with a government which treats its word thus lightly, becomes difficult if not im- possible." If the Soviet government insisted upon this demand and carried the war into the heart of Poland in an effort to impose it, "no free govern- ment can recognize or treat with the Soviet oligarchy."[5] From the French point of view, August 23 was a happy day; Lloyd George and Giolitti had apparently accepted Millerand's and Wilson's views. "The understanding is therefore perfect today between the four great nations: France, England, America, Italy."[6] From Lucerne, Lloyd George and Giolitti sent friendly greetings to Millerand, and Giolitti proposed a separate meeting with the French Premier on French soil.[7]

Moderately emboldened by Poland's victory, the Western powers were tempted to take, and, in less important matters such as the transshipment of Allied cargoes of war supplies through Danzig, did take, a stronger line. Even the American government became somewhat more active. The am- bassador in Paris was instructed to express the hope in the Council of

Ambassadors that this traffic "may be facilitated" provided that Poland used the supplies for defensive purposes.[8] At long last, the Council of Ambassadors ordered Towers, the High Commissioner, on August 24, to use all means to assure the free movement of these cargoes through Danzig and promised him French and British military reinforcements for this purpose.[9] Assisted by the depressing effect of the Red Army's defeat upon the recalcitrant dockworkers, there was a prompt and effective result. On the very next day, the American Consulate in Danzig informed the Legation in Warsaw that munitions were being unloaded without trouble because of energetic action by the French and British.[10]

In regard to Soviet Russia, the American government was not to be moved from the high moral ground of the Colby note into any positive commitments. Yet the secretary of state yielded to the temptation to let General Wrangel know his conception of what the proper policy was and thereby unintentionally encouraged hopes of American aid. On August 27, Colby dispatched a long questionnaire for Wrangel's consideration. Phrased in such a way as to suggest the desired answers, which in fact were quickly forthcoming, these questions revealed the thought that he should remain upon the defensive, nourish democratic institutions, tackle the agrarian problem, and build up a "nucleus of national regeneration."[11] In a matter of days, his representatives in Paris were talking of the American government's willingness to furnish economic assistance in the form of clothing, agricultural machinery, etc. and of the desirability of the co-ordination of American and French aid with the result that the embarrassed secretary of state found it necessary to issue a denial to the press.[12]

Returning to his post in Warsaw early in September, Hugh Gibson, the American minister, resumed his pleas for Allied unity in support of Poland[13] and urged a notable development of American policy toward Soviet Russia. Aware that force was out of the question, he was convinced that the United States government should initiate a similar but stronger declaration than the Colby note on the part of the Western powers. "It would be a serious perhaps mortal blow to Bolshevism if the powers were to unite in a solemn declaration along the line already taken by you [Colby] that on moral ground there can be no compounding with [the] Bolshevik system. If it were not only a declaration but in some sense a mutual pledge it would end all doubts in Russia and give strength to those opposed to the present regime." France would welcome the idea, and Italy's industrial disturbances would convince her of the danger. If the three governments were to approach Lloyd George "with the statement that they were resolved on this course and should like to have British support Mr. Lloyd George would be faced with the dilemma of joining the civilized powers of the world in a declared resolution to boycott Bolshevism or admitting that he preferred to remain aloof on ground of expediency and place his trust in the triumph of the Soviet system." More than anything else, this would "undermine the infinite [!] strength of the Soviet regime."[14] After a considerable delay, American influence in the Council of Ambassadors was exerted without much effect for "as complete agreement as possible" in regard to Poland,[15] but Gibson's proposal for an international boycott of Soviet Russia apparently got no further than the files of the Department of State. The administration's hands were tied by the president's illness, the presidential election, and the defeat of the Democratic candidates in November. Poland could expect no support from the United States for the continuation of the war.

The key to the situation still lay in Great Britain. The much stiffer tone of the British communications to Soviet Russia seemed to foreshadow a complete break, although Lloyd George was probably still bent upon peace.[16] On August 23, Balfour transmitted the Lloyd George–Giolitti statement to the Soviet delegation with a demand that the Soviet government explain by the evening of August 27 whether it intended to insist upon the terms it had presented to Poland at Minsk. "On the answer the future policy of the British government will depend."[17] Well in advance of this deadline, August 25, Chicherin withdrew the demand for a workers' militia and declared that the Minsk terms had not been intended as an ultimatum but only as a basis for discussion,[18] but the British government refused to be appeased.

Meanwhile, the earlier alignment of Liberal-Labor opinion against action, momentarily weakened by the Minsk terms, reasserted itself as a result of the harshness of the Lloyd George communiqué and of the Balfour note. Labor's Council of Action denounced the communiqué "as a move in the direction of war" and called for immediate peace negotiations with Soviet Russia, the withdrawal of all support from Poland and of all British warships from Russian waters.[19] More significant was the reaction of Liberal opinion. The *Manchester Guardian* (August 27) condemned the "violent and insulting language" of the Lloyd George–Giolitti statement as severely as the Soviets' demand for a workers' militia which "was probably never meant to be insisted upon." In the *Westminster Gazette*'s view (August 25), expressed even before its cancellation was known, that demand could not "in the present state of the negotiations, justify the high language used regarding it by the Prime Minister and Mr. Balfour." Thoroughly disgruntled, the radical *Nation* (August 28) denied the basic assumptions of the Lucerne statement—for the detailed organization of the militia would decide whether or not it constituted a threat to Poland's independence—and described the "thunderbolt launched at Lucerne" as a startling example of Lloyd George's "vacillating mind...opportunism, and lack of policy." It believed the country's temper to be such that "Mr. George will soon and finally have to return to the conviction that we must have trade and peace with Soviet Russia."

In these circumstances and, without much doubt, in accordance with Lloyd George's real purposes, the British government lowered its sights from a complete break with Soviet Russia to the expulsion of Kamenev which was ordered on September 10. Balfour, for the first time in the prolonged effort to reach an agreement, challenged the Soviet's propaganda line on September 1, but he addressed Kamenev, not Chicherin. Balfour dismissed the claim that the proposed militia was a favor to Poland as a manifest "jest" and denied that the British government had recognized, as Chicherin had claimed, the justice of the demand for the reduction of the Polish army. Its position had been that the demand would not warrant "active intervention" on its part. Replying to the charge of economic inequalities in Britain, Balfour agreed that he had never personally doubted "the efficacy of Soviet methods for making rich men poor." It was more difficult and also more important to make "poor men richer." Therein, it was to be feared, Soviet Russia had failed.[20]

Chicherin, not Kamenev, replied. The Minsk terms, Chicherin maintained as before, were merely bases for discussion, but on other matters he gave as good as he received. Blandly ignoring Balfour's clarification of Britain's attitude on the Polish army, Chicherin asserted that its change of front resulted from an erroneous estimate of the relative strength of Soviet Russia and Poland; the "reinforcements sent to the front" made the Red Army stronger than ever. Balfour's patronizing superiority in regard to economic conditions came with poor grace from a country that had imposed the blockade and participated in the Civil War. Moreover, the wealth of the rich in Russia had not been destroyed; it was being used for the benefit of the people(!).[21]

Nevertheless, the grounds given for Kamenev's expulsion on September 10 were based upon his personal conduct, not upon Soviet policy. He had violated, it was charged, his privileges as a guest by his complicity in the affair of the smuggled Russian jewels and in the subsidies for the *Daily Herald,* by his contacts with the Council of Action, and the calculated distortion of his government's terms for an armistice and preliminary peace. Kamenev tried to clear himself for the benefit of British and, especially, Labor opinion on the eve of his expulsion. Addressing Lieutenant Commander Kenworthy and other Labor members of Parliament, he made a sweeping denial of the first two charges and maintained that he had been approached by the Council of Action to which he had merely given information. In regard to the workers' militia, he had repeatedly advised his government to withdraw this demand, and, in any event, it was a matter of no importance since it had in fact been withdrawn.[22]

The British government then unveiled its heaviest guns for Labor's benefit in a letter to the same members of Parliament. It possessed documentary evidence showing that Kamenev's dispatches to his government had mentioned the smuggling affair and that he had personally omitted the compromising description of the "civic militia" from the text his government had sent for unavowed purposes.[23] Moscow's reaction was one of defiance. *Pravda* denounced Balfour's note of September 1 as "most shameless, impudent, cynical and bloodthirsty." It was clear that "when we are strong they will trade with us and flatter us, but when we suffer defeat the capitalists will attempt to crush us" and urged working for "the defeat of world capitalism."[24] Some three weeks later, Chicherin announced to Curzon the lapse of the agreement reached between the two governments at the beginning of July since Britain's treatment of Russian representatives meant that it intended to prevent peaceful relations. It was, moreover, incompatible with the "standing of the Russian Government."[25]

However, neither Kamenev's expulsion, nor the Soviets belligerent reaction to it, nor even the curious incident of the alleged launching of a new Soviet submarine in the Black Sea,[26] seriously disturbed Krassin's status in London. France had withdrawn her representative from the Permanent Committee of the Supreme Economic Council which concerned itself with the question of trade with Soviet Russia on behalf of the Allies,[27] but the British Inter-Departmental Committee, of which Wise was also chairman, continued the intermittent and wearisome negotiations. Early in October, the British committee gave a draft of a complete treaty to the press, doubtless to show that the commercial negotiations still continued.[28]

The Western world was of two minds about the use that Poland should make of her victory. To some, it was an opportunity to hasten the downfall of the Bolshevik regime which was generally expected in the near future,[29] but the prevailing mood and the intentions of Western governments were quite different. Poland's success had swiftly dispelled the fear of the Red Army; everywhere dispatches from the front disappeared from first pages of the press. It was generally felt that if anything could revive the danger it would be another Polish invasion of Russia and that, if Russian national sentiment was not again aroused, the Bolshevik regime would shortly collapse from its failure at home.[30] This was Washington's estimate of the situation. On August 21, before Sapieha's appeal for Allied support for continued war arrived,[31] Colby instructed the chargé in Warsaw to deliver a note to the Polish Foreign Minister urging that "every reasonable effort be made to terminate the present bloodshed. It could not approve the adoption of an offensive war program against Russia by the Polish Government." In order to avoid incitement to Russian patriotism, Colby thought that Poland should publicly announce her intention to respect the Curzon Line pending the settlement of the definitive eastern frontier by direct agreement with Russia.[32]

There is no reason to believe that the Allies, to whom the American note was later (August 27) confidentially communicated, were of a different opinion at this time. In London, virtually the entire press, including some of the most extreme anti-Bolshevik journals, took the position that the Allies should advise Poland to stop at the Curzon Line.[33] The Polish chargé confided to the American Embassy that he was advising Sapieha, doubtless because of the British attitude, on no account to "go beyond ethnographic frontiers even if military successes of present campaign continue."[34] As for Italy, Sforza, Giolitti's Foreign Minister, was telling the American Ambassador less than a week after the blast against the Soviet government in the Lloyd George–Giolitti communiqué that Italy did not rule out full recognition in the longer view and that, in his opinion, the blockade and the recognition of Wrangel had been a help to the Soviets.[35] It would be a mistake to assume that France's influence was thrown at once in favor of extreme measures.

On the contrary, the Paris press was just as definite as the British that the Poles should be advised to respect the Curzon Line. The *Temps* (August 21) promptly, though tactfully, warned Poland not again to give the Soviets an opportunity to appeal to Russian national feeling. "We must," wrote P. Bernus, "pledge our allies of Warsaw not to thrust themselves again across the perilous Russian steppes." While Poland's eastern frontier could not yet be determined in detail, "the line that Lloyd George traced in July is a good one."[36] Gaston Doumergue held that France and her Allies should "advise circumspection and moderation to the victorious Poles. Poland should have no ambitions beyond the frontiers fixed by the treaties of peace."[37] According to Millet, France's contributions to the victory placed her under the obligation to make Poland listen to reason "in the interest of the peace of Europe."[38] Since Poincaré evidently regretted that the Allies had not in good time secured her acceptance of an eastern frontier that would have restrained her aspirations, it is reasonable to conclude that he accepted the Curzon Line as in general the limits of the advance of the Polish Army. The reprieve won by Poland's victory should be used to restore Franco-British unity, since independent action by either would mean the Entente's suicide.[39]

These indications of a change in attitude toward Britain and, to some extent, in general policy received a degree of confirmation when Philippe Berthelot replaced Maurice Paléologue in September as the permanent secretary general of the French Foreign Ministry.[40] The dominant place that Paléologue wished to give Hungary in France's Central European policy was shifted to the succession states in the Little Entente (Czechoslovakia, Yugoslavia, and Rumania), and while Poland by no means lost her preferential standing, there were some hints of a somewhat less intransigent attitude toward Soviet Russia.[41] Sapieha made it a point to tell White, the American chargé, on August 21 "that the French Government which has recognized Wrangel has expressed no objection to the conclusion of peace by the Poles."[42] The communiqué issued after the meeting between Millerand and Giolitti at Aix-les-Bains, September 13, was distinctly milder than the Lloyd George–Giolitti statement. For French sensibilities, there was an assertion of an agreement in the desire for changes within Russia that would permit her return to the concern of peaceful peoples, but freedom of action in regard to Russia was assured to both countries and there was a reference to the resumption of trade as useful to the world as well as to Russia.[43]

The Poles had no intention of halting their army on the Curzon Line, however much they differed about the continuation of the war. The American note (August 21) elicited from Sapieha a forthright declaration that he did not recognize it as "the ethnographic frontier of Poland" in view of the large Polish population beyond it. Lloyd George had "no right to insist that Poland which had triumphed by its own efforts should be held to a stricter observance" than that of Soviet Russia, especially since he had done nothing for six weeks to restrain the Reds or to aid the Polish defenders. Sapieha's hint that the White Russians were less accommodating than the Bolsheviks in fact indicated the direction in which the Polish wind was blowing.[44]

In rejecting the Soviets' terms at Minsk on August 23, the Polish delegation specifically repudiated the Curzon Line as without justification, and for the next few days it did little but complain about the conditions under which it worked, especially in regard to the difficulties of communications with Warsaw.[45] The Poles finally lost patience—with the increased confidence due to their victories—but when they moved it was not to break off the negotiations but to propose that the meeting place be changed, asserting at the same time their desire of peace. On September 1, Chicherin agreed to Riga—Poland had secured the Latvian government's consent—provided that the diplomatic immunity of the entire Soviet delegation and the complete freedom of its communications with Moscow were guaranteed.[46] The

Polish government not only undertook to secure these guarantees but it also urged as early a date as possible for the resumption of negotiations.[47]   When the Soviets' requirements were satisfied, Sapieha informed them: "Our delegation, furnished with full powers to conclude, not only an armistice and peace preliminaries, but ultimately also a definitive Treaty of Peace, will be ready to start by the first boat from Danzig, due to leave September 12."[48] While the Soviets complained of Poland's delays, it was probably something of a conditioned reflex for they admitted that the Polish government had shown unexpected signs of "a peace-loving character" because, however, of the Red Army's offensive operations at certain points and of American and Italian advice against a revival of Polish imperialism.[49]   By September 16, both delegations had arrived in Riga and the resumption of negotiations soon followed.[50]

After the move to Riga, there could be little doubt that both sides wanted peace, and the intercepted messages made at least Sapieha's intentions clear to the Allied governments. It was by no means certain, however, that he would be able to control Polish policy in the final resort, since Pilsudski's military clique, which was represented on the Polish delegation at Riga, intrigued for continued war. In Gibson's opinion, it might succeed if the other parties were forced to seek guidance from different countries as a result of Allied disunity.[51]

Confident that the Soviet regime was doomed in any event, Western opinion for the most part continued to urge moderation and peace,[52] but the prospects for immediate peace inspired second thoughts in certain quarters. The *Temps* (September 21) thought that Poland needed every possible guarantee of her security since peace to the Soviets meant nothing more than a truce so that they might face up to the threat from Wrangel and other internal enemies.[53]   What a Polish-Russian peace would mean in a military sense was painfully evident to that White Russian general. His Foreign Minister, Baron Struve, appealed to France to see that Poland continued the war on a defensive basis in order to keep an important part of the Bolshevik forces on the Polish front and to give "us time to reinforce our army, to equip it with the cooperation of the powers in preparation for definitive operations." Otherwise, "all of the Red armies will concentrate against us and crush us by their numerical superiority."[54]   Here and there a voice was publicly raised that Poland should demand the total disarmament of the Red Army,[55] but it made little impression upon the general public since it clearly meant all-out war.[56]

If Sapieha's confidences to the American minister are to be believed, France did take steps on Wrangel's behalf, her minister in Warsaw writing privately to the chief of the Polish General Staff on the advisability of sending an agent to Paris to discuss a military alliance with Wrangel's representatives. As a result, the French Minister was advised to address himself to the Foreign Ministry, that is to Sapieha himself. For weeks the Italian diplomatic mission had "almost openly urged [the] Poles to go on fighting—no peace until the overthrow of Soviet Government"—certainly a sharp departure from the official Italian policy! Even in the British attitude, Sapieha detected bellicose views, especially in their harping upon the menacing character of Bolshevik troop concentrations, and he thought that Lloyd George might in some circumstances "join the chorus against peace." Sapieha would, however, consider continued "hostilities only on condition that the Allies come out openly and declare that it is their united purpose to crush [the] Bolshevists, that for this work they require the aid of Poland, and that in return for Poland's contribution of man power, they are prepared to finance the operations and assure Poland definite frontiers so that she may settle down and go to work when her task is finished."[57]

However belligerent the Allied representatives in Warsaw may have been, the British government decided to throw Wrangel to the wolves. On October 1, it fixed another deadline for the Soviets to yield to its demands. After noting the violations of the July pledge against hostile propaganda, Curzon denounced the failure to carry out the February agreement to exchange prisoners, threatening to take whatever action was required to secure their release if clear proof was not furnished by October 10 of the agreement's execution.[58] These tough words did not deter the British from accepting the Soviets' prompt assurances. Curzon professed to see in them proof of a "sincere desire" to carry out the promises made in July, although he listed specific acts of an unfriendly nature.[59] In fact, a few days later arrangements were concluded and carried out for the final exchange of prisoners.[60]

As at Brest-Litovsk more than two years earlier, Soviet Russia was the defeated power and again, as the desperate internal crisis of the coming winter was to show, she needed a "breathing spell." Defeat, however, had not destroyed the Soviet leaders' confidence. Tactical considerations doubtless played a part in Lenin's boasts of the narrowness of the margin between defeat and victory, his identification of the Soviet cause with the "revisionist" aspirations of Germany, and his profession of faith in the victorious result of a winter campaign against the Poles if one became necessary.[61] The defeat, contrary to Pilsudski's and Western opinion's wishful thinking, had not destroyed the Red Army or exhausted Russia's manpower reserve, nor, indeed, had it brought immediate disillusionment about the prospects of world revolution. In Labor's Council of Action, though dominated by "unrepentant Mensheviks," Lenin saw an immature Soviet that had restrained the bellicose intentions of the British government, and in October, Zinoviev went to Germany in an effort to bring the Independent Social Democrats into the Bolshevik camp. In the end, what decided Lenin's policy at Riga was the shocking revelation of the indifference of the Polish peasants to the red flag of revolution and hostility to their self-appointed liberators.[62] He consoled himself with the dubious thought that the industrial proletariat of Warsaw and the cities of western Poland would have risen had the Red Army reached them, but his confidence was not sufficiently firm to resist Trotsky's desire to liquidate the Polish adventure. As soon as the defeat on the Vistula was confirmed, it seems clear that Lenin went along with the majority in the Politburo in the decision to turn against Wrangel and that troops were diverted from the Polish front even before the hostilities there had been suspended.[63]

Fearing "overwhelming disaster" from continued war, especially in the absence of firm Allied pledges,[64] Sapieha and the Witos government were willing to sacrifice Pilsudski's ambitious plans and Wrangel in return for territorial gains in White Russia that far exceeded what the Allies regarded as just. Their renunciation of further adventures in the Ukraine, which seems to have been clearly indicated during the conversations at Minsk, was, according to Karl Radek, the key consideration from the Soviet point of view, since the material resources of the Ukraine were essential to the future of the Soviet Union.[65] On this assurance, the Russians offered enough White Russian territory to interpose Polish territory between themselves and friendly Lithuania, and they made no protest when, October 9, the Polish General Zeligowski occupied Vilna. Determined to secure a quick peace, the All-Russian Central Executive Committee warned the Poles at Riga on September 25 that, if the peace preliminaries were not signed by October 5, "the Council of People's Commissars will have the right to alter its terms."[66] This threat apparently gave the upper hand to Sapieha and the partisans of peace, and a cease-fire was agreed upon on the stipulated date apparently without consulting the Allies.

The preliminary peace was signed a week later on October 12.[67] With about 100,000 square miles of territory east of the Curzon Line, Poland acquired an additional population of approximately 4,000,000 of which even Polish sympathizers have not claimed that more than 30 per cent were Poles. The Soviets also undertook to pay financial, economic, and cultural reparations for Russia's participation in the various partitions, but the far-reaching demands for damages arising from the revolution and Russia's involvement in the World War were dropped. In return, Poland washed her hands of Wrangel and of any foreign effort against Soviet Russia. The concluding sentence of Article 2 read as follows: "From the moment of the ratification of the present agreement both contracting parties undertake that neither will support any foreign warlike operations against the other party."[68]

Although the Poles, like many of their Western friends, doubtless feared a new Soviet aggression in the spring, it was the Soviet government that charged that the treaty was not being observed—that Poland, on the excuse of the need to await the exact delineation of the frontier, was not withdrawing her troops, and that she was supporting the hostile operations of Boris Savinkov and of General Balakhovich.[69] The Polish government at once showed its desire of peace by disavowing these leaders who, with Wrangel, represented the fading hopes of the White Russians and of Western interventionists. Perhaps under Polish pressure, Savinkov and Balakhovich crossed the Polish frontier in an effort "to win a decisive victory over the Bolshevist usurper,"[70] and, on November 9, the Polish government publicly denied the Soviets' charges. The Council of Ministers had decided on October 15, it claimed, to request the Supreme Army Command to sever all connections with Petlyura and Balakhovich and this had been done. All liaison had been ended and a detachment of the latter's troops, still on Polish soil, had been disarmed.[71] Despite all difficulties, hostilities were not resumed at least on a serious scale.

In assessing the effect of Poland's victory and the preliminary peace of Riga, Germany presents a special case, for she alone regarded the Soviet-Polish peace, for the most part, as clearly disadvantageous. The unavowed hopes revealed in Foreign Minister Simons' speech of July 26 had collapsed, and he could only cite the avoidance of civil war as the outstanding accomplishment of Germany's strict neutrality.[72] Nevertheless, the German government gave visas to a some half dozen Bolshevik leaders, including Zinoviev, the President of the Third International, whose mission was to swing the Independent Social Democrats into the Bolshevik fold at their congress in Halle in October. Taunting them with what amounted to, in his view, a cowardly aversion to revolutionary violence in a four-hour speech in German, he succeeded in splitting the congress, a large majority agreeing to accept terroristic methods and the dictatorship of the proletariat.[73] Poland's victory helped Germany to move promptly without fear of serious complication; charging Zinoviev and Lozovsky, who also spoke at Halle, with incitement to violence, both were expelled from Germany. The foreign minister made it clear, however, that he was not seeking a break with Soviet Russia. Announcing the expulsion to the Reichstag, October 20, he explained that no other people was as popular in Germany as the Russians; it was felt instinctively "that Germany's recovery can be achieved with, not against, the Russian people in the innumerable opportunities for working together...."[74]

The conclusion was inescapable that Germany's position had deteriorated. Although the Red Army's advance had improved it "a little," the Polish victory, according to a moderate observer who had not shared the extravagant expectations of the extremists, had brought "a frightful worsening of Germany's position in foreign politics."[75] Social Democrats feared that a blow had been struck at Germany's chances in the plebiscite that was to be held in Upper Silesia whose coal mines were indispensable to German industry and to full employment.[76] For those who had expected the Bolshevik danger to facilitate an arrangement with the Allies to Germany's advantage for common action against Soviet Russia, the results were also disappointing, thanks to French intransigence toward concessions to Germany. Lloyd George had not acted, as they anticipated, as if the Bolsheviks were Britain's mortal enemy.[77] The new situation colored and depressed the views of Chancellor Fehrenbach when he addressed the Reichstag on October 27. Involvement on either side in the war would have completed Germany's ruin; she must continue to avoid adventures of any kind. "We are broken from the military point of view, and we are struggling for the merest breath of economic life." With reason Scheidemann called attention to the chancellor's "tone of deepest resignation," in contrast to the note of confidence in his government's first pronouncements.[78]

The Allies had reason to be pleased at the turn of events in Eastern Europe, although their satisfaction was not unalloyed. The menace of militant bolshevism, the cause briefly of intense anxiety and fear, had been averted or, as many believed, even eliminated forever. France, where the crisis had acquired hysterical overtones, experienced a resurgence of confidence. Some of the foremost leaders claimed for French military genius a major share of the credit for Poland's victory and hailed it as a striking exoneration of Millerand's policy.[79] Since many assumed as a matter of course that Germany had united with Soviet Russia in some sort of agreement and that she had furnished the Red Army with officers and arms, the conclusion was inevitably drawn that Germany as well as the Soviets had been defeated, and Germany's attitude seemed indeed to confirm this judgment.[80]

The use that Poland had made of its victory was not, however, a source of complete satisfaction, even for the French. It had paid little heed to Allied advice and had rejected the Curzon Line. Indeed, it does not seem even to have informed the Allies on the progress of the negotiations after the move from Minsk to Riga. If it correctly informed American Minister Gibson, the French as well as the British handed notes to Pilsudski on October 12, when the Riga treaty had already been or was about to be signed, urging moderation in victory, and respect for Russia's legitimate interests and for Grabski's commitments at Spa, one of the most important of which was his acceptance of the Curzon Line.[81] As the full extent of the victory became apparent, the French, usually desirous of as large and as powerful a Poland as possible, lost interest in that line. Moreover, a representative of the *Times* who was in Warsaw at this time later discounted the sincerity of France's moderate advice. The French minister, he wrote, carried out his official instructions "in correct and formal language . . . then sat down over an informal cup of coffee, and the gist of his remarks was hard to reconcile with the purport of his official communication."[82]

Although the Poles concluded the Riga treaty in defiance of British policy and advice, there was little that the Lloyd George government could do about it. British Liberal opinion was, however, unrestrained in its condemnation. To the *Nation* (October 16), it was "Another Punic Peace" which would result in "Jones and Smith marching cheerfully to fight for Polish independence" in response to appeals to save a small nation, in defense of the sanctity of treaties and the authority of the League of Nations. An occasional voice was raised in France to much the same effect. Because it had advised Poland to disregard the Curzon Line, one insisted that France should redeem her sin by intervening actively to prevent the definitive Polish-Soviet treaty from sealing the triumph of Polish imperialism. "The security of all is at stake, but also the good repute of French policy."[83]

If doubts about Poland's action existed in France's governing circles, the reason was not so much the territorial settlement as it was Poland's renunciation of active hostility to the Soviet regime and, above all, the timing of the treaty. It was plain for all to see from the Soviets' hasty acceptance of Poland's demands that they intended to turn in full force against General Wrangel, as Foreign Minister Struve had warned.[84] A military expert emphasized the imminence of "serious repercussions upon General Wrangel's theatre of operations,"[85] and the sober *Figaro* (October 7) assumed that Trotsky's sole thought would be "to throw all his forces against Wrangel." Exaggerating Wrangel's strength and underestimating Soviet Russia, the situation was not taken too seriously or, at least, the danger was not seen as immediate. In the view of the *Temps,* the Soviets were "incapable of sustaining a winter campaign"; the real risk—another offensive against Poland in the spring—might arise from the opportunity the winter would offer for recovery. The treaty, it feared, would retard the fall of the Bolshevist regime.[86] Everywhere there was a sudden revival of confidence in its approaching collapse, which France shared to the full, that was nourished by the wildest sort of rumors.[87] The *Temps* accepted as fact that "large numbers of commissars" were fleeing to Germany, that the leaders were sending their "wealth to safe places abroad," and from these signs of dissolution, together with the frantic appeals to the world proletariat, it concluded that, after many disappointments, the end was at last certain.[88] The Red Army had lost all of its discipline, according to A. Gauvain, as a result of the failure of the commissars' promise of loot. Red troops were fleeing into the heart of Russia demanding peace as they went. "With coolness and energy the Soviet regime can be disposed of this winter."[89] Confident of the impending overthrow of bolshevism and of Wrangel's defensive strength, the French suppressed their resentment of what they undoubtedly regarded as Poland's premature signature of the preliminary peace.

2. The Abandonment and Defeat of General Wrangel

In the eagerness to turn to other problems, there was little inclination to assure at least Wrangel's survival. Churchill's silence testified to the hopeless prospect of Britain's participation in a vigorous exploitation of Poland's victory. When he broke that silence, November 4, in a speech to the United Wards Club, his tone was one of sad resignation. He still judged world events and tendencies, he said, "from the point of view of whether they were Bolshevist or anti-Bolshevist," but he confessed that "we could do little" for Russia. "The fearful series of events must run their course. One could only hope that some day in our own time deliverance would come to the Russian people...."[90] Anti-bolshevism was as bitter as ever, but it had become little more than a sentiment. Although the *Daily Telegraph* (November 6) agreed with Churchill that bolshevism was the paramount issue of the time "in comparison with which all other divisions of opinion and sentiment in public affairs fall into second rank," it had nothing positive to propose.

As usual, the Bolsheviks were frank about their calculations and intentions. The *Izvestia* was not far wrong in claiming "that the Bourgeois countries are quite incapable of fighting against us" since all were preoccupied with internal affairs, except France which was concerned about its relations with England, and the United States was too far away. The respite must be used to "defeat and destroy the autocrat of the South, Wrangel, behind whom stands reactionary France."[91]

Notwithstanding the moral commitment implied in France's *de facto* recognition of Wrangel's government, France did nothing effective to restrain Poland from leaving him to fight alone or to help him to survive the ultimate test. On the first news that things were going badly for him, the authoritative *Temps* could only say, "It was certainly not the French government that pushed Poland into a premature signature of the peace with the

Bolsheviks."[92] As earlier, such aid as France sent was too little and too late. Not until almost the end of October, on the very eve of the Soviet offensive, did French High Commissioner de Martel arrived in Sevastopol with a small military mission of twenty officers. His public advice that the conflict could be won by winning the peasants, that France insisted upon democratic practices, and that a liberal regime should be consolidated in the territory already held before further advances were attempted, though sound enough if Wrangel survived, was rather ludicrous in view of the immediately impending events. More to the point were the three French merchant vessels laden "with clothing, aeroplanes, artillery and other supplies" that arrived along with the battleship that had carried De Martel to his post.[93] Even these supplies seemed to have had little or no influence upon the battles that were about to begin.

Greatly superior in numbers, the Red Army launched its offensive late in October and forced Wrangel to seek refuge within the narrow confines of the Crimea, although it failed to destroy his army before this operation was completed. Again, however, Western reliance upon the defensive strength of the Perekop Isthmus—the narrow strip of land uniting the Crimea with the mainland—proved a delusion. Within a matter of days after the final assault began on November 7, three successive defense lines were pierced or outflanked, and the disastrous results of the fighting on November 11 left Wrangel no other course than evacuation. On that day, Admiral McCully, the American agent with the White Russian general, addressed a moving appeal to his government for its aid in saving the many refugees from the Bolsheviks. "To allow them to perish miserably would be a reproach to all civilization."[94] The response, though meager, was prompt. The main burden was rightly on the Allies, but with President Wilson's approval and after the Russian Embassy in Washington agreed to meet the expense involved—there were no American funds available—some half dozen Shipping Board merchant vessels in the area in addition to American warships were assigned to the evacuation of civilian refugees.[95] The Allies, too, acted swiftly, contributing ships for the transport of Wrangel's troops as well as civilian refugees and they secured temporary safe havens for them on Turkish and Greek islands. If he had expected the Allies, or at least France, to maintain his army intact for later use against the Bolsheviks, events soon revealed the harsh reality. The French, as he informed an American official, had deprived them of their weapons and had seized his fleet of naval and merchant ships in order to reimburse themselves for what they had spent on his behalf. No wonder that his relations with them no longer seemed cordial![96] In due course, the Wrangel army was scattered to the four winds, a considerable fraction settling in Yugoslavia where they and their sons fought on Hitler's side in World War II.

A few die-hard interventionists in the West refused to accept this catastrophe as the end of their hopes. Even in Britain, the *Times* (November 15) hailed General Balakhovich as the "New Enemy of the Reds," estimating that he could rally about fifty thousand men on the White Russian front.[97] This was grasping at straws, an example which few followed. Others, however, tried to put the best possible face on these events, while tacitly conceding at last the end of all hopes for successful armed intervention. To the Conservative *Daily Telegraph* (November 15), the wonder was that Wrangel had held out so long, and his defeat meant little in comparison with the inability of the Bolsheviks to bring peace or order in Russia. They were, like the Tartars of old, "wholly incapable of building anything upon the ruins they create." It was as bitter as ever. Commenting on H. G. Wells' judgment that Lenin was at least "honest," it replied: "We have never doubted it. He has an honest disbelief in all goodness. He has an honest contempt for all who have the slightest qualms of conscience.... He is an honest, cold-blooded fanatic of the type which is vastly more dangerous than the hot-blooded type, and he doubtless includes in his universal contempt Mr. Wells and all the other unintelligent intelligentsia who will not see that the world can only be saved by the Dictatorship of the Proletariat...."[98] The Tory *Morning Post* (November 15) also minimized the Soviets' victories as won against "by no means formidable foes" and insisted that they would be unable to survive the approaching economic struggle which would be decisive, for the Soviet system was "a complete and ludicrous failure."

Far more directly involved in Wrangel's fate, the French were naturally more concerned than the British about its causes. There was a lively postmortem in the press in which blunt words were spoken. In the *Avenir,* Maurice Geneste wrote of the "Riga armistice as the equivalent of a death sentence for the government of South Russia,"[99] and others blamed the Poles in still more forthright terms. Bernard de Lacombe recalled his earlier thought that they should have required the disarmament of the Red Army instead of demanding territory beyond the Curzon Line.[100] In an article that Lenin cited as evidence of France's incurable hostility, the *Temps* again asserted that Poland had made peace against France's advice.[101]

There was an occasional admission of France's responsibility. Poincaré still regarded her isolated recognition of Wrangel as a mistake, since, as he claimed, her military advisers had warned against supporting generals "whose collaborators were recruited among the most detestable agents of the old regime and whose troops fought poorly allowing the Red Armies to capture the guns and ammunition France had sent."[102] While Pertinax had nothing but praise for Millerand's insistance throughout September that the Poles should not negotiate without Wrangel ("ne traitez pas les uns sans les autres"), a change, Pertinax asserted, had taken place in French policy early in October in regard to the Crimea in order to conciliate Britain and, he added, on the foolish advice of Czech leaders.[103] It remained for a relatively obscure commentator to put his finger upon what was perhaps France's decisive mistake: "From the moment the Polish armistice was signed, Wrangel should have been reinforced with all the necessary material. It could have been done. It was not done."[104]

The general tendency was, however, to blame the lack of Allied unity, which meant of course the failure of France's allies to follow Millerand's lead.[105] "Never have the great powers," declared a publicist of considerable penetration, "given a more frightening demonstration of powerlessness. Those who, in 1918, had assumed the task of remaking the world are incapable of settling accounts with this band of brigands and a few fanatical anarchists." He ended on a note of profound pessimism: even if the 100,000 men necessary for the overthrow of bolshevism had been available, the task of occupying and governing Russia would have involved burdens beyond the capacity of any country or group of countries.[106]

3. *The Internal Soviet Crisis and the Anglo-Russian Trade Agreement, March 16, 1921*

There were doubtless many who, like Pertinax,[107] continued to see in force the only solution of the Russian problem. In the prevailing climate of opinion, armed intervention was, however, a lost cause for the foreseeable future. If the Russians were to be saved, they must do it themselves. "We are then reduced to waiting," admitted Auguste Gauvain sadly, "for the Russian people to rescue themselves from the frightful tyranny of the Soviets without the assistance of military expeditions. That waiting will not be brief." [108] After reproaching the *Times* for its support of Balakhovich, a British weekly that could not be reproached for softness toward the Bolsheviks concluded: "The truth is that if the Russians become able to overthrow Bolshevism, they will do it of their own accord, and that they will never do it in any other way."[109] While Poincaré and other French leaders urged that the winter be employed in working out an agreement among the Allies and the United States upon a common policy, his purpose was defensive.[110] Not even the extremists openly advocated anything more concrete than the defense of Poland, whom they expected to be the victim of another Soviet offensive in the spring.[111] In London, the *Daily Telegraph* (November 16) agreed with French opinion "in taking the fall of Wrangel as a new menace to Poland, and through Poland to Europe," and the *Morning Post* (October 14) had been certain from the first news of the Riga treaty that the Bolsheviks "are looking forward and doubtless preparing for another attack on the barrier which keeps them from the promised lands of the west." Pilsudski's state visit to Paris in February, 1921, resulted in a Franco-Polish defensive alliance, but it is certain that no Allied agreement was reached either for the defense of Poland or upon a common Russian policy. As for the United States, the Allies' official recognition of Rumania's possession of Bessarabia, a move to strengthen its anti-bolshevism and perhaps to guard against a deal with the Soviets similar to that of Riga, aroused American displeasure as going counter to the policy of conserving Russia's territorial integrity.[112]

Meanwhile, Lenin was taking stock of the results of the prolonged crisis. Striking the balance in a speech, November 20, to the Bolshevik organizations of the Moscow area, he acknowledged that an "international victory [i.e., the world revolution], the only kind that is important and lasting for us" had not been won, and that the capitalist states had warded off the immediate threat to their institutions. Soviet Russia, nevertheless, had won in effect a victory over Poland and the powers. In Poland's acceptance of a frontier, at certain points fifty to a hundred kilometers west of the line that Soviet Russia had offered before the invasion of the Ukraine, he claimed a victory for the Red Army. The tensions between the capitalist powers, of which the Japanese-American and the German-Entente were especially valuable for Soviet Russia, offered fruitful opportunities for exploitation. Not a step did he retreat from his ultimate objective of world revolution, and he did not rule out the use of the Red Army to achieve it. Advantage would be taken of international tensions "but as soon as we are strong enough to destroy capitalism in its entirety, we will seize it by the gullet." For the immediate future, however, he moved in the direction of co-existence. In spite of their vastly superior strength, the capitalist powers had not been able to destroy Soviet Russia, and "we have conquered by force the possibility of existing side by side with the capitalist powers which are now constrained," he added, "to enter into commercial relations with us." Moreover, the Bolsheviks had never been "so insane as to claim that they intended to remake the world with Russia's own strength alone. We have always said that our revolution will win when it has the support of the workers of all countries." In staying the hands raised against Soviet Russia, they had given half-support and had thereby rendered "an appreciable service."[113] Indeed, contrary to his expectation, it was a greater service than they were ever to give again.

In another speech in December, Lenin played upon the Allies' treatment of the German people in the Versailles Treaty and their reactions as only less advantageous to Soviet Russia than the divisions among the Allied powers. With some exaggeration, he spoke of the marching of the "German Black Hundreds" with "the Russian Bolsheviks and the Spartacists" in the ferment caused by the Red Army's approach. Against its will, for the "German bourgeois government madly hates the Bolsheviks . . . the interests of the international situation are pushing towards peace with Soviet Russia. . . ." It was, as a distinguished historian of Soviet Russia concludes, "a step on the road to Rapallo."[114]

Despite the evidence that the Bolsheviks' ultimate revolutionary purposes had not changed and that a winter respite might enable them to tighten their hold upon Russia, even to invade Poland again in the spring, there was little support in the West for anything more energetic than nonintercourse. In the United States, the idea took the form of a reaffirmation of the secretary's note of August 10. The complete embargo it preached was, according to the *New York Times* (November 18), "the wise and sound policy" and it "has the well-nigh universal approval of the American people."[115] When, in December, administrative measures were taken allegedly for the purpose of implementing the removal (July 7) of restrictions upon trade with Soviet Russia, the permission to send money there may have made purchases possible, but it was a one-way street for the mint was directed not to accept gold (the only substantial form of payments the Soviets possessed) suspected of Soviet origin.[116] Many Frenchmen clung to the hope of at least an Allied agreement for the defense of Poland, but some called for a do-nothing or a waiting policy.[117] In London, the die-hard Tories, like Churchill, had abandoned armed intervention as impracticable. Without saying so openly, they manifestly favored at least a *de facto* economic blockade on the theory that the Bolsheviks would, through their inability to construct anything, destroy themselves.

Lloyd George, however, still disagreed, for he saw no alternative to the Soviet regime. In his Guildhall speech, November 9, he minimized the danger of bolshevism as an ideology and program of action. It was "a passing phase that cannot survive, it is such an impossible creed, such a ludicrous creed, such a crazy creed, it cannot survive, but what may survive is anarchy." If anything was worse than a bad government, it was, he declared, no government at all, and for that reason he was persisting in his effort to make peace.[118] Already a government spokesman, Bonar Law, had affirmed the intention of making a trade agreement. "Trade relations have been renewed by other governments, and this government," he said, "must do its best to get its share of the trade."[119]

On November 9, the day of Lloyd George's Guildhall speech and short-ly after the beginning of the final Red offensive against the Crimea, Chicherin addressed a note that was one long complaint about Britain's delays ending with a blunt demand for a "yes" or "no" in regard to its intentions. He hoped for a favorable reply and that a commercial accord would be accompanied or immediately followed by peace negotiations and the establishment of normal relations.[120]

The bitter-enders at once moved to the attack. To the *Daily Telegraph* (November 16), the Soviet note was merely "5,000 words of vituperation" and (November 17) "insolent." For the benefit of the foreign secretary, R. T. Nugent, who was Director of the Federation of British Industries, laid down what his group considered to be the essential prerequisites of a trade agreement: the recognition of all Russian debts, public as well as private; the payment of all interest charges; and provision for the amorti-zation of the principal—conditions that would doubtless have been rejected by the Soviets.[121] In the House of Commons, full compensation for British investments in Russia was demanded by a member who had just spent two "weary" hours explaining to the representatives of fifteen hundred shareholders what had happened to their investment of £2,500,000 in Baku oil wells. In any case, he was against a trade agreement that would pro-duce no trade. He derided those who expected as a result of an accord that "the hens will begin to lay, the flax will grow, and the corn bins will bulge once more."[122] Besides the absence on Soviet Russia's part of the good faith essential to all sound business relations, the opponents of Lloyd George's Russian policy relied most heavily upon the poor prospects that an appreciable trade would result from an agreement. "Russia, at the moment, is as fruitful as the desert, as rich in goods as an ice-bound continent."[123] Devastating evidence of the poor condition of Russian wheat shipped to Italy was belatedly picked up from the Italian press. On Sep-tember 2, the *Giornale d'Italia* had reported a large part of the S. S. "Pietro Calvi's" cargo had consisted of rotten barley, moldy corn, and seven hun-dred tons of wheat "three or four years old, mixed with manure, old boots, illustrated postcards, British and French unexploded cartridges."[124]

Although these arguments made a good deal of sense, they failed to carry conviction, doubtless in part because of the past record in the Rus-sian problem of those who advanced them. The dominant trend, tired of past deceptions, was obviously ready to try Lloyd George's recipe. Nor was it diverted by clear evidence that the Soviet government, through the Third International, continued to try with little success to needle British labor into a revolutionary frame of mind.[125] The chorus in favor of a trade pact began to swell. Naturally the Labor *Daily Herald* favored it, as always. The Council of Action, after a period of somnolence, resumed its activity. The fight "to secure peace and trade with Russia," it announced, would be resumed.[126] Russian trade was quite unrealistically presented as a solution of mounting unemployment. On December 22, a deputation representing 200,000 unemployed in London presented resolutions to the Labor party calling for the immediate opening of that trade. "The idea that trade with Russia will relieve unemployment," said William Adamson, member of Parliament and of the Council of Action, "has taken hold of the imagination of a great section of the people, and personally, I am in complete agreement with the idea."[127] Even the Sunday *Observer* (November 21) predicted that "orders to the tune of 100,000,000 pounds" would be placed by Russia in the first year after trade was resumed, but it had already gone farther. Wrangel's defeat had moved it (November 14) to declare: "Our business now and hereafter is to recognize the effective Government of Russia whatever it may be. Foreign force cannot smash the Bolshevist system. Trade is far more likely to transform it into a more moderate regime." Although the weekly *Spectator* had been consistently and bitterly anti-Bolshevik, it now (November 20) accepted Lloyd George's thesis as to the effect of trade upon the Bolshevik regime. "The hard angles of Bolshevism would begin to lose their sharpness by attrition." From the Liberal press, there was no dissent,[128] although the *New Statesman* (November 20) was convinced that Lloyd George and the coalition government acted from purely opportunistic motives. Support also came from the Conservative *Pall Mall Gazette* (November 17) and in the penny press; although Northcliffe's *Daily Mail* (November 9) was hostile, Beaverbrook's *Daily Express* (November 19) regarded trade as the best way to help the Russian people "out of their present evil plight."[129]

Although the details are not available, there is no possible doubt that the Cabinet had authorized the resumption of these trade negotiations. To sidestep anti-Bolshevik opposition, a distinction was drawn for the benefit of the public between bolshevism and the Soviet government, thus accepting for tactical reasons Moscow's own version of the separate and independent status of the Soviet government and the Third International. Speaking in the House of Commons, December 22, Sir Robert Horne, the President of the Board of Trade, repeated the usual castigation of bolshevism: "We detest and loathe the practices of Bolshevism. We believe that there could scarcely be a greater boon to the world at the present time than if you succeeded in destroying Bolshevism. . . ." When he was reproached from the Labor side, he replied that he had not meant the Soviet government. He was not disturbed by the unlikelihood of large-scale trade at once, but a beginning would be made. The only way to destroy bolshevism "will be by bringing Russia and the Russians under the civilizing influence of the rest of the world, and you cannot do that in any better way than by beginning to enter into trade and commerce with them." As for Bolshevik propaganda, which apparently was again a principal stumbling block as it had been before the July agreement, Horne abandoned the pretense of accepting the independence of the Bolshevik party organizations. The government, he said, was seeking from the Soviet government "assurance that they will themselves give directions to their Russian nationals to cease their propaganda." A recognition in principle of Russia's debts, and he specifically mentioned only those owed to private interests, was being sought, and he indicated that an agreement, because of the *de facto* recognition it would imply, might protect Soviet cargoes or gold in payment for British goods from seizure by the courts as the property of the Soviet government.[130] The virtuous insistence at the beginning of the trade negotiations that only the Russian co-operatives were involved and that no contact with the Soviet government would be tolerated had been long since conveniently forgotten.

In France, the same evolution began as a result of the changes in policy that accompanied the formation of George Leygues' ministry and Berthelot's control of the Quai d'Orsay. According to the *Petit Parisien* (November 26), Leygues told the Chamber's Foreign Affairs Commission on the eve of his departure for London (November 25) that "he was disposed to authorize commercial relations between French and *Russian merchants and industrialists* . . ." and for humanitarian reasons he would end the blockade if, indeed, it still existed.[131]

On January 8, 1921, Krassin left for Moscow with the text of the agreement he had reached with the Board of Trade. There would soon be, the American Ambassador was informed by a source conversant with the negotiations, "a trade agreement but no trade."[132] To insure against any backsliding on the government's part, a special Labor Conference, comprising representatives of the Trade Union Congress and the Labor party, listed trade with Russia as the first of its recommendations for Britain's economic recovery, but Liberal opinion, though still favorable, warned against exaggerated expectations especially in regard to the effect of Russian trade upon unemployment.[133]

The prospects were gloomier than ever during the winter for the Soviets were confronted by a more serious internal crisis than any they had faced since Brest-Litovsk in 1918 and the peak of Admiral Kolchak's fortunes in 1919. With the end of the Polish war and Wrangel's defeat, the pressures, arising from foreign intervention and the danger of a restoration, that had made the crushing burdens of the Bolshevik dictatorship somehow bearable lost much of their effectiveness. The apparently inexhaustible endurance and patience of the Russian people reached the breaking point when the most resented practices of War Communism, the forced collection of grain and other food stuffs, continued unchanged. The poor harvest in 1920 had reduced the available food, and acute fuel shortages hampered or prevented its transport to where it was needed most. While Lenin may have envisaged the tactical retreat to the New Economic Policy (NEP) before the full onset of winter, he did nothing about it until the following March, and the Bolshevik leaders seemed to be far more concerned with doctrinal disputations than with the people's distress. Their indifference to human misery and their utter lack of the milk of human kindness were never more convincingly shown. Among the rank and file, there were party members who renounced their faith at this bitter fruit of the revolution.[134]

Peasants and workers rose in a wave of rebellions here and there throughout Russia against the self-styled workers' government. In Moscow and Petrograd, workers struck against the reduction of food rations. Makhno, the anarchist guerrilla leader, was a scourge to the Bolsheviks in the southern Ukraine. In the province of Tambov, not far from Moscow, a large portion of the peasants rose under Antonov, a leader of indeterminate ideological aims, so effectively that the writ of the Soviet did not run outside the larger towns for a period of months. Tukhachevsky seems to have employed more than a score of rifle divisions (doubtless undersized) to suppress a peasant rebellion in Saratov province in the middle Volga basin.[135] Better known and more important was the Kronstadt rebellion (March 1-18) at this naval base near Petrograd, where under leftist leadership,[136] the naval garrison, despite its large part in the Bolshevik seizure of power and in the Civil War, fought off the élite of the Red Army for more than a fortnight. Never once appealing for foreign aid, the rebels hoped by their example to precipitate a third revolution for the end of the Bolshevik dictatorship, for freedom of speech and assembly by the opposition, and for the popular election of the Soviets by secret ballot.[137]

Embarrassed as the Bolshevik leaders were by the undeniably working class and peasant origins of these uprisings, they stood their ground. For the benefit of the outside world, they represented the Moscow strikes as proof of "the determination of the Russian workers to reach a better achievement," but they gave the show away by claiming to have traced the source of the trouble to the Latvian legation. True, Russia was experiencing "a serious food crisis, due to fuel shortages, but now as before, the Russian workers will prove to the world that their revolutionary solidarity and determination to stand by their achievements know no weakness."[138] While the Kronstadt rebels might have been won over by a compassionate approach, General Cavaignac, the author of the June Days in France (1848), and General Galliffet, the conqueror of the Paris Commune (1871), would have understood the Bolsheviks' intolerance. Trotsky, himself taking command, warned (March 5) that only those who surrendered unconditionally could expect mercy, but there was no response. After several assaults over the ice were repulsed with heavy losses, the defenses were finally penetrated during the early hours of March 18, and the Cheka then proceeded to carry out Trotsky's threat of no mercy.[139]

Reluctant to acknowledge the working class and peasant origins of the rebellion, the Bolsheviks borrowed a time-honored device from bourgeois practice and blamed their foreign enemies. First, the Moscow wireless station, March 3, then Zinoviev, the President of the Third International, in a speech to the Petrograd Soviet on March 4, and finally Lenin in an address, March 10, to the Congress of the Russian Bolshevik party then meeting in Moscow singled out the Entente, and especially the French secret services, as responsible.[140] What part, if any, these undercover agencies played will doubtless never be known—it is extremely doubtful that the leftist leaders of the rebellion would have worked with them—but it was possible that Kronstadt might have become the spearhead of a new interventionist campaign if the rebellion had managed to hold out indefinitely. To prevent this was undoubtedly a reason why Trotsky was determined to capture Kronstadt before the ice melted in the Gulf of Finland and thus opened a route for the arrival of foreign aid.[141]

In the West, the Kronstadt rebellion was an enormous sensation and its fortunes were followed with the utmost sympathy. Although the *Manchester Guardian* (March 7) doubted its success, it had none of the reactionary connotations that had assured the hostility of British Liberals against the White Russians. As late as the fourteenth, the *Daily Chronicle* noted with no indication of skepticism or displeasure that the insurrection seemed to be "gaining strength and extending" and that the Soviets were reported to have lost Kiev, Tambov, and Orel. It was, of course, the day of vindication for the Tory *Morning Post* (March 14): "The peasant . . . is breaking Lenin, as we all along thought he would." Thanks to the general expectation of the Soviet regime's internal collapse, the wildest reports from Scandinavian and Finnish sources were widely credited throughout the West. In Germany, the press unanimously, except for journals on the extreme left, predicted the impending collapse of the Soviet government, and in many instances this confidence survived the fall of Kronstadt.[142] The *Matin* in Paris (March 8, 10, 12) had more than fifty "commissars" arriving in Revel, most of them supplied with "a considerable quantity of gold, platinum, and jewels." "Petrograd is almost entirely in the hands of the Kronstadt insurgents." "The revolution is spreading to all parts of Russia. It seems impossible that Lenin and his partisans can resist much longer." On March 5, the London *Times* announced from Copenhagen that the "white flag is hoisted over the Winter Palace and the Kremlin in Moscow."

It is possible that a relatively small but determined military effort might have destroyed the Soviet regime at this time. So at least General Wrangel thought in his Near East refuge, for he told an American agent that he expected to lead his "fighting force of about 60,000 men" against the Bolsheviks before the end of the year.[143] The White Russians in Berlin, however, according to the resident American diplomatic agent, thought differently. They were convinced that "any effort by reactionaries or even moderates to mix in the present situation," which was "a spontaneous effort by seamen, workmen and peasants," would play into Lenin's hands. They thought that "as before all factions would unite against foreign invasion."[144]

Whatever their undercover agents were doing, neither Poland nor her Western friends had any intention of intervening again. On the contrary, the Poles, in spite of the alliance they had signed with France on February 19, seem to have identified their interests with the survival of the Soviet government and the suppression of the Kronstadt rebellion.[145] Their peace delegation in Riga pressed for the conclusion of the definitive peace treaty, which was signed on March 18, the date of the Bolsheviks' capture of Kronstadt,[146] in which Poland contented herself with the advantages she had won in the preliminary peace.

Nor was Poland, the only traditional enemy among Russia's neighbors that found it to its interest to conclude peace at this time. Despite subversive propaganda addressed to the Turkish people, including the followers of Mustapha Kemal, Soviet policy had already supported, with arms and money, Kemal's struggle with Greece for Turkey's national revival.[147] On March 2, just as the Kronstadt Rebellion began, the Moscow wireless station announced the opening of a Russo-Turkish Conference in Moscow on which occasion Chicherin aligned Soviet Russia with "the struggle for the liberation of the peoples of the East, who have been oppressed by Western imperialism." Yusuf Kemal Bey, the chief Turkish delegate, responded with a repudiation of the Treaty of Sèvres which the Allies had imposed upon Turkey. The Russian and Turkish peoples, Yusuf declared, "will naturally advance hand in hand."[148] On March 16, two days before Kronstadt's fall, a treaty was signed in Moscow returning Batum, which Kemalist forces had occupied on March 11, to Soviet Russia, ceding Kars and Ardahan to Turkey, and pledging solidarity in the struggle against Western imperialism.[149]

On the same day, March 16, the year-old negotiations culminated in London in the signature of the Anglo-Soviet trade agreement. It was a high point in Soviet Russia's successful foreign policy at this time. It was facilitated, if not made possible, by Lenin's announcement, March 10, to the Tenth Congress of the Russian Communist party of the New Economic Policy. While the uprising caused by the French and the Social Revolutionaries would, he said, be crushed in a few days, it forced the consideration of the peasants' complaints. The essential changes were the substitution of a food tax in kind for forced collections and a large measure of economic freedom for the peasant, but he also acknowledged the necessity of agreements with bourgeois governments.[150]

In regard to President Harding and the new Republican administration, the hopes nourished by L. Martens,[151] the Soviet agent who had finally been deported by the American government, and by the concession-hungry American, W. B. Vanderlip, for a reversal of the Wilson administration's attitude were rudely disappointed, but the British government was prepared to come to terms with the approval of a large part of British opinion. The Liberal *Daily Chronicle* (March 8) frankly warned: "Nor can any fighting element in Russia again look to the rest of Europe for any military support whatsoever. The Allies certainly will never repeat the experiment which failed in the cases of Koltchak [*sic*] and Denikin." In contrast to the sympathetic if platonic interest with which the Liberals followed the fortunes of the ill-fated Kronstadt Rebellion, the Labor *Daily Herald* (March 3), blindly accepting the Soviet regime as a true workers' and Socialist government, did not say a kind word for the rebels, who, it insisted, were playing into the hands of the British enemies of the trade agreement. It caustically referred to the press reports that "Trotsky and Lenin are in flight, or, at any rate, in rumoured flight . . . and we expect to hear very shortly that the Tsardom is re-established." It echoed Moscow's estimate that the rebellion was of no importance. "This revolution is an old friend. It usually comes to us . . . via Helsingfors. The sailors are always in it. Revolutionary fellows, the sailors! It must be something in the sea air. . . . Obviously, the only way to stop this sort of thing is to get the Trade Agreement signed, and then the revolution will have no excuse for happening again."

Since Krassin had left Russia for London, stopping en route in Berlin before the outbreak of the Kronstadt Rebellion,[152] both the British and the Soviet governments had probably decided to reach a conclusion. On his arrival in London, March 4, his first effort was to correct the press's version of Russia's internal situation. To the *Daily Herald's* diplomatic correspondent (March 5) he remarked at Victoria Station, "Well, I see from the English papers that Lenin has gone to South America." In a formal interview, Krassin claimed that the counter-revolution "exists mainly in the columns of the English newspapers." True, there had been "small disturbances" at Tambov, but even in regard to the "only real trouble" in Kronstadt it was "quite unimportant." Nowhere in Russia was there anything comparable to "what is going on in Ireland" (!). Kronstadt was "insignificant" when the other troubles the Soviet government had already surmounted were remembered. It would be "dealt with in the usual way"; the true situation would be explained to the rank and file, who would then surrender, and the leaders "will be quietly arrested and tried" (!). The French were to blame, as the Paris *Matin's* (February 13) article had shown, but "it is really of no importance at all—except in its political repercussion here."[153]

Despite the Foreign Office's apparent opposition,[154] the Board of Trade, to which Lloyd George continued to entrust the negotiations, was determined to go ahead. On March 9, Sir Robert Horne, ignoring the Foreign Office's attitude, told the House of Commons, "I am all for trading with Russia." He detested the crimes of the Soviet government as much as anyone, but he believed that "nothing will so upset the Communist system there as to resume trade, and if you will resume trade with gold you will find the system existing to-day will be so upset that the Russian people will soon become ready to adopt individual effort to produce goods which can be exchanged for commodities."[155] He conceded that the Soviets had little besides gold with which to trade but that gold, tainted or not, would make a beginning, and he stated more clearly than ever that a trade agreement, carrying with it the *de facto* recognition of the Soviet government, would protect Soviet gold and other goods from judicial seizure by Russia's creditors.[156]

While public interest largely centered upon Russia's internal crisis, the Conservative and anti-Bolshevik press belatedly awoke to the government's decision. It was greatly scandalized. The *Morning Post* (March 14) could see no necessity for "taking tainted or stolen gold, overriding law, and the countenancing of a régime which is tottering to its fall." As the *Daily Telegraph* (March 16) saw the situation in Russia, the world had witnessed no comparable disaster since the Great Flood.

Ignoring these and other arguments, the agreement was completed and signed, March 16, a fortnight after Krassin's return to London and two days before the fall of Kronstadt.[157] It provided for an exchange of commercial representatives who were to enjoy semi-diplomatic status, and, what was essential for the Soviet side in any resulting trade, the British government pledged itself not to initiate any steps to take possession of any funds or commodities that Russia might export.[158] Britain's renunciation of the blockade and other obstructions to trade formalized a decision long since made, but, as is usual in treaties, the renunciation was mutual. As for hostile propaganda—long a major obstacle from the British point of view—the Soviet government promised to refrain from hostile action or propaganda against British interests in Asia, especially in India and Afghanistan, but the intention Horne had mentioned in December of securing a specific guarantee that it would restrain its nationals in these respects had apparently been dropped. On its part, the British government gave a similar pledge in regard to the border countries that had formerly been in the Russian Empire. The question of Russia's private debts, although recognized in principle, was reserved for later settlement.

While the lengthy series of treaties which Soviet Russia was concluding with individual countries suggested a preference for bilateral treaties, there is little doubt that Lloyd George valued the agreement in large part as a step toward a general peace settlement in an international conference. It was for him a way station on the road to the conference that finally met, with far less success than he had hoped, at Genoa in 1922. From Lloyd George's as well as the Soviet point of view, the agreement, however, was intended to initiate a period of what was later to be called "co-existence," neither side then being so naïve as to expect the other to abandon its principles or ideology.[159] Doubtless as a reminder of British alertness, Horne addressed a list of specific instances of hostile propaganda in India to Krassin on the same day that the agreement was signed, to which the Soviets naturally replied, after a month had passed, that their hands had been free before the agreement. Since March 16, everything was being done to carry it out.[160]

Except in Labor circles, the earlier illusions about the Russian market had long since been dispelled. Increasing unemployment kept hope alive for large orders of British products, and Beaverbrook's *Daily Express* (March 17) acclaimed contracts for the repair of Russian locomotives as the first fruits.[161] Once the agreement was signed, Krassin immediately poured cold water upon excessive expectations, telling the *Daily Herald* (March 17), "We must not expect miracles. . . . A trade agreement isn't trade. The Treaty of Versailles was a Peace Treaty. But—." For the *Herald* (March 17) in its moment of triumph, the apparent demonstration of Labor's power over "the hard-faced men" of the government's majority in the House of Commons and the Foreign Office was apparently more important than the prospect of trade and its supposed relief of unemployment. *"What British Labour has done in this matter, British Labour could do in all. . . .* The Churchills, the Curzons, the Northcliffes hate and fear the Soviet Republic of Russia—because it is Socialist."

Their feelings were doubtless expressed in the unyielding anti-Bolshevik press. While the *Times* (March 17) assumed that the government whips would assure a majority in the House of Commons for the agreements, it awaited "with interest" the ministry's case for this "accommodation with this government of bandits, permitting them to sell their plunder in this country. . . ." Lenin and his accomplices would use "the credit and prestige" of this *de facto* recognition "to spread the tentacles of their poisonous influence throughout the world." The *Morning Post* (March 16) was filled with disgust and frustrated rage even before the agreement was signed. It waged a last-ditch defense against the recognition of what it described as "The Unclean Thing," that "illegitimate administration blackened with the commission of every crime in the calendar, whose agents in every part of the world are at this moment actively plotting the destruction of the British Empire." The *Morning Post* reminded the Unionists in the government coalition that the deal involved more than trade for "The honour of Great Britain is to be bought and sold." Why, above all, did the government select this moment "when the Soviet Government is reeling under a counter-revolution. . . ?" In a week or a month, that government might no longer exist, and, in any event, the agreement would be worthless as the Soviet government "respects neither bond nor pledge." Why, Mr. Lloyd George? The answer was clear to the Liberal *Manchester Guardian* (March 17). While no one would condone its sins, neither moral condemnation nor force had accomplished anything against the Soviet government. "We had tried the cold shoulder and the mailed fist, and neither . . . had apparently done anything to lead the sinner to repentance. . . . If we could neither persuade nor bully the Russians into virtue, was it not time that we tried what a good square meal would do?" Such was essentially Lloyd George's defense of the agreement in the House of Commons, March 22.

In his speech the prime minister for the first time specifically spoke of the agreement as "recognizing the Soviet government as the *de facto* Government to Russia . . ." and acknowledged that Soviet Russia's own actions had alone blocked his effort to obtain a general peace settlement. He obviously did not share the moral indignation expressed by preceding speakers; their speeches "do not seem to have penetrated beyond the walls of this House, and they do not seem to have raised that great moral indignation" which they had expressed so eloquently. No one could say how long the Soviet regime would last, but he did know that every prediction of its end had been mistaken. Was there, he asked, never to be any trade with Russia? "You cannot rule out half of Europe and a vast territory in Asia by ringing down the fire curtain and saying that until it has burnt itself out you will never send a commercial traveller there." Every prediction of the end of the Soviet regime had so far been mistaken. For the moment, he saw no alternative to it, but he did see a change in it. Reports of "the most remarkable declarations" in Moscow indicated "a complete change in the attitude of the Bolshevik Government to what is called capitalism, towards private enterprise," for Lenin had discovered that "you cannot patch up locomotives with Karl Marx's doctrines." In fact, Lenin's speeches might have been delivered by the secretary of state for colonies (Churchill), and it would be a good thing if they were circulated as "an antidote to the propaganda of the Labour Party in this country." In making the trade agreement, the government, Lloyd George said in substance, was not as charged "shaking hands with murderers," but it was rather "converting them. This is a gentlemanly process of instruction that has been going on."[162]

Britain's *de facto* recognition of the Soviet government as the first by one of the former Allies shocked the Western world, especially the United States and France. Following the example of the London *Morning Post,* the *New York Times* (March 17) captioned its editorial comments "The Unclean Thing" and was only restrained from concluding that "all established governments now sustaining relations of amity with Great Britain might describe it [the agreement] as the Unfriendly Thing" by the probability that nothing would come of it. Yet trade and diplomatic relations would strengthen the Soviet regime "very much at a time when most of the civilized peoples of the earth have begun to hope for its overthrow. He [Lloyd George] is not merely dealing with an unclean thing, he is petting mad dogs on the head." True, Herbert Hoover, Secretary of Commerce in the Harding Cabinet, was so little shocked that he instantly wrote the State Department that it seemed unfair to him to refuse to American traders the right to accept Russian gold that British merchants would presumably enjoy. He would like to have the State Department do something about it.[163] Although Secretary of State Hughes coldly rejected the All Russian Central Executive Committee's proposal to send a Soviet delegation to the United States for trade negotiations, until there existed convincing evidence that conditions existed "essential to the maintenance of commerce, personal safety, firm guarantees of private property, and of the rights of free labor,"[164] his reply lacked something of the moral fervor of the Colby note of August 10, 1920, and, of course, there was no appeal for an international non-intercourse pact. Moreover, the State Department and

Secretary Hughes did, in fact, concern themselves thereafter with certain practical problems involved in the promotion of trade in Russia.[165]

The French point of view had not changed sufficiently to assure a favorable reception of the Anglo-Soviet agreement. It would, the *Temps* (March 21) insisted, strengthen the Soviet regime and threaten French interests. Pertinax saw the situation in a somewhat different light. In his view, Lloyd George had seized an opportunity to reap a political profit at home without risk abroad in view of the certainty of the collapse of bolshevism, but he too feared for France's interests. Would Britain remain neutral in the event of another invasion of Poland to whose defense France had just obligated herself or if Russia attacked Rumania for the recovery of Bessarabia? Explanations, at any rate, were in order.[166] There was also the concern for the Russian imperial debts to France that always loomed large in French calculations.[167]

The approaching showdown with Germany in May, 1921, on the reparations question exerted greater influence upon French policy. Less than ever was there thought of further adventures in Russia. On March 8, the Allies under French leadership extended the zone of occupation to Duisburg, Ruhrort, and Düsseldorf as a reminder of the desirability of an acceptable German proposal for a permanent settlement. While France was not among the many countries that concluded trade agreements with Soviet Russia at this time, her attitude was more than ever strictly defensive. She was, for example, preparing to wash her hands completely of General Wrangel. The latter informed Dulles that the French High Commissioner had demanded the immediate liquidation of the Crimean Army "as the French will be forced to relinquish their support."[168]

Increasing Allied pressure upon Germany tended to neutralize the effect of the Bolsheviks' manifest complicity in the Communist uprising in March and to hasten the conclusion of a trade pact with Soviet Russia. What happened was a striking example of the ambivalence of Soviet policy between the Third International's commitment to world revolution and the Soviet government's new opportunistic adjustment to hard realities. While Victor Kopp negotiated about trade, Béla Kun, representing Zinoviev, the International's president, arrived in Berlin with advice that probably influenced the narrow vote in the Executive Committee of the German Communist party on March 3 for an effort to overthrow the government by force. The revolt began in the Mansfeld mining area in central Germany on March 17, spreading to other localities notably to "red" Hamburg, but, poorly prepared and disavowed by the greater part of the workers, it was suppressed with the usual ruthlessness before the end of the month.[169] It was in this context that Germany reacted to the Anglo-Russian trade agreement. Except in the demand for guarantees against Bolshevik meddling in Germany affairs,[170] the Communist Putsch had little effect upon either opinion or official policy.

Liberal and democratic opinion was sharply divided. The *Vossische Zeitung* (March 18), clinging to its expectation of the collapse of the Soviet regime which had lost forever the workers and peasants, attributed Britain's action not to confidence in the Soviet government's survival but to the desire to prevent those Russians who could assure its recovery from regaining control of their country. So far did it wander from reality that it, on March 19, identified Germany's interests with those of France and the Little Entente in their essentially anti-Bolshevik policy, regardless of the French attitude on reparations or perhaps in the hope of concessions on that question. Far more general was the feeling that Soviet Russia's position had been strengthened by the London trade pact. "The men in power in Moscow," the *Frankfurter Zeitung* (March 19) wryly remarked, "have had almost too much good fortune." Certainly, Great Britain would not have concluded the agreement, declared the moderately nationalist *Kölnische Zeitung* (March 18), if it had anticipated the Soviets' fall in the near future, and the liberal *Berliner Tageblatt* (March 18) saw in the suppression of the Kronstadt Rebellion another demonstration of the regime's "extraordinary skill" in surmounting its difficulties if not an assurance of its viability.

The *Frankfurter Zeitung* (March 19) called for the conclusion of a Soviet-German trade agreement, and, except for the *Vossische Zeitung,* there is no reason for thinking that it was vigorously opposed on any side. It was foreshadowed when Foreign Minister Simons (April 28) clearly if unrealistically distinguished between the responsibility of the Third International and the Soviet government for the Communist Putsch. The German government, he said, had no evidence of any complicity on the part of the Soviet government.[171] The increasing tension over reparations doubtless gave the final impetus to the Eastern orientation, although Simons had spoken of Germany's intellectual and economic surpluses as its chief reason. An unacceptable German proposal to the Allies (March 1), followed by the extension of the zone of occupation (March 8), led to the final Allied demand (May 5) for Germany's recognition of 132 billion gold marks as the total of her reparation obligations. On the next day, May 6, the Soviet-German trade agreement was signed in Berlin. Aside from an exchange of trade representatives with certain diplomatic privileges and technical arrangements relating to trade between private interests and the Soviet state monopoly, it severed such contacts as remained between the German government and the White Russians, since the former pledged itself to treat the Soviet trade mission as Russia's sole representation in Germany.[172]

Compared with the narrowness of Soviet Russia's escape from catastrophe during the internal crisis of 1921, her successes in foreign relations were almost spectacular. Soviet trading delegations were established in many countries by the end of the year: all of the Baltic states including Finland, Great Britain, Germany, Sweden, Norway, Poland, Czechoslovakia, Austria, Italy, Persia, and Turkey.[173] Soviet Russia was no longer isolated, although full diplomatic recognition was still withheld in most cases. These countries had, nevertheless, agreed in substance to repudiate the White Russians and intervention in Russia's internal affairs. Of the border states from Finland to Turkey, Rumania alone had not limited her freedom of action in this way, and her attitude was the result of the Soviet government's refusal to recognize the seizure of Bessarabia. No convenient base, therefore, remained for renewed military intervention as long as these treaties were observed. That the small countries within the immediate reach of the Russian colossus, whose strength would not remain crippled forever, decided to come to terms was not surprising in view of the attitude of the great powers. Not one of them even remotely contemplated renewed resort to armed force, and the policy of economic strangulation was almost as dead. None allowed the emotional hatred of bolshevism, which, while still a reality, perhaps no longer burned with its original intensity, to dictate its relations with Soviet Russia. Secretary of State Colby's note of August 10, 1920, had no lasting effect except upon American policy.[174] With the Republican administration of President Harding, the rejection of all relations as with an "Unclean Thing" was, however, not quite as absolute, for Secretary of State Hughes, after all, did state the conditions on which trade would be possible and unadvertised consideration was given to the means by which the American interest in that trade might be advanced.

Notes

CHAPTER I

1. David Lloyd George, *Memoirs of the Peace Conference* (New Haven, 1939), I, 271.

2. Would the German Spartacists and Communists, if they had led a successful revolution of their own, have welcomed this transfer with its implication of the continued leadership of the Russian Bolsheviks?

3. American Peace Mission to Secretary of State, Paris, September 26, 1919. National Archives, 763.72 112/12525.

4. In 1920, the British Foreign Office issued an obviously slanted collection of official documents and interviews on conditions in Russia from the summer of 1918 to March 1919. Great Britain, Foreign Office, *Collection of Reports on Bolshevism in Russia* (London, 1920).

5. *Figaro*, January 24, 1920.

6. General Viraux was the author of these articles in *Oeuvre*. *Annales de la Chambre des Députés*, 1920, I, 563. Hereafter cited as *Annales* (C.D. or S.).

7. V. Poliakoff, "The Entente, Germany, and the Bolsheviks," *Nineteenth Century and After*, LXXXVIII (September, 1920), 432-33. Hereafter cited as *Nineteenth Century*.

8. Bertrand Russell's critical articles, which appeared in the liberal weeklies, *Nation* (London) and *New Republic* (New York), were reprinted in book form, *Practice and Theory of Bolshevism* (London, 1920; 2d ed., 1949).

9. A. Ransome, *Russia in 1919* (New York, 1919). See also his *The Crisis in Russia* (New York, 1921).

10. "A Test of the News," *New Republic*, August 4, 1920 (Supplement).

11. Bertrand Russell reached a different conclusion at the time. Seeing in it a combination of characteristics of the French Revolution and of the early days of Islam, he believed that the truth "can only be understood by a patient and passionate effort of the imagination." *Practice and Theory of Bolshevism*, p. 7.

12. For the details see F. Borkenau, *The Communist International* (London, 1938).

13. Beatrice Webb noted the irresistible pull of the Third International among the "rebels." Margaret J. Cole, ed., *Beatrice Webb's Diaries, 1912-1924* (London, 1952), p. 177 (February 25, 1920).

14. *Parliamentary Debates*, Commons, 1919, X, 690-91 (November 17, 1919). Hereafter cited as *Parl. Deb.* (H.C. or H.L.).

15. *Ibid.*, p. 763. (Brigadier Croft, November 17, 1919.)

16. A. Duff Cooper, *Old Men Forget* (London, 1953), p. 131.

17. C. E. Callwell, *Field Marshal Sir Henry Wilson* (London, 1927), II, 221 (January 2, 1920); 222 (January 15); 226 (February 2).

18. Paul Cambon, *Correspondance, 1870-1924* (Paris, 1946), III, 347 (July 24, 1919); 348 (July 24); 351 (August 9).

19. J. St. Loe Strachey, "The Mechanism of Revolution," *Nineteenth Century*, LXXXVIII (October, 1920), 582-88.

20. Josephus Daniels, *The Wilson Era: Years of War and After, 1917-1923* (Chapel Hill, N.C., 1946), 546.

21. F. L. Paxson, *Post-War Years: Normalcy, 1918-1923* (Berkeley and Los Angeles, 1948), pp. 27-29. Cf. R. K. Murray, *Red Scare: A Study in National Hysteria, 1919-1920* (Minneapolis, 1955).

22. S. Huddleston, "French Politics Today," *New Europe*, August 5, 1920.

23. L. Dumont-Wilden, "La politique extérieure: La défense de l'Europe," *Revue politique et parlementaire* (*Revue bleue*), 58th yr. No. 2 (July 24, 1920), 56. Hereafter cited as *Revue bleue. Annales* (C.D.), 1920, I, 108 (February 6, 1920).

24. *Die Aufzeichnungen des Generalmajors Max Hoffmann.* (Berlin, 1928), II, 319-23.

25. In the spring of 1920, Victor Kopp arrived in Berlin as the Soviet representative, and on April 19 an agreement was signed in Berlin. The granting of diplomatic immunities, July 7, 1920, for representatives of both governments engaged in the exchange of prisoners foreshadowed the eventual resumption of full diplomatic relations. Gustav Hilger and Alfred G. Meyer, *The Incompatible Allies: A Memoir-History of German-Soviet Relations, 1918-1941* (New York, 1953), p. 25.

26. The matter was debated in the Reichstag, October 23, 24, 1919. L. Kochan, *Russia and the Weimar Republic* (Cambridge, 1954), pp. 22-24.

27. A. Chaumeix, "Chronique," *Revue des deux mondes*, November 1, 1919, p. 237; M. Hoschiller, "La politique extérieure des Soviets," *Revue de Paris*, January 15, 1920, p. 423; J. Bainville in *Action française*, January 30, 1920; J. Bainville, *La Russie et la barrière de l'est* (Paris, 1937), p. 37.

28. *Parl. Deb.* (H.C.), 1919, X, 729 (Lt. Col. Guinness).

29. L. Dumont-Wilden, "La défense de l'Europe," *Revue bleue*, January 24, 1920, pp. 56-58.

30. *Knickerbocker Press*, in *Literary Digest*, August 28, 1920.

31. For a critical examination of the authorship and sources of the *Protocols*, see

Notes

J. S. Curtiss, *An Appraisal of the Protocols of Zion* (New York, 1942). H. Arendt, *The Origins of Totalitarianism* (New York, 1951), pp. 347-50.

32. "Episodes of the Month," *National Review*, No. 442 (December, 1919), 442.

33. "Episodes of the Month," *National Review*, No. 448 (June, 1920), 448; A Student of History, "The Vendetta against Poland," *ibid.*, No. 450 (August, 1920), 783 f. Another contributor stated as a fact that Lenin's real name was Sederbaum and that his wife had long been known to be a Jewess. B. J. Wilden-Hart, "If Poland Perish," *ibid.*, No. 452 (October, 1920), 219-30.

34. *Times*, January 5, 1920.

35. *The History of the Times*, Part II, 1912-1920 (London, 1952), has nothing on this point. It is, in fact, completely silent on Russia for 1920 and the Polish-Russian War.

36. R. A. Ussher, "The Council of Action and Poland," *Nineteenth Century*, LXXXVIII (September, 1920), 441. In France and Germany, even the press of the extreme right apparently did not go as far as the British Tory press in using the myth of a Jewish conspiracy. The Bolshevik Revolution was, however, occasionally interpreted as the vengeance of the oppressed Jewish race. Dumont-Wilden, "La défense de l'Europe," *Revue bleue*, January 24, 1920; F. Wieser, "Die Revolutionen der Gegenwart," *Deutsche Rundschau*, CLXXXII (March, 1920), 327, 330.

37. F. Mury, "La première république bolcheviste," *Revue des deux mondes*, September 1, 1919, p. 167; Baron Nolde, "Le règne de Lénine," *ibid.*, November 15, 1919, p. 313; E. K. Mason, "A Military Appreciation of Bolshevik Russia," *National Review*, No. 440 (October, 1919), 272.

38. *Der zweite Kongress der Kommunist. Internationale. Protokolle der Verhandlungen vom 19. Juli in Petrograd und vom 23. Juli bis 7. August 1920 in Moskau* (Hamburg, 1921), pp. 313ff., 324. Rosa Luxemburg, especially, was never a real convert, nor probably was Karl Liebknecht, of the Spartacist leaders.

39. G. B. S.'s review of H. M. Hyndman, *The Evolution of Revolution*, in the *Nation* (London), February 19, 1920.

40. A. Heichen, "Die Problem der Minderheitsregierung," *Die neue Zeit. Wochenschrift der Deutschen Sozialdemokratie*, I (January 9, 1920), 399.

41. V. Poliakoff, "The Entente, Germany, and the Bolsheviks," *Nineteenth Century*, LXXXVIII (September, 1920), 432-433.

42. *Illustrated London News*, in *Literary Digest*, September 4, 1920.

43. See his first article, *Nation* (London), July 10, 1920, and his *Practice and Theory of Bolshevism*, pp. 26-27.

44. Ransome, *Russia in 1919*, p. ix.

45. *Nation* (London), October 18, 1920.

46. "They hit the Trail," *New Republic* (New York), August 11, 1920.

47. J. Y. Simpson, "Russia and Allied Policy," *Nineteenth Century*, LXXXVII (January, 1920), 76.

48. "Bertrand Russell on Russia," *New Republic*, September 1, 1920.

49. Chap. I, "What is Hoped from Bolshevism," Russell, *Practice and theory of Bolshevism*, pp. 17-23.

50. "B. Russell's Impressions of Bolshevik Russia," *Nation* (London), August 7, 1920. It was, according to the *New Republic* (New York, September 1, 1920), contributing enormously to the rescue of "a demoralized people from complete disintegration."

Notes

51. Russell, *Practice and Theory of Bolshevism*, p. 21.
52. Capt. F. McCullagh, "Leninism: The Design of the Bolsheviks," *Nineteenth Century,* LXXXVIII (July, 1920), 201-2.
53. G. Lansbury, *My Life* (New York, 1930), p. 229.
54. *Nation* (London), October 18, 1920.
55. See the concluding paragraph of the report of "The British Labor Delegation to investigate conditions in Russia." *Nation* (New York), September 25, 1920 ("International Relations Section").
56. *Nation* (London), August 14, 1920. Sir Basil was in charge of internal security.
57. *New Statesman,* April 24, 1920.
58. B. Russell, "Impressions of Bolshevik Russia," *Nation* (London), August 7, 1920.
59. A. Chaumeix, "Chronique," *Revue des deux mondes,* February 1, 1920, p. 720.
60. F. P. Walters, *A History of the League of Nations* (London, 1952), I, 95.
61. *Annales* (C.D.), 1920, I, 565 (Marcaine, March 25).
62. *Ibid.* (S.), 1920, I, 436, 439-40 (March 26). G. R. Labry, "Notre politique en Russie: Les méthods, les hommes," *Mercure de France,* February 15, 1920, pp. 5-24.
63. *Annales* (C.D.), 1920, I, 242f. (February 25).
64. *Ibid.,* p. 2108 (June 25).

CHAPTER II

1. American Peace Mission to Secretary of State, Paris, September 26, 1919. National Archives, 763.72 112/12525.
2. *Annales* (C.D.), 1919, p. 59 (December 23).
3. This did mean that the American government had softened towards Bolshevism and Soviet Russia. The Cabinet had considered an official and public statement "which would disclose the extent of the so-called Bolshevik movement," although no action was taken. The State Department provided the Congressional Committee on Foreign Affairs with a confidential memorandum on the Bolshevik program of world revolution. Lansing to J. P. Tumulty, Department of State, October 29, 1919. Woodrow Wilson Papers, File VI, Vol. 59, Folder 40, Library of Congress.
4. Curzon to Balfour, Foreign Office, August 21, 1919. *Documents on British Foreign Policy, 1919-1939,* 1st Series, II, 744-48. Hereafter cited as *D.B.F.P.*
5. Curzon's comments on (Sir Walford) Selby's minute, October 11, 1919, Foreign Office. *Ibid.,* 1st Series, III, 591-92.
6. Crowe to Hardinge, Paris, November 15, 1919. *Ibid.,* 1st Series, III, 647-48.
7. G. A. Craig and F. Gilbert, eds., *The Diplomats, 1919-1939* (Princeton, 1953), Chap. I, "The British Foreign Office from Grey to Austen Chamberlain."
8. *Old Diplomacy: The Reminiscences of Lord Hardinge of Penshurst* (London, 1947), p. 245.
9. *Lord Riddell's Intimate Diary of the Peace Conference and After, 1918-1923* (London, 1933), p. 198.
10. While it is not possible to adduce documentary evidence in support of this analysis in its entirety, especially in regard to diplomatic recognition, even this would seem implicit in his general attitude and actions.
11. W. Churchill, *The Aftermath, 1918-1928* (New York, 1929), p. 270 (Memorandum, September 15). No known evidence shows any significant German contribution to the Soviet military build up.

12. *Times,* October 29, 1919. Although this was substantially correct, the military specialists with Denikin in South Russia, who remained into 1920, seem to have done some fighting under the pretext of giving instruction in the use of British weapons.

13. *Parl. Deb.* (H.C.), 1919, X, 766-67.

14. See his Guildhall speech, November 8, *Daily Telegraph,* November 10, 1919.

15. Minute by Sir Walford Selby, October 11, 1919. *D.B.F.P.,* 1st Series, III, 591-92.

16. *Parl. Deb.* (H.C.), 1919, X, 766-67.

17. *Annales* (C.D.), 1919, p. 59 (December 23).

18. Summarized in Curzon's circular for the confidential information and guidance of the British representatives in Helsingfors, Vladivostok, Riga, Warsaw, Tiflis, and Rostov, January 1, 1920. *D.B.F.P.,* 1st Series, III, 746.

19. Notes of a conversation held at 10 Downing Street, December 12, 1919. *Ibid.,* 1st Series, II, 744-48.

20. Curzon's circular to Revel, Riga, Helsingfors, and Warsaw, September 25, 1919. *Ibid.,* 1st Series, III, 569-70. Cf. Curzon to Tallents, December 19, 1919. *Ibid.,* 1st Series, III, 679.

21. Philippe Berthelot, Director of Political Affairs, Quai d'Orsay, December 17, 1919, in a dispatch quoted by Pertinax in *Écho de Paris,* January 8, 1920. Pertinax credited the *New Statesman* (January 3) with the revelation of this document.

22. E. H. Carr, *The Bolshevik Revolution, 1917-1923* (London, 1951-53), III, 156.

23. *Daily Telegraph,* November 10, 1919.

24. "A New Edition of Prinkipo," *New Europe,* November 13, 1919.

25. *Parl. Deb.* (H.C.), 1919, X, 726, 728.

26. *Ibid.,* 728 (Lt. Col. W. Guiness).

27. Curzon was in charge of the Foreign Office during the absence of Balfour, the Foreign Secretary, at the Paris Peace Conference.

28. Petrograd broadcast, received by Foreign Office, July 20, 1919. *D.B.F.P.,* 1st Series, III, 472 fn. 2.

29. Curzon to Grahame (Paris) for Chicherin, Foreign Office, August 5, 1919. *Ibid.,* 1st Series, III, 471-72.

30. Chicherin to Curzon, August 13, 1919. *Ibid.,* 1st Series, III, 486-87.

31. *Ibid.,* 1st Series, III, 487, fn. 2.

32. Curzon's instructions suggest the possibility that the choice was Lloyd George's. Robert Nathan, of the Foreign Office, was attached to O'Grady as adviser (and possibly as his mentor and watchdog). O'Grady was specifically directed that his reports were to be sent directly to the Foreign Office by the British minister in Copenhagen, and he was to submit his final report to it. Curzon to O'Grady, Foreign Office, November 13, 1919. *Ibid.,* 1st Series, III, 643-44.

33. Curzon to Grant Watson (for O'Grady), Foreign Office, November 26, 1919. *Ibid.,* 1st Series, III, 663-64.

34. Sir C. O'Grady to Curzon, Copenhagen, December 10, 1919. *Ibid.,* 1st Series, III, 691.

35. O'Grady to Gregory, Copenhagen, December 10, 1919, with enclosure. *Ibid.,* 1st Series, III, 692.

36. Litvinov to O'Grady, Copenhagen, December 22, 1919 (letter and footnote). *Ibid.,* 1st Series, III, 738-40.

37. Curzon to Mackinder, Foreign Office, November, 1919. *Ibid.,* 1st Series, III, 672-78.

38. Curzon's minute, December 28, 1919. *Ibid.*, 1st Series, III, 740.

39. L. Fischer, *The Soviets in World Affairs* (2d ed.; Princeton, 1951), I, 250-51.

40. Writing from Helsinki in March, 1920, a German observer advised that the emphasis upon economic reconstruction should be taken seriously. The Bolshevik press was filled with propaganda about productive work. C. von Kügelgen, "Die russische Sphinx," *Deutsche Rundschau*, CLXXXIII (May 1920), 188.

41. Carr, *Bolshevik Revolution*, II, 211-12, 215-16.

42. *Ibid.*, II, 370-71.

43. Translations of these documents are available in J. Degras, *Soviet Documents on Foreign Policy* (London, 1951-53), I, covering the years 1917-24.

44. Lenin, Trotsky, Joffe, and Litvinov all gave such interviews during February 1920 in which they spoke of peace and of trade. Carr, *Bolshevik Revolution*, III, 160.

45. "Où va la Russie," *Temps*, January 3, 1920.

46. J. Bainville, *La Russie et la barrière de l'est* (Paris, 1937), p. 63.

47. *Times*, January 5, 1920; *Nation* (London), January 10, 1920.

48. George Lansbury's editorial, "Peace with Russia," *Daily Herald*, January 3, 1920.

49. E. F. Wise's memorandum, January 6, 1920. *D.B.F.P.*, 1st Series, II, 867-70, fn. 2. Wise's estimates as to the quantities of grain and other commodities available for export were obviously much exaggerated.

50. Curzon's minute on R. H. H[oare], memorandum, December 22, 1919. *Ibid.*, 1st Series, III, 735-38.

51. Notes of a meeting of the Heads of Delegations, Paris, January 14, 1920. *Ibid.*, 1st Series, III, 866-75. Kammerer and Marguis della Toretta were the French and Italian members. On the same day, Captain O'Grady suggested from Copenhagen that the Supreme Council should be asked to raise the blockade. Grant Watson to Curzon, January 14, 1920. *Ibid.*, 1st Series, III, 757-58.

52. Notes of a meeting of Ministers of Foreign Affairs, Quai d'Orsay, Paris, January 10, 1920. *Ibid.*, 1st Series, II, 796-97.

53. *Ibid.*, 1st Series, II, 725-26.

54. Appendix, January 12, 1920. Notes of a Meeting in M. Pichon's Room, Quai d'Orsay, Paris, January 19, 1920. *Ibid.*, 1st Series, III, 925-26. For his part Field Marshal Wilson dissented vigorously against the military support of these states whose conquest by the Bolsheviks he regarded as certain. He was certain that the only feasible defense of the Middle East was a line considerably to the South. C. E. Callwell, *Field Marshal Sir Henry Wilson* (London, 1927), II, 221-22 (January 12, 1920).

55. Fischer, *Soviets in World Affairs*, I, 218.

56. *World* (New York), January 16, 1920.

57. Callwell, *Wilson*, II, 223 (January 15).

58. *New York Times*, January 17, 1920, Edwin L. James, Paris, January 16.

59. See also *Matin*, January 16, 1920, London, January 15; *Journal des débats*, *Figaro*, January 17.

60. Callwell, *Wilson*, II, 223.

61. Notes of a Meeting of the Heads of Delegations, Quai d'Orsay, Paris, January 16, 1920, 10:30 A.M. *D.B.F.P.*, 1st Series, II, 804-05.

62. Curzon's telegram was marked "Very Confidential, not for circulation." *Ibid.*, 1st Series, II, 911, fn. 5.

63. A Catholic review offered no objection in principle and even discounted the

Notes

immediacy of the Bolshevik danger. *Correspondant*, N.S., CCXLII (January 20, 1920), 381-83.

64. Draft telegram to French Ambassador, Washington. *D.B.F.P.*, 1st Series, II, 944-45.

65. Lansing to President Wilson, Department of State, January 20, 1920. Woodrow Wilson Papers, File II, Box 166, Library of Congress.

66. *Morning Post*, January 19, 1920.

67. *Daily Telegraph*, January 29, 1920. Cf. W. P. and Zelda K. Coates, *A History of Anglo-Soviet Relations* (London, 1944), p. 14.

68. *Lord Riddell's Intimate Diary*, p. 161.

69. Notes of a meeting held in M. Pichon's Room, Quai d'Orsay, Paris, January 19, 1920. *D.B.F.P.*, 1st Series, I, 915-25.

70. *Parl. Deb.* (H.C.), 1920, I, 40 ff.

71. *Lord Riddell's Intimate Diary*, pp. 162, 163.

72. *Times*, February 16, 1920.

73. L. Broad, *Winston Churchill* (New York, 1952), pp. 182-83.

74. Lansing to Davis, Washington, February 2, 1920. *Papers Relating to the Foreign Relations of the United States*, 1920, III, 701-2. This series will henceforth be cited as *Foreign Relations*.

75. Davis to Secretary of State, London, February 7, 1920. *Ibid.*, 1920, III, 702-3.

76. For H. Fabre in *Journal du peuple*, and M. Geneste in *Avenir*, see *Matin*, February 1, 1920; for Buré in *Éclair*, see *Matin*, February 2.

77. *Victoire*, in *Matin*, February 2, 1920.

78. A. Chaumeix, "Chronique," *Revue des deux mondes*, February 1, 1920.

79. *Annales* (C.D.), 1920, I, 105.

80. *Foreign Relations: The Paris Peace Conference*, X, 681-83 (February 6, 7, 1920).

81. According to his informants, the government's decisions on Russia (and Constantinople) were being made by the prime minister "almost without reference to the Cabinet." Curzon, the Foreign Secretary, was reportedly dissatisfied but his resignation seemed improbable. Davis to Secretary of State, London, February 24, 1920. National Archives, 861.01/197.

82. *Europe nouvelle*, June 13, 1920.

83. *Parl. Deb.* (H.C.) 1920, I, 1501-3 (February 24). For the communiqué, see *Manchester Guardian*, February 25. On March 12, the League's council informed the Soviet government of its decision to send a commission of inquiry and requested assurances in regard to facilities for its investigations and to its safety. F. P. Walters, *A History of the League of Nations* (London: 1952), I, 95-96.

84. See Paul Cambon's jaundiced remarks about Nitti, in *Correspondance, 1870-1924* (Paris, 1946), III, 376 (February 27, 1920), and Nitti's statement in *Atti del Parlamento Italiano*, Camera del Deputati, sessioni 1919-1920, Discussioni, II, 1034 (March 22). "Il ritorno della Russia," *Giornale d'Italia*, February 25; A. Zanetti, "Verso la Russia di oggi," *ibid.*, February 26; *Corriere della Sera*, February 26.

85. Polk to Wallace (Paris), Washington, March 6, 1920; Colby to Wallace, April 2. *Foreign Relations*, 1920, III, 703-704, 708. Cf. W. A. Williams, *American-Russian Relations, 1781-1947* (New York, 1952), p. 174.

86. *Matin*, February 25, 1920. Some forty-five businessmen having secured orders were reported to have organized to protect their interests. *Ibid.*, March 9.

87. *Annals* (C.D.), 1920, II, 562-63. The public reaction to Barthou's speech shows

Notes

the strength of the passions he had offended. According to the Socialist *Humanité* (*Matin,* March 26, 1920), the Chamber seemed partly stupified, and Auguste Gauvain, writing in the *Journal des débats* (March 27) declared that Barthou had disqualified himself for the succession to the presidency of the council.

88. Some thousands of Reichswehr troops had pursued armed Communist bands into the areas demilitarized under the Treaty of Versailles on April 3.

89. F. Polk, Under-Secretary of State, to President Wilson, Department of State, March 19, 1920; President Wilson to Polk, White House, March 19. Woodrow Wilson Papers, File II, Box 167, Library of Congress.

90. President Wilson to Colby, White House, April 7, 8, 1920. Woodrow Wilson Papers, File II, Box 168, Library of Congress.

91. Enclosure in Wallace to Secretary of State, Paris, April 9, 1920. *Foreign Relations,* 1920, III, 709-10. On April 17, representatives of European neutral states, Denmark, Sweden, Norway, Holland, and Switzerland, met in Switzerland and agreed that their claims upon Russia should conform to a pattern. Fischer, *Soviets in World Affairs,* I, 251.

92. Colby to President Wilson, State Department, April 16, 1920; Wilson to Colby, White House, April 19. Woodrow Wilson Papers, File II, Box 168, Library of Congress. This note was occasioned by the Italian government's desire for America's presence at San Remo—which may well have been inspired by Lloyd George. Colby to Wilson, Department of State, April 16. Wilson Papers, File II, Box 168, Library of Congress.

93. He frankly acknowledged his awareness of the true situation in private conversations. *Lord Riddell's Intimate Diary,* p. 175 (March 6, 1920).

94. *Parl. Deb.* (H.C.), 1920, II, 1792, 1793 (March 15). According to the conservative *Spectator* (April 24), the delegation represented "the terrorists of Moscow," and Krassin, its leader, "was understood to be a German agent." According to Fischer, Lloyd George's pretense was regarded as a joke by the Bolsheviks, Chicherin always chuckling when he spoke of it. *Soviets in World Affairs,* I, 251.

95. Such was the American Embassy's conclusion, Wright to Secretary of State, London, April 2, 1920, *Foreign Relations,* 1920, III, 708, 709. The delegation did not, in fact, arrive in London until May 27.

96. American Commission to negotiate Peace, Paris, 1918-19, Vol. 101. Cases 180.038-180.0401, National Archives.

CHAPTER III

1. E. H. Carr, *The Bolshevik Revolution, 1917-1923* (London, 1951-53), III, 91-94. For further discussion of the Allied decision not to employ German troops against the Bolsheviks, see E. H. Carr, *German-Soviet Relations between the Two World Wars, 1919-1939* (Baltimore, 1951), pp. 13-16; L. Kochan, *Russia and the Weimar Republic* (Cambridge, 1954), pp. 14-16; H. R. Rudin, *Armistice 1918* (New Haven, 1944), pp. 310-12; Charles Seymour, *Intimate Papers of Colonel House* (Boston, 1928), IV, 334; David Lloyd George, *Memoirs of the Peace Conference* (New Haven, 1939), II, 245-246; *Foreign Relations: The Paris Peace Conference,* IV, 207-12; *D.B.F.P.,* 1st Series, III, Chap. I; G. Noske, *Erlebtes aus Aufsteig und Niedergang eines Demokratie* (Offenbach-Main, 1947), pp. 122-23; Colmar von der Goltz, *Als politischer General im Osten* (Leipzig, 1936), pp. 82-83.

2. *Der polnisch-sowjetrussische Krieg, 1918-1920. Herausgegeben vom Generalstab*

Notes

des Heeres. Kriegswissenschaftliche Abteilung 2 (Berlin, 1940), I, 13. The Library of Congress has only the first volume of this useful publication of the Historical Division of the German General Staff. Based upon Polish and Russian sources, the first volume ends with the situation at the time of Pilsudski's capture of Kiev, May 6, 1920.

3. According to a French officer who served with the Allied mission observing the German evacuation, France delivered the following war supplies to Poland by the spring of 1920: more than 327,000 rifles; 2,800 machine guns; almost 1,500 guns ranging from 75 to 155 mm. in caliber; more than 10,000,000 shells; 291 airplanes; 800 trucks; 400,000 overcoats; 540,000 pairs of trousers; 830,000 shirts; 780,000 pairs of boots; 226,000 blankets. O. d'Etchegoyen, *The Comedy of Poland* (London, 1927), pp. 218-19. (Translated from: *Pologne, Pologne*... [Paris, 1923].) This disillusioned witness claimed that these supplies were lost during the Red Army's offensive in 1920 and had to be replaced by France. For the number of divisions and organizational problems, see General W. S. Sikorski, *La campagne polono-russe de 1920* (Paris, 1928), p. 271. Sikorski commanded the 9th Polish Division in 1920.

4. A. Przybylski, *La Pologne en lutte pour ses frontières* (Paris, 1929), pp. 100-1.

5. J. Piksudski, *L'année 1920*... (Paris, 1929), p. 177.

6. Rudin, *Armistice 1918*, pp. 299-300; *The Treaty of Versailles and After: Annotations of the Text of the Treaty* (Washington, 1947), p. 208. The Minorities Treaty, which the Allies and Poland signed June 28, 1919, contained the same provision concerning the eventual determination of the Polish boundary. *The Treaty of Versailles and After*, p. 793.

7. German General Staff, *Der polnisch-sowjetrussiche Krieg, 1919-1920*, I, 104-5.

8. M. Baumont, *La faillité de la paix* (3d ed.; Paris, 1951), I, 82.

9. A. L. Kennedy, *Old Diplomacy and the New, 1876-1922: From Salisbury to Lloyd George* (London, 1922), p. 137.

10. M. K. Dziewanowski, "Pilsudski's Federal Policy, 1919-1921," *Journal of Central European Affairs*, X (July, 1950), 119-20.

11. While Paderewski estimated that Poland would require a daily subsidy of some £600,000, Lloyd George thought it would more probably amount to £1,000,000. Notes of a meeting of the heads of delegations of the Five Great Powers, Paris, September 15, 1919. *D.B.F.P.*, 1st Series, I, 689-704.

12. *Ibid.*, 1st Series, I, 714.

13. While an official spokesman explained to the House of Commons, November 11, 1919, that the responsibility for supplying the Poles with equipment and ammunition had heretofore been France's, he admitted that some British money had been spent for this purpose and that the possibility of drawing upon surplus stocks was being considered. *Times*, November 12, 1919.

14. See the notes of meetings of the heads of delegations of the Five Great Powers in Paris, October 2, 29, 1919, and the notes of the Anglo-French Conversations in London, December 13. *D.B.F.P.*, 1st Series, I, 849-85; II, 30, 31, 776.

15. D'Etchegoyen, *Comedy of Poland*, pp. 145-47.

16. Rumbold to Curzon, Warsaw, October 20, 1919, No. 371. *D.B.F.P.*, 1st Series, III, 605.

17. Rumbold to Curzon, Warsaw, October 26, 1919, No. 392. *Ibid.*, 1st Series, III, 605-6, fn.

18. Rumbold to Curzon, Warsaw, October 24, 1919, No. 393. *Ibid.*, 1st Series, III, 610-11.

19. After an interview with Pilsudski on November 5, 1919, Hugh Gibson, the American Minister, told Rumbold of the acceptance of German supplies as the possible basis of a German-Polish agreement. Rumbold to Curzon, Warsaw, November 7, 1919, No. 432. *Ibid.,* 1st Series, III, 635.

20. Rumbold to Curzon, Warsaw, November 7, 1919, No. 432. *Ibid.,* pp. 633-36.

21. Rumbold was officially informed that the Polish representatives had repulsed the efforts made by the Soviet delegates to discuss the possibility of peace (Rumbold to Curzon, Warsaw, October 19, 1919, No. 336. *Ibid.,* p. 630, fn. 1) and that the Soviets had offered all of White Russia (Rumbold to Curzon, Warsaw, November 3. *Ibid.,* p. 630).

22. Dziewanowski, "Pilsudski's Federal Policy, 1919-1921," *Journal of Central European Affairs,* pp. 124, 125. For other references to this obscure episode, which the Bolsheviks later used as evidence of Poland's betrayal of Denikin, see L. Fischer, *The Soviets in World Affairs* (2d ed.; Princeton, 1951), I, 239-41; Carr, *Bolshevik Revolution,* III, 154-55; K. Radek, *Die auswärtige Politik Sowjetrusslands* (Hamburg, 1921), pp. 56-57. A visiting British Socialist, H. N. Brailsford, was given the essential data by Y. Markhlevsky, a Polish Communist who had been personally involved. H. N. Brailsford, "Russian Impressions: v. The Armed Doctrine," *New Republic,* December 29, 1920.

23. Carr refers to the record of a decision by the Politburo, November 14, 1919, in the Trotsky archives relating to such terms. Carr, *Bolshevik Revolution,* III, 154, fn. 3. The Poles claimed later to have been offered the frontiers of 1772.

24. Curzon to Crowe, Foreign Office, October 24, 1919, No. 1329. *D.B.F.P.,* 1st Series, III, 897. An unlimited tenure would, in his view, mean in practice direct annexation, although the same consideration was not to affect his attitude toward the mandates Great Britain and the Commonwealth were shortly to receive at San Remo in April, 1920, for former German and Turkish possessions.

25. Curzon to Crowe, Foreign Office, November 7, 1919, No. 1533. *Ibid.,* 1st Series, III, 898; Curzon to Crowe, Foreign Office, November 12, No. 1352. *Ibid.,* 1st Series, III, 900.

26. Notes of a conversation at 10 Downing Street, London, December 11, 1919. *Ibid.,* 1st Series, II, 729-30, 737.

27. Crowe to Curzon, Paris, December 23, 1919, No. 1733. *Ibid.,* 1st Series, III, 909.

28. G. M. Gathorne-Hardy, *A Short History of International Affairs, 1920-1939* (4th ed.: London, 1950), p. 95.

29. Notes of a meeting of the heads of delegations of the Five Great Powers, Paris, September 25, 1919. *D.B.F.P.,* 1st Series, I, 785-86.

30. Notes of meetings of the heads of delegations of the Five Great Powers, Paris, December 1, 2, 1919. *Ibid.,* 1st Series, II, 442 (December 1); 470 (December 2). For the final text of the communication, see *British and Foreign State Papers,* CXII (1919), 971-72.

31. Rumbold to Curzon, Warsaw, Nov. 7, 1919, No. 432. *D.B.F.P.,* 1st Series, III, 634.

32. Appendix E. Notes on a meeting of the heads of delegations of the Five Great Powers, Paris, November 29, 1919. *Ibid.,* 1st Series, II, 431.

33. Carr, *Bolshevik Revolution,* III, 154 fn. 3, on the basis of Trotsky's private papers in the Houghton Library of Harvard University.

34. *Ibid.,* I, 303-4.

Notes

35. For an English translation, see J. Degras, *Soviet Documents on Foreign Policy* (London, 1951-53), I, 177-78. Cf. R.S.F.S.P. Commissariat du peuple pour les affaires étrangères, *Livre Rouge* (Moscow, 1920), pp. 87-88. This is a collection of Soviet documents in French translation dealing with Soviet-Polish relations down to Pilsudski's invasion of the Ukraine. In a foreword, Chicherin explained that every Soviet note was addressed to the workers and peasants as well as to the government in question. The note to Poland—and most of the other notes—conformed to this standard practice of Soviet diplomacy.

36. Rumbold to Curzon, Warsaw, December 31, 1919. Tel. 522. *D.B.F.P.*, 1st Series, III, 745.

37. Gibson to Secretary of State, Warsaw, January 17, 1920, Tel. 27. *Foreign Relations*, 1920, III, 371-75.

38. Rumbold to Curzon, Warsaw, December 31, 1919, Tel. 522. *D.B.F.P.*, 1st Series, III, 745.

39. Rumbold to Curzon, Warsaw, January 17, 1920, Tel. 36. *Ibid.*, 1st Series, III, 759-60.

40. Rumbold to Curzon, Warsaw, January 19, 1920, Tel. 41. *Ibid.*, 1st Series, III, 764-66.

41. Gibson to Secretary of State, Warsaw, January 18, 1920, Tel. 28. *Foreign Relations*, 1920, III, 375-76. Cf. Gibson to Secretary of State, Warsaw, January 17, Tel. 27. *Ibid.*, pp. 371-75.

42. Since Poland and Soviet Russia were already engaged in hostilities even if there had been no formal declarations of war, what he meant was doubtless a sizable offensive.

43. Curzon to Rumbold, Foreign Office, January 27, 1920, Tel. 46. *D.B.F.P.*, 1st Series, III, 803-5.

44. *Daily Telegraph, Manchester Guardian*, January 28, 1920.

45. *Morning Post*, February 2, 1920. The *Temps* (February 4) insisted that Patek's press statement contained no trace of a promise by Lloyd George.

46. See "The Bolsheviks Propose Peace to Poland" in *Matin*, January 31, 1920. Its tone suggests official inspiration.

47. Davis to Secretary of State, London, January 28, 1920, Tel. 155. *Foreign Relations*, 1920, III, 376-77.

48. See R. Pinon's bitter reproaches in "The Future of Franco-British Friendship," *New Europe* (February 19, 1920), and the editor's (R. W. Seton-Watson) rejoinder that France's efforts to inflate Poland into a country of forty or even sixty million was a disservice to the Polish people.

49. *Journal des débats*, February 19, 1920.

50. Gibson to Secretary of State, Warsaw, January 30, 1920, Tel. 51. *Foreign Relations*, 1920, III, 377; Gibson to Secretary of State, Warsaw, January 30, Tel. 52. *Ibid.*, pp. 377-78.

51. Lansing to Gibson, Washington, February 5, 1920, Tel. 54. *Ibid.*, p. 378. Testifying before the House Ways and Means Committee, January 15, on proposed loans to European countries for the purchase of food, General Tasker H. Bliss, a member of the American Peace Commission, said that the government should require as a condition that the Allies provide the Poles with military supplies. Secretary of War Newton D. Baker was reported as telling the committee that the Allied and American governments were considering definite plans for supplying Poland with "war materials and

Notes

food" to help in checking the westward expansion of Bolshevism. *Washington Post,* January 16, 1920. Cf. *Nation* (New York), January 17. There is no evidence that any action was taken.

52. Degras, *Soviet Documents on Foreign Policy,* I, 179-80. Cf. *Livre rouge,* pp. 90, 91. In this Soviet publication, the document carries the signatures of Lenin, Chicherin, and Trotsky.

53. V. I. Lénine, *Oeuvres complètes* (Paris, 1928), XXV, 33. On February 7, he wrote that the time had come for a war against hunger, cold, typhus, and destruction. *Ibid.,* XXV, 36-37.

54. *Livre rouge,* pp. 92-95.

55. See the dispatches of British press correspondents from Warsaw in mid-January, 1920, above. Cf. *New York Times* January 22, February 16; *World* (New York), January 29, Arno Dosch-Fleurot, Warsaw, January 28. On March 26, a French Senator foresaw the occupation of Warsaw and Bucharest next summer (1920) by an army of two million and eventually the invasion of Western Europe by an army of eight to ten million Tartars, Musulmen, Chinese, and Slavs under German command. *Annales* (S.), 1920, I, 443 (Gaudin de Villaine).

56. *Times,* February 14, 1920, Warsaw, February 9.

57. *Écho de Paris,* February 23, 1920, Charles Bonnefou, Warsaw, February 21.

58. *Matin,* February 19, 1920, "From our own special representative," Warsaw, February 13.

59. Gibson to Secretary of State, Warsaw, March 3, 1920, Tel. 123, National Archives, 760 c 61/28.

60. *Livre rouge,* p. 92. English translations of this and many of the ensuing messages relating to the Soviet-Polish crisis were printed in the *Nation* (New York), August 14, 1920.

61. "Pologne, Russie et Bolchévisme," *Journal des débats,* February 2, 1920.

62. Count Alexander Skrzyński, *Poland and Peace* (London, [1923]), pp. 40-41.

63. Gibson had apparently not yet received Lansing's instructions of February since he cautioned Patek not to do violence to Polish national opinion. He also again urged that the Allies should give Poland a lead as to the course she should follow. Gibson to Secretary of State, Warsaw, February 8, 1920, Tel. 68. *Foreign Relations,* 1920, III, 378-80.

64. *Matin,* February 17, 1920, Warsaw, February 12, under headline, "Poland demands Europe make Peace with Russia."

65. *Ibid.,* February 20, Henry de Korab, Warsaw, February 15, under the headline, *"Le moment de faire la paix avec la Russie est arrivé pour tous les pays de l'Entente, déclare ... le Général Pilsudski...."* Cf. excerpt quoted in Dziewanowski, "Pilsudski's Federalist Policy, 1919-1921," *Journal of Central European Affairs,* p. 271.

66. *Times,* February 14, 1920, Warsaw, February 9.

67. *Écho de Paris,* February 23, 1920, Charles Bonnefou, Warsaw, February 21.

68. Gibson to Acting Secretary of State, Warsaw, February 19, 1920, Tel. 86. *Foreign Relations,* 1920, III, 381.

69. The French were encouraging the Poles by holding out the prospect of an early visit by Marshal Foch to Warsaw, of "generous material support from France," or of an early internal collapse in Soviet Russia. Gibson's claim that the Italian minister was vigorously urging the refusal of the Soviet peace offer contradicts the general attitude of the Nitti government, but this is not the only instance at this time of such

253

Notes

a pronounced difference between an Italian diplomat and his government. Gibson to Acting Secretary of State, Warsaw, February 10, 1920, Tel. 86. *Ibid.*, 380-81. A French press correspondent quoted General Henrys, the Chief of the French Military Mission, as saying that Foch was coming to carry out Bismarck's prophecy of "the organization of a strong French army on the Vistula." *Matin,* March 3, 1920, Warsaw, n.d.

70. *Parl. Deb.* (H.C.), 1920, I, 282, 286, 308 (February 12).

71. *Ibid.* (H.C.), 1920, I, 502.

72. *Écho de Paris,* February 12, in Dziewanowski, "Pilsudski's Federalist Policy, 1919-1921," *Journal of Central European Affairs,* p. 271.

73. In the absence of a peace treaty between the Allies and Hungary—the terms were submitted to the Hungarians on January 15, 1920, at the Quai d'Orsay—formal diplomatic relations between Hungary and other states, including Poland, were impossible. For the above mentioned conversations see Csekonič to Count Somssich, Warsaw, February 13, Tels. 7, 8; Csekonič to Somssich, Warsaw, February 20. Tel. 11. F. Déak and D. Ujváry, eds., *Papers and Documents Relating to the Foreign Relations of Hungary,* I (1919-20), (Budapest, 1939), 149-50, 160.

74. *Ibid.,* I, 149-50 (Csekonič, Warsaw, February 13).

75. In Gibson's opinion, these requests were made to France, not in expectation of their acceptance, but rather to make a case for concluding peace with the Soviets. Gibson to Secretary of State, Warsaw, February 13, 1920, Tel. 73. *Foreign Relations,* 1920, III, 380.

76. Gibson to Secretary of State, Warsaw, February 19, 1920, Tel. 86. *Ibid.,* pp. 380-81.

77. Charles R. Crane to Secretary of State, Prague, March 3, 1920, Tel. 46. National Archives, 760 c. 61/27.

78. A report from Major H. S. Howland, the American liaison officer to the Polish Military and Diplomatic Mission in Paris, enclosed in Wallace to Secretary of State, Paris, February 17, 1920, Report 860. National Archives, 760 c. 61/29.

79. Gibson to Secretary of State, Warsaw, March 3, 1920, Tel. 123. National Archives, 760 c. 61/28.

80. I. Deutscher, *The Prophet Armed: Trotsky, 1879-1921* (New York and London, 1954), p. 459, on the basis of information in the Trotsky unpublished papers. According to the German General Staff study, *Der polnisch-sowjetrussische Krieg, 1918-1920,* this reinforcement had not made much progress before the final negotiations in March-April before the Polish offensive, April 25.

81. He continued, however, to depict the reasons for the victory over the White Russians and Allied intervention as Bolshevik unity, disunity among the enemy, and the inability of the Allies to rely upon their own troops to use their immense superiority in weapons against the Revolution. (Valid or not, these arguments presumably fostered confidence in any further conflicts.) Lénine, *Oeuvres complètes,* XXV, pp. 63-82.

82. *Nation* (New York), August 14, 1920. The date is March 6 in *Livre rouge,* pp. 99-100.

83. *Europe nouvelle,* May 16, 1920. This useful French weekly occasionally printed documents, such as this, which are not to be found elsewhere.

84. The well-informed anonymous author of "La tache de M. Deschanel" (*ibid.,* February 21, 1920), doubted the official thesis as to Poland's effectiveness as a barrier

between Germany and Russia and warned that support of the White Russians would end by turning the Russian nation toward Germany. Louis Barthou was of essentially the same opinion. *Annales* (C.D.), 1920, I, 555-56, March 25, 1920.

85. *Rätezeitung,* February 17, in A. Hartung, "Die englische Politik," *Deutsche Grenzboten,* CLXXXIII (April, 1920), 88.

86. F. von Rabenau, *Seeckt* (Leipzig, 1940), p. 252. Not all conservative German opinion agreed with Seeckt, for there were those who were sincere Westerners as well as those who believed that a Western orientation would be the best approach to the revision of the Versailles treaty. Cf. W. Schotte, "Das falsche Pferd! Eine erdichtete Rede und ein ernsthaftetes Nachwort." *Prüssische Jahrbücher,* CLXXIX (March, 1920), p. 179. Schotte was the new editor of this influential conservative review.

87. W. von Blücher, *Deutschlands Weg nach Rapollo* (Wiesbaden, 1951), p. 97.

88. K. Radek, "Deutschland und Russland," *Zukunft,* February 7, 1920, pp. 78-189. Cf. Social Democratic reaction in A. Heichen, "Russland und Wir," *Neue Zeit,* March 12, 1920, pp. 545-51.

89. Blücher, *Deutschlands Weg nach Rapallo,* p. 98.

90. Crane to Secretary of State, Prague, March 3, 1920, Tel. 46. National Archives, 760 c. 61/27.

91. It was not until April, 1920, that Herbert von Dirksen arrived in Warsaw as German chargé d'affaires to establish formal diplomatic relations and to prepare for the later coming of Count Oberndorff, the German Minister, who seems to have bespoken Germany's collaboration in an anti-Bolshevik front with Allied representatives to no avail. H. von Dirksen, *Moskau-Tokio-London: Erinnerungen und Betrachtungen zu 20 Jahren deutscher Aussenpolitik, 1919-1939* (Stuttgart, 1950), pp. 35-36.

92. Gibson to Secretary of State, Warsaw, March 13, 1920, Tel. 143. National Archives, 760 c. 61/34.

93. Gibson to Secretary of State, Warsaw, March 22, 1920. *Foreign Relations,* 1920, III, 381-82. A standard chronicle of contemporary events gives March 22 as the date of the communication to the Entente powers. *Deutsche Geschichtskalender,* January-June 1920, p. 177.

94. Gibson to Acting Secretary of State, Warsaw, March 22, 1920, Tel. 163. *Foreign Relations,* 1920, III, 381-82.

95. Gibson to Secretary of State, Warsaw, April 6, 1920, Tel. National Archives, 760 c. 61/44.

96. Colby to the American Legation in Warsaw, Washington, March 25, 1920, Tel. 140. National Archives, 760 c. 61/34.

97. *Hungarian Papers and Documents,* I (1919-20), 895 (App. I, March 16, 1920); 897 (March 18); 898 (March 19, 20); 902 (March 23). For the later phases of Paléologue's dealings with the Hungarians, see below.

98. Gibson to Secretary of State, Warsaw, April 6, 1920, Tel. 210. National Archives, 760 c. 61/44.

99. *Livre rouge,* pp. 101-2. Although it is said that the Poles also sent a "comprehensive note" presumably containing their peace terms on the same day (Dziewanowski, "Pilsudski's Federal Policy, 1919-1921," *Journal of Central European Affairs,* p. 273), the present writer has not found its text.

100. Lénine, *Oeuvres complètes,* XXV, 85-87.

101. *Ibid.,* p. 116.

102. Deutscher, *The Prophet Armed,* p. 459, on the basis of Trotsky's papers.

Notes

103. *Livre rouge,* p. 102; Degras, *Soviet Documents on Foreign Policy,* I, 183-84.
104. *Livre rouge,* pp. 103, 105.
105. *Ibid.,* pp. 106-8.
106. The Chinese and North Korean Communists later negotiated with the representatives of the United Nations in 1953-54 at Panmunjom under almost exactly the same circumstances which the Russian Bolsheviks rejected in 1920; the site was on the battle line, like Borisov, and the truce was limited to the immediate vicinity.
107. Chicherin to London, Paris, Rome, April 7 (Wireless). *Europe nouvelle,* May 16, 1920.
108. Degras, *Soviet Documents on Foreign Policy,* I, 185-86.
109. Cf. the note (No. 1212) of the Polish Minister in Washington, Prince Lubomirski, April 18, 1920. *Foreign Relations,* 1920, III, 383-84.
110. Skrzyński, *Poland and Peace,* pp. 40-41.
111. H. Gibson, *Diplomat between Wars* (New York, 1941), p. 117.
112. *Daily Herald,* April 7, 1920, Copenhagen, April 6. Thanks to its editor's (George Lansbury) sympathetic attitude and contacts, this Labor journal is a valuable source for the Soviet point of view.
113. Curzon to Chicherin, April 11, 1920, in *ibid.,* August 17. Soviet agents used the *Daily Herald* for the publication of British as well as Soviet notes.
114. Degras, *Soviet Documents on Foreign Policy,* I, 184-85 (April 14).
115. Cf. *Nation* (London), April 10, 1920.
116. *Parl. Deb.* (H.C.), 1920, VIII, 970 (July 26, 1920).
117. Paléologue, Memorandum for the Hungarian Government, Doc. 226, Paris, April 15, 1920. *Hungarian Papers and Documents,* I, 235-38. The alleged *aide mémoire* of the same date, April 15, signed by Paléologue and Sir Francis Barker for Great Britain which Louis Fischer accepted as authentic (Fischer, *Soviets in World Affairs,* I, 258) and which provided that France should equip and lead a force of 100,000 Hungarians across the Carpatho-Ukraine to the defense of Poland in return for the surrender of twelve important cities by Rumania is almost certainly a forgery. The British were not involved in Paléologue's dealings with the Hungarians and were outraged when they later learned of them. Even Paléologue was not prepared to undermine France's case for the enforcement of Germany's disarmament by agreeing at this time to the rearmament of Hungary.
118. Despite this radical reversal of French policy, the *Temps* (April 26, 1920) reported a wireless from Moscow to this effect without contradicting it then or later. The agreement is dated April 20 in Fischer, *Soviets in World Affairs,* I, 250-51.
119. *Matin,* April 29, 1920, Warsaw, April 28. According to this dispatch, the normal freedom of communication abroad was resumed during the evening of April 28. Not until the evening of April 29 did the *Temps* (April 30) publish its first news of the offensive.
120. France is said to have been completely surprised. Dziewanowski, "Pilsudski's Federal Policy, 1919-1921," *Journal of Central European Affairs,* pp. 273-74.
121. J. C. White to Secretary of State, Warsaw, April 22, 1920, Report 405. National Archives, 760 c. 61/66.
122. *Parl. Deb.* (H.C.), V, 1239 (May 18, 1920). What he described as a Soviet attack in "great force" with the obvious purpose of giving the Polish offensive the color of a defensive counterattack, was obviously, because the Soviet concentration had scarcely begun, a local operation.

Notes

123. Poland promised to equip four Ukranian infantry divisions, each of fifteen thousand men, a promise which throws a curious light upon her constant complaints of shortages in her own army. For the text see R. Martel, *La Pologne et nous* (Paris, 1928), cited in Dziewanowski, "Pilsudski's Federal Policy," *Journal of Central European Affairs*, p. 273. Another article, originally secret, provided that the claims of Polish landlords should be satisfied before any settlement was made of the agrarian problem by an Ukranian national assembly. S. L. Sharp, *Poland: White Eagle on a Red Field* (Cambridge, 1953), pp. 119-20.

CHAPTER IV

1. J. Pilsudski, *Erinnerungen und Dokumenten*, 4 vols. (Essen, 1936), I, 59-60 (April 26).
2. Chamberlin's analysis of Pilsudski's aims still seems valid. W. H. Chamberlin, *The Russian Revolution, 1917-1921* (New York, 1935), II, 301.
3. Early in April, Pilsudski learned that one cavalry and five rifle divisions had apparently arrived on the northern front. German General Staff, *Der polnisch-sowjetrussische Krieg*, I, 113.
4. The comparative numerical strengths in the area of the offensive were approximately 64,000 for the Polish and 17,000 for the Red Army. *Ibid.*, p. 115. The fact that a journal of the *Journal des débats* standing could state (May 12, 1920) that the Bolsheviks had concentrated the bulk of their forces there shows how completely at sea the Western press was about the military situation.
5. This conclusion is supported by the text of General Haller's order (he was in operational command) of May 7, 1920, which also directed Polish support of an eventual Ukrainian effort to take the Black Sea port of Odessa. *Der polnisch-sowjetrussische Krieg*, I, 112, 268.
6. In his book on the crisis of 1920, Pilsudski quoted, with approval, the following estimate of the strength of Red Army forces in this attack and of its purposes by a Soviet military historian; at the time of the capture of Kiev, " 'our troops on the western front were so unprepared that a counter-attack was impossible; they lacked sufficient reinforcements, were badly equipped, almost without supply trains, inadequately numerous. Despite all that, they had to give blow for blow in order to distract the attention of the Poles from the southwestern front. . . .' " E.-N. Serghieieff, *De la Duna à la Vistule* (Warsaw, 1925), quoted in J. Pilsudski, *L'année 1920* . . . (Paris, 1929), pp. 32-33. Pilsudski's judgment in military matters was presumably more reliable than that of a Polish politician who wrote: "The extraordinary rapidity of this counter-offensive justified the Polish headquarters in making provision for the Russian preparations for war." Count Alexander Skrzynski, *Poland and Peace* (London, [1923]), pp. 42-43.
7. L. Trotsky, *Stalin: An Appraisal of the Man and His Influence* (New York, 1941), pp. 327-28 (April 30).
8. I. Deutscher, *The Prophet Armed: Trotsky, 1879-1921* (New York and London, 1954), p. 459.
9. Chamberlin, *Russian Revolution*, II, 303. Cf. Trotsky, *Stalin*, p. 328.
10. Poland's defeat, Radek wrote in an article transmitted by the Moscow wireless station, would reveal the necessary social fissures. *Daily Herald*, May 5, 1920.

257

Notes

11. Speech at the All-Russian Congress of Glass and Porcelain Workers. V. I. Lénine, *Oeuvres complètes* (Paris, 1928), XXV, 301-4.

12. *Ibid.*, pp. 308-12.

13. *Livre rouge*, pp. 107-9. It is the last document in this official Soviet publication.

14. The party newspaper, *Pravda* (May 7, 1920), printed Brusilov's letter offering his services and proposing a conference of Tsarist officers for the improvement of the Red Army. E. H. Carr, *The Bolshevik Revolution, 1917-1923* (London, 1951-53), III, 274, fn. 3.

15. The Russian delegation did not arrive in London from Copenhagen until May 27.

16. The Politburo shared this conviction. Deutscher, *The Prophet Armed*, pp. 461-62, on the basis of Trotsky's private papers.

17. J. Degras, *Soviet Documents on Foreign Policy* (London, 1951-53), I, 184-85.

18. Lénine, *Ouevres complètes*, XXV, 301-3.

19. Chicherin to Curzon, May 5. *Daily Herald*, August 17, 1920.

20. Chamberlin, *Russian Revolution*, II, 321 ff.

21. F. P. Walters, *A History of the League of Nations* (London, 1952), II, 96.

22. For Lenin's letter see *The Times*, June 11, 1920.

23. Carr, *Bolshevik Revolution*, III, 243, 248-50.

24. Deutscher, *The Prophet Armed*, pp. 461-62.

25. "The initiation of active warfare against the Bolsheviks," J. W. Davis, the American Ambassador, informed his government from London, "attracted at the start little attention, except in the Northcliffe press." Davis to Secretary of State, May 28, 1920, Rep. 2930. National Archives, 760 c/ 61/67.

26. While Patek was quoted to much the same effect in a press interview in Rome (*Matin*, May 14, Rome, May 13, 1920), there is no support in the known texts of Patek's message to Moscow. It is scarcely likely that Pilsudski would have allowed his hands to be tied by such a promise.

27. "The Poles and the Bolsheviks," *Times*, May 1, 1920; *Temps*, May 6; "Polish Defense or Aggression," *Spectator*, May 8; G. Doumergue, *Soir*, May 8; *Journal des débats*, May 12; "France et Pologne," *Revue bleue*, June 5; Joseph Barthélemy, "L'alerte polonaise," *ibid.*, November 1920, pp. 166-67.

28. *Matin*, May 14, 1920, Rome, May 13.

29. *Temps*, May 6, 1920. Of the Russians who gave their services to the Bolsheviks because of the Polish invasion of the Ukraine, the *Journal des débats* (May 12) wrote their "misfortunes had completely unbalanced their judgment."

30. W. Churchill, *The Aftermath, 1918-1928* (New York, 1929), pp. 276-77.

31. Cecil rejoined, May 13, with a reminder of the evidence of Poland's intentions which the press had reported as early as January, 1920. These letters were printed in the *Times*, May 17, 1920.

32. "The Storm Breaks," *Daily Herald*, April 30, 1920.

33. "The Polish-Ukrainian Agreement," *New Europe*, May 13, 1920.

34. *Annales* (C.D.), 1920, I, 111 (February 6) [Ernst Lafont].

35. Berthélemy, "L'alerte polonaise," *Revue bleue*, p. 167.

36. P. Millet, "L'adventure polonaise," *Europe nouvelle*, May 16, 1920.

37. M. Pernot, "L'Épreuve de la Pologne," *Revue des deux mondes*, October 1, 1920, pp. 493-94.

38. *Annales* (C.D.), 1920, II, 1368 (May 26).

39. *Lord Riddell's Intimate Diary of the Peace Conference and After, 1918-1923* (London, 1933), p. 191.

40. *Ibid.*, p. 197 (May 23).

41. This message, whose text has not been seen, is summarized in the standard Soviet diplomatic history. V. Potiemkine, *Histoire de la diplomatie* (Paris, n.d.), III, 89.

42. Riddell reported Churchill as marvelling during a luncheon "that we have been able to work together on such terms of personal friendship notwithstanding the divergence of our views regarding Russia," and Riddell agreed that it was extraordinary. *Lord Riddell's Intimate Diary*, p. 203.

43. Davis to Secretary of State, London, May 28, 1920, Rep. 2930. National Archives, 760 c. 61/67.

44. It was belatedly communicated to the press; the *Times* printed it on May 10, 1920.

45. *Parl. Deb.* (H.C.), 1920, V, 237.

46. *Nation* (London), July 17, 1920.

47. American embassy to Secretary of State, London, June 4, 1920, Tel. 897. National Archives, 860j. 24/5.

48. The Conservative *Spectator* (May 8, 1920) was unkinder: "The public have never known from one week to another which method was in favour in Downing Street," denunciations or "proposals for Prinkipos.... The Government's Eastern policy is a kind of nightmare, and we can make nothing of it."

49. Davis to Secretary of State, London, May 3, 1920, Tel. 720. *Foreign Relations, 1920*, III, 710-11.

50. Garvin also insisted that the "Polish War and the invasion of historic Russian territory must be brought before the judgment of the Powers" and that the Russo-Polish boundary must be determined by a general conference at which Russia was represented. "From San Remo to Spa," *Observer*, May 2, 1920.

51. "Pentecost and Politics," *ibid.*, May 23, 1920.

52. C. E. Callwell, *Field Marshal Sir Henry Wilson* (London, 1927), II, 240.

53. In revealing that the Russians were not openly registered at the small, obscure hotel where they were lodged, the *Times* (May 28, 1920) doubtless wished to suggest that this was typical of their secretiveness.

54. "Lloyd George said that when Krassin arrived, Winston came to him and said, laughing, 'I suppose you have shaken the baboon's hairy hand?'" *Lord Riddell's Intimate Diary*, p. 225 (July 24).

55. *Ibid.*, p. 198 (May 30).

56. L. Krassin, *Leonard Krassin: His Life and Work, by His Wife* (London [1929]), p. 129.

57. *Soir*, May 30, 31, 1920; *Temps*, June 1; "M. Lloyd George et M. Krassine," *Journal des débats*, June 2.

58. Cambon assumed as a matter of course that Lloyd George's purpose was the diplomatic recognition of the Soviet government. Paul Cambon, *Correspondance, 1870-1924* (Paris, 1946), III, 383-84 (May 31).

59. *Times*, June 2, 1920, "From our own correspondent," Paris, June 1.

60. Henri Dié in *Soir*, May 30, 31, June 1, 1920; E. du Mesnil in *Rappel*, quoted by *Matin*, June 5.

61. "Kief et Enzeli," *Temps*, June 1, 1920. Cf. Pertinax, in *Écho de Paris*, June 2; G. Doumergue, in *Soir*, June 5.

Notes

62. *Parl. Deb.* (H.C.), 1920, V, 2030-31. What he meant was that the Wise Committee of the Supreme Economic Council would negotiate the trade agreement in the name of the Allies after the British government had settled the political questions. Cf. American embassy to Secretary of State, London, June 7, 1920, Tel. 905. National Archives, 661. 4116/43.

63. *Parl. Deb.* (H.C.), 1920, VI, 164 ff.

64. Krassin to Lloyd George, June 29, 1920. *Daily Herald,* July 10.

65. L. Fischer, *The Soviets in World Affairs* (2d ed.; Princeton, 1951), I, 261 (June 9).

66. Chicherin to Curzon, June 11, 1920, text quoted in Kamenev's memorandum to Lloyd George, August 15. *Europe nouvelle,* September 26, 1920. Chicherin and Radek told a left-wing American journalist about this time "that Great Britain is forcing Russia into a war *à outrance,* a war never desired, but which, once commenced, may shake the British Empire to its foundations." Henry G. Alsberg, "Will Russia drive the British from China?" Moscow, June 16, *Nation* (New York), August 14, 1920.

67. On June 25, 1920, the Labor Party Conference voted down a motion to join the Third International by a majority of 2,715,000 votes.

68. *Lord Riddell's Intimate Diary,* p. 204 (June 13).

69. To his brother, Jules Cambon, June 14, 1920. Cambon, *Correspondance,* III, 384. An Allied conference at Boulogne, nevertheless, decided, June 16, that the negotiations should continue if political recognition were ruled out. W. P. and Zelda K. Coates, *A History of Anglo-Soviet Relations* (London, 1944), pp. 30-31.

70. *Lord Riddell's Intimate Diary,* p. 204 (June 13).

71. Krassin to Curzon, October 6, 1920. *Daily Herald,* October 8; *Europe nouvelle,* October 17.

72. Degras, *Soviet Documents on Foreign Policy,* I, 191, 192.

73. *Daily Herald,* July 10, 1920.

74. Degras, *Soviet Documents on Foreign Policy,* I, 192, 193.

75. *Parl. Deb.* (H.C.), 1920, VI, 2369-71.

76. *Ibid.*

77. *Ibid.*

78. *Ibid.,* p. 2371. The Narkomindel's summary included this threat. Krassin took the note in person to Moscow. Degras, *Soviet Documents on Foreign Policy,* I, 193. For the Soviet reply, July 7, see below.

79. After the Red Army's capture of Kiev, December 16, 1919, General Bredow, who had commanded Denikin's troops there, escaped into Poland where he was interned with the remnants of his command. Chamberlin, *Russian Revolution,* II, 281.

80. The council finally referred the matter to the heads of government. C. A., 55. Notes of a meeting at the Quai d'Orsay, June 30, 1920, 10:30 A.M. Leland Harrison Papers, Library of Congress.

81. He claimed that railway rolling stock had been delivered. Lincoln Colcord, "America Aids the Polish Drive," *New Republic,* June 23, 1920. Of food and medical supplies, America gave liberally. The administration's attitude toward Colcord may have been soured by his letter to the Secretary of State Colby in which he dismissed a public statement by Dewitt C. Poole, the chief of the Eastern European Division of the State Department, linking the Soviet government and the Third International as an "an interesting example of the futility of the State Department's methods in

dealing with the Russian situation." That connection, he wrote, was self-evident; the real defense against Bolshevik propaganda was the correction of the conditions that nourished bolshevism. The recognition of the Soviet government would remove a grievance and therefore weaken the effect of its propaganda. Colcord to Secretary of State, Washington, April 20, 1920. National Archives, 861.01/215. There was no reply.

82. Davis to Secretary of State, London, May 3, 1920, Tel. 720. *Foreign Relations,* III, 710-11.

83. Davis to Secretary of State, London, May 26, 1920, Tel. 848. *Ibid.,* p. 712.

84. Walter Lippmann and Charles Merz, "More News from the *Times,*" *New Republic,* August 11, 1920. Walter Duranty reported that the French were equally optimistic: "France believes that the sands of the Bolshevik regime are fast running out." *New York Times,* June 4, 1920.

85. Newton D. Baker, the Secretary of War, volunteered at a Cabinet meeting to ascertain the facts from Military Intelligence. The results were reassuring: "...while there has been much talk on this subject by persons in the various nations, there has been very little actual resumption of commercial relations." Baker to President Wilson, War Department, May 10, 1920. Papers of President Wilson, File II, Box 168, Library of Congress.

86. He acted after the British unofficially intimated that the presence of an American representative would be welcome. Davis to Secretary of State, London, May 19, 1920, Tel. 711; Colby to Davis, Washington, May 21, Tel. 530. *Foreign Relations,* 1920, III, 711-12.

87. Colby to Davis, Washington, June 5, 1920, Tel. 589. National Archives, 661.4116/36.

88. *Parl. Deb.* (H.C.), 1920, VI, 1433-34 (June 17).

89. Colby to Davis, Washington, June 19, 1920, Tel. 654. *Foreign Relations,* 1920, III, 713. Being informed, June 25, that Skinner had been invited to attend a meeting of the Wise Committee on June 26 at which Krassin and other Russian delegates would be present, the department ordered him: "Do not attend." Skinner to Secretary of State, London, June 25, 1920, Tel. [no number]; Norman Davis, Acting Secretary of State, to Skinner, Washington, June 25, Tel. [no number]. *Ibid.,* p. 716.

90. Davis to Secretary of State, London, June 21, 1920, Tel. 972. *Ibid.,* p. 714.

91. The embassy reached this conclusion by including the Liberal journals that doubted the attainment of positive results from the negotiations with Krassin as a part of the opposition, although that skepticism was more the result of doubt as to the prime minister's persistence and of the pressures operating upon him than of disapproval of an agreement with the Russians. Davis to Secretary of State, London, June 5, 1920, No. 2994. National Archives, 841.00/349; Davis to Secretary of State, London, June 28, No. 3096. *Ibid.,* 841.00/3522.

92. President Wilson to Norman Davis, White House, June 23, 1920. Woodrow Wilson Papers, File II, Box 169, Library of Congress.

93. Norman Davis, Acting Secretary of State, to J. W. Davis, Washington, June 24, 1920, Tel. 671. (For repetition to Paris, Rome, Warsaw.) *Foreign Relations,* 1920, III, 715-16.

94. Norman Davis to President Wilson, Department of State, July 2, 1920; President Wilson to Davis, White House, July 3. Woodrow Wilson Papers, File II, Box 169, Library of Congress.

Notes

95. Norman Davis to Wallace, Washington, July 7, 1920, Tel. 1215. *Foreign Relations*, 1920, III, 717.

96. *New York Times*, July 10, 1920. Special to the *Times*, Washington, July 9.

97. Norman Davis to J. W. Davis, Washington, June 24, 1920, Tel. 671. *Foreign Relations*, 1920, III, 716.

98. *Annales* (C.D.), 1920, III, 2084. ["A Socialist Deputy" refers to Ernst Lafont.]

99. Hennessy's passing question, "Pourquoi soutenons-nous la Pologne dans ses tentatives d'expansions?" on June 24 showed clearly enough what he thought of it. *Ibid.*, p. 2066.

100. Such encouragement and support as was given General Wrangel's offensive (June 8, 1920) were the last feeble manifestations of France's earlier championship of the White Russians and their hope of preserving intact the substantial territorial integrity of Poland. Wrangel's victory would have been embarrassing for he would certainly not have handed the Ukraine over to Poland.

101. Millerand to Count Apponyi, President of the Hungarian Peace Delegation, Paris, May 6, 1920; Declaration of Fouchet, French High Commissioner, to Admiral Horthy, Budapest, May 18; Teleki (Hungarian Foreign Minister) to Csáky (Hungarian representative in Paris), Budapest, June 5; Fouchet to Teleki, Budapest, June 5; Csáky to Teleki, Versailles, June 22; Fouchet to Teleki, Budapest, June 24. *Hungarian Papers and Documents*, I, (1919-20) 287-91, 310-11, 328-30, 385, 391.

102. Csáky to Teleki, Paris, May 5, 1920. *Ibid.*, pp. 279-84.

103. Csáky to Teleki, Paris, June 18, 1920. *Ibid.*, pp. 371-72.

104. Csáky to Teleki, Versailles, June 28, 1920. *Ibid.*, pp. 404-8.

105. Teleki to Csáky, Budapest, June 5, 1920. *Ibid.*, p. 328.

106. Memorandum on British Representations concerning Negotiations with France, June 30, 1920. *Ibid.*, pp. 415-16.

CHAPTER V

1. E. H. Carr, *The Bolshevik Revolution, 1917-1923* (London, 1951-53), III, Chapter 25; I. Deutscher, *The Prophet Armed: Trotsky, 1879-1921* (New York and London, 1954), Chapter XIII.

2. W. H. Chamberlin, *The Russian Revolution, 1917-1921* (New York, 1935), II, 304 f.

3. Deutscher, *The Prophet Armed*, p. 472.

4. W. S. Sikorski, *La campagne polono-russe de 1920* (Paris, 1928), p. 27.

5. V. I. Lénine, *Oeuvres complètes* (Paris, 1928), XXV, 348-52.

6. See S. Kamenev's report to the Revolutionary War Council, July 19, 1920, in N. C. Kakourine and W. A. Mielikoff, *La guerre contre les polonais blancs en 1920* (Moscow, 1926), quoted in J. Pilsudski, *L'annee 1920 . . .* (Paris, 1929), pp. 279-80.

7. Count Alexander Skrzyński, *Poland and Peace* (London, [1923]), p. 44.

8. M. K. Dziewanowski, "Pilsudski's Federalist Policy, 1919-1921," *Journal of Central European Affairs*, X (July, 1950), 279.

9. White to Secretary of State, Warsaw, June 12, 1920, Tel. 323. National Archives, 760 c. 61/66.

10. Colby to American Legation, Washington, June 17, 1920, Tel. 77. *Ibid.*

11. Crane to Secretary of State, Prague, July 3, 1920, Tel. 162. *Ibid.*, 760 c. 61/83.

12. G. P. Pink, *The Conference of Ambassadors* (Geneva, 1942), pp. 89-90. On

Notes

July 11, 1920, the Supreme Council agreed to fix the Czecho-Polish boundary in the Teschen area.

13. Admiral Horthy to Marshal Pilsudski, Budapest, June 6, 1920; Count Csekonics to Teleki, Warsaw, June 21. *Hungarian Documents and Papers,* I (1919-20), 331-32, 381-84.

14. Csekonics to Teleki, Warsaw, June 26, 1920. *Ibid.,* p. 400.

15. Csekonics to Teleki, Warsaw, July 3, 1920, Tel. 95. *Ibid.,* 425; Teleki to Csekonics, Budapest, July 8. Tel. 78. *Ibid.,* p. 437.

16. Csekonics to Teleki, Warsaw, July 10, 1920, Tel. 96. *Ibid.,* p. 445.

17. Teleki to Csekonics, Budapest, July 13, 1920, Tel. 92. *Ibid.,* p. 451.

18. Teleki to Praznovsky, Budapest, July 14, 1920, Tel. 376. *Ibid.,* pp. 456-57.

19. Praznovszky to Teleki, Paris, July 19, 1920, Tel. 305. *Ibid.,* p. 472.

20. Praznovszky to Teleki, Paris, July 26, 1920, Tel. 311. *Ibid.,* pp. 503-4. On July 26, he finally explained that the Quai d'Orsay was of divided mind about Hungary, not because of "dislike of Hungary," but for factional reasons. Berthelot and others, as representing the Clemenceau regime, were against Paléologue on all questions, including Hungary. Praznowszky to Teleki, Paris, July 26, Report 89. *Ibid.,* pp. 508-10.

21. *New York Times,* July 7, 1920, Spa, July 6.

22. "Narkomindel Statement on Anglo-Russian Negotiations," Moscow, July 9, 1920. J. Degras, *Soviet Documents on Foreign Policy* (London, 1951-53), I, 191-94. The text as read in the House of Commons, July 14, by Bonar Law, the government's leader in the House, omitted the last sentence. *Parl. Deb.* (H.C.), VI, 2371-74. It was included in the press telegram in *Daily Herald,* July 10, Christiania, July 8. Cf. *Daily Herald,* October 8, 1920; *Europe nouvelle,* October 17, 1920.

23. A. L. Kennedy, *Old Diplomacy and the New, 1876-1922; From Salisbury to Lloyd George* (London, 1922), p. 322; H. Nicolson, *Curzon, The Last Phase, 1919-1925: A Study in Post-War Diplomacy* (London, 1937), p. 204.

24. *Lord Riddell's Intimate Diary of the Peace Conference and After, 1918-1923* (London, 1933), p. 219 (July 12).

25. *Times,* July 15, 1920. Cf. *Parl. Deb.* (H.C.), VI, 2371-74 (July 14). The tone of Grabski's press interview did not altogether confirm Poland's accommodating spirit. While Poland would fight only in self-defense, the military situation was not as serious as some were saying. She would seek peace in accord with her allies, but she was also confident that they, in appreciation of her role as the bulwark of Western civilization, would aid her. *Vossische Zeitung,* July 12, 1920, Spa, July 11.

26. *Annales* (C.D.), 1920, III, 2622, 2623. At this time, the news kiosks carried P. Millet's slashing view of Polish policy leading to the invasion of the Ukraine. He accepted the sincerity of the Soviet government's efforts to reach a peaceful settlement. P. Millet, "Les fautes de la Pologne," *Europe nouvelle,* July 18, 1920.

27. "Le spectacle imprévu," *Temps,* July 14, 1920.

28. L. Dumont-Wilden, "La Pologne en danger," *Revue bleue,* July 17, 1920, quoting the nationalist *Tägliche Rundschau.* The conservative *Deutsche Allgemeine Zeitung* (July 14) warned France that continued oppression might drive Germany to decisions that would not be to France's liking. Even the liberal *Frankfurter Zeitung* (July 13) took a detached attitude toward the Russo-Polish War; the Allies, not Germany, were responsible for the preservation of peace.

29. *Les Annales,* in *Matin,* July 16, 1920.

30. R. Pinon, "The Future of the Franco-British Friendship," *New Europe,* July 15.

Notes

31. By a Student of Politics, Westminster, July 14. *Times,* July 15.

32. The weekly *Spectator* (July 17, 1920) regretted what it suspected would turn out to be the use of Wrangel as a pawn but it was philosophically resigned: "Still, we suppose that as the Poles have made a mess of things, pawns have to be given away if there are to be negotiations at all. . . ."

33. "Poland, Russia, and the Allies," *Daily Telegraph,* July 13, 1920.

34. *Times,* July 13, 1920. After they had won the war, the Poles, who should have known the facts, testified that the Red Army included virtually no German officers. They informed Gibson that only five had been captured during the entire campaign and that even these were "casual adventurers." Gibson to Secretary of State, Warsaw, September 15, 1920, Tel. 510. National Archives, 760 c. 61/321.

35. The *New York Times* (July 13, 1920) relied more upon the threat of Allied action, but it conceded that the prospect of "a fair field in which to show whether they can make their system work or not" would also help.

36. The author fitted the British and French Russian policies into the general picture. "Mr. Lloyd George wants to spare the Germans, conciliate the Russians, and crush the Turks. The French would like to pamper the Turks, skin the Germans alive, and crush the Russians. Between them they may succeed in relighting the war again over the greater part of the Continent. . . . We cannot fight Turks, dictate to the Russians, and coerce Germans simultaneously." "Illusions and Realities at Spa," *Nation* (London), July 17, 1920. It had indicated the significance of Russia's choice in the preceding number. "The Breaking of the Polish Barrier," *ibid.,* July 10.

37. H. N. Brailsford, "Poland and Spa." *Daily Herald,* July 13, 1920.

38. These views, which largely coincided with Moscow's, were repeated in the *Daily Herald's* leading editorial, July 16, 1920.

39. *Nation,* July 17, 1920. This organ of American intellectual radicalism allowed itself to be carried away by the different standards the Allies were applying to Poland and Soviet Russia. After doing nothing to restrain Poland, they "rush to their [the Poles] aid" who "are being properly punished for their imperialistic folly. . . ." Would the Bolsheviks stop at their own boundaries "or at those of Germany," would they "do the world the service of chasing the Grabskis, Pilsudskis, and Hallers out of Warsaw?" Would Lenin be bluffed by Lloyd George's blustering manifesto? Yet the *Nation* ended by advising Lenin "to set an example of self-restraint even when victory is apparently in his hands."

40. Wireless News, No. 524, London, July 12, 1920. Enclosure in Davis to Secretary of State, London, July 19, 1920. National Archives, 861.00/7194. "Wireless News" was an official British compilation of intercepts from Soviet and other foreign wireless stations.

41. The following analysis of the difference between the two Bolshevik leaders is largely based upon Deutscher (*The Prophet Armed,* pp. 463-65), who has used Trotsky's private papers.

42. M. Tukhachevsky, *La marche au delà de la Vistule,* in Pilsudski, *L'année 1920,* p. 232.

43. Kakourine and Mielikoff, *La guerre contre les polonais blancs en 1920,* in *ibid.,* pp. 279-80.

44. Deutscher, *The Prophet Armed,* pp. 464-65.

45. Wireless News, No. 528, July 16, 1920. Enclosure in Davis to Secretary of State, London, July 27, 1920. National Archives, 861.00/7221.

Notes

46. Kakourine and Mielikoff, *La guerre contre les polonais blancs en 1920*, in Pilsudski, *L'année 1920*, pp. 280-81.
47. C. E. Callwell, *Field Marshal Sir Henry Wilson* (London, 1927), II, 253 (July 16).
48. *Lord Riddell's Intimate Diary*, pp. 220-21 (July 18).
49. Chicherin to Curzon, July 17, 1920. Degras, *Soviet Documents on Foreign Policy*, I, 194-97. Cf. *Observer*, July 25. The divergences between these texts are verbal rather than of substance. The reference to the League of Nations seems to have been occasioned by rather numerous unofficial suggestions in press and parliament that the Russo-Polish problem should be referred to the League's council; no such proposal was officially made to the Soviet government.
50. *Lord Riddell's Intimate Diary*, pp. 220-21.
51. To a member of the extreme left who cried, "It means war," he replied that he was as sure of Britain's loyalty to her word as he was of France's. *Annales* (C.D.), 1920, III, 2622-23.
52. *Ibid.*
53. *Daily Herald*, July 22, 1920.
54. As reported in "A Confusion of Ideas," *Westminster Gazette*, July 20, 1920.
55. At least until the Red Army's invasion of ethnographic Poland became clear, Lloyd George evidently thought of his pledge in the Curzon note as limited to the furnishing of material aid. *Parl. Deb.* (H.C.), 1920, VII, 482-84, 539-40. This is confirmed by Cecil's warning in the course of the debate: "You cannot make war under a system of limited liability" (*ibid.*, p. 520).
56. Cf. Colonel Wedgwood's remarks. *Ibid.* (H.C.), 1920, VII, 522-23.
57. *Ibid.* (H.C.), 1920, VII, 535ff, 541-42. The *Times* (July 22) also thought that Lloyd George's attitude meant that aid might not stop with advice and munitions. "Mr. Lloyd George is like one hastening after lost time and trying to catch it by the back hair."
58. See below, Chapter VII, Section 2.
59. "Full Peace or New War," *Observer*, July 18, 1920.
60. *Parl. Deb.* (H.C.), 1920, VII, 542 (July 21).
61. "The Great Unrecognized," *Nation*, July 24, 1920.
62. Deutscher, *The Prophet Armed*, pp. 463-66.
63. Kakourine and Mielikoff, *La guerre contre les polonais blancs en 1920*, in Pilsudski, *L'année 1920*, pp. 286-87.
64. Carr, *Bolshevik Revolution*, III, 211-12; L. Fischer, *The Soviets in World Affairs* (2d ed.; Princeton, 1951), I, 268-69.
65. W. Churchill, *The Aftermath, 1918-1928* (New York, 1929), p. 279.
66. S. Kutrzeba, "The Struggle for the Frontiers," *The Cambridge History of Poland: From Augustus II to Pilsudski (1697-1935)* (Cambridge, 1951), II, 526-27.
67. His omission of troops from the aid that would be sent to Poland is indicative of the state of French and British opinion. *Annales* (S), 1920, II, 1460. Paderewski, then in Paris, advised D'Abernon to see that airplanes were attached to the mission to assure its escape since the fall of Warsaw was "almost certain." Masaryk warned his friend Jusserand in Prague not to organize any military assistance for Poland as it would be useless and would weaken the Allies' position in the subsequent peace negotiations. Viscount d'Abernon, *The Eighteenth Decisive Battle of the World: Warsaw, 1920* (London, 1921), pp. 18-19 (July 22); 20-21 (July 24).

Notes

68. The Labor *Daily Herald* printed most of them, but some (especially those that passed between Poland and Soviet Russia) appeared in the *Europe nouvelle* and others in the *Observer*. As earlier, members of the British government sometimes read or otherwise communicated such material to the House of Commons, but later, after Poland's final victory, the proposal for preparing a White Paper was turned down for the reason that it might disturb the Russo-Polish peace negotiations then in progress and the subject seems never to have been revived. The indispensable series, *Documents on British Foreign Policy, 1919-1939,* when it covers this period will not, of course, remove all difficulties, since it will presumably be restricted to the British side. It may, moreover, be reasonably expected to illuminate Anglo-French relations at this time about which comparatively little is known. [*Ibid.,* 1st series, XI, 198-748, covers the Russo-Polish War. Ed.]

69. American Embassy to Secretary of State, London, July 20, 1920, Tel. 1093. National Archives, 760 c. 61/97.

70. He could say that the Soviet government was offering a more favorable frontier than the Curzon Line. Curzon to Rumbold, July 19, 1920, *Observer,* July 25. Lloyd George informed the House of Commons that this step had been taken. *Parl. Deb.* (H.C.), 1920, VII, 484 (July 21).

71. While the pen that signed the note was Curzon's, the directing mind was obviously Lloyd George's. Curzon to Chicherin, July 20, 1920. *Observer,* July 25; *Europe nouvelle,* August 8.

72. Havas Agency dispatches in *Europe nouvelle,* August 15, 1920. The substance of these notes was reported in Rumbold to Curzon, Warsaw, July 23. *Observer,* July 25.

73. Havas Agency dispatch, *Europe nouvelle,* August 15, 1920.

74. *Observer,* July 25, 1920.

75. *Europe nouvelle,* August 15, 1920.

76. The Moscow wireless station interpreted Tukhachevsky's justification of the long delay somewhat differently. The Red Army's advance was so rapid, it claimed, that several days were required for the establishment of communications with the front and "to allow the necessary measures being taken for the reception of [the] enemy parlementaires." Moscow, July 25, 1920. Wireless News, No. 536, July 26. Enclosure in Davis to Secretary of State, London, August 4. National Archives, 861.00/7259.

77. Supreme Polish Command to Supreme Russian Command, July 27, 1920. *Europe nouvelle,* August 15. No reply has been located.

78. White to Secretary of State, Warsaw, July 29, 1920. Tel. 410. National Archives, 760 c. 61/126.

79. Russian communiqué on the rupture of the armistice negotiations, Moscow, August 3, 1920. *Europe nouvelle,* August 15.

80. Wróblewski to Prince Sapieha, August 2, 1920. *Ibid.,* August 15.

81. Russian communiqué, Moscow, August 3, 1920. *Ibid.,* August 15. Nothing like as definite a phrase as "the principal conditions of peace" appeared in the Russian correspondence.

82. For Poland's decision to go to Minsk but at a later date, see below. Radek chose this moment to reveal, in *Izvestia,* Pilsudski's dealing with the Bolsheviks and the unofficial truce in the autumn of 1919 and to put his article on the air from the Moscow wireless station. Radek on Markhlevsky-Polish Negotiations in 1919, Moscow, August 3, 1920, Wireless News, No. 547, August 9. Enclosure in Wright to Secretary of State, London, August 13. National Archives, 861.00/7295.

83. *Lord Riddell's Intimate Diary,* p. 225 (July 24).

84. Although Chicherin called this conference a British proposal without being contradicted, its origins are not entirely clear. It was mentioned by Kamenev in a letter to Lloyd George dated August 5 as having appeared in a "communication" of July 22, which is probably a mistake for Chicherin's note of July 24 since such a document so dated has not been found. Chicherin seems to have brought together the proposed London conference in the Curzon note (July 11) and Curzon's explanation in the note of July 19 that it would bring Soviet Russia into relations with the "Peace Conference" or, in other words, with the Allies, and he has described the result as a British proposal for a general conference between Soviet Russia and the Allies. For the text of Chicherin to the British government, July 24, see *Daily Herald,* July 25, 1920. Cf. *Parl. Deb.* (H.C.), 1920, VIII, 974-75 (July 26).

85. *Lord Riddell's Intimate Diary,* p. 226 (July 25).

86. *Parl. Deb.* (H.C.), 1920, VIII, 974-75. According to the *Daily Herald's* (July 29) "diplomatic correspondent," the government interpreted Chicherin's note (July 24) as meaning Russia's agreement that the conference would concern itself with the Russo-Polish treaty as the prerequisite for a general settlement between the Allies and Soviet Russia. He doubted that this was a correct inference as to the Soviet government's attitude.

87. Curzon to Chicherin, July 26. *Daily Herald,* July 30, 1920.

88. "Peace in the Balance," *Nation* (London), July 31, 1920.

89. *Parl. Deb.* (H.C.), 1920, VII, 500 (July 21).

90. Curzon to Chicherin, July 29. *Daily Herald,* July 30, 1920.

91. Davis to Secretary to State, London, July 30, 1920, Tel. 1151. National Archives, 760 c. 61/125.

92. *Lord Riddell's Intimate Diary,* pp. 229-30 (August 8).

93. R. Poincaré "Chronique de la quinzaine," *Revue des deux mondes,* August 1, 1920, pp. 670-71.

94. *New York Times,* July 28, 1920, Edwin L. James, Boulogne, July 27.

95. Harrison to Secretary of State, Paris, July 30, 1920, Tel. 1475. National Archives, 861.00/7195.

96. *Washington Post,* August 2, 1920. Special cable to the *Washington Post* and the *New York Sun-Herald.*

97. "La rencontre de Boulogne," *Temps,* July 28, 1920. The London *Times* (July 28) at once hoped, obviously with Lloyd George in mind, that France would not be compelled to choose between Great Britain and the United States.

98. *New York Times,* August 1, 1920. Special to the *New York Times,* Washington, July 31.

99. Davis to Secreary of State, London, July 30, 1920, Tel. 1151. National Archives, 760 c. 61/125.

100. Colby to Davis, Washington, August 2, 1920, Tel. 821. *Foreign Relations,* 1920, III, 461-63.

101. K. Radek, *Die auswärtige Politik Sowjetrusslands* (Hamburg, 1921), p. 63.

102. *Lord Riddell's Intimate Diary,* p. 227 (July 31).

103. "The Sphinx and the Answer," *Observer,* August 1, 1920.

104. Lloyd George read this note in the House of Commons on August 5. *Parl. Deb.* (H.C.), 1920, VIII, 2628-29.

105. Callwell, *Wilson,* II, 255.

106. V. Potiemkine, *Histoire de la diplomatie* (Paris, n.d.), III, 93.
107. Radek, *Die auswärtige politik Sowjetrusslands,* p. 63.
108. Potiemkine, *Histoire de la diplomatie,* III, 93.
109. Kamenev to Lloyd George, 123 New Bond St., W., August 5, 1920. *Daily Herald,* August 7. Cf. also *Manchester Guardian,* August 7.
110. The British Embassy delivered the letter to the White House, with its seals unbroken, on August 18, that is, after the beginning of the decisive battle of the Vistula. Besides Russia and Poland, it covered Anglo-French relations, Italy's attitude, the Adriatic question, Britain's debts, and the Turkish problem. The prime minister reminded the president of their co-operation in Paris in "endeavoring to lay the foundations of the postwar world on just and fair lines. . . ." David Lloyd George to President Wilson, 10 Downing Street, London, August 5, 1920. (Private and Confidential.) Woodrow Wilson Papers, File II, Box 171, Library of Congress.
111. Woodrow Wilson to David Lloyd George, White House, November 3, 1920. Woodrow Wilson Papers, File II, Box 171, Library of Congress.

CHAPTER VI

1. In regard to economics, Social Democrats, like Friedrich Stampfer, editor of the Socialist *Vorwärts,* held that Germany was neither capitalistic in the Western sense nor, of course, Communist. *Verhandlungen des Reichstags,* CCCXLIV, 273 (July 27, 1920).
2. Zinoviev, president of the Third International, denounced the stand taken by the Central Committee of the U.S.P.D. on these matters, but Dittmann and Crispien stood their ground. *Der zweite Kongress des Kommunist. Internationale. Protokolle* (Hamburg, 1921), pp. 246-50, 313ff., 324 (July 29, 1920).
3. J. S., "Krassin's Heimreise," *Berliner Tageblatt,* July 3, 1920; T[heodor] W[olff], "Beginn der Konferenz in Spa," *ibid.,* July 5.
4. Bernhard, "Der Erfolg von Spa," *Vossische Zeitung,* July 18, 1920.
5. *Berliner Tageblatt,* July 19, 1920.
6. From the coal settlement there was fear of increased unemployment, because of shortages of coal, fear of being recruited for the revolutionary left-wing, and fear that the military agreement would weaken means for the maintenance of internal peace. *Kölnische Zeitung,* July 18, 1920. Cf. *Frankfurter Zeitung,* July 15; Fritz Kern, "Spa als Beginn einer Geschichtsepoche," *Deutsche Allgemeine Zeitung,* July 19.
7. "Promesses," *Temps,* July 15-16, 1920.
8. L. Dumont-Wilden, "La Pologne en Danger," *Revue bleue,* July 17, 1920.
9. Erwin Barth "Das Resultat von Spa," *Die Neue Zeit: Wochenschrift der Deutschen Sozialdemokratie* II (July 30, 1920), 419-20. The Social Democratic party conceded Poland's right to independence within her ethnographic boundaries.
10. T. W., "Beginn der Konferenz in Spa," *Berliner Tageblatt,* July 5, 1920; *ibid.,* July 9; Dr. Paul Nathan, "Der Weissen von Spa," *ibid.,* July 10; T. W., "Allenstein," *ibid.,* July 12.
11. H. Kr. "Zwischen Spa und Lenin," *Deutsche Allgemeine Zeitung,* July 14.
12. Cf. F. Meinecke, *Die Deutsche Katastrophe: Betrachtungen und Erinnerungen* (2d ed.; Wiesbaden, 1946), pp. 35, 41, 153, 163, 164, for the attraction such ideas held even after World War II.
13. "Illusionen über Russland," II, *Kölnische Zeitung,* July 9, 1920. The movement,

originating among the extreme leftists in Hamburg, under Heinrich Lauffenburg and Fritz Wolffheim, had contacts with such conservative revolutionaries as Count Ernst zu Reventlow. A. Möhler, *Die Konservative Revolution in Deutschland, 1918-1932* (Stuttgart, 1950), pp. 60-61. Its Communist founders were excommunicated by Moscow after Soviet Russia's defeat in the Polish war.

14. *Parl. Deb.* (H.C.), 1920, VII, 528-29.

15. Rathenau, the head of the German General Electric Company (A.E.G.), had himself talked with Radek and had sent economic emissaries to Soviet Russia to report on the prospects for doing business there, but he condemned Stinnes's advice as meaning national suicide. Harry Graf Kessler, *Walter Rathenau: Sein Leben und sein Werk* (Berlin-Grünewald, 1928), pp. 295-96.

16. *Manchester Guardian,* July 23, 1920, Berlin, July 21.

17. W. Phillips to Secretary of State, The Hague, July 20, 1920, Report 197. National Archives, 862.00/993.

18. *Philadelphia Public Ledger,* in *Literary Digest,* July 24, 1920.

19. *Manchester Guardian,* July 23, 1920, Special Correspondent, Berlin, July 22.

20. E. L. Dresel to Secretary of State, Berlin, August 4, 1920 Report 506. National Archives, 861.00/7271.

21. V. Potiemkine, *Histoire de la diplomatie* (Paris, n.d.), III, 98-99. For von Seeckt's attitude in April, see above. In regard to his views in July and August, there seems to be no available evidence. However, it was perhaps significant that he went on leave on August 1. L. Kochan, *Russia and the Weimar Republic* (Cambridge, 1954), p. 30.

22. This, and the second note of July 30, was signed by Goeppert, the German delegate to the Peace Conference, and was addressed to the "President of the Peace Conference." *Vossische Zeitung,* July 25, 1920.

23. Council of Ambassadors, Interim Meeting, August 5, 1920, Appendix F. Woodrow Wilson Papers, Acc. 9712, Box 21, February-October 1920, Library of Congress.

24. *Action française,* in *Matin,* July 24, 1920. Cf. *Écho de Paris* (July 23, Zurich, July 22) for a report of important concentrations of German troops on the Polish frontier and of a German press campaign for an aggression against Poland. For fears of what the troops that the Allies had approved for Allenstein and Marienwerder might do, see "Pologne, Allemagne, Russie," *Temps,* July 24, 1920.

25. The *Berliner Tageblatt* (July 21, 1920) credited the French legation in Bern with a report that Millerand possessed proof that such an agreement existed, which the *Tageblatt* denied. Under the sensational caption of "Red Understanding with Germany," the London *Times* (August 5) printed a communication alleging that a definite agreement had been reached even before the Red offensive was launched and the leader of the *Times* "The Menace in Poland," held that the report merited serious consideration. The *Petit Parisien* added the information that the agreement had been signed by Kopp, the Soviet representative in Berlin, and Baron Ago von Maltzan, the chief of the East European Division of the German Foreign Ministry. For the Wolff Telegraph Bureau's semi-official denial, see *Berliner Tageblatt,* August 6.

26. *Reichsanzeiger,* July 20, 1920, in *Berliner Tageblatt,* July 21.

27. *Verhandlungen des Reichstags,* CCCXLIV, 262-63. Even the Kiel Canal was closed to shipping loaded with war supplies for Poland. R. Buell, *Poland: Key to Europe* (3d ed.; New York, 1939), p. 337, fn. 32.

28. *Verhandlungen des Reichstags,* CCCXLIV, 263.

Notes

29. E. H. Carr, *German-Soviet Relations between the Two World Wars, 1919-1939* (Baltimore, 1951), p. 35.

30. *Verhandlungen des Reichstags*, CCCXLIV, 275-79. (July 27).

31. *Vorwärts*, July 23, 1920.

32. *Ibid.*, August 8, 1920. For weeks German dock workers made Danzig useless as a port of entry for supplies destined for the Polish Army.

33. Teleki to Forster (Berlin), Budapest, July 22, 1920, Tel. 81. *Hungarian Documents and Papers*, I, 478.

34. Forster to Teleki, Berlin, July 24, 1920, Tel. 154. *Ibid.*, pp. 495-97.

35. Forster to Teleki, Berlin, July 29, 1920, Tel. 41; Forster to Teleki, Berlin, July 29, Report 156; Forster to Kánya, Berlin, July 29. 5077/pol. *Ibid.*, pp. 495-97.

36. W. von Blücher, *Deutschlands Weg nach Rapallo* (Wiesbaden, 1961), pp. 98-99; Gustav Hilger and Alfred G. Meyer, *The Incompatible Allies: A Memoir-History of German-Soviet Relations, 1918-1941* (New York: 1953), p. 65, fn. Blücher, who was a member of the Ministry's East European Division at this time, unfortunately failed to pin events to specific dates in his otherwise valuable memoirs. Simons took office with the new Fehrenbach Cabinet on June 20, 1920.

37. Blücher, *Deutschlands Weg nach Rapallo*, p. 100. Blücher was not certain that the Red Army generals would live up to this promise, and the *Frankfurter Zeitung* (August 3, 1920) shared this doubt at the time.

38. N. C. Kakourine and W. A. Mielikoff, *La guerre contre les polonais blancs en 1920* (Moscow, 1926), quoted in J. Pilsudski, *L'année 1920* . . . (Paris, 1929), pp. 289-90. As this did not accord with Lenin's plans of a revolutionary war and the presence of the Red flag on the German frontier of 1920, nothing came of this thought.

39. Kopp's interview with representatives of the *National Zeitung* in *Vossische Zeitung*, July 23, 1920, and of the *Berliner Tageblatt*, July 23. See also Bronski-Warszowski's interview in Vienna with a correspondent of the *Berliner Tageblatt* (July 26). *Izvestia*'s friendly views on Soviet-German relations at this time were put out by the Moscow wireless. In contrast to the Allies' implacable hostility at Spa, "between Germany and Russia there are no differences." Wireless News, July 28, No. 538, enclosure in Davis to Secretary of State, August 4. National Archives, 861.00/7259.

40. *Rote Fahne*, July 22, 1920, in *Vossische Zeitung*, July 23, and in *Kölnische Zeitung*, July 23.

41. Blücher, *Deutschlands Weg nach Rapallo*, p. 100.

42. E. H. Carr, *The Bolshevik Revolution, 1917-1923* (London, 1951-53), III, 325.

43. *Verhandlungen des Reichstags*, CCCXLIV, 262-64 (July 26); 282 (July 27); 347-48 (July 28); 571-72 (August 2).

44. Dresel to Secretary of State, Berlin, July 30, 1920, Tel. 903. National Archives, 862.00/989. Dresel had promptly cabled a full summary of the passages relating to Russia and Poland. Dresel to Secretary of State, Berlin, July 27. *Ibid.*, 862.00/988. Privately Simons spoke to Dresel of Russia somewhat differently: "he was in favor of a self-governing Poland but he was convinced the Poles could not maintain their complete independence and he eventually looked for a greater Russia which would include Poland as a federated province. The Bolshevik regime would he thought disintegrate at no distant date by contact with the outside world." Dresel to Secretary of State, Berlin, July 31. *Ibid.*, 861.00/7199.

45. Wireless News, No. 543, August 4, 1920. Enclosure in Wright to Secretary of State, London, August 13. National Archives, 861.00/7295.

46. Allied officers, they claimed, were allowed to examine the weapons of Soviet troops that had been forced into East Prussia and interned. Potiemkine, *Histoire de la diplomatie*, III, 99.

47. This is one of the unpublished documents from the archives of the German Foreign Ministry which E. H. Carr has seen. Carr, *Bolshevik Revolution*, III, 325.

48. Interview in *Neue Freie Presse, August 3*, in J. Bardoux, *De Paris à Spa: La bataille diplomatique pour la paix française* (Paris, 1921), p. 354. Simons' statement was sent out by the German wireless station at Plauen. Wireless News, No. 543, August 4, 1920. Enclosure in Wright to Secretary of State, London, August 13. National Archives. 861.00/7295.

49. *Verhandlungen des Reichstags*, CCCXLIV, 299-300 (July 27).

50. *Ibid.*, p. 288 (July 27).

51. *Ibid.*, p. 273 (July 27).

52. *Ibid.*, pp. 278-79 (July 27), 570-72 (August 2).

53. *Ibid.*, p. 282 (July 27). To the author of the document known as the Stresemann diary (possibly Fritz Rauch, his private secretary), Simons attributed the friendliness of his remarks on Russia to his desire to destroy "every possibility of seeing Germany [represented] as the champion of reactionary capitalism against free Russia in the possibly eventual conflict between Germany and Soviet Russia." Gustav Stresemann's Private Papers, *Nachlass, Series 7375, H165739*, National Archives. These are microfilm taken from Gustav Stresemann's private papers that his later secretary, Henry Bernhard, deposited in the archives of the German Foreign Ministry. While the above entry may throw light upon one aspect of Simons' motivation, it by no means tells the whole story as the facts brought out above clearly show.

54. Blücher, *Deutschlands Weg nach Rapallo*, pp. 96-97.

55. *Ibid.*

56. Dresel to Secretary of State, Berlin, July 24, 1920, Tel. 870. National Archives, 760 c. 61/117.

57. Von Seeckt, in his opinion, had disqualified himself by his dealings with the Social Democrats, and his conduct during the Kapp Putsch had cost him the confidence of the officer corps. Rechberg to Stresemann, Berlin, June 5. Gustav Stresemann's *Nachlass, Series 6927H, H138762-63*, National Archives.

58. Given the direction that Fehrenbach's views and those of his foreign minister Simons, in regard to Russia, Hoffmann was the last man he would consider for this important post in view of his known anti-Bolshevik activities.

59. Both felt, however, that Poland could not survive in the long run. Rechberg to Stresemann, Munich, July 10. Stresemann's *Nachlass, Series 6927H, H138791-92*, National Archives.

60. Tagebuch, Sunday, July 24, 1920. *Ibid.*, Series 7351H, H165733-34.

61. [Rauch] to Georges Deslaurens, Berlin, July 17, 1920; [Rauch] to Dr. H. Freigang, Berlin, July 19. *Ibid.*, Series 6930H, H139260-62, H139341-44.

62. "Richtlinien," *Ibid.*, Series 6930H, H139276-77, 139281.

63. Tagebuch, July 6, 1920. *Ibid.*, Series 7351H, H165723.

64. [Rauch] to Stresemann, Berlin, July 23, 1920. *Ibid.*, Series 6929H, H139020-25.

65. W. Görlitz, *Gustav Stresemann* (Heidelberg, 1947), pp. 111-12.

66. Joint Session of the Reichstag Fraction, the Executive Committee, and the Policy Committee of the Prussian Landtag Fraction of the German Peoples Party, July 26, 27, 1920, in the Reichstag. Stresemann's *Nachlass, Series 6929H, H139031-39*, National

Notes

Archives. On the same day (July 26), Stresemann talked with a Russian prince, identified as "A" in the diary, who told Stresemann to his obvious astonishment and skepticism that France had approved his formation of an army of 200,000 men in Latvia and Estonia under General Hoffmann with the eventual purpose of restoring Germany's 1914 frontier in the East and, even the disappearance of Poland! Tagebuch, Stresemann's *Nachlass,* Series 7351H, H165735-37, National Archives.

67. Joint Session . . . , July 27. Stresemann's *Nachlass,* Series 6929H, H139056, National Archives.

68. *Verhandlungen des Reichstags,* CCCXLIV, 317-18 (July 28). Clara Zetkin, the Communist deputy, regarded Stresemann's attack on Soviet Russia as more serious than that of Otto Hoetzsch. *Ibid.,* pp. 328-32.

69. The Stresemann diary contains an entry dated July 31, 1920, on a luncheon given by Rechberg at which the progress of his ideas was discussed. The guests included Stresemann; Lord Kilmarnock, the British chargé d'affaires; Rauch; and Colonel Stuart-Rodde, identified as a close friend of the Prince of Wales. Tagebuch, July 31, Stresemann's *Nachlass,* Series 7351H, H165740, National Archives.

70. It reprinted a Berlin dispatch in the *Petit Parisien* on alleged negotiations between British groups in Berlin and Ludendorff and on an alleged German plan for the suspension of the Treaty of Versailles for the duration of the campaign, for the restoration of Germany's 1914 frontier, etc., that resembled Rechberg's draft of an Anglo-German alliance. Later, the editor of the most influential conservative German review wrote of negotiations at this time for the revision of Versailles between agents who could easily be disavowed. W. Schotte, "Prolegomena zur Aussenpolitik," *Preussische Jahrbücher,* CLXXXIII (January, 1921), 283.

71. *Lord Riddell's Intimate Diary of the Peace Conference and After, 1918-1923* (London, 1933), p. 222 (July 22, 1920).

72. *Evening News,* July 28, 1920, quoted in *New York World,* July 29.

73. Memorandum for Mr. Bliss, Department of State, 7/29/20, attached to Dresel to Secretary of State, Berlin, July 24. Tel. 870. National Archives, 760 c. 61/117.

74. *Parl. Deb.* (H.C.), 1920, XIII, 1994-95.

75. V. Poliakoff, "The Entente, Germany, and the Bolsheviks," *Nineteenth Century,* LXXXVIII (September, 1920), 429-30.

76. "Episodes of the Month," *National Review,* No. 451 (September, 1920), pp. 18-19.

77. "Peace Hanging in the Balance," *New Europe,* August 5, 1920.

78. *Atti del parlamento italiano: Camera dei Deputati, 1919, 1920, Discussioni,* V (July 30), 4399. Hereafter cited as *Parl. Ital.* (C.D.), *1919-1920.*

79. Count Carlo Sforza, *Europe and the Europeans* (New York, 1936), p. 232.

80. *Parl. Ital.* (C.D.), *1919-1920,* V (August 6), 4987.

81. Cf. B. de Lacombe, *Correspondant,* N.S., CCXLIV (August 5, 1920), 570, 571.

82. *Deutsche Allgemeine Zeitung,* August 9, 1920.

83. *Verhandlungen des Reichstags,* CCCXLIV (July 28), 348.

84. Simons, "Kreuzzüge und Koalitonskriege," *Deutsche Allgemeine Zeitung,* August 2, 1920. A full summary of this article was sent out by the German wireless station at Plauen. Wireless News, No. 543, August 4. Enclosure in Wright to Secretary of State, London, August 13. National Archives, 861.00/7295.

85. In regard to the League of Nations, in which membership was generally assumed to be the reward for accepting Churchill's proposal, he thought the time for that had not arrived. *Verhandlungen des Reichstags,* CCCXLIV, 570-72.

Notes

CHAPTER VII

1. According to Trotsky—and Deutscher agrees—Josef Stalin, then the chief political commissar of the southern army, persuaded its commander, Yegorov, to disregard an order to turn north until it was too late, in the hope of a victory at Lvov that would rival Tukhachevsky's achievements. L. Trotsky, *Stalin: An Appraisal of the Man and His Influence* (New York, 1941), pp. 328-30; I. Deutscher, *Stalin: A Political Biography* (New York, 1949), pp. 216-17; I. *Deutscher, The Armed Prophet: Trotsky, 1879-1921* (New York and London, 1954), pp. 466-67. Overconfidence seems also to have played a part.

2. The motive was perhaps less to cut the Warsaw-Danzig communications, since the Danzig dockworkers were effectively blocking the flow of war supplies, than to carry out Lenin's wish to plant the red flag on the German frontier. "Danzig," reported the American consul, "is virtually worthless to Poland during the present emergency." W. Dawson to Secretary of State, Danzig, August 23, 1920, No. 89. National Archives, 760 c. 61/312.

3. Four-fifths of its casualties since November, 1918 (a total of 251,329 officers and men), were lost in 1920. General W. S. Sikorski, *La campagne polono-russe de 1920* (Paris, 1928), p. 280.

4. Pilsudski's version was that Weygand favored the evacuation of Warsaw and then an attack while he himself insisted upon the capital's use as the base for the counter-offensive. For this reason Weygand refused his offer of the operational command. Pilsudski, *L'année 1920*, as cited in M. K. Dziewanowski, "Pilsudski's Federal Policy, 1919-1921," *Journal of Central European Affairs*, X (July, 1950), 282.

5. *Manchester Guardian*, August 14, 1920. Special correspondent, Warsaw, August 10. 1920.

6. C. R. Crane to Secretary of State, Prague, August 7, 1920. National Archives, 760 c. 61/150.

7. Cf. fn 6. General Weygand had designated Danzig as the chief reliance since "all other means of communications may fail at short notice." Weygand to Foch, Prague, July 24, 1920. No. 612. Tel. Interim Meeting, Council of Ambassadors, Paris, August 5. Woodrow Wilson Papers, Acquisition 9712, Box 21 (February-October, 1920), Library of Congress.

8. Viscount d'Abernon, *Eighteenth Decisive Battle of the World: Warsaw, 1920* (London, 1921), p. 56.

9. *Ibid.*, pp. 59-60, 72.

10. B. de Lacombe, *Correspondant*, N.S., CCXLIV (August 5, 1920), 567-68.

11. *New York Times*, August 2, 1920. Walter Duranty, Paris, August 1.

12. J. Bardoux, *De Paris à Spa: La bataille diplomatique pour la paix française* (Paris, 1921), p. 352.

13. T. Weiss, "La frontière de l'est européen," *Europe nouvelle*, August 8.

14. B. de Lacombe, *Correspondant*, N.S., CCXLIV (August 5, 1920), 567-68. Jules Cambon, the distinguished French diplomat, deplored the tendency to blame Poland for everything at a meeting of the Council of Ambassadors, August 5, but he said nothing of going to war for her sake. Woodrow Wilson Papers, Acquisition 9712, Box 21, Library of Congress.

15. He defied Labor's demands that he deny charges of pressure upon Poland's neighbors as reported in the case of Czechoslovakia or to desist from it "if it becomes

Notes

clear that the Soviet authorities mean to destroy Poland." *Parl. Deb.* (H.C.) 1920, VIII, 2628-32 (August 5).

16. See below, Section 2.

17. C. E. Callwell, *Field Marshal Sir Henry Wilson* (London, 1927), II, 256 (August 6).

18. *Daily Telegraph,* August 9, 1920, Reuter's dispatch, August 6. Cf. *Soir,* August 8, 9, 1920.

19. Sapieha to Chicherin, Warsaw, August 5, 1920. Wireless News, No. 547, August 9. Enclosure in Wright to Secretary of State, London, August 13, No. 3273. National Archives, 861.00/7295. Cf. *Daily Telegraph,* August 19, where the Polish legation in London is given as the source. This wireless is mistakenly dated August 6 in *Europe nouvelle* (August 15).

20. To foreign correspondents in Warsaw and to Sir Eric Drummond, the Secretary General of the League of Nations, he explained that the Moscow station first refused to receive it during the late hours of the night and again at an agreed upon hour on August 6 on grounds of weak reception. *Daily Telegraph,* August 9, 1920.

21. Chicherin to Sapieha, Moscow, August 6, 1920. Wireless News, No. 546, August 7. Enclosure in Wright to Secretary of State, London, August 13. National Archives, 861.00/7295.

22. Sapieha to Chicherin, Warsaw, August 7, 1920. *Daily Herald,* August 9.

23. Chicherin to Sapieha, Moscow, August 7, 1920. *Ibid.,* August 9.

24. Callwell, *Wilson,* II, 257 (August 8). The biographies of Lloyd George, Curzon, Bonar Law, and Balfour are silent on the crisis over the Polish-Soviet War. [See *D.B.F.P.,* 1st Series, XI, 198-748, for the Russo-Polish War. Ed.]

25. Soviet declaration, August 8, 1920. *Daily Herald,* August 9.

26. Chicherin to Lloyd George, Moscow, August 8, 1920. *Europe nouvelle,* September 26.

27. *Der zweite Kongresse des Kommunist. Internationale. Protokolle,* pp. 680-81; Wireless News, No. 547, August 9, 1920. Enclosure in Wright to Secretary of State, London, August 13. National Archives, 861.00/7295.

28. These statements appeared in the *Daily Telegraph* (August 9, 1920) under the headline, "Allies defied by Moscow Soviet." To Lord Riddell, Lloyd George lamented Soviet Russia's refusal to see how much more advantageous peace with Great Britain and France would be than the conquest of Poland, and he recalled that revolutionary France had compelled Pitt to go to war over Holland. *Lord Riddell's Intimate Diary of the Peace Conference and After, 1918-1923* (London, 1933), pp. 229-30.

29. *New York Times,* August 9, 1920, A.P., Hythe, England, August 9.

30. Callwell, *Wilson,* II, 257; "No Troops for Poland," *Westminster Gazette,* August 10.

31. D'Abernon, *Eighteenth Decisive Battle,* pp. 68-69.

32. Harrison to Secretary of State, Paris, August 11, 1920, Tel. 1534. National Archives, 760. c. 61/16T.

33. *Morning Post,* August 5, 1920; *Times,* August 6; *Daily Telegraph,* August 10.

34. "Britain Plunging into War with Socialist Russia," *Daily Herald,* August 5, 1920.

35. The *Morning Post* (August 7, 1920) and the *Daily Telegraph* (August 7)

printed the Polish chargé d'affaires' (John Ciechanowski's) detailed indictment of Soviet tactics.

36. "Will Poland be Saved?," *Daily Telegraph,* August 6, 1920.
37. "A National Crisis," *ibid.,* August 10.
38. "A Fateful Day," *ibid.,* August 9.
39. Churchill to Secretary, Leicester and District Trades Council, August 5, 1920. *Ibid.,* August 7.
40. The above summarizes the views expressed by the *Westminster Gazette* on August 9 and 10, 1920. In the reports of efforts to enlist Hungary's military assistance for Poland in return for the revision of the terms of peace, it saw another manifestation of "mad hatter" policy. "Our London Letter," *ibid.,* August 10.
41. "Poland and the British Bolsheviks," *Morning Post,* August 9, 1920.
42. Lloyd George's attitude, and that of his colleagues, according to the American Embassy, "has united the bulk of British workingmen in the belief that none of the Labor ideals are possible of attainment by the present Government." J. Butler Wright (chargé d'affaires) to Secretary of State, London, August 16, 1920, No. 3303. National Archives, 841.00/363.
43. Dismissed by Harvard University, Laski had recently assumed the post at the London School of Economics that he was to hold for more than thirty years. Laski to Holmes, London, July 18, 1920. Mark de Wolfe Howe, *Holmes-Laski Letters: The Correspondence of Mr. Justice Holmes and Harold J. Laski, 1916-1935* (Foreword by Felix Frankfurter) (Cambridge, 1953), I, 271.
44. On January 30, 1920, Beatrice Webb, who with her husband Sydney, was among the moderate leaders, noted in her diary that the press had failed to see one characteristic of the Labor Party: its assumption of the right outside Parliament "to settle imperial and foreign affairs here and now without becoming H.M. Government." Margaret J. Cole, ed., *Beatrice Webb's Diaries, 1912-1924* (London, 1952), p. 174.
45. The delegation arrived back in England on June 30. Carefully choosing from its members, the pro-Bolshevik *Daily Herald* (July 30, 1920) printed a number of statements whose unrealistic praise of bolshevism misrepresented the sharp differences of opinion within the delegation. However, Mrs. Philip Snowden, one of the sharpest critics, joined seven other members in a sweeping condemnation of intervention and in a warning as to the need of peace. *Ibid.,* July 8. Bertrand Russell, who traveled with the delegation but was not a member, shared this point of view.
46. "The Slippery Pole," *Ibid.,* August 4, 1920.
47. "Britain Plunging into War with Socialist Russia," *ibid.,* August 5.
48. *Morning Post,* August 7, 1920.
49. *Daily Herald,* August 10, 1920. Because the Lympne Conference had carried over to August 9, Lloyd George's statement had been delayed one day. It has not been possible to determine exactly when the joint committee issued the call for the National Labor Convention to meet in London on August 13.
50. *Ibid.,* August 11. The Labor delegation's secretary kept a verbatim record of everything said at this unique meeting.
51. *Parl. Deb.* (H.C.), 1920, IX, 253-72 (August 10).
52. *Ibid.,* pp. 273-87.
53. *Ibid.,* pp. 351-52.

Notes

54. *Times, Daily Herald,* August 14, 1920. Cf. Bonar Law's statement in the House of Commons, August 16. *Parl. Deb.* (H.C.), 1920, IX, 666-67.

55. Quoted in *Matin,* August 13, 1920.

56. In view of the *Daily Herald's* campaign and of Arthur Henderson's circular telegram as Secretary of the National Labor party, there is ground for doubting the complete authenticity of this spontaneity. *Daily Herald,* August 6, 1920.

57. Harold J. Laski, London, August 15, in *Nation* (New York), September 15, 1920.

58. *Daily Herald,* August 14, 1920. By our Parliamentary Correspondent, August 13. Cf. J. T. Murphy, *Labour's Big Three* (London, 1948), pp. 79-80. The radical journalist, Robert Dell, thought it was the *serment de jeu du paume* of the English revolution. *Nation* (London), August 21.

59. *Nation* (New York), September 15, 1920.

60. Beatrice Webb, who with Sydney was on the Continent, doubted that a general strike, if one were called, would have been "sufficiently universal to be effective," but she was convinced that much of middle class opinion approved Labor's stand. Cole, ed., *Beatrice Webb's Diaries,* p. 187 (August 20).

61. *Literary Digest,* September 25, 1920.

62. Callwell, *Wilson,* II, 259-61 (August 19).

63. *Parl. Deb.* (H.C.), 1920, IX, 665 (August 16).

64. *Ibid.,* pp. 594-95.

65. *Ibid.,* p. 706. That evening after Lloyd George's speech, the Council of Action reaffirmed Labor's stand in still stronger terms, demanding, under threat of "any and every form" of strike, guarantees against the use of British armed forces in support of Poland or Wrangel or a blockade of Soviet Russia, the recognition of and trade with the Soviet government, and the repudiation of alliances or other association with France or other countries involving the furnishing of war supplies to Poland or Wrangel. It acknowledged the receipt of a telegram of appreciation from the All-Russian Central Council of Trade Unions and recommended the observance of August 22 as "Peace with Russia" Sunday. *Daily Herald,* August 17.

66. As a Labor journal, it was handicapped in selling advertising space, normally a newspaper's principal source of revenue. Although the trade unions were represented on the board of directors—Ernest Bevin was a member among others—they gave it considerable sums only occasionally but no regular subsidies. *Nation,* September 18, 1920. Lansbury never acknowledged himself at fault in turning to the Soviets. He himself had raised funds and contributed his own money to help Socialist newspapers in other countries. In his opinion, the only grounds for criticism in such circumstances were "secrecy and dictation." Even in later years, he saw no reason to distinguish between the revolutionary activities of the Third International and the international campaigns of the churches and temperance societies. G. Lansbury, *My Life* (New York, 1930), p. 194.

67. That they were retained for possible use later is evident from the fact that none of them were included in the "Wireless News" along with other wireless intercepts.

68. Davis to Secretary of State (Winslow to Hurley), London, August 14, 1920, Tel. 1235. (urgent). National Archives, 841.00 B/5.

69. Callwell, *Wilson,* II, 259 (August 18).

70. The *Daily Chronicle, Westminster Gazette,* and *Manchester Guardian* all remained silent, but it is not without significance for the attitude of Liberal opinion that the *Guardian's* political correspondent wrote (August 19, 1920): "I doubt if the Government have done themselves much good by the carefully selected telegrams they have published about Mr. Lansbury's efforts to get paper for the *Daily Herald* through Russia." He thought that there had been omissions since those that were published, standing alone, were incomprehensible even to the persons immediately concerned.

71. Trevor Evans, *Bevin of Britain* (New York, 1946), pp. 103-6. In September, the directors, staff, and holders of the newspaper's debentures reached a formal decision against an arrangement with the Soviet government, despite the favorable results of a poll of the *Daily Herald's* readers. R. Postgate, *George Lansbury* (London, 1951), pp. 210-13. Postgate was the *Herald's* sub-foreign editor in 1920.

72. This was the sense of numerous clippings from the provincial press assembled by the *Temps* (August 17, 1920) under the caption "Opinions de Province."

73. J. Roujon, "L'Allemagne ménace," *Figaro,* August 8.

74. On August 10, a joint Anglo-French note demanded that it define its attitude as a condition of their aid. Sir Maurice Hankey's (the secretary of the British Cabinet) report on the discouraging political situation in Warsaw and on the apparent half-heartedness of the military effort had echoes in the Paris press. *Matin,* August 10, 1920. J. Sauerwein, Hythe, August 9.

75. Litvinov was quoted to this effect. *Ibid.,* August 10, 1920, Copenhagen, August 8.

76. The Allies, he apparently added, might be compelled to equal the Soviets' bid in order to secure Germany's co-operation. *Ibid.,* August 10, Hythe, August 9.

77. *Temps,* August 11, 1920, Special Correspondent, Berlin, August 7.

78. Reventlow in *Deutsche Tageszeitung* (August 3, 1920) in *Berliner Tageblatt,* August 16; *Vorwärts,* August 3; *Kölnische Zeitung,* August 13, Berlin, August 11; *Frankfurter Zeitung,* August 13.

79. T. Wolff, "The Way of the Boulevards," *Nation,* August 14, 1920.

80. *Victoire,* in *Matin,* August 9, 1920.

81. "Les Alliés, la Pologne et la Russie," *Temps,* August 11, 1920.

82. Bernus, "Le Discours de M. Lloyd George," *Journal des débats,* August 12, 1920.

83. They were printed in full by the morning newspapers of August 11, 1920. Cf. *Figaro,* August 12, under, *Dernière heure.*

84. Enclosure in Hugh C. Wallace to Secretary of State, Paris, August 18, 1920, No. 1544. National Archives, 661.00/7335.

85. *Journal des débats,* August 13, 1920.

86. D'Abernon, in Warsaw, thought the Polish government would not even consider such "extravagant terms." D'Abernon, *Eighteenth Decisive Battle,* p. 71 (August 11).

87. In Germany, Simons, the Foreign Minister, as well as the press was insisting that the Allies should not repeat the mistake they had made in the Paris Peace Conference and try to settle the Eastern European problem without Germany. Cf. Wolff, "The Way of the Boulevards," *Nation,* August 14.

88. "L'explication franco-britannique," *Temps,* August 13; R. Poincaré, "Revue de la quinzaine," *Revue des deux mondes,* August 15, 1920, pp. 891-92.

Notes

89. The morning newspapers in Paris had, however, printed the essentials. See above, fn. 81.

90. A press report that Kamenev had twice offered in writing to De Halbouët, the French commercial attaché, Russia's recognition of the debts of preceding regimes and and proposing negotiations in Paris for this purpose may have been the immediate occasion for this decision. *Matin*, August 10, 1920. For the communiqué, see "Pour une vraie paix," *Temps*, August 12; *Matin*, August 12.

91. *New York Times*, August 13, 1920. Edwin L. James, Paris, August 12. Paléologue in fact showed the American chargé a circular dispatch to certain French diplomatic missions explaining that "the French Government considered that the British notification to the Poles was contrary to the Hythe [Lympne] decisions which had for their object the encouragement of Poland to defend its independence whereas the Soviet terms would place Poland at the mercy of her enemies." Harrison to Secretary of State, Paris, August 13, Tel. 1547. National Archives, 760 c. 61/181.

92. *Matin*, August 15, 1920. The French authorities acted at once when William Adamson, a Labor M.P., and Harry Gosling, appeared in Paris as delegates from the Council of Action to arouse and co-ordinate French labor unions and Socialists. On orders from the Paris police, they cut their visit short by some hours on August 16. *Daily Telegraph*, August 18, Paris, August 17; *Daily Herald*, August 18.

93. *Humanité* (August 14, 1920) in *Manchester Guardian*, August 16.

94. A. Tardieu, "Les alliés et le bolchèvisme," *Illustration*, August 14, 1920.

95. *Europe nouvelle*, August 22, 1920.

96. *Action française* (August 12, 1920), in J. Bainville, *La Russie et la barrière de l'est* (Paris, 1937), pp. 71-72.

97. The *Nation* (August 14, 1920) reported it was received with "incredulity."

98. "Le choix de M. Lloyd George," *Temps*, August 15, 1920.

99. "Faults on Both Sides," *Times*, August 13, 1920.

100. The *Matin* (August 13, 1920) translated the views of the *Evening Standard*, the *Pall Mall Gazette*, and also the declaration of the *Star* that Great Britain would send neither men nor money nor munitions to Wrangel's troops.

101. "The Misunderstanding with France," *Manchester Guardian*, August 13, 1920.

102. "The Vice of French Policy," *Nation*, August 14, 1920.

103. "Mad Doggery," *Daily Herald*, August 13, 1920.

104. Yvon Delbos, who was to be a foreign minister of a Popular Front government in the 1930's, was among the exceptions. "Our government declares that it will not make war on the Soviets under any circumstances. Why, then, does it wish others to make it? . . . Since everyone, including France desires peace, let us make peace at last!" *L'ère nouvelle*, in *Matin*, August 16, 1920.

105. "Wrangel Consequences," *New World*, August 19, 1920.

106. "The Only Way to Peace," *Spectator*, August 14, 1920.

107. "No War with Russia," *Observer*, August 15, 1920.

108. Davis to Secretary of State, London, August 4, 1920, Tel. 1170; Colby to Davis, Washington, August 6, Tel. 846. *Foreign Relations*, 1920, III, 386, 387.

109. In any event, the sealed letter was not in the President's hands until August 18 and he replied with a refusal on November 3.

110. *Literary Digest*, August 7, 1920.

111. *Ibid.*

112. It was perhaps not a coincidence that the affair followed shortly after the

Curzon note of July 19 which, because of its proposal of a conference of East European governments in London with Soviet representation, marked the beginning of Millerand's independence in the Russo-Polish problem.

113. Norman H. Davis to President Wilson, Department of State, July 23; Woodrow Wilson to Colby, White House, July 24. Papers of Woodrow Wilson, File II, Box 169, Library of Congress. It would have been most unusual for a French diplomat, especially a counselor of embassy, to have been ignorant of protocol or to have violated it without a calculated purpose.

114. *New York Times,* August 5, 1920, Special to the *New York Times,* Washington, August 4.

115. *Ibid.,* August 6, 1920, Special to the *New York Times,* Washington, August 5.

116. Colby to President Wilson, Department of State, July 18, 1920. Papers of Woodrow Wilson, File II, Box 169, Library of Congress.

117. Woodrow Wilson to Secretary of State Colby, White House, July 20, 1920. *Ibid.*

118. *New York Times,* August 7, 1920, Special to the *New York Times,* Washington, August 6.

119. Colby to Davis, Washington, August 7, 1920, Tel. 851. National Archives, 760 c. 61/151a. After an exchange of telegrams on the extreme length of some of these messages, the department settled for a full summary (instead of the complete texts) which, however, arrived days after the dispatch and publication of Colby's famous note on August 10. Davis to Secretary of State, London, August 15. National Archives, 760 c. 61/198.

120. *Washington Post,* August 5, 1920.

121. *New York Herald,* Paris Edition, August 10, 1920. The text has never been revealed.

122. Italy's absence from the Boulogne Conference between Lloyd George and Millerand was explained, semi-officially, on the ground that the British Prime Minister and Count Sforza, the Foreign Minister in the Giolitti government, were "in perfect accord on the Russian question." *La Tribuna,* in *Matin,* July 28, 1920. On August 6, Sforza announced to the Italian Chamber of Deputies the conclusion of an agreement with the Soviet government for an exchange of agents, the arrival soon of a Russian agent, and Italy's opposition to the revival of the blockade, but, at the same time, he strongly affirmed Poland's right to independence despite her error in invading Russia. *Parl. Ital.* (C.D.), *1919-1920,* V, 4987.

123. *New York Herald,* Paris Edition, August 11, 1920.

124. The *Herald's* treatment of the featured story attracted special attention in the press and diplomatic circles. The headline read, "Note issue by the United States backs up Russia" and an introductory editorial statement declared "that the United States Department of State—evidently at the direction of President Wilson—has issued a statement. . . ."

125. *Figaro, Écho de Paris,* August 10, 1920.

126. *New York Herald* (Paris edition), August 10, 1920. On August 12, the *Herald* added the point comparing the spirit of the Russian Army of 1920 to that of the American Army of 1776, without attributing it to a Russian Tsarist officer as Fox had done. It appeared, however, in the French original in the *Matin* (August 10) and in the *Temps* (August 11) that evening.

127. In the American chargé's first telegram on this incident, he summarized the

Notes

New York Herald's story and reported the reaction to the Department's denial as reserved. Harrison to Secretary of State, Paris, August 10, 1920, Tel. 1522. National Archives, 760 c. 61/157.

128. Harrison to Secretary of State, Paris, August 10, 1920, Tel. 1527. National Archives, 760 c. 61/160.

129. Colby to American Embassy, Washington, August 11, 1920, Tel. 1361. National Archives, 760 c. 61/160a. Cf. *New York Times,* August 14, Special, Washington, August 13.

130. Harrison to Secretary of State, Paris, August 14, 1920, Tel. 1551. National Archives, 760 c. 61/184.

131. Although the understandably mystified press was assured that a full clarification would be forthcoming, the mystery was never satisfactorily cleared up. On August 14, the *Écho de Paris* mentioned the part played by Fox's article, and a Washington dispatch (August 13) in the *New York Herald* (Paris Edition), August 14, explained clearly enough what had happened there but not the actions of the Quai d'Orsay. A statement in the *Temps* (August 28) added no new information of significance: the *Washington Post* had summarized "a communication representing the ideas of Secretary of State Colby" and the omission of quotation marks had been responsible for the misunderstanding. Hugh C. Wallace to Secretary of State, Paris, September 3, 1920, Tel. 1581. National Archives, 760 c. 61/304. Imaginations ran riot in seeking a reasonable solution. There was the fantastic story "gravely circulated in the Conservative papers last night," according to the *Manchester Guardian's* (August 14) Paris correspondent (August 13) that a Bolshevik agent "had got hold of the French code and sent a forged note from Mr. Wilson," but the correspondent's own version was not much more credible. The Paris story contained, he alleged, the essentials of a first draft of the Colby note, prepared by President Wilson's secretary, which, reaching the Quai d'Orsay from the French Embassy in Washington, had been leaked to the Paris press.

132. A draft telegram to the Paris Embassy was prepared for Colby's signature suggesting that Jusserand should be informed and persuaded to secure De Béarn's recall. Although Colby approved the text and agreed that it should be sent, it never was dispatched, doubtless as a result of France's favorable reaction to the Colby note of August 10. Draft telegram, with attached memoranda, Department of State, August 13, 1920. National Archives, 760 c. 61/160.

133. See above, fn. 120.

134. Colby to Avezzana, Department of State, August 10, 1920. *Foreign Relations,* 1920, III, 463-68.

135. *New York Times,* August 12, 1920. Special, Washington, August 11.

136. *Journal of Commerce* (New York), *Bulletin* (Philadelphia) in *Literary Digest,* August 21, 1920.

137. *Literary Digest,* August 21, 1920.

138. *New York Times,* August 12, 1920, A. P., Washington, August 11.

139. *Ibid.,* August 15, Washington, August 14.

140. *Ibid.*

141. "Pour une vraie paix," *Temps,* August 12, 1920; *Journal,* in *Écho de Paris,* August 14.

142. De Béarn to Secretary of State Colby, French Embassy, Washington, August 14, 1920. *Foreign Relations,* 1920, III, 469-70.

143. Van S. Merle-Smith, 3d Assistant Secretary of State, Department of State. *Ibid.,* p. 471.

144. *New York Times,* August 13, Paris, August 12. Robert Dell, the radical British journalist, attributed the stiffening of France's stand on Poland to the Colby note. "Poland and the Entente," *Nation* (New York), September 18, 1920, London, August 26.

145. Bardoux, *De Paris à Spa,* p. 361.

146. P. Millet, "Une erreur: la reconnaissance de Wrangel," *Europe nouvelle,* August 22.

147. Dresel to Secretary of State, Berlin, August 20, 1920, Tel. 527. National Archives, 760 c. 61/296.

148. The *Tribune* and *Popolo romano* quoted in translation in Johnson to Secretary of State, Rome, August 17, 1920, Tel. 309. *Ibid.,* 861.01/232.

149. Johnson to Secretary of State, Rome, August 30, 1920, Tel. 324. *Ibid.*

150. Wright to Secretary of State, London, August 21, 1920. *Ibid.,* 841.00/364.

151. Davis to Secretary of State, London, August 12, 1920, Tel. 1213. *Ibid.,* 760 c. 61/171.

152. *Morning Post,* August 13, 1920, Washington, August 12.

153. *Daily Telegraph,* August 12, 1920, Washington, August 10. This was also the *Spectator's* view (August 14).

154. Czech chargé (Masaryk) to Secretary of State, Washington, September 27, 1920. *Foreign Relations,* 1920, III, 472.

155. L. Fischer, *The Soviets in World Affairs* (2d ed.; Princeton, 1951), I, 308-10.

156. E. H. Carr, *The Bolshevik Revolution, 1917-1923* (London, 1951-53), III, 280, fn. 1.

157. J. Degras, *Soviet Documents on Foreign Policy* (London, 1951-53), I, 207-11.

158. Martens to Italian Ambassador (Avezzana), October 4, 1920. *Foreign Relations,* 1920, III, 474-78.

159. D'Abernon, *Eighteenth Decisive Battle,* p. 79. Because of differences that included divergent conceptions of time and place, General Weygand had refused Pilsudski's offer of the operational command.

160. *Manchester Guardian,* August 16, 1920. Special correspondent, Paris, August 15.

161. Wireless News, No. 552, August 14, 1920. Enclosure in Wright to Secretary of State, London, August 20, No. 3312. National Archives, 861.00/2320. Cf. *Temps,* August 15. For the foreign press, correspondents were present from the *Times, Daily Express, Morning Post* of London, the Associated Press, *Public Ledger* (Philadelphia), *Chicago Tribune* of the American Press, the *Temps, Journal, Matin, Liberté* of Paris, and the *Corriere della sera* of Milan.

162. *Temps,* August 15, 1920.

163. Chicherin to Litvinov, Moscow, August 22, 1920. Wireless News, No. 559, August 23. Enclosure in Wright to Secretary of State, London, August 27, No. 3336. National Archives, 861.00/7319. They insisted at the first business meeting on August 17 that the second should convene on the nineteenth and then that the next meeting should not be held until the twenty-third.

164. Wireless News, No. 554, August 17, 1920. Enclosure in Wright to Secretary of State, London, August 20, No. 3312. National Archives, 861.00/7320.

165. Chicherin to Kamenev, Moscow, August 26, 1920. Wireless News, No. 564,

Notes

August 28. Enclosure in Wright to Secretary of State, London, September 3, No. 3379. National Archives, 861.00/7366.

166. *Daily Herald,* August 16, 1920.

167. Moscow, August 20 (?), 1920. Wireless News, No. 557, August 20. Enclosure in Wright to Secretary of State, London, August 27, No. 3336. National Archives, 861.00/7319. Cf. Degras, *Soviet Documents on Foreign Policy,* I, 201-2.

168. Although Mason's dispatch appeared in the *Berliner Tageblatt* (August 15, 1920, Moscow, August 11), it does not seem to have been circulated elsewhere. The London *Times* (August 17) mentioned under the heading "Red Trickery" an intercepted wireless from Moscow, dated August 11, to much the same effect which described the arming of the workers as "unprecedented in history." This exact phrase appears in an intercept identified as a message from Harrison to Gerfalk, A[ssociated?] P[ress?] in Copenhagen, Moscow, August 11. Wireless News, No. 551, August 13. Enclosure in Wright to Secretary of State, London, August 20, No. 3312. National Archives, 661.00/7320.

169. It is possible, as a contributor to the *Times* later suggested, that Kamenev took it upon himself to edit this item for fear of his immediate expulsion from England at the time when, in view of Warsaw's expected fall, his presence would be most useful to the Soviet government. A well-informed correspondent, "A Scheme that Failed," *Times,* August 26, 1920.

170. *Daily Herald,* August 18, 1920, H. N. Brailsford, our special correspondent, Minsk, August 16; *Manchester Guardian,* August 18, special correspondent, Minsk, August 16.

171. Chicherin to Curzon, August 24, 1920. *Europe nouvelle,* September 26.

CHAPTER VIII

1. *Daily Chronicle,* August 31, 1920, Warsaw, August 20.

2. White replied that the American government would not, in his opinion, object to Poland's concluding peace, but he personally believed that her best course would be to "continue the war with the aid of the Entente." He reported the general feeling in Warsaw to be that Wrangel might succeed in overthrowing the Soviet regime if the Poles continued the war for several months. "Such a possibility," he added for Washington's benefit, "is not one to be lightly discarded by the Western world." White to Secretary of State, Warsaw, August 20, 1920, Tel. 459. National Archives, 760 c. 61/243.

3. *Lord Riddell's Intimate Diary of the Peace Conference and After, 1918-1923* (London, 1933), pp. 232-33 (August 22, 23).

4. The presence of Simons, the German foreign minister, in Switzerland at this time, which the suspicious *Temps* (August 19) noted, was apparently a coincidence. That Lloyd George had seen him was officially denied in the *Times* (August 24, 1920).

5. *Times,* August 24, 1920, Lucerne, August 23.

6. *Matin,* August 25, 1920.

7. *Europe nouvelle,* October 3, 1920. The French and Italian Prime Ministers met at Aix-les-Bains in September with somewhat different results than the Lucerne meeting. *Ibid.*

8. He was, however, to take no part in the discussion of the instructions to the High Commissioner, Sir Reginald Tower, since he was an official of the League of

Nations! Nor was force to be used against an unwilling populace. Colby to Wallace, Washington, August 21, 1920, Tel. 1391. *Foreign Relations, 1920,* III, 391.

9. Secretariat General to Towers, Paris, August 24, 1920 (Tel.) in Wallace to Secretary of State, Paris, August 27, No. 1565. National Archives, 760 c. 61/291.

10. White to Secretary of State, Warsaw, August 27, 1920, Tel. 468. *Ibid.,* 760 c. 61/259.

11. Colby to American High Commissioner (Admiral Bristol, Constantinople), Washington, August 27, 1920, Tel. 48. *Ibid.,* 861.01/232. A. Wrangel's answers followed the indicated lines. Bristol to Secretary of State, Constantinople, September 8, Tel. 487. *Ibid.,* 861.01/238.

12. Wallace to Secretary of State, Paris, September 13, 1920, Tel. 1694. Colby to Admiral Bristol (Constantinople), Washington, September 16, Tel. 58. *Ibid.,* 661.00/7359.

13. Gibson to Secretary of State, Warsaw, September 2, 1920, Tel. 483. *Foreign Relations, 1920,* III, 401-3.

14. Gibson to Secretary of State, Warsaw, September 15, 1920, Tel. 506. National Archives, 760 c. 61/320.

15. Colby to Wallace (Paris), Washington, September 25, 1920, Tel. 1507. *Foreign Relations, 1920,* III, 405.

16. According to Riddell, the prime minister's confidant, he was "still keen on making peace with them." *Lord Riddell's Intimate Diary,* p. 233 (August 23).

17. *Times, Daily Herald,* August 25, 1920.

18. Chicherin to British government. Tel. August 25, 1920. J. Degras, *Soviet Documents on Foreign Policy* (London, 1951-53), I, 203.

19. There was, however, no appeal for or threat of a general strike. *Daily Chronicle,* August 26, 1920. Cf. *Daily Herald,* August 26.

20. Balfour to Kamenev, September 1, 1920, *Daily Herald,* September 3.

21. Chicherin to Kamenev (for Balfour), September 8, 1920. Degras, *Soviet Documents on Foreign Policy,* I, 204-6. Cf. *Daily Herald,* September 9.

22. Kamenev to Lt. Commander Kenworthy *et al.,* September 11, 1920. *Europe nouvelle,* October 3.

23. British government to Kenworthy *et al.,* September 15, 1920. *Ibid.,* October 17. On the way back to Russia, Kamenev told a Stockholm newspaper, the *Social Demokraten* (September 17), that he had known about the smuggling of jewels into England. He had seen nothing objectionable in it! Enclosure in Wheeler to Secretary of State, Stockholm, September 22, No. 1982. National Archives, 861.00/7502.

24. Moscow, September 5, 1920. Wireless News, No. 572, September 7. Enclosure in Wright to Secretary of State, London, September 10. National Archives, 861.00/7404.

25. Chicherin to Curzon, September 24, 1920. Degras, *Soviet Documents on Foreign Policy,* I, 211-12. Cf. *Europe nouvelle,* October 17, where this document is dated September 26.

26. In view of repeated declarations by leaders of the Soviet government that it considered itself to be at war with England, Curzon warned the Soviets that British warships would fire on sighting the submarine which, the British government was informed, the Soviet had launched in the Black Sea. Curzon to the Soviet government, September 26, 1920. This order was extended to the Baltic Sea. Curzon to Chicherin, October 2. *Daily Herald,* October 11. Cf. *Europe nouvelle,* October 17.

Notes

The collapse of Russian industry naturally tends to discredit the existence of this new submarine; it is, of course, possible that the craft had been virtually completed before the Bolshevik Revolution.

27. Wise's statement as its chairman, Minutes, Permanent Committee, S.E.C., September 17, 1920. Enclosure in Wright to Secretary of State, London, September 23. National Archives, 661.4116/91.

28. *Times, Morning Post,* October 5, 1920.

29. Emile Buré proposed the delivery of a "mortal coup." *Éclair* in *Écho de Paris,* August 27, 1920. The voice of Hungary was raised in favor of Europe's making a supreme effort "against the Bolshevist danger." She was "ready to make sacrifices in that cause." Budapest, August 26. Wireless News, No. 563, August 27. Enclosure in Wright to Secretary of State, London, September 3, No. 3379. National Archives, 861.00/7366.

30. David Francis, the former American Ambassador to Russia, predicted its fall within six months. *Literary Digest,* August 28, 1920.

31. White's telegram of August 20 (No. 459) was not received by the Department of State until August 24 at 11:35 P.M. National Archives, 760 c. 61/243.

32. Colby to chargé in Poland (White), Washington, August 21, 1920, Tel. 363. *Foreign Relations,* 1920, III, 391, 392. For Sapieha's reaction, August 23, see below.

33. *Times,* August 23, 26; *Daily Telegraph,* August 23; *Westminster Gazette,* August 25; *National Review,* September, 1920, pp. 17, 18; *Spectator,* August 28.

34. Wright to Secretary of State, London, August 21, 1920, Tel. 1267. (Received August 21, 10:13 A.M.) National Archives, 760 c. 61/223.

35. Johnson to Secretary of State, Rome, August 30, 1920, Tel. 325. National Archives, 861.01/233.

36. P. Bernus, "Les succès polonais et les conditions de la paix," *Journal des débats,* August 22, 1920.

37. *Soir,* August 28, 1920.

38. P. Millet, "La politique polonaise de la France," *Europe nouvelle,* August 29, 1920.

39. R. Poincaré, "Chronique de la quinzaine," *Revue des deux mondes,* September 1, 1920, p. 219.

40. G. A. Craig and F. Gilbert, eds., *The Diplomats, 1919-1939* (Princeton, 1953), p. 70. Professor Challener, the author of this essay on Berthelot, misses the immediate significance of this appointment.

41. Speaking to the Czech Parliament, September 1, Beneš, the Czech Foreign Minister, referred to the policy of neutrality in the Russo-Polish war as quite feasible for the Little Entente and asserted that Czechoslovakia would do all it could to establish economic relations with Soviet Russia. R. Machray, *The Little Entente* (New York, 1930), p. 133.

42. White to Secretary of State, Warsaw, August 21, 1920, Tel. 459. National Archives, 760 c. 61/243.

43. *Europe nouvelle,* October 3, 1920.

44. White to Secretary of State, Warsaw, August 24, 1920, Tel. 463. *Foreign Relations,* 1920, III, 392-93. This interview took place on August 28. Much the same line was taken in Poland's formal reply to the American note. Lubomirski, Polish note, No. 2864, Washington, August 30. *Ibid.,* pp. 397-98.

45. The Soviets could scarcely be blamed, in view of Minsk's location on lines of

Notes

communication behind the Red Army, for not permitting the Poles to have their own transmitting apparatus. On August 23, Chicherin denied that engagements on these matters had been broken. All messages from and to the Polish delegation had been expeditiously transmitted by the Moscow station, and if difficulties had arisen, the responsibility rested with the Warsaw station. Chicherin to Sapieha, August 23, 1920. *Europe nouvelle,* September 26.

46. Chicherin to Sapieha, September 1, 1920. Wireless News, No. 568, September 2. Enclosure in Wright to Secretary of State, London, September 10, No. 3407. National Archives, 861.00/7404.

47. Sapieha to Chicherin, Warsaw, September 6, 1920. Wireless News, No. 572, September 7. Enclosure in Wright to Secretary of State, London, September 10, No. 3407. *Ibid.*

48. Sapieha to Chicherin, Warsaw, September 9, 1920. Wireless News, No. 574, September 9. Enclosure in Wright to Secretary of State, London, September 17, No. 3440. *Ibid.,* 861.00/7445.

49. Moscow, September 9, 1920. Wireless News, No. 575, September 10. Enclosure in Wright to Secretary of State, London, September 17, No. 3440. *Ibid.*

50. The Poles finally left Danzig by sea, September 14, and arrived in Riga on the sixteenth. Sapieha to Chicherin, Warsaw, September 12. Wireless News, 577, September 13. Enclosure in Wright to Secretary of State, London, September 17, No. 3440. *Ibid.* Danzig, via Berlin, September 16. Wireless News, No. 580, September 16. Enclosure in Wright to Secretary of State, London, September 24, No. 3485. *Ibid.,* 861.00/7486. Cf. L. Fischer, *The Soviets in World Affairs* (2d ed.; Princeton, 1951), I, 274-75.

51. Gibson to Secretary of State, Warsaw, September 18, 1920, Tel. 514. *Foreign Relations,* 1920, III, 403-4. On September 23, Colby again indicated the American government's approval of a serious effort for peace, although Gibson was not to express this opinion unless asked. Colby to Gibson, Washington, September 23. *Ibid.,* p. 405.

52. Poincaré, for example, held that France's services had been sufficient to justify her counsels of restraint, although he noted that Poland had never accepted the Curzon Line. Poincaré, "Chronique de la quinzaine," *Revue des deux mondes,* September 15, 1920, pp. 442-43.

53. It presumed that Poland would propose the frontier of 1793, the second partition. "Avant les négotiations de Riga," *Temps,* September 21, 1920.

54. Commandant d'Etchegoyen, Sebastopol, September 30, 1920. *Matin,* October 10.

55. B. de Lacombe, "Chronique politique," *Correspondant,* N.S., CCXLV (October 6, 1920).

56. From Warsaw, the press reported Moscow as willing to accept all of Poland's terms no matter how severe except on disarmament. *Écho de Paris,* September 30, 1920, Warsaw, September 29. Despite signs of Soviet Russia's military collapse—entire regiments were said to be surrendering almost without fighting—the same journal concluded (October 2) that Russia could only be saved by the Russians.

57. Gibson to Secretary of State, Warsaw, September 23, 1920. Unnumbered Tel., National Archives, 760 c. 61/344.

58. Curzon to Soviet government, October 1. *Europe nouvelle,* October 17, 1920.

59. Curzon to Chicherin, October 5, 1920. *Ibid.,* October 17. Cf. *Daily Herald,*

285

Notes

October 11.

60. On October 13, one day after the signature of the Russo-Polish preliminary peace at Riga, Krassin gave Curzon details of the exchange on the Finnish frontier. *Europe nouvelle,* October 31, 1920.

61. V. I. Lénine, *Ouevres complètes* (Paris, 1928), XXV, 449-53 (September 22); 497-502 (October 15).

62. His confidences to the German Communist, Clara Zetkin, have the ring of truth. Clara Zetkin, *Reminiscences of Lenin* (New York, 1934).

63. I. Deutscher, *The Prophet Armed: Trotsky, 1879-1921* (New York and London, 1954), p. 468. Trotsky mobilized the reserve of the Bolshevik faithful for the Crimean campaign.

64. Gibson to Secretary of State, Warsaw, September 23, 1920, Unnumbered Tel., National Archives. 760 c. 61/344.

65. K. Radek, *Die auswärtige Politik Sowjetrusslands* (Hamburg, 1921), pp. 65-66.

66. This message was signed by Kalinin, President, and Yenudidze, Secretary of the Central Executive Committee. Wireless News, No. 589, September 27, 1920. Enclosure in Wright to Secretary of State, London, September 30, No. 3515. National Archives, 861.00/7515.

67. The definitive Treaty of Riga was not signed until March 18, 1921, but its terms were substantially the same as those of the Preliminary Peace.

68. The text was not reported in England until a translation appeared in the *Contemporary Review,* CLXXXVIII (December, 1920), 857-66. Cf. S. Kutrzba, "The Struggle for the Frontiers," *Cambridge History of Poland, From Augustus II to Pilsudski (1697-1935)* (Cambridge, 1951), II, 528-29. Ratifications were expeditiously exchanged at Riga on November 2. Moscow, November 2, 1920. Wireless News, No. 621, November 3. Enclosure in Wright to Secretary of State, London, November 12, No. 3736. National Archives, 861.00/7732.

69. Moscow, November 2, 1920. Wireless News, No. 621, November 3. General Balakhovich, who had commanded the White Russian forces in Kiev before its capture by the Ukrainian Bolsheviks early in 1920, fled with his corps to Polish soil.

70. Warsaw, November 3, 1920. Wireless News, No. 621, November 3.

71. Warsaw, November 9, 1920. Wireless News, No. 626, November 9. Enclosure in Wright to Secretary of State, London, November 12. National Archives, 861.00/7732.

72. Cf. his remarks to the Reichstag's Foreign Affairs Commission on September 1. *Deutsche Allgemeine Zeitung; Vorwärts,* September 2, 1920. In a private letter, Stresemann noted that the foreign minister's July speech had been forgotten, overshadowed by the revolutionary significance of the Congress of the Third International in Moscow. Stresemann to Gravenhoff, Berlin, September 6. Serial 6924H, H138267-68, National Archives.

73. The vote was 237 to 156. The majority joined with the small German Communist Party (KPD) in December, 1920, to form the United German Communist party. E. H. Carr, *The Bolshevik Revolution, 1917-1923* (London, 1951-53), III, 222-23.

74. *Verhandlungen des Reichstags,* CCCXLV, 762-63.

75. "Politische Rundschau," *Deutsche Rundschau,* CLXXXV (October, 1920), 116-19.

76. N. Osterroth, "Der Kampf um Oberschlesien," *Neue Zeit,* 38th year, II (September 10, 1920), 531. The plebiscite was held on March 20, 1921.

77. An illuminating article by the new editor of Germany's foremost conservative

review contains references to contacts between this group and unnamed British leaders. W. Schotte, "Politische Korrespondenz: Die Russische Frage," (2), *Preussische Jahrbücher,* CLXXXIII (January, 1921), 277-86.

78. *Verhandlungen des Reichstags,* CCCXLV, 786-87 (Fehrenbach); 803-4 (Scheidemann).

79. De Lacombe, "Chronique politique," *Correspondant,* N.S., CCXLIV (September 6, 1920), 955; M. Pernot, "L'épreuve de la Pologne," *Revue des deux mondes,* September 15, 1920, p. 498; R. Poincaré, "Chronique de la quinzaine," *ibid.,* October 15, 1920, p. 887.

80. E. Fournol, "Qui a été vaincu en Pologne," *Europe nouvelle,* September 5, 1920.

81. The Poles replied the next day that the preliminary peace had been signed and, in any event, that Britain's failure to support Poland had voided the Spa agreement. Gibson to Secretary of State, Warsaw, October 15, 1920, Tel. 667. National Archives, 760 c. 61/394.

82. A. L. Kennedy, *Old Diplomacy and the New, 1876-1922: From Salisbury to Lloyd George* (London, 1922), p. 332.

83. P. Millet, "Les nouvelles frontières de la Pologne," *Europe nouvelle,* October 17, 1920.

84. In London, the *Daily Herald* (October 7, 1920) bluntly declared after the cease-fire that "the peace of Riga sounds the doom of Wrangel."

85. Commandant Civrieux in *Matin,* October 7, 1920.

86. "L'armistice polono-bolchéviste," *Temps,* October 8, 1920.

87. In Washington, Secretary of State Colby was quoted as predicting, on the basis of the department's confidential information "that the regime now controlled by Lénine and Trotzky will utterly collapse within a few months" as a result of the peasants' hostility. *Washington Post,* October 22, 1920. This article is attached to document 861.01/257 in the archives of the Department of State. According to the *New York Times* (October 10) "the Soviet government is already tottering to its inevitable collapse."

88. "Le déclin de bolchévisme," *Temps,* October 6, 1920.

89. *Journal des débats,* October 7, 1920. Cf. *ibid.,* October 13.

90. *Times,* November 5, 1920.

91. Moscow, October 22, 1920. Wireless News, No. 613, October 25. Enclosure in Wright to Secretary of State, London, October 29, No. 3670. National Archives, 861.00/7669.

92. "Les leçons d'une rétraite," *Temps,* November 7, 1920.

93. Bristol (Admiral McCully) to Secretary of State, Constantinople, October 25, 1920, Tel. 541. National Archives, 861.00/7604.

94. "I am in the midst of this passionate distress, and know and love this people and hope because their cry for help is faint and far away our government and people will not remain indifferent to it." Bristol (McCully) to Secretary of State, Constantinople, November 11, 1920, Tel. 572. National Archives, 861.00/7674. Cf. W. H. Chamberlin, *The Russian Revolution, 1917-1921* (New York, 1935), II, 329-32; Fischer, *Soviets in World Affairs,* I, 277-78.

95. Colby to President Wilson, Washington, November 12, 1920, initialed "W. W." Colby to High Commission (Admiral Bristol, Constantinople), Washington, November 14, Tel. 105. National Archives, 861.00/7678, 7674. According to Wrangel, 145,693 persons were evacuated. Chamberlin, *Russian Revolution,* III, 329.

Notes

96. Bristol (Imbrie) to Secretary of State, Constantinople, December 28, 1920, Tel. 654. National Archives, 861.00/7895. The State Department did not even reply to Wrangel's request that he and his troops be transported to Vladivostok. A draft telegram stating its disapproval of the project was cancelled on the ground that it was none of "our business." See S. Merlesmith's note on draft. National Archives, 861.00/7895.

97. The *New York Times* (November 16, 1920) was more realistic; it described the wandering armies of Balakhovich and others as "mere guerrilla bands. They can give no more serious annoyance to the Red leaders than Ferdinand Schill did to Napoleon." Before the end of November, the remnants of his command were forced back into Poland where, as the Moscow wireless acknowledged, "they were immediately disarmed by the Poles in the presence of a representative of Soviet Russia." Wireless News, No. 651, December 8. Enclosure in Davis to Secretary of State, London, December 14, No. 3869. National Archives, 861.00/7886.

98. "The Honest Bolshevik," *Daily Telegraph,* November 17, 1920. Clipping enclosed in Davis to Secretary of State, London, November 24, No. 3794.

99. *Matin,* November 15, 1920.

100. *Correspondant,* N.S., CCXLV (November 21, 1920), 763.

101. "Le désastre de Crimée," *Temps,* November 16, 1920. Lénine, *Oeuvres complètes,* XXV, 568 (November 20).

102. "Revue de la quinzaine," *Revue des deux mondes,* December 1, 1920, pp. 666, 667.

103. *Écho de Paris,* November 14, 1920. Pertinax quite correctly blamed the Poles for fearing the White Russians more than the Bolsheviks.

104. A. Oulman, in *Petit bleu. Matin,* November 16, 1920.

105. J. Roujon, *Figaro,* November 14, 1920; M. Geneste, *Avenir* in *Matin,* November 15.

106. L. Dumont-Wilden, "Venizelos et Wrangel," *Revue bleue,* 58th yr., No. 23 (December 4, 1920), 723; "Quelques nouveaux aspects du probleme russe," *ibid.,* No. 24 (December 18, 1920), 750 ff.

107. *Écho de Paris,* November 14, 1920.

108. Auguste Gauvain, "Les Bolchévistes en Crimée," *Journal des débats,* November 15, 1920.

109. "The Right Attitude toward Russia," *Spectator,* November 20, 1920.

110. Poincaré, *Revue des deux mondes,* December 1, 1920, p. 667.

111. Gauvain, *Journal des débats,* November 15; De Lacombe, *Correspondant,* N.S., CCXLV (November 23, 1920), 763; Poincaré, *Revue des deux mondes,* December 1, 1920, p. 668. The assumption that the Bolsheviks were capable only of destruction offers something of a rational explanation why those who expected the collapse of their regime also feared, at the same time, new Soviet offensives.

112. For Colby's protest, see *Foreign Relations,* 1920, III, 433 (October 5), and for Ambassador Wallace's action in the Council of Ambassadors, National Archives, 763.72119/10551 (Tel. 1793, October 11). For the Soviet government's protest, see Degras, *Soviet Documents on Foreign Policy,* I, 219.

113. Lénine, *Oeuvres complètes,* XXV, 569 ff. This speech was published as a pamphlet, *Our External and Internal Situation* (Moscow, 1920).

114. E. H. Carr, *German-Soviet Relations between the Two World Wars, 1919-1939* (Baltimore, 1951), p. 40. The Treaty of Rapallo between Germany and Soviet Russia

was signed in April, 1922.

115. This was probably true, although there were protests from the liberal intelligentsia. Of the claim that the world "should let Russia alone, should neither fight nor make peace with Russia," the *New Republic* (December 1, 1920) declared: "There is no such line between peace and war" as Colby had claimed. There was, in its view, no alternative to war to the end or *de facto* recognition. The Colby note, it charged, was merely a cover for continued "intrigue, sabotage, illicit intervention...." Cf. *Nation* (New York), December 1.

116. S. P. Gilbert, Assistant Secretary of Treasury, to Acting Secretary of State, Washington, December 20, 23, 1920. *Foreign Relations, 1920,* III, 724-27.

117. P. Millet spoke for the first and L. Dumont-Wilden for the second course. Millet, "L'Effondrement de Wrangel," *Europe nouvelle,* November 21, 1920; Dumont-Wilden, "Quelque nouveaux aspects du problème russe," *Revue bleue,* December 18.

118. *Times,* November 10, 1920.

119. *Parl. Deb.* (H.C.), 1920, IX, 1519-20 (October 26).

120. *Daily Herald,* November 16, 1920.

121. *Morning Post,* November 11, 1920. Clipping in Davis to Secretary of State, London, November 24, No. 3794. National Archives, 661.4116/112.

122. *Parl. Deb.* (H.C.), 1920, XII, 1884-87 (Major Barnett, December 22).

123. *Morning Post,* November 11, 1920, National Archives, 611.4116/112.

124. Translation in Johnson to Secretary of State, Rome, September 2, 1920, Tel. 331. National Archives, 761.65/8. Cf. *Daily Telegraph,* November 18.

125. See the provocative and insulting letter of November 17 to the International Congress of Trade Unions then meeting in London signed by Zinoviev, the Third International's President, Lenin, Bukharin, Radek, and others in which the rank and file were summoned to turn against their "yellow leaders." Moscow, November 17, 1920. Wireless News, No. 636, November 20. Enclosure in Davis to Secretary of State, London, December 3, No. 3819. National Archives, 861.00/7884.

126. *Daily Herald,* November 16, 1920.

127. *Parl Deb.* (H.C.), 1920, XII, 1851. Captain James O'Grady declared on the same day that sixty thousand would find employment in his constituency in Leeds at the moment that the trade agreement was concluded. *Ibid.,* pp. 1858-59 (December 22).

128. See clippings from the *Daily News* (November 18), *Daily Chronicle* (November 19), and *Star* (November 22) in Davis to Secretary of State, London, November 24, 1920, No. 3794. National Archives, 661.4116/112.

129. See clippings in above Davis dispatch, November 24, 1920, No. 3794. National Archives, 661.4116/112.

130. *Parl. Deb.* (H.C.), 1920, XII, 1865-76 (December 22). Adamson had warned that it would be almost as difficult for the Russian government to give an absolute guarantee against propaganda as it would for the British government "to undertake to keep the right honorable Gentleman the Secretary of State for War [Churchill] quiet on this question." *Ibid.,* p. 1854.

131. The italics are mine. *Europe nouvelle,* December 5, 1920.

132. Davis to Secretary of State, London, January 7, 1921. National Archives, 661.4113/29.

133. *Daily Chronicle,* January 27, 1921.

134. Chamberlin, *Russian Revolution,* II, 432-33.

Notes

135. Deutscher, *The Prophet Armed*, pp. 511-12.

136. While Deutscher flatly asserts that it was anarchist, it seems more reasonable to conclude that it comprised Menshevik and Social Revolutionary elements as well. *Ibid.*, p. 510.

137. Chamberlin, *Russian Revolution*, II, 441-42.

138. Moscow, February 26, 1921. Wireless News, No. 719, February 28. Enclosure in Davis to Secretary of State, London, March 8, No. 4299. National Archives, 861.00/8382.

139. In contrast, the rebels had treated their Bolshevik prisoners humanely. Deutscher, *The Prophet Armed*, pp. 512-14. On the day of their surrender, March 18, 1921, the anniversary of the Paris Commune, Alexander Berkman, the American Anarchist whose original enthusiasm for Bolshevism had cooled as the result of his first-hand experiences, noted in his diary: "Trotsky and Zinoviev denounce Thiers and Galliffet for the slaughter of the Paris rebels." The *Bolshevik Myth*, in Chamberlin, *Russian Revolution*, II, 444.

140. Moscow, March 3, 1921. Wireless News, No. 724, March 5. Enclosure in Wright to Secretary of State, London, March 16, No. 4346. National Archives, 861.00/8411; Wireless News, No. 725, August 7. *Ibid.;* Moscow, March 10, Wireless News, No. 728. *Ibid.* They picked out an alleged dispatch from Helsingfors in the Paris *Matin*, February 13, as proof of foreknowledge of coming events. Actually the *Matin* carried the telegram on the fourteenth as based upon news from the Finnish port via Copenhagen and London. It reported the arrest of representatives of the Soviet government by the Kronstadt sailors and claimed that Red Army units were showing "marked repugnance" to fight the latter. "Since the guns of Kronstadt dominate Petrograd, the city is more in the hands of the rebels than of the Soviet."

141. Deutscher, *The Prophet Armed*, p. 513.

142. *Vossische Zeitung*, March 5, 7, 11, 1821; *Berliner Tageblatt;* March 10, 18; *Deutsche Tageszeitung*, in *Kölnische Zeitung*, March 8; *Frankfurter Zeitung*, March 14. Some felt that the overthrow of the Bolsheviks would help Germany's cause in the Upper Silesia plebiscite scheduled for March 20, 1921, by diverting Poland's attention and forces to her eastern frontier.

143. High Commissioner (Dulles) to Secretary of State, Constantinople, March 12, 1921, Tel. 92. National Archives, 861.00/8322. His appeal to the world for aid was referred to President Harding with negative results. On March 31, Secretary of State Hughes cabled that non-interference in internal Russian affairs would not permit American aid even if funds were available. G. B. Christian, Secretary of the President to Secretary of State Hughes, White House, March 14; Hughes to High Commissioner (Constantinople), Washington, March 31, Tel. 25. National Archives, 861.00/8324.

144. Nevertheless, they asked if the United States would be prepared to provision a liberated Petrograd and the Baltic area. Dresel to Secretary of State, Berlin, March 14, 1921, Tel. 279. National Archives, 861.00/8323.

145. In this view, the entire Polish press from the Socialists to the extreme right was agreed, according to the Warsaw correspondent (March 10, 1921) of the *Frankfurter Zeitung* (March 11). Cf. *Kölnische Zeitung*, March 14, Warsaw, March 9, 12. While Pilsudski, according to Gibson, the American Minister, expected the Soviets to survive the current crisis, he did foresee a violent clash between Lenin and Trotsky "resulting in the complete collapse of the regime." Gibson to Secretary of State, Warsaw, March 12, Tel. 49. National Archives, 861.00/8320.

146. It was perhaps no accident that the treaty was signed in advance of the plebiscite in Upper Silesia on March 20, since a definitive eastern frontier would in a measure free Poland's forces for trouble with Germany. Germany's interest was manifestly in continued Russo-Polish tension which would be best served by the success of the rebels.

147. Fischer, *Soviets in World Affairs*, I, 391.

148. Moscow, March 2, 1921. Wireless News, No. 723, March 4. Enclosure in Davis to Secretary of State, London, March 8, No. 4299. National Archives, 861.00/8382.

149. The treaty also recognized Constantinople as a part of Turkey and provided for a possible Soviet effort to change the status of the Straits in a conference of the Black Sea Powers to be called on that question. Carr, *Bolshevik Revolution*, III, 303; Fischer, *Soviets in World Affairs*, I, 392-93.

150. Since his speech was sent out by the Moscow wireless station, Lenin's retreat on the home front was known at once throughout the West. Moscow, March 10, 1921. Wireless News, March 10, No. 728. Enclosure in Davis to Secretary of State, London, March 16, No. 4346. National Archives, 861.00/8411. The essentials of Lenin's speech, credited to "wireless press, Moscow, March 10," appeared in the *Daily Telegraph*, March 11, although these intercepts were usually treated as classified material.

151. On his return to Russia, he was quoted as saying that "relations with Russia will undergo a complete change" under the Harding administration. Moscow, February 23, 1921. Wireless News, No. 718, February 26. Enclosure in Davis to Secretary of State, London, March 8, No. 4299. National Archives, 861.00/8382.

152. In Berlin, Krassin told Phillips Price, the *Daily Herald*'s special correspondent, that he had placed an order in Germany for one hundred locomotives and would shortly order six hundred more. Britain, however, held the key to Russia's economic relations with Europe since the Germans feared that France would claim any gold or goods that Russia sent in payment under the reparations clauses of the Treaty of Versailles unless prevented by Great Britain. *Daily Herald*, February 28, 1921, Berlin, March 26.

153. *Ibid.*, March 7.

154. Replying to questions in the Commons, its under-secretary, Harmsworth, indicated its doubt as to the Soviet Government's survival. The situation in Petrograd would be determined by the outcome of the fighting still in progress there. General Koslovsky, the former Tsarist and Red Army artillerist, who commanded the rebels, was reported to be advancing on Moscow, but it was "not yet known whether he has established contact with the anti-Bolshevik workmen within the city." *Parl. Deb.* (H.C.), 1921, II, 476 (March 9). Cf. *Manchester Guardian*, March 10.

155. The Bolsheviks, of course, were aware of this calculation, and their reaction had been stated over the Moscow wireless station on December 1, 1920. The British capitalists hoped "to inoculate us with the 'Bourgeois virus,'" but Soviet Russia "has a definite plan of action and struggle against every attempt to frustrate it." Moscow, December 1, 1920. Wireless News, No. 647, December 3. Enclosure in Davis to Secretary of State, London, December 14, No. 3869. National Archives, 861.00/7886. Cf. Radek, *Die auswärtige Politik Sowjetrusslands*, p. 81.

156. *Parl. Deb.* (H.C.), 1921, II, 537.

157. Lloyd George announced its signature by Horne and Krassin during the question period on the same day. *Ibid.*, p. 1440 (March 16).

Notes

158. The British government could not prescribe by treaty or otherwise determine the attitude of the courts in private suits, but it had been advised that an agreement that amounted to *de facto* recognition would be interpreted by the courts as ruling against such suits on the ground that the goods in question were the property of the Soviet Russian state. And so it proved, for no individual thereafter sued successfully.

159. Fischer, *Soviets in World Affairs,* I, 294-95. Carr, *Bolshevik Revolution,* III, 287-88. Cf. *Times,* March 17, 1921.

160. Chicherin's instructions to Krassin, April 16. Degras, *Soviet Documents on Foreign Policy,* I, 245-46.

161. Enclosure in Wright to Secretary of State (Hughes), London, March 17, 1921, No. 4360. National Archives, 641.6131/18. Wright correctly attributed the agreement in large part to E. F. Wise of the Ministry of Food and reported the general view that the government's loss of several by-elections accounted for Lloyd George's support. Actually he had never abandoned the idea since the beginning of the negotiations. Cf. Wright to Secretary of State, London, March 17, Tel. 320. *Ibid.,* 641.6131/20.

162. *Parl. Deb.* (H.C.), 1921, III, 2506-11. Neil MacLean more accurately described the changes in Russia as acts of expediency, not an abandonment of principles. *Ibid.,* II, 2512.

163. Hoover to Secretary of State (Hughes), Department of Commerce, March 16. *Foreign Relations,* 1921, II, 762-63.

164. Litvinov to (the United States) Congress and President Harding, Revel, March 20, 1921. Hughes to Albrecht (Revel), Washington, March 25. *Ibid.,* pp. 763-64.

165. Hoover disagreed when the Russian Division of the State Department recommended that Germany should be used as the intermediary for the development of Russo-American trade. Hughes commented that the department had in mind only supplementary trade. Secretary of State to Hoover, December 1, 1921; Hoover to Secretary of State, December 6; Hughes to Hoover, December 27. *Foreign Relations,* 1921, II, 785-88.

166. "Le pacte anglo-russe et les intérêts français," *Écho de Paris,* March 19, 1921.

167. "L'accord anglo-bolchéviste," *Temps,* March 21, 1921. Cf. Bernus in *Journal des débats,* March 24.

168. Stanav (Dulles) to Secretary of State, Constantinople, March 19, 1921, Tel. 106. National Archives, 861.00/8373.

169. Carr, *German-Soviet Relations,* pp. 41-46. In view of the importance Lenin always attributed to Germany, it seems most unlikely that even his preoccupation with the internal Russian crisis would have caused him to leave the initiative entirely to Zinoviev. He, too, doubtless saw the advantage of a diversion from Soviet Russia's troubles and of a demonstration of the vitality of international Communism.

170. *Frankfurter Zeitung,* March 19, 1921.

171. *Kölnische Zeitung,* April 29, 1921.

172. Wiedenfeld arrived in Moscow as Germany's trade representative in September, 1921, and N. Krestinsky was appointed to the equivalent post in Berlin in October. Carr, *Bolshevik Revolution,* III, 339, 365; Carr, *Soviet-German Relations,* p. 51; L. Kochan, *Russia and the Weimar Republic* (Cambridge, 1954), p. 41.

173. Carr, *Bolshevik Revolution,* III, 340.

174. Winston Churchill apparently took no public notice of it at the time and he did not even mention it in his history of this period (*The Aftermath, 1918-1928*).

Index

Index

Baltic Sea area, 28, 36, 115, 131, 156, 175, 206, 283n

Baltic states, 7, 21, 24-25, 33, 34, 37, 51, 52, 58, 59-60, 241

Barthou, L., 20, 46, 111, 248-49n, 255n

Béarn et de Chalais, Count de Galard de, 190-97 *passim,* 279n, 280n

Beneš, E., 68, 70-71, 106, 159, 284n

Berliner Tageblatt, 137, 182, 240, 269n

Berthelot, P., 72, 102, 163, 215, 230, 263n, 264n

Bessarabia, 105, 226, 239, 241

Bevin, E., 171, 172-73, 181, 276n

Black Sea, 206, 213, 257n, 283n, 291n

Bolsheviks, ideology, 5, 6, 12, 17, 63, 69, 162, 227, 236, 238; propaganda, 5, 11, 13, 27, 31, 33, 71, 91, 95-96, 100, 120, 143, 151, 152, 212, 230, 236, 261n, 289n; favor world revolution, 50, 65, 82, 90, 91, 103, 113, 126, 152, 153, 166, 168, 169, 172, 180, 181, 182, 194, 201, 213, 217, 220, 222, 227, 239, 245n, 253n; mentioned 7, 8, 52. *See also* Lenin

Borisov, 58, 73-84 *passim,* 122, 256n

Boulogne, 126, 128, 153, 155, 260n, 267n

Breitscheid, R., 140, 147, 151, 157

Brest-Litovsk, 29, 114, 122, 144, 201, 217, 230n

British Empire, 4, 91, 96, 167, 178

Brusilov, A., 81, 109, 192, 259n

Budënny, S. M., 28, 80, 91, 104, 158

C

Cabinet, British, 8, 22, 23, 27, 32, 42, 89, 97, 120, 121, 153, 229, 248; American, 98, 245n; German, 140, 150; French, 184, 197

Cambon, P., 9, 91-92, 94, 248n, 259n

Cecil, R., 8, 66, 76, 83, 85, 88, 258n, 265n

Central Europe, 11, 33, 59, 62, 101-2, 113, 117, 145, 159, 215

Chicherin, G. V., 24-26, 29, 47, 58-75 *passim,* 82, 93, 95, 96, 114-30 *passim,* 141-46 *passim,* 152, 163, 164, 180, 201-4 *passim,* 211, 213, 228, 233, 249n, 252n, 260n, 267n, 287n

Churchill, W. S., and intervention, 4,

23, 30, 43, 88-89, 113, 168, 179, 187, 222, 227; and Germany, 23, 31, 33, 40, 42, 43, 72, 148-57 *passim;* and Lloyd George's Russian policy, 23, 30-31, 36, 40-43, 64, 67, 88, 152-55 *passim,* 259n, 272n; anti-bolshevism, 23, 30-31, 88-90, 94, 152, 155, 156, 168, 176, 222, 237; mentioned, 13, 32, 34-35, 78, 84, 177, 178, 206, 238, 256n, 289n, 292n. *See also* Middle East

Civil War, 5, 6, 28, 29, 32, 49, 57, 212, 231

Clemenceau, G., and Russia, 3, 21, 24, 36, 37, 52, 53, 57, 64, 68, 92; mentioned, 33, 38, 43, 56, 59, 72, 185, 263n

Clynes, J. R., 39, 174, 179, 180

Colby, B., note, 129, 133, 191, 193-202, 206, 210, 227, 238, 241, 280n, 281n, 292n; mentioned, 72, 98, 190, 260n, 285n, 287n

Communists, American, 10; Italian, 45; Polish, 55, 120, 203, 251n; German, 74, 135, 140-41, 142, 182, 242n, 249n, 269n, 286n; Hungarian, 76, 82, 106, 141; British, 154; Chinese, 256n; mentioned, 8, 15. *See also* Bolsheviks

Commissariat of Foreign Affairs (Narkomindel), 47, 95, 108, 125

Conservative party. *See* Tory party

Containment and co-existence, 5, 21, 24, 29, 30, 52, 53, 57, 68, 226, 236

Co-operative Societies, 33, 36, 37, 45, 47, 48, 77, 90, 91, 230

Cordon sanitaire, 20, 21, 24, 57, 157

Council of Action, 10, 171-73, 177, 180, 181, 206, 211, 212-13, 217, 229, 276n, 278n

Council of Ambassadors, 96, 209-10, 211, 260n, 273n

Crimea, 26, 76, 82, 93, 114, 117, 164, 223, 225, 228, 286n

Curzon, Earl, and Lloyd George, 36, 85, 91, 125, 248n, 266n; mentioned, 22, 25-26, 27, 32, 33-34, 85-94 *passim,* 98, 102, 110-130 *passim,* 143, 175, 184, 213, 217, 228, 237, 246n, 251n, 265n, 267n, 274n, 283n, 286n

Curzon Line, 110, 114-20 *passim,* 127,

Index

Polish material aid, 88, 120, 131, 160, 214, 250n, 253n, 254n, 265n; Tsarist debts, 100, 128, 129, 132, 166, 184, 278n; Polish alliance, 226, 233, 239; mentioned, 4, 20-25 *passim*, 65, 72, 74, 127, 145, 210, 213, 232, 234, 235, 261n, 291n. *See also* Colby, Clemenceau, Germany, Hungary, Middle East, Millerand, Ruhr, United States, Wrangel

Frankfurter Zeitung, 137, 147, 157, 240, 263n

G

Galicia, 54, 55-56, 58, 78, 109, 110
Garvin, J. L., 30, 31, 40, 89, 112, 118, 187, 259n. See also *Observer*
Gauvain, A., 63, 65, 222, 225, 249n
Georgia, 33, 37, 83, 177
Geraud, A. *See* Pertinax
Germany, frontiers, 3, 104, 127, 132-51 *passim*, 158, 167-75 *passim*, 182, 270n, 272n; workers, 5, 81, 139-45 *passim;* coal deliveries, 10, 94, 101, 111, 135, 136, 138, 268n; Bolshevik domestic revolt, 11, 29, 62, 73-74, 81, 84, 85, 91, 103, 109, 113, 119, 134, 138, 139, 141, 151, 152, 153, 163, 169, 197, 219, 239-40, 242n; Russian prisoner exchange, 11, 142, 243n; Russian recognition, 11, 142-51 *passim;* French fears of Russian contacts, 12, 135-40 *passim*, 148-57 *passim*, 181-82, 198; reparations, 30, 197, 240; Russian trade 32, 33, 70, 135, 142, 144, 151, 182, 198, 239, 240-41, 269n, 291n; officers in Red Army, 41, 112, 220, 245n, 264n; Russian alliance, 42, 111, 112, 137-43 *passim*, 166, 206, 255n, 269n; French occupation, 46-47, 74, 139, 141, 185, 206, 239; defeat, 49, 134, 161, 167; Allied enforcement of Versailles on, 70, 106, 134-41 *passim*, 156, 205, 239, 240, 269n; mutual hostility with France, 84, 101, 126, 138, 155-56, 159, 183, 198, 220, 263n; attack on Poland, 84, 112, 156, 185; disarmament, 94, 101, 102, 107, 135, 136, 140, 149-50, 151, 156, 256n; transit of Polish supplies through, 105, 140, 159,

195, 269n; neutrality, 105, 134, 135, 140-59 *passim*, 206, 219; anti-Russian alliance with Allies, 134-48 *passim*, 157, 220, 249n, 255n, 272n; and Russian peace conference, 135, 167, 184; blackmail of Allies, 136, 138, 140, 150, 156, 249n; hostility to Poles, 137, 139, 140, 149-50, 151, 156, 265n; Bolshevik invasion of, 137, 139, 144, 147; national bolshevism in, 137-38, 157, 182, 269n; anti-bolshevism, 148, 157, 198, 227, 240; mentioned, 13-34 *passim*, 39, 44, 53-63 *passim*, 87, 107, 117, 160, 166, 196, 226-27, 232, 250n, 251n, 253n, 268n, 270n, 271n, 277n. *See also* Armistice, Colby, Churchill, Kapp Putsch, Reichswehr, Ruhr, Versailles
Gibson, H., 58-76 *passim*, 105, 190, 196, 210-11, 216, 220, 250n, 251n, 253n, 264n, 285n, 290n
Giolitti, G., and Lloyd George, 155, 198, 209, 211, 214, 215, 279n
Grabski, L., 64, 66, 106, 108, 109, 110, 221, 263n, 264n
Great Britain, workers, 9, 19, 81, 90, 168, 170, 171; fleet, 21, 36, 125, 131, 156, 164, 173; intervention, 23-24, 28, 52, 76, 81, 83, 119, 161, 168, 172, 176, 212, 228, 246n; Russian prisoner exchange, 25, 68, 77, 217, 286n; Russian trade, 32-33, 82, 93, 96, 97, 108, 119, 124, 125, 127, 147, 160, 161, 184, 186, 227-41 *passim*, 249n, 289n; Russian recognition, 44, 45, 96, 99, 127, 129, 160, 161, 169, 200, 229, 235, 237, 238, 292n; Russian peace, 65, 89, 91, 96, 108, 109-10, 121-30 *passim*, 143, 150, 153, 167, 170, 176, 186, 228, 267n; Polish aid, 72, 88, 109-21 *passim*, 131, 159, 162, 166, 188, 211, 276n; Bolshevik revolt in, 83, 179, 228; and Russo-Polish peace, 108, 115, 116, 132, 174, 209-21 *passim;* and Polish independence, 109, 110, 112, 160-61, 165, 209; anti-bolshevism, 114, 151, 152, 199, 222, 229, 237; pacifism, 118, 165, 168, 170, 177; mentioned, 10, 27, 54-63 *passim*, 69-98 *passim*, 105, 106, 107, 141, 170,

Index

Q

Quai d'Orsay, 19, 37, 46, 72, 77, 101, 102, 128, 163, 188-93 *passim*, 215, 230, 263n, 280n

R

Radek, K., and Poland, 80-81, 103, 115, 129-30, 131, 257n; mentioned, 29, 70, 114, 218, 260n, 266n, 269n, 289n

Rapallo, 134, 144, 227, 288n

Rechberg, A., 149-52, 271n, 272n

Red Army, defeats White Russians, 27-28, 29, 32, 40-41; Polish offensive, 34, 63, 65, 80, 135-41 *passim*, 147, 150, 151, 160-66 *passim*, 173, 183, 191, 202, 209, 218, 220, 227, 250n, 265n; Crimean campaign, 82, 223, 224, 228; mentioned, 49, 54-66 *passim*, 83, 84, 86, 122, 143, 158, 159, 169, 182, 200, 206-17 *passim*, 222, 226, 231, 257n, 258n, 264n, 266n, 270n, 285n

Red Scare, 14, 38, 39, 189

Reichswehr, 49, 70, 74, 84, 111, 112, 135, 139, 140, 249n

Republican party, 189, 196, 234, 241

Rhine region, 135, 141, 156, 185

Riddell, Lord, 42, 88, 109, 116, 124, 130, 152, 209, 259n, 274n, 283n

Riga, 50, 94, 208, 215-26 *passim*, 233, 251n, 285n, 286n

Ruhr, 74, 136, 137, 143, 148

Rumania, and Poland, 51, 105, 107, 115; and Hungary, 73, 77, 101, 102, 105; mentioned, 44, 59, 114, 183, 215, 226, 239, 241, 253n, 256n

Rumbold, H., 54-72 *passim*, 121

Russell, B., on Russia, 7, 16, 17-18, 19, 174, 243n, 275n

Russia, revolution, 3, 4-5, 105, 113, 143, 231, 284n; peasants, 4, 15, 64, 223, 231-34 *passim*; aggression, 4, 11, 30, 32, 38, 59, 63, 78, 84, 85, 173, 186, 219, 226, 227, 288n; violence, 5, 15, 16, 65, 135, 146, 174, 201, 219, 224, 230-31; terrorism, 5, 8, 18, 45, 92, 135, 146, 147, 153, 219; workers, 6, 7, 16, 26, 64, 115, 116, 146, 174, 201, 203, 205, 231-34

passim, 291n; lack of information about, 6-8, 25, 85, 95, 112; expected collapse, 7-8, 11, 15, 17, 27, 55, 79, 133, 208, 213, 216, 221-22, 225, 232, 237-40 *passim*, 261n, 284n, 287n, 288n, 290n; border lands, 24, 35, 41, 53, 67, 71, 75, 79, 126, 129, 185, 236; diplomatic techniques, 25-26, 120, 143, 176, 194, 204, 222; economic situation, 28-33 *passim*, 37, 75, 82, 104, 113, 144, 147, 151, 212, 217, 224, 231, 247n, 253n; peace campaign, 29, 30, 51, 57, 58, 59, 64-65, 68; transport, 65, 66, 84, 113, 151, 236, 238; nationalism, 80, 81, 86, 87-88, 183-92 *passim*, 213, 214. *See also* Allies, Baltic states, Entente, France, Germany, Great Britain, Lenin, Lloyd George, Poland, Red Army

S

San Remo Conference, 46-47, 48, 76, 77, 91, 92, 98, 249n, 251n

Sapieha-Rożański, E., Prince, 88, 120, 122, 159, 163, 176, 179, 202, 208-9, 213-18 *passim*

Seeckt, H. von, 70, 71, 74, 111, 139, 255n, 269n, 271n

Seton-Watson, R. W., 25, 86, 154-55, 187, 252n

Sforza, C., 155, 198, 214, 279n

Simons, W., and Russia, 111, 141-47 *passim*, 157, 182, 219, 240, 271n, 277n; and Spa, 148-56 *passim;* mentioned, 138, 270n, 272n, 282n

Social Democrats, 5, 11, 15, 74, 137, 139, 141, 147, 149, 157, 220, 255n, 268n, 271n. *See also* Independent Social Democrats

Socialists, 10, 12, 15, 16, 19, 20, 39, 64, 86, 181. *See also* Social Democrats

Spa Conference, and Germany, 94, 111, 137, 139, 143, 150, 151; and Poland, 108, 115, 221, 287n; mentioned, 95, 101, 107, 110, 117, 126, 135-36, 268n

Spectator, and Russia, 84, 186, 187, 225, 229, 249n, 264n; mentioned, 178, 259n

State Department, 45, 46, 72, 97, 99, 105-

Index